HO...

Patrick Robinson is author of six previous books – three of them on the breeding and racing of thoroughbred horses, *Classic Lines*, *The Golden Post* and *Decade of Champions*. A leather-bound volume of the latter was the official gift of the United States to the Queen in 1982 from President Reagan.

In 1985 he wrote the international bestseller *Born to Win*. In 1988 he wrote another bestseller *True Blue*, which won the 'Sports Book of the Year' Award.

His 1992 No.1 bestseller, written with Admiral Sandy Woodward, was *One Hundred Days*, the memoirs of the Falklands Battle Group Commander.

Nick Robinson, publisher of the leading bloodstock magazine *Pacemaker International* from 1973 to 1988, is a past President of the Racehorse Owners' Association. He is an inaugural member of the British Horseracing Board.

Horsetrader was runner-up in the William Hill 'Sports Book of the Year' Award for 1993.

HORSETRADER

Robert Sangster and the Rise and
Fall of the Sport of Kings

Patrick Robinson
with
Nick Robinson

HarperCollins*Publishers*

HarperCollins*Publishers*
77–85 Fulham Palace Road
Hammersmith, London W6 8JB

This paperback edition 1994
1 3 5 7 9 8 6 4 2

First published in Great Britain by
HarperCollins*Publishers* 1993

ISBN 0 00 638105 7

Set in Linotron Ehrhardt

Printed in Great Britain by
HarperCollinsManufacturing Glasgow

To Joe Thomas and Northern Dancer.
They are both gone now, but they left behind
an eternal flame in the Vale of Tipperary

Contents

List of Illustrations

Pages 232 to 233

Sheikh Mohammed al-Maktoum receives the trophy for the 1988
   Champion Stakes from his elder brother Hamdan (*courtesy of* Racing
   Post)
Snaafi Dancer (*courtesy of* The Blood-Horse)
El Gran Senor defeated by Secreto in the 1984 Derby (*Alan Johnson*)
The gates of Spendthrift Farm (*courtesy of* The Blood Horse)
Brownell Combs (*Skip Dickstein, courtesy of* The Blood-Horse)
Leslie Combs (*Anne M. Eberhardt, courtesy of* The Blood-Horse)
Spendthrift Farm (*Tony Leonard, courtesy of* The Blood-Horse)
Lester Piggott with Vincent O'Brien at the Curragh (*courtesy of* Racing
   Post)
Lester winning the 1990 Breeders' Cup Mile in New York on Royal
   Academy (*courtesy of* Racing Post)
Vincent with Michael Smurfit (*Gerry Cranham*)
Danny Swartz (*courtesy of* Racing Post)
John Gaines (*John C. Wyatt*)
Franklin Groves (*Anne M. Eberhardt, courtesy of* The Blood-Horse)
J. T. Lundy (*Anne M. Eberhardt, courtesy of* The Blood-Horse)
Tommy Gentry (*courtesy of* The Blood-Horse)
Farm for sale (*Nick Robinson*)
Nelson Bunker Hunt (*Anne M. Eberhardt, courtesy of* The Blood-Horse)
Sue Sangster congratulates Lester Piggott on Rodrigo de Triano
   having won the 2000 Guineas in 1992 (*Alec Russell*)

Authors' Note

Throughout this narrative there are frequent references to huge sums of money, some of them in US dollars and some of them in pounds sterling. We did not attempt to convert these into one single currency, which is the standard editorial practice, because the sums – such as the $10·2 million for a Keeneland yearling – were often such well-known figures that conversion would have been misleading and almost certainly inaccurate since exchange rates can vary by the hour. A sterling rate of 1·75, for instance would have converted to 'the £5,828,571·40 Keeneland yearling'. This would plainly have been absurd. The yearling was bred in the USA, the bidding was in dollars, and when in England or Ireland we have used pounds – occasionally Irish ones, when a stallion involved an Irish-trained horse going to Coolmore Stud in Tipperary.

There is also the occasional mention of the old-fashioned 'guineas' (one pound and one shilling). This is still used at English bloodstock auctions, and where appropriate we have utilized this measurement. The title of the one-mile classics remains in the old racehorse currency – the 2000 Guineas and the 1000 Guineas. These do not, however, bear any relationship to the modern prize money for these rates, which is nowadays over £100,000.

Prologue: The Historic Blackballing of Lord Soames

It was always tense in The Rooms when they were proposing to elect a statesman to membership. Actually, it was always tense in The Rooms whomever they were proposing to elect to membership. But a statesman created a special feeling of apprehension. Such an event happened only every fifty years or so, because, by and large, the Jockey Club did not see statesmen as the right calibre of chap. Most of them had depressingly brilliant intellects coupled with dazzling charm and tact. Or, put in the more ducal vernacular of the Club, they were too clever by half, 'too smarmy'.

The Earl of Rosebery, during his Lordship's tenure as Prime Minister of England, had of course been a member of the Club back in 1894 when his colt Ladas had won the Derby at Epsom. However, having been a member since the age of twenty-two, the touchy business of electing a statesman had never really applied.

The Jockey Club had admitted an Under-Secretary of State for War, Earl Cadogan, in the middle of the nineteenth century, in the knowledge that he was much preoccupied with the unrest along India's north-west frontier. The same applied, in smaller measure, to the Marquis of Londonderry and the Earl of Zetland in the 1880s when they were appointed as successive Lords-Lieutenants of Ireland. Different frontier, similar unrest among the natives and one or two furrowed brows in the Club. Lord Randolph Churchill, Chancellor of the Exchequer and owner of an Oaks winner in 1889, had *had* to be elected. And they could not quite avoid accepting his often fractious son Sir Winston, who won the Jockey Club Cup in 1950 with his stout-hearted grey Colonist II shortly before becoming Prime Minister for the second time.

Of course the greatest of all England's horse-racing monarchs, King Edward VII, was a member. He would have to be included as a statesman – Emperor of India and Ruler of the Lands Beyond the Seas and all that – but like Rosebery he had not really been considered as such when proposed for membership. Elected at twenty-three, he already owned two Derby winners (Persimmon and Minoru) and, during his frequent stays in Newmarket, he usually took the Jockey Club Rooms, in a private apartment with a private entrance – a discreet little throughway not entirely unfamiliar to the occasional visiting mistress. Upon the death of his mother Queen Victoria in 1901, Edward ascended the throne a few months off his sixtieth birthday in 1901 and by this time he assuredly was 'one of us'.

These very few apart, then, the Jockey Club had stuck for the past two hundred years to its own kind: land-owning horsemen who understood who was to be trusted and who was not. But today, 3 May 1967, in the hours following the running of the first English classic of the season, the 2000 Guineas, on nearby Newmarket Heath, there was an unmistakable apprehension in the Rooms. Before them this evening was written the name of Arthur Christopher John Soames, former Secretary of State for War, Prime Minister Harold Macmillan's Minister of Agriculture and Fisheries and a Coldstream Guards officer of the highest quality who had been awarded the Croix de Guerre from a grateful, liberated French nation. He was also the son-in-law of the recently deceased member Sir Winston Churchill.

The eighty-five-year-old Earl of Rosebery, son of the nineteenth-century PM, was worried. The Club employed a legendary, not to mention brutal, 'blackballing' system, which ended would-be members' aspirations with the suddenness of a guillotine. The blackballing box is a tall shiny, wooden case, with a round, tube-like aperture close to the top in which the forearm is placed. The ball can be dropped to either side: left in the 'YES' slot, right into the 'NO' slot. One ball, dropped in the 'NO' slot, by any member, was all it took. No one would ever know precisely *who* had dropped it in. Far less, *why* it had been dropped in.

Lord Rosebery did not like it. He and the industrialist Sir Foster Robinson had argued about the system just a couple of years previously. Rosebery believed it was a 'damned bad idea' because news of a blackballing of someone important would one day get out and there would be hell to pay in the press. With much apprehension, he envisaged 'the kind of thing Cardigan had to put up with after the "Black Bottle" incident in the officers' mess of his personal regiment of Hussars'. In the case of Mr Soames the Club had sent letters to all members sounding out the strength of feeling towards his election, conscientiously

heading off the possibility of an unseemly blackballing. Indeed no
member had intimated even a dislike of the rotund bon vivant Christopher Soames, far less an intention to throw him out of the Club before
he was even elected. But Lord Rosebery still did not like it.

He walked slowly into the Jockey Club Rooms, leaning on his walking
stick owing to a slight touch of gout that day. The master of the massive
castellated Buckinghamshire manor of Mentmore, with its £7 million
collection of French furniture and art, breeder of two Derby winners
and a Steward as long ago as 1929, was filled with misgivings.

One by one, as the sun slipped below the long western horizon of
Newmarket Heath, his fellow members arrived. There was the Chairman of the meeting, the formidable figure of the former Coldstream
Guards Major General, Sir Randle 'Gerry' Feilden, future High Sheriff
of Oxfordshire. There was the Duke of Devonshire, owner of the greatest house in England, Chatsworth, together with fifty-six'thousand acres
of Derbyshire. There was Bernard Marmaduke Fitzalan Howard, the
sixteenth Duke of Norfolk, Earl Marshal of England, owner of the lovely
Arundel Castle and twenty-five thousand acres of Sussex. There was
Lord Tryon, Keeper of the Privy Purse, Treasurer to Her Majesty
Queen Elizabeth II; the Earl of Halifax, son of Neville Chamberlain's
Foreign Secretary, a former Captain in the Royal Horse Guards, Master
of Foxhounds, married to Lord Rosebery's niece; and the fabulously
wealthy Jakie Astor, owner of Hatley Park in Bedfordshire, son
of Viscount 'Waldorf' Astor and the legendary Nancy Lady Astor,
Britain's first female Member of Parliament.

Quietly reading *The Times* in the Coffee Room sat The Hon. Major
General Sir Harold Wernher, owner of the great English mansion of
Luton Hoo, with its four thousand surrounding acres, where the Queen
spent her honeymoon. (Sir Harold's wife, the fabled Lady Zia Wernher,
was the Queen's godmother and daughter of Grand Duke Michael of
Russia, first cousin of Czar Nicholas. Lord Rosebery thought she would
make a damned good Empress of All the Russias if they ever got fed
up with those Bolsheviks . . .) Lord Howard de Walden (proprietor of
three thousand acres and a sizeable portion of central London) was
chatting to the wealthiest of all the Scottish whisky heirs, Major Sir
Reginald Macdonald-Buchanan, Chairman of Distillers; the eighteenth
Earl of Derby, with twenty-two thousand acres of Lancashire, had
slipped in after the short drive from his Newmarket home, Stanley
House, and was enjoying a quiet drink with the old Cavalry officer
Lord Willoughby de Broke, the twentieth Baron, Lord Lieutenant of

Warwickshire. This was a rather poetic duo, both the Derby and the Willoughby titles had been awarded by King Henry VII after the Battle of Bosworth Field in 1485. Both of the first Lords had fought against King Richard III with enormous courage, and here we were, five hundred years later, with Derby and Willoughby still standing, in a sense, shoulder to shoulder.

They all made their way along to the Committee Room, past the bust of the most fearsome Jockey Club president of all, that of Admiral Henry John Rous who completely dominated the English Turf from 1846 until his death in 1877. The Admiral's creed had been well known: 'I do not believe in heavy gambling, and any member of this club who wins more than £50,000 on a horse should be expelled.' Even in 1967 some of the members were a bit reticent to look the white stone bust directly into its dead, but still withering, eye. Most of the thirty or so members seated themselves around the main table with the Chairman. But the great, venerable names of the Jockey Club, such as Rosebery, Derby, Astor and Norfolk, sat in their big personal chairs strategically set around the room.

'My Lords and Gentlemen,' said Sir Randle, 'there is one candidate for the Jockey Club: Mr Christopher Soames, proposed by Mr Blackwell, and seconded by Mr Astor.' At this point the formal ballot was taken. The official Jockey Club 'servants' from the old racing firm of Weatherbys carried round to each member the polished wooden blackballing box. Each one of these extraordinarily influential men, who could be said to own a lion's share of England rather than merely run it, placed his hand into the ballot box. The little wooden balls rattled into the slot which signified 'YES' to Mr Soames. Well, all but one. Whether misfired or maliciously misdirected, a solitary ball landed in the 'NO' slot. Sir Randle hesitated for a few moments before he said flatly, and without declaring the actual number of 'blackballs', 'My Lords and Gentlemen, Mr Soames is not elected.'

The room went stone silent, every member, except perhaps for one, embarrassed at what they had somehow managed to achieve. 'My God!' whispered Sir Harold Wernher. 'Someone's blackballed Winston's son-in-law.' But the Major General recovered swiftly and said nothing of the blackballing. In a murderously contrived anti-climax, he declared, 'My Lords and Gentlemen, the minutes of the last meeting have been circulated. Can I sign them as the correct record?'

A few voices muttered assent and Sir Randle reached for his fountain pen. But the sixth Earl of Rosebery, godson of His Late Majesty (and distinguished former member) King Edward VII, was on his feet, and he was absolutely furious. His words came out in growling torrent.

'May I say something on that?' he said. 'The blackballing, I mean, not the damned minutes. We have all had confidential letters round and presumably you, sir, have read all those replies and come to the conclusion that the Club thought this was an excellent candidate for the Club. Well, if these letters go out ... and you yourself read them, and feel a man should be elected, and he is then not elected ... well, it does not seem to me there is much good going on this way ... not if you are trying to get members into the Club.'

'I could not agree more, Lord Rosebery,' replied the Major General.

By now there was an air of great consternation in the Committee Room. The Duke of Devonshire, a former Commonwealth Minister of State in his Uncle Harold's Government, was mentioning that he was quite sure that his former Tory Party colleague Christopher Soames was to become Britain's next ambassador to Paris, which would probably carry with it a peerage.

The Duke of Norfolk, sitting forward at the table with his natural magisterial authority, observed that as a result of 'this damned blackballing' there were certain people he was not absolutely dying to encounter. He knew beyond all doubt that trouble involving a statesman is apt to be ten times more awkward than that involving anyone else. As seconder to Mr Soames's candidature, Jakie Astor, himself a former Member of Parliament, was very, very angry.

The previous year's Senior Steward Tom Blackwell, Brigade Major to the 5th Guards Armoured Division in the Second World War, was now on his feet. It was this former Coldstream Guards officer who had proposed Mr Soames in the first place. He also was not pleased. 'Look here,' he said, 'I support every word Lord Rosebery said. It is pointless going on with this. We would not have put Christopher Soames up if we had not understood that people approved. If they have changed their minds at the last minute, they might have let the Senior Steward know.'

Major General Feilden declared helplessly, 'What Mr Blackwell says is absolutely correct. I advised them there was no doubt Mr Soames would be elected to the Club. It must be that people have changed their minds ... They should have let me know, I think. My Lords and Gentlemen, do I take it that the Club wants to go back to the original method of election?'

'The original what?' asked Lord Rosebery grumpily.

'The old method of election,' said the Major General.

'Oh, yes, that,' replied his Lordship. 'We'd better get a sub-committee or something to go into it, rather like they did after the First War. They'd better present it to the Club at the Summer Meeting. Because if it goes on like this people will refuse to be put up for Membership.'

'And I', stated the still-irritated Earl Marshal of England, 'am quite prepared to second Lord Rosebery's suggestion.'

'Would that be the wish of the Club?' asked Sir Randle. The members muttered 'Agreed', with each man glancing sideways to see if there was a dissenting voice – perhaps belonging to the men who had embarrassed them all so utterly by 'blackballing' the Rt. Hon. Christopher Soames.

The meeting droned on for another hour, discussing a modernization plan for the racecourse at Newmarket. But nobody's heart was really in it. This packed formal gathering of the great, the landed, the titled and the highest officer classes, was nervous. 'Damned nervous', in the words of Tom Blackwell. 'Because this is not going to reflect at all well on us – and it's made a damned sight worse because even *we* do not know who blackballed Soames. We should have listened to Harry Rosebery two years ago and scrapped the blackballing system once and for all.'

The Duke of Norfolk, was widely reputed to be an organizational genius, having masterminded the arrangements for the Coronation of Queen Elizabeth II and managed an England Cricket Tour of Australia. Now, as he walked slowly back to the more comfortable morning room, there gathered about him a group of fellow members seeking not only comfort from his great wisdom, but also some guidance as to how to explain the aberration which had just taken place, should the news become public.

Lord Rosebery was not among them. Still furious, he stumped out of the Jockey Club Rooms and headed for his car, uttering only the words: 'Absolutely ridiculous. Like some bloody secret society. This has to stop . . .' Lord Rosebery, who in his prime was properly recognized as a truly formidable orator and a man of serious intellectual power, was oblivious to the fact that, on this black night, the blackball had been deliberately dropped by one of his closest colleagues.

Back in the morning room, Andrew Devonshire was at the Duke of Norfolk's side, as were John Derby, Jakie Astor, Gerry Feilden, Jocelyn Hambro, Tom Blackwell, and Major General Sir George Burns, who privately thought someone might have merely 'got a bit muddled up' and blackballed Soames by sheer carelessness. His Grace did not share this view.

They all stood beneath George Stubbs's near-priceless oil of the immortal racehorse Eclipse, painted outside the old 'rubbing house' on the nearby heath in the less stressful times of the late eighteenth century. 'Well,' said Bernard, sipping boldly from a large tumbler of J&B Scotch and soda, 'this is a real bugger's muddle. There is someone here with a clear feeling against Christopher Soames. We'll meet again tomorrow morning and I think we can count on Harry Rosebery to put forward a proposal which will at least prevent this happening again. For the moment I suggest we say nothing, but perhaps make it clear to Mr Soames that such a 'technicality' will not happen again, and that he may look forward to becoming a full member at the very next opportunity.'

There was no argument with such a sure-footed course of action, but the members with strong Tory Party connections – Devonshire, obviously, Astor (close friend of the next Prime Minister Edward Heath), and Hambro (friend of the former Chancellor of the Exchequer Reginald Maudling) – were bitterly unhappy. No less so was Gerry Feilden who had chaired this disastrous meeting.

On the Newmarket racecourse that afternoon, the day had held such promise. Royal Palace, a grand-looking bright bay colt owned by Jockey Club member Jim Joel, had won the first English classic, the 2000 Guineas, without even a warm-up race as a three-year-old. In a dramatic, driving finish he had held off the French challenger Taj Dewan by a short head. The joy that always pervades the Jockey Club Room at Newmarket racecourse when an English classic race is won by a member was both sincere and sportsmanlike. Mr Joel, heir to a gigantic South African diamond fortune, was a popular owner-breeder, and his colt had carried a few sizeable wagers on behalf of several of the members. Three hours ago everything had seemed very pukka. And now this . . . The possibility of open, hostile, national ridicule loomed tiresomely upon the horizon.

As Lord Rosebery had gruffly phrased it: 'This has to stop.'

At 11 o'clock the following morning, they all gathered once more at the Jockey Club Rooms in Newmarket High Street. A couple of glasses of port and a good night's sleep had done precisely nothing for his Lordship's mood. Harry Rosebery was still furious. 'Good morning, m'lord,' a member of staff greeted him as he walked through the main door.

'I can think, offhand, of nothing, absolutely nothing', he replied, 'that is good, or even remotely acceptable about this particular morning.'

He walked steadily along the corridor to find the Senior Steward.

They spoke for several minutes together and then joined the meeting in the Committee Room. Above the fireplace hung another magnificent oil by George Stubbs, which was, in fact, shortly to be removed in favour of a large portrait of Sir Winston Churchill, whose son-in-law the Club had just irrevocably humiliated. Major General Feilden called the members to order, which was not a difficult task. This was a very subdued gathering, since, even now, no one had the slightest idea which members had perpetrated the blackballing. The High Tory group were still extremely embarrassed and there was a dignified silence from them.

But there was a deafening silence from the corner occupied by one of the most popular sportsmen in England, the twentieth Baron Willoughby de Broke. For it was he who had blackballed Christopher Soames. Lord Willoughby, with the deadly subversiveness the system encouraged, had registered a secret and decisive protest to the proposed membership.

Major General Feilden proceeded. 'My Lords and Gentlemen,' he said, 'Lord Rosebery has given notice to the Stewards that he wants to raise a point before we get to the main agenda.'

There was again silence as the Club's most venerable member rose to his feet. He spoke firmly, in that blunt aristocratic manner which has always outlawed any form of interruption:

'My Lords and Gentlemen,' said Harry Rosebery, 'I want to thank the Stewards for their courtesy in letting me bring up Any Other Business at the start. But I have to catch a train, at 12 o'clock.

'Now then,' he began, 'I want to recall to your minds what happened last night when we had a candidate put up and blackballed. Every single person had been asked if they were in favour and every single person – except one – replied to say they were. Well, as I said last night, his subsequent rejection knocks on the head our method of election completely.' He gazed around the historic room very slowly, and very carefully, before adding, 'If you cannot trust members of the Club to carry out what they write, I am ashamed to think that you cannot trust them at all.'

He addressed the possibility of a blackballing-by-error in the following words: 'There is to my mind just a chance – and it is more than just a chance, I think – that a black ball, or even two, can get in by mistake . . . you know, into the wrong aperture. It has happened in the past, I know. And it might always happen. I am not saying it did happen last night, but I am hoping, for the credit of members of the Club, that it did.'

'So am I,' whispered the Duke of Norfolk. But there was an atmosphere of mistrust in the room. Who had blackballed Christopher Soames? And why? The Duke of Norfolk shook his head, conveying his exasperation. Lord Rosebery spoke again.

'I am proposing', he said, 'that we go back to what happened forty-three years ago. At that time there was a general reluctance among people who were put up for the Jockey Club, not at all sure whether they would get elected or not. I myself missed the blackballing system – they never had an opportunity to get me – which is perhaps the only reason why I'm here at all! But in 1924 they passed a resolution making membership the province of a Membership Committee. The late Lord Derby was made chairman, as I remember. A few of us were elected under that system and then, suddenly, they went back to the old method of blackballing . . . Can't remember why.

'Personally I dislike blackballing. I always have. Doesn't give a man a fair chance. I have never blackballed anyone in my life. For anything. Also I think this system leaves a possibility of one of us making an error. I mean, you might be talking to someone, and put the damn thing in, and it goes into the wrong 'NO' or the wrong 'YES'. There is the possibility for error. I don't like it.'

He then proposed, formally, that the Club return to the method which was adopted in 1924. 'I am not a great believer in thinking that the things of the past were better than things of the present. But I do think the 1924 method is superior. I think we are all agreed that it is quite impossible to go on as we are going on now, when people write one thing, and then vote in another way. I propose that the Order of 1924 be re-enacted and made a Rule of the Club.'

The Duke of Norfolk seconded the motion and, although it took almost a year to implement, the return to 1924 was carried out. It would never again be quite such a searching challenge to become a member of England's Jockey Club, which still remains the most exclusive gathering of men in the history of the free world, with the possible exception of the Last Supper.

Lord Willoughby never did come clean and admit what he had done, although he felt extremely strongly about it. Very late one night, Lord Willoughby, pressed on the subject, put the blackballing down to events in the North African campaign of the Second World War, where Christopher Soames served in the Coldstreams. 'Tobruk,' snapped his Lordship. There was not another word. Not another clue.

Christopher Soames was finally elected in May 1968, by which time he was indeed Britain's ambassador to France, and a Peer of the Realm,

as Andrew Devonshire had forecast on that most awful of nights a year
previously. His election went some way towards stabilizing relations with
the diplomatic world, but it was always overshadowed by his blackballing.
The outlook of many members, not least the Duke of Norfolk, had been
changed irreconcilably. For them it was essential to recruit new blood
into the Club, to make contact with new younger racehorse owners and
breeders, who had experience beyond that of the land and the military.
But despite some powerful voices in the Jockey Club pushing for a more
enlightened and forward-looking approach to the new decade of the
1970s, there remained many reactionaries in the world's oldest sporting
club. They refused to elect to membership Mr David Robinson, England's biggest racehorse owner, presumably because he made his vast
fortune in renting television sets rather than fields of turnips or corn to
tenant farmers. As a result Robinson turned his back on racing to fund
the most beautiful new college at Cambridge University and dispense
charitable largess around the country totalling some £26 million.

However, an era had passed. No longer could the membership be
founded on quasi-medieval families, whose main qualifications had been
derived through the execution of *noblesse oblige*: fighting wars, acquiring
money and land from the peasant classes and displaying a sycophantic
devotion to various dull-witted monarchs. Times were changing. This
was the twentieth century. Had been for some time now. It was time to
wake up, to breathe new life into the two-hundred-year-old organization
which rules, runs and organizes horse-racing in Great Britain, and sets
a standard of excellence and integrity for the Sport of Kings which is
unmatched anywhere in the world.

Over the centuries the Jockey Club established itself firstly as the
supreme rulers of Newmarket and all of the heathland gallops which
surround it, virtually all of which the Club now owns. Then, with inordinate speed, before 1800, it became the sole ruler of all racing in Great
Britain. In 1967 its traditions were without parallel, its authority unques-
tioned, its power in racing absolute over all men. Each member wears
a little silver badge to admit him to every racecourse in the country,
almost all of them with a private room for members. Royal Ascot is run
principally for, and essentially by, the Jockey Club. Members have total
priority in every aspect of a day at the races.

The Jockey Club still enjoys considerable royal patronage. The Queen
and the Queen Mother are its two Patrons; Prince Philip, Prince Charles
and Princess Anne are honorary members, and in addition there are
the two dukes, Devonshire and Sutherland. One way and another, it is

an organization to which any owner of any racehorse might longingly aspire. Today it has more than one hundred and twenty members, still drawn from a frightfully narrow social stratum. With any one of the Queen's subjects having only a 467,000 to 1 chance of ever being elected, the odds of acceptance are depressingly daunting for the socially ambitious, notwithstanding the 1967 outlawing of the hated blackball. Its membership is still heavily loaded with the military: high-ranking officers combined with haughtily born captains and majors who spent time in Her Majesty's Service but never threatened to reduce the importance of Field Marshal Lord Montgomery in the roll of British Army strategists. There is certainly no record of a former private, lance corporal or even sergeant ever being elected.

It has always been difficult to assess the precise criteria required for membership, principally because the members have historically behaved in such an arbitrary way. Collectively they have demonstrated a whim of iron. Until the early 1970s there might be said to have been ten 'Rules' which had served as general electoral guidelines. They were never, of course, formalized, but they were unfailingly observed:

1. The Club does not like trade, nor the people involved in it.
2. The Club does not like 'other ranks' from any branch of the Armed Services.
3. The Club does not like professional sportsmen, or trainers.
4. The Club does not like jockeys.
5. The Club does not like journalists.
6. The Club does not like bookmakers.
7. The Club does not like commercial horsetrading.
8. The Club does not like ostentation – film stars, play actors, entertainers of any type.
9. The Club does not like foreigners.
10. The Club does not like persons of low rank, not Honoured by Her Gracious Majesty.

These 'Rules' for membership, unwritten, unspoken, but rigid, have stood the test of time. The centuries-old contempt for all jockeys was encouraged historically by Admiral Rous himself, a man who was proud of the fact that he 'never shared his dinner table with one'. From the ranks of the race-riders, only one, the late Sir Gordon Richards, was ever made a member. No active trainer has ever been elected to membership. Among journalists, the three exceptions were men whose interest in racing and breeding was equal to their chosen trade. On the other hand, anyone even remotely connected with the betting industry was unmentionable. Owners and breeders showing too keen an interest in the monetary value of horseflesh, with inclinations to deal in bloodstock on a totally commercial level, were unacceptable – might result in a conflict of interest in the future. Show business people were also banned. Period.

However, politicians, undesirable though they may be, did not fall into any banned category. The outrageous breach of etiquette on the night of 3 May 1967, with the blackballing of the Rt. Hon. Christopher Soames, changed everything.

As the great men of the Jockey Club had stared in horror at that black ball in the wrong slot, a Rolls Royce had been moving swiftly away from Newmarket Heath, through the dark English countryside up towards the wooded borders of the ancient county of Cheshire. In the passenger seat sat the smiling figure of the thoughtful northern trainer Eric Cousins.

The driver of the car wore a similar smile, having just had a 'rather nice little each-way touch' in the 2000 Guineas, on a horse called Missile which had finished fast at 40–1, right behind Royal Palace and Taj Dewan. His trainer was the somewhat devilish little Irishman from Tipperary, Vincent O'Brien, whom the driver had admired since his schooldays. He had never of course met him, but one day he would become his most trusted friend.

The man at the wheel would, also, one day in the not-too-distant future, sail into the Jockey Club as a full member, without any questions. He would do so in total defiance of 'Rules' 1), 2), and 6). He would take 'Rule' 7) and single-handedly strangle it. And as for the section of 'Rule' 8) which deals with ostentation, well, he would somewhat unwittingly reduce that to rubble. As for the old creeds of Admiral Rous about gambling fortunes on bloodstock, the man driving the Rolls Royce would one day turn the entire thoroughbred breeding world into nothing short of an international commodity market. He would habitually risk gigantic fortunes, on the running of a racehorse. He would back his judgment on a scale never hitherto even dreamed about, by anyone. He would ultimately make Harry the Horse look like Winnie the Pooh.

His name was Robert Edmund Sangster.

== 1 ==

Chalk Stream

The once-great English seaport of Liverpool ought, in fairness, to hold a truly commanding view across the wide Mersey to the far-off mystic mountains of north Wales. Indeed it would do so, but for a mighty headland which juts like a giant fist straight out of the picturesque Roman city of Chester. The Wirral peninsula measures some fifteen miles by six, and it divides the two broad estuaries of the Mersey and the River Dee. On its north-eastern side are the heavy industrial ports of Birkenhead, Wallasey, Bebington and Ellesmere, which more or less wreck the mystic aspect of Liverpool's view.

On the far, western coast, however, is a true romance of water and flatlands, of a great river swirling out into the Irish Sea, of west winds from Ireland, perfumed by the heather of County Wicklow. Breathtaking vistas of the sea – the same waters over which Admiral Nelson once sailed his fleet – not to re-store in Liverpool, but for a secret tryst with the most famous and elegant of the local beauties, Lady Emma Hamilton of Parkgate. J. M. W. Turner memorably painted the Welsh mountains from here.

Just to the north of Lady Hamilton's childhood home stands the eastern seaward point of the headland. Here lies the historic golf links of Hoylake, home of the Royal Liverpool Golf Club, the scene of ten Open Championships and the course which beat Jack Nicklaus. And here, with glorious gardens lapping down almost to the fairways, are some of the most expensive residences in this most exclusive stretch of north-western England. They form a millionaire's row, known since the age of Queen Victoria as The Golden Mile. What the Hamptons are to New York's Long Island, so West Kirby is to the Wirral peninsula.

This is Sangster Country. It has been Sangster Country for most of this century. The grand family house, where Robert was raised, is called West Lodge. It stands behind solid, red sandstone pillars, among beautifully clipped lawns. Providentially it always possessed a fine stable block and groom's cottage within its grounds. The family has been wealthy since Edwardian times. Robert's grandfather Edmund Sangster founded the fortune with a large warehousing and wholesale business in nearby Manchester shortly after Lord Rosebery's godfather ascended the throne of England in 1901. Fourteen years later his teenaged son Vernon – Robert's father – set off with the Manchester Regiment to fight on the Western Front in the Great War. He survived that most awful of conflicts, and returned to a depressed and demoralized England with a view to taking over the family business.

But by nature, Sangsters tend not to take over things. They are more inclined to start things. They are entrepreneurs by instinct, blessed with a touch of daring, but equally blessed by a certain sure-footedness. Young Vernon Sangster and his father proceeded to launch a business, essentially a lottery. They called it Vernons Pools and their plan was to give every working man, for just a few pence, a chance to win a fortune. Every week.

It was built around the results of the Football League matches played in England all through the autumn, winter and spring of the year. Success depended on the devotion of millions of ordinary people who sent in their coupons and their small amount of money, in the hope of scooping up thousands of pounds for correctly forecasting the drawn matches. One unlikely 'save' from an unseen goalkeeper playing hundreds of miles away in the pouring rain and mud, could smash millions of dreams. It happened every week. But it did not cost much, and the hopes of millions stayed high. The coupons and the little cheques and money orders kept coming.

Profits grew steadily each year and in the mid 1920s Vernon Sangster and his father moved the operation thirty miles to Liverpool. In the 1930s, with the business of football pools making the family rich, there were two major relocations: Vernon, now married to Peggy, bought West Lodge; and Vernons Pools set up their new headquarters in the north-eastern suburb of Liverpool, Aintree, home of the world's most famous steeplechase, the Grand National.

Robert was born on 23 May 1936. He was to be an only child and sole heir to a sprawling business which would, before he was out of school, employ six thousand people. Under the umbrella of Vernon Industries there were factories making products to help Britain's war effort, factories making kitchen and domestic products, factories making plastics, factories making children's toys. And all the time the great 'cash cow' of the football pools increased the vast and diverse fortune of Vernon Sangster.

He was a nice man, rather quiet, but immensely well-liked by both his peers and employees. He was extremely generous to charities, a trait inherited by his son. Vernon was not given to ostentation in any form, and usually had lunch with his wife in a private businessmen's club in Liverpool. He was, however, obsessed by sports, choosing for Robert's godfather Dr Joe Graham, a British Boxing Board of Control official fight doctor. He also ensured that Robert was taught the game of golf at a very young age under the tutelage of one of England's finest players, his friend Henry Cotton, three times winner of the Open Championship and, belatedly, a Knight of the Realm.

Vernon, who played off a handicap of twelve and would one day be elected to membership of the Royal and Ancient at St Andrews, was of course a member of Royal Liverpool Golf Club. He and his wife played the daunting 7000 yards of Hoylake a couple of times a week. This was no ordinary golf club. Royal Liverpool is redolent with legend. Here it was that one of the finest amateurs of all time, Mr Harold Hilton, a local member and the *only* man who had ever held both the US and British Amateur Championships in the same year, won the 1897 Open beating the five-times professional winner James Braid. Here too the immortal Edwardian golfer James Taylor won the first of his five Open Championships by eight shots in 1913. Also it was at Hoylake that the great American Walter Hagen won the second of his four Open Championships, in 1924, playing the last nine holes in 36, despite visiting three bunkers. Bobby Jones sailed into Liverpool in 1930 and nearly blew his Grand Slam – with a seven at the par-five eighth hole, right at the bottom of the Sangster garden – in the last round of the Open Championship at Royal Liverpool. Ultimately he won by two strokes, but to the end of his life he always said: 'I'll never forget Hoylake.'

In the 1967 Open Championship here, in mild conditions, only 19 of the 370 rounds played were under 70. The winner was the Argentinian Roberto de Vicenzo who finished on 278. The holder, Jack Nicklaus, failed by two shots to shoot the 67 which would have given him a tie. Afterwards he stood alone, memorably, outside the Victorian clubhouse, and he gazed out towards the far-distant eighth hole at the end of the formidable links, and he shook his head in disbelief. It is one thing for a local businessman to play off twelve on a well-watered park golf course, but quite another to be able to score like that over Hoylake. Both Vernon and Peggy Sangster became Captains of the Club in 1975, the year their only son set off on his mission to revolutionize The Sport of Kings.

As the Second World War drew to its close and Robert Sangster attained the age of eight, he was sent as a weekly border to the nearby Leas School which was also situated with panoramic views across the golf course. Unsurprisingly he swiftly came to love sports and, by the time he left for public school, Repton (founded 1577), he was a very reasonable cricketer, an enthusiastic rugby player and, at thirteen, a pretty long hitter of a golf ball. But what he could really do was box. Dr Joe Graham had seen to that, having personally shown his godson at a very young age the basics of the straight left, the jab, the hook and the uppercut. Robert even knew how to throw combinations, knew how to shift his weight, to move to the left away from a 'southpaw'. Above all, he knew how to punch correctly, how to take the impact.

He had accompanied Joe on trips to London. At the age of eleven he had seen the British heavyweight champion Bruce Woodcock suffer a broken jaw at the hands of the American Joe Baksi. Engraved on his memory is the post-fight scene in the dressing room, where the badly hurt Woodcock sat with a white towel over his head, muttering over and over to his manager: 'I'm sorry, Tom. I'm so sorry. I've let you down.'

In 1951 he watched the brilliant British Middleweight Champion Randolph Turpin beat Sugar Ray Robinson for the world title at London's Earls Court Stadium. A few years later he was ringside with his godfather at Liverpool Stadium when the British Middleweight Champion Johnny Sullivan entered the ring first for his title fight with Pat McAteer of Birkenhead, and insisted on occupying Pat's traditional corner. He can still recall the sound and the fury of the packed ranks of the dockers at this affront to their hero; the uproar in the stadium as the referee spun a coin and then led the arrogant ex-booth fighter Sullivan to the opposite corner. 'No one,' says Robert, 'I promise you, no one who was there could ever forget the eruption of joy from that crowd when Pat knocked Sullivan out. I flew out of my seat with my arms in the air.'

He also remembers to this day nearly every punch thrown in the 'toughest fight I ever saw', when Dennis Powell fought George Walker for the vacant British cruiserweight crown at Liverpool Stadium on 26 March 1953. He sat behind Dr Joe while the two grim, determined contestants fought it out.

Walker, felled in the first round by a right hook, took an eight count. In the fourth Powell was down for nine from a momentous right from

Walker. Then they both went down together, Powell for 'six', Walker rising immediately. In the seventh Walker lost his gum shield, Powell's eye was cut, Walker's left eye was closing and still they went at it, with thunderous punches.

By the eighth round Walker could see only through his right eye. In the ninth they were considering stopping the fight in favour of Walker, so badly was Powell's eye bleeding. But the referee let it go on, through a murderous tenth and through the eleventh, with George Walker, fighting for his life, now being hit too often for anyone's taste. His eye was so badly injured, his chief second Dave Edgar refused to let him come up for the twelfth round. He called the referee over and asked him to stop it. George Walker was heartbroken, begging for a chance, for just one more round. But Edgar was having none of it, and neither was the ref. They named Powell the winner and Robert remembers watching George Walker, sitting on his stool, devastated, alone, as we all must be at such times. 'I thought then, as I think now,' says Robert, 'what a man'. (George Walker was to make and lose a gigantic fortune as Chairman of Brent Walker, owners of bookmakers William Hill, in the late 1980s.)

Whenever he was home from school Robert attended the big fights at Liverpool Stadium. He saw all of the top British fighters of the 1950s: Freddie Mills, Dave Charnley, Terry Downes, Jack Gardner. Dr Joe even took him down to London, to the promoter Jack Solomons's gymnasium in Windmill Street, off Piccadilly. There the trainers taught him to spar. He used to hold the padded gloves for Freddie Mills to swing at, and he learned to move them quickly, listening to Freddie tell him, 'Watch my eyes, Bobby, watch carefully, that's how you read a fighter, that's how you know when the punches are coming.'

Robert loved to watch Freddie Mills, and he was not yet fourteen years old when Dr Joe took him down to London to watch his hero defend the world cruiserweight championship against the American Joey Maxim. 'It was', recalls Robert, 'the worse night of my life thus far.' Maxim knocked Freddie out in round ten. He also knocked out three of his front teeth and Mills never fought again. But he still turned up to spar with Robert at Windmill Street.

This involvement with the sport of professional boxing was not absolutely what one might have expected from a young gentleman of Robert's social standing. But Vernon Sangster was not some old lord crusting around the battlements wondering why the devil his son could not show a decent interest in something less violent, like hunting or shooting. Vernon Sangster was a man of the real world and he understood the excitement of professional sport at that level, and he believed his son would benefit later in life from the raw hardness of such a world. He believed it was excellent training for a boy to understand sacrifice, courage, determination, the joy of winning, and the pain and disappointment of defeat. He saw no harm in Robert's early devotion to the brutality of the prize ring, and the men who worked in it. He even allowed his son to take eight friends, on his tenth birthday, to the fights at Liverpool Stadium.

Robert was not in fact a great scholar at school, but he was good at maths and long on common sense. He was a very formidable front-row forward on the rugby field and he pleased the Repton cricket coach, the former Derbyshire spin-bowler Eric Marsh, so much that he allowed his wealthiest pupil to keep his car in a garage at his home. Considering that Repton had now been waiting nigh-on half a century for someone to replace their immortal England and Oxford University batsman C. B. Fry (and it clearly was not going to be Robert) this must rank as a gesture of the highest nobility. At boxing, Robert was never defeated in twelve fights in the ring at Repton.

Like all young men leaving school in the 1950s, Robert was required for two years of National Service and he selected one of England's historic fighting regiments, the 22nd Regiment of Foot, The Cheshires, the headquarters of which were in Chester Castle down at the end of the Wirral peninsula. The regiment had been founded in 1689 by the Duke of Norfolk, the direct ancestor of the one so upset at the Jockey Club blackballing, who sailed his men from Liverpool to fight at the Battle of the Boyne. For nearly three centuries the Cheshires had fought for King, Queen and Country. They had defeated the Americans during the Revolution at the Battles of Rhode Island and New York; they had fought, on and off, in India for a hundred years; they fought in the great battles for Afghanistan in the 1840s under General Sir Charles Napier, once defeating 30,000 Baluchis when outnumbered by ten to one. They fought in the Boer War, and they fought and died by the hundreds at the Somme, at Ypres, all over Passchendaele, and at Gallipoli. In the Second World War the regiment fought with enormous heroism at El Alamein, Sicily, Salerno and Anzio.

Dearly wanting to be an officer in the Cheshires, Robert applied for training but the officer selection board wanted to assess him twice and after his first interviews they requested him to serve a little more time in the regiment and come back in a few weeks in order that they might talk to him again. In the meantime, however, fate intervened and he leapt at a posting with the Commanding Officer in exciting postwar Berlin and, casting his ambitions of leadership to the west winds of the Wirral, he flew to Germany. Private Sangster, foot soldier, reported for duty.

During the first couple of days men were assessed for sports activities. It was viewed as something of a joke among the ranks when this wealthy young chap from Repton College – famed mainly for producing four Archbishops of Canterbury including Dr Ramsay – stuck his hand up to volunteer for, of all sports, boxing. Also he was apt to make the occasional remark which branded him among instructors as something of a 'smartass' – and on the first day of training the PTI was expounding the rules of 'non-hitting' areas (back of the head, kidneys, and so on), when Robert uttered one wisecrack too many. The instructor chose to teach him a short, sharp lesson in Army etiquette. Summoning to the fore the big, beefy Brigade shot-putt champion, Private 'Tiny' Davies, he said, 'Right men, I am looking for someone to box a demonstration with Tiny here in the ring. Ah yes, Private Sangster, I think you'll do very nicely.'

Robert gazed at the massive, six-foot-four-inch Tiny, nodded curtly, checked his gloves and climbed into the ring. At eighteen, he was five feet ten inches, weighed one hundred and seventy-two pounds, and he was giving away about forty-two pounds and several inches. But as Tiny advanced in round one, the words of Freddie Mills rang clearly in his mind: 'Bobby, if ever you're fighting a man who might be a bit short on experience, and he comes at you, bang him on the nose early – it'll make his eyes water, unsettle him.'

Tiny came forward, swung twice. Robert, on his toes, backed away waiting for the next advance. Tiny, almost inviting Robert to hit him, again swung wildly. Robert ducked to his right, slipped inside and banged his opponent on the nose with a short left hook. Hard. The soldiers yelled with excitement. Tiny reacted with instant, unutterable rage. He wiped his smarting eyes, leaned back on the ropes for extra leverage and catapulted himself across the ring at Robert. His face was puce with fury, and his fists were drawn back behind his ears.

Robert backed up to the ropes, stood his ground and stared hard into Tiny's angry eyes. His stance was slightly crouched, with his left jab ready. At the final split second, he shifted his weight to his left foot, and let fly with a text-book straight right hand that would have knocked down a stud bull. The force was doubled by the on-rushing momentum of Tiny, and Robert caught him flush on the jaw, just to the left of centre. Everything was correct, his wrist was locked, his elbow was locked, and his shoulder took the impact, just as Freddie Mills had instructed. Tiny, by the way, was unconscious before he hit the floor, where he remained, with the lights out, for a little over thirty seconds.

The soldiers went wild. Robert was unable to stop laughing, and the Army doctors were busy trying to revive Tiny. It was, upon reflection, Robert's finest hour in the ring. He went on to win the Berlin Brigade Heavyweight Championship and was never defeated in more than a dozen fights, though most of them, against better boxers, were decided on points. 'I never once had a chance to hit anyone that hard ever again,' he recalls. 'Actually, Freddie would have been proud of me that evening.'

For a young man so naturally captivated by heroism, both in the boxing ring and indeed in the history of his regiment, it was curious that he entirely abandoned his plans to become a second lieutenant and the vague ambition to become Captain Robert Sangster, which does after all possess a rather authoritative ring. But deep down he knew that his time in the Army was limited to just a few months and that back home the challenging, rewarding and glamorous world of big business awaited him. He had already acquired a taste for fast, expensive cars, beautiful girls, vintage champagne and the kind of well-tailored country clothes that young gentlemen of his wealth and education were apt to wear. Having bought himself a car in Berlin, Robert made the most of the great city. He was always zipping in and out of the Russian sector in search of the occasional pot of caviar and his memories of notorious forays into the more expensive night spots with a small group of adventurous, but largely impoverished fellow 'squaddies' still bring a beaming smile to his cheerful face even today.

Robert returned to the Wirral in 1957. By now the Vernon Organization was building parts for aircraft and owned a factory that produced a little three-wheel car which did eighty miles to the gallon, in sharp contrast to Robert's new Mercedes Sports which was pushed to get eighteen to the gallon going downhill. He was glad to be home and was quickly absorbed with the many improvements and expansions his father had implemented during his time in the Army. One of the least successful was in horse-race betting: a credit bookmaking business run in conjunction with the football pools, an innovation which Robert noted swiftly was not making much money. He was also at a loss as to how to help improve it, since his knowledge of horse racing was extremely limited.

He knew one fact about the sport. It was a schoolboy belief that the best trainer of a racehorse lived somewhere in southern Ireland, and was named Vincent O'Brien. This man had trained the winner of the Grand National Steeplechase in each of the last three years Robert had spent at Repton, 1953–55, and achieved this with three different horses too. Robert reasoned that, since no one else had ever achieved this, O'Brien must be the best there is. At school the experts among his friends had asserted that the Grand National was for big, slow plodding 'chasers' and that the real kings of National Hunt racing were those who won the two main races at Cheltenham – the Gold Cup and the Champion Hurdle. One fifteen-year-old Irish tipster had then confided that a trainer called O'Brien had won each of those races as well, three times in a row. And that settled it in Robert's mind. O'Brien must be the best.

Flat racing was essentially a mystery to him but, with Vernons now involved in credit betting, it was his bound duty to understand the basics of all gambling, the odds and the risks. As such he usually noticed the winners of big races like the Derby, where there might be a major pay-out. The 1957 Derby was run just a few days after he returned to the family fold and he saw that it had been won by Crepello. He also noted that the second horse, beaten only a length and half, was named Ballymoss. His price had been 33–1 and, happily for Vernons Credit, not many people had risked more than a few shillings each way. 'I might have had a few quid on it if I'd known he was running,' thought Robert. The horse was trained in County Tipperary by Vincent O'Brien.

Three weeks later Robert missed Ballymoss again when he won the Irish Derby by miles. But he did not miss much, since the horse started at an impossible price of 9–4 on. An entire year then slid by without Robert taking a shred of interest in flat racing, until the Royal Ascot meeting of 1958 took place. Because of pressure of work, he was not able to join a group of friends who had travelled south for the Gold Cup, all dressed up, complete with badges for the Royal Enclosure. He glanced rather enviously at the papers the following day to see if any of them had had their photographs taken, but none had. Every inch of the papers were devoted to the great Irish mare Gladness who had beaten all the colts to win the Gold Cup. She had been trained by O'Brien. That *really* settled it. Robert, at the age of twenty-two, reckoned he knew one shining, copper-bottomed, indisputable fact about flat racing. 'Vincent O'Brien is the best trainer there has ever been,' was how he phrased it to his friends, none of whom knew a whole lot more about it than he did.

Like many men of a steady temperament, but with a very busy mind, Robert Sangster was apt to come out with these slightly high-powered remarks from time to time. The fact that they were sudden, and usually sounded arrogant in the extreme, occasionally unnerved people. But they were always followed by a deep, good-natured chuckle at himself. Pompous he was not, but a mind like his needed an outlet, even though he had never actually heard of such legendary trainers as Dick Dawson, Frank Butters, Alec Taylor, John Porter, Fred Darling or Joe Lawson.

The usual setting for these pearls of modern wisdom from young Sangster was Liverpool's Kardomah Coffee House, the lunchtime gathering place of 1950s' upwardly mobile Liverpudlians. It was divided essentially into three sections: those set to inherit a considerable fortune; those who had a plan to amass a considerable fortune; and those who were merely *working* on a plan to earn a considerable fortune. Robert was a founder member of all three groups and, as the only one to already possess a fortune, he naturally became the unchallenged social leader.

The membership at table at which they gathered became an object of immense envy, admittance being unobtainable to those who did not fit these elite criteria. With Rugby Union only played at public schools in the 1950s, Robert and two or three of his colleagues from the highly reputable Birkenhead Park Rugby Football Club saw the playing of this esteemed sport as a qualification to their group. Several of their number were the sons of friends of Robert's father. Every provincial city in England at that time had such a table in one of the new, expensive coffee houses and country towns had their groups of wealthy young farmers, but big places like Liverpool had trainee businessmen who would one day run financial empires.

Amidst the huge amount of laughter generated by these chosen few, many a great business plan was hatched in the Kardomah. Robert was more inclined than the others to think very carefully before he spoke, because he was the one person at that table who had the financial clout actually to launch a new idea. He knew that a well-thought-out business proposition to his father would be backed, because Vernon Sangster had a firm belief in the inherent entrepreneurial talents of his only son and heir. Now that he had given up his youthful ambition to change his name by deed poll to Rocky Sangster and win the Heavyweight Championship of the World, Robert was eager to make his mark and knew that he deserved to be taken seriously and, if necessary, supported. This was just as it had been between Vernon and *his* own father Edmund Sangster in the years immediately following the Great War.

Robert fitted into the business world of Liverpool surprisingly well. To meet him it was impossible to avoid the impression of a well-tailored young bon vivant, with several girl friends and eight powerful cylinders to maintain. But he worked hard and was watchful of the firm's money, ever mindful of how to make more. He also cherished an unspoken, even to himself, ambition to start something of his own within the Vernons Organization just as his father had done so many times.

By the spring of 1960 Robert, now coming up to twenty-four, was planning to get married. He had met and spent almost a year with the very beautiful, tall, dark-haired, Manchester model Christine Street, whose career was on a major upswing with several television appearances to her credit and increasing work in London. Her parents owned the George Hotel in Penrith, a market town in Cumbria, fifteen miles south of the border town of Carlisle. Unsurprisingly Christine was not your average model. She was extremely well educated, having attended one of the best girls' boarding schools in the north of England – Queen Ethelburga's at Harrogate – and completed her studies at the Swiss finishing school Brillantmont in Lausanne. She was also extremely well mannered.

A grand society wedding was being planned at Penrith for the month of May, and the lunch club at the Kardomah was heavy with advice for the prospective bridegroom, particularly about the importance of the lunch club, even to a married man. It was into this slightly restless atmosphere that a stranger, named Nick Robinson, walked one morning in early March. He was new to the city and had been brought to the Kardomah by one of the regulars who worked in the giant packaging business built up by Nick's grandfather, the eighty-year-old Sir Foster Robinson.

Nick's background was not dissimilar to Robert's. He had been head boy at his famous prep school, Hawtreys, on the edge of the Savernake Forest in Wiltshire, and had completed his education at Harrow. He had entered the family business at their headquarters in Bristol, but upon his grandfather's specific instructions had been sent to their Liverpool office for two years to learn the technique of the Sales Department. But where Robert was addicted to hard contact sports like boxing and rugby football, Nick's game was horse racing. He had been brought up to it, as Robert had been to championship golf.

As they all sat in the Kardomah, the talk turned gradually to the sport which was so important to the newcomer. He told them of his grandfather's sprawling Wicken Park Stud, in Buckinghamshire, where racing fillies became broodmares and spent almost all of the rest of their lives in foal. He told them of the great breeding stallions of the day, horses who thought nothing of covering forty mares in a season, like Palestine, Court Martial, Swaps, Nashua, Court Harwell, Alycidon and the new young Crepello who had beaten Ballymoss in the 1958 Derby. At that Robert remembered with a blinding flash: 'That's my man O'Brien.' He seriously considered issuing the old 'Greatest trainer of all time' line across the young Mr Robinson, but decided against it. Instead he observed, more typically, that upon reflection he'd rather be a stallion than a broodmare.

For a table of young men so profoundly ignorant about the subject of racing thoroughbreds, Nick Robinson was getting a substantial amount of attention. They actually found it rather a fascination. But he really got them when he disclosed the deathless piece of information that the stable which trained for his grandfather thought he might win the Lincolnshire Handicap with his five-year-old bay gelding Chalk Stream. 'And', added Nick darkly, 'it might just be possible to have a really nice touch, at about 20–1.'

Now he was really talking. This group understood money, perhaps above all else, and the chance of landing a sizeable chunk of it without working was, as they say in New York, hitting 'em right where they lived. Robert, already interested, was teetering on the verge of enthralment. 'OK, Nick,' he said. 'Let me just get this straight. The Lincolnshire Handicap is a race, over what distance? One mile? Right. Now, how many are in it? About thirty? Christ, that's rather a lot, isn't it? Right. Now why do you think Chalk Stream might win?'

'Well, for a start, he is a pretty good racehorse. He has some experience, plenty of speed without being a champion or anything, he's been working extremely well for the past week or so, and above all he runs off a very light weight – under seven stone. We think he has a decent chance.'

'What do you mean a light weight?' said someone. 'I thought they all carried the same weight, otherwise it wouldn't be fair, would it?'

'Now this is a tricky subject.' said Nick doing his best to simplify it. 'In big races they do all carry the same weight, but this is a handicap and all the horses are weighted differently. The Jockey Club handicapper is basically trying to get them all to finish in a line, a dead heat. So he piles weight on the good horses to slow them up and leaves the less good ones with just a little. The idea being that every horse has a fair chance.'

'What kind of weight?'

'Oh, just lead weight slipped into the saddle cloth.'

'You mean, if the jockey weighs eight stone and the horse has to carry nine stone, they just put fourteen pounds of lead in the cloth?'

'That's it. Chuck in a couple of pounds for the saddle and there'll be six pounds of lead either side of the horse's flanks.'

'Yes, but how do they *know* what weight to put in? How does the handicapper know that his weights will slow the good horse down enough for the slower ones to catch him?'

'Well, that is a real speciality which can take almost a lifetime to master. But in the broadest possible terms, if, in a one-mile race, Horse A beats Horse B by three lengths at level weights, the handicapper will calculate it at two pounds a length, and he will ask Horse A to carry six pounds more than Horse B the next time they meet over a mile. In theory this should bring them across the line together. Of course it may not, because Horse A may have more in hand than everyone thought, and he may again win by three lengths, and the handicapper will give him six pounds more the next time. Eventually the handicapper *will* stop him from winning.'

'So,' said Robert, 'if a horse keeps losing, his weight is likely to get a lot lighter?'

'Precisely. And some trainers deliberately keep a horse losing – it's called "working him down the handicap" – until he has a weight so light he could not possibly be beaten. I mean, for example, he's carrying seven stone, when he should really be carrying nine stone . . .'

'And that's when they have a real bet?' said Robert.

'Correct.'

'Christ! Is that what's happening with Chalk Stream?'

'I am not sure about that, but Arthur Budgett, his trainer, says he is "very nicely weighted" – and that'll do for me. I'm backing him to win the Lincoln, 23 March.'

'Where do they run the Lincoln?'

'Lincoln. On a Wednesday. The race is always like the Charge of the Light Brigade. They try to go flat out from start to finish and if our horse wins . . . well, there's no feeling of elation quite like it.'

'Especially if your pockets are full of the bookmaker's money,' said Robert. 'OK, Nick,' he added, seeking some final assurance, 'now just tell me very simply why you think Chalk Stream is actually going to win.'

'Well, mainly because he damn nearly won it last year, dead-heated for second place. He has won three races, but last season he was very unlucky, placed second five times. Now I hear he is very well, working sharply in the morning and he has that low weight.'

Robert decided then and there that he would join the owner's grandson and place a bet of £25 each way on the horse. He did so with another bookmaker, not Vernons Credit Betting, and they all waited, with almost daily conferences at the Kardomah, for the great day to come.

On Saturday morning, 19 March, they met at the coffee house early, prior to Robert driving his colleagues fast back out to the Wirral to play rugby that afternoon for Birkenhead Park. Nick was there first, poring over the *Sporting Life*, the specialist newspaper for the horse-racing industry. As far as the others were concerned it might have been printed in Latin. But Nick had known his way around that publication almost since birth, and now he had the page open at the Four-Day Acceptors, and he was studying precisely who the opposition would be, the booked jockeys and, above all, the weights.

'The first thing to check', he said, 'is the top weight . . . damn it. Sovereign Path's stood its ground.'

'I suppose there is no possibility of you breaking into English?' said Robert. 'What d'you mean "Damn it. Sovereign Path's stood its ground"?'

'Well, Sovereign Path, who is a very tough grey horse, has already won six races, one of them by ten lengths. He nearly won a classic trial last season and he is the best horse in the Lincoln. I was rather hoping he would not be ready this early in the season. But he's in and his jockey is booked. He'll run. Still, he has a huge amount of weight – nine stone five pounds. No horse has carried that much to win the Lincoln this century. Anyway, I don't really think he will be happy giving us thirty pounds.'

'Could you tell me how you know all that stuff, about the biggest weight this century and everything?' asked Robert.

'Oh, those are just little facts that all horse-racing people know, or somehow get to know, round about the time of the Lincoln. I think the biggest weight was carried by Dorigen who won in 1933. I'm not sure of the exact amount, but it was less than nine-five.'

'Well, it would take me about fifty years to learn it all,' said Robert, and then, '*Hey!* What about this horse, Courts Appeal, he's from the O'Brien stable in Ireland. Vincent O'Brien, best trainer in the world.'

Nick looked up, grinning. Robert, flushed with success, having detonated his one shining fact about racing, decided to elaborate, and he charged on. 'Trained the runner-up in the Derby for the same owner, John McShain, a couple of years ago, as I remember. A very shrewd man.'

Nick replied, 'Yes, and he trained Mr McShain's mare Gladness to win the Gold Cup a couple of years ago, and they'll probably make Courts Appeal favourite just because O'Brien is bringing him over from Ireland. But he won't win, not with eight stone twelve pounds.'

At this stage Robert shuddered at the thought of his early view that this was a rather 'uncomplicated sport', since such a notion could clearly have been considered only by a lunatic. This was the most complicated sport he had ever known. It would, he thought, take a lifetime to comprehend it.

On the day of the race, all of them were strategically placed around the city with phone lines open to Robert's credit office to hear the result. This was, of course, long before the days of commentaries being beamed into betting shops and call-in phone lines. And when they heard the result there was a terrible hush. Chalk Stream had finished nowhere. In fact he had finished twenty-ninth out of thirty-one. Understandably Nick Robinson was a bit sheepish and did not call Robert until he had ascertained that the gelding had been very hesitant at the start, had lost his place in the general mêlée for position, and never got into the race at all. Such things happen every day in racing, but Nick was nonetheless quite upset that his new friend had lost so heavily and told him they would have another chance. Chalk Stream would come good, of that he was sure.

What he did not know was that Robert Sangster did not give a tinker's cuss about the result, or the £50. He could not remember having had such fun (at least, not since he had flattened Tiny Davies). For weeks now he had been personally involved in this major horse race. Somehow he had lived that Lincolnshire Handicap in his mind. It was almost as if he had been there at the racecourse, listening to the roar of the crowd as the field thundered into the last furling.

In his mind he could almost hear the vicarious pounding hooves, as Sam Hall's lightly weighted chestnut gelding Mustavon, hard under the whip, fought a gripping battle with Jim Joel's Major General to win by three parts of a length. It had been a terrific race. There was less than a length between the first three. The big weight had beaten Sovereign Path, as it also had beaten the O'Brien-trained favourite Courts Appeal. In a strange way Robert felt a part of all this, as if their studied calculations in the Kardomah had somehow influenced the result.

There was now only one thing Robert wanted in this life. He wanted to buy a racehorse. And the racehorse he wanted to buy was Chalk Stream.

Quite frankly, Nick was flabbergasted. But Robert did not habitually make jests about matters like £1000, the sum he was offering. Nick knew his grandfather had paid only 620 guineas for Chalk Stream's dam, Sabie River, and he set about trying to get the horse for racing's brand new devotee. There were many conferences between Sir Foster and his trainer Arthur Budgett, but after several weeks of negotiation they agreed to sell. Robert gave the son of the stallion Midas to Christine as a wedding present. Chalk Stream would henceforth be campaigned in the colours of Mrs Robert Sangster.

The first thing Robert needed was a trainer and he wanted one close to Chester so that he and Christine could visit the horse. He chose the thirty-nine-year-old Eric Cousins, a rather dashing ex-RAF pilot who had ridden fifty winners as an amateur over the jumps. He was a top-class horseman, a keen fox-hunter and had won the great long-distance handicap, the Ascot Stakes, at the Royal Meeting in 1957, just three years after taking out his licence to train. Better yet, he was developing a burgeoning reputation for his ability to place highly trained horses into exactly the right spot on the handicap. He had just moved his horses from Rangemore, near Burton-on-Trent, right into the heart of Cheshire, at Sandy Brow Stables, outside the country town of Tarporley, less than an hour's drive from the Wirral.

Chalk Stream journeyed north from the historic Budgett stables of Whatcombe in Berkshire and met his new trainer. He was already fit and sharp, but Cousins set about trying to improve him. He ran him often and the horse showed courage running into the first four on four occasions and then winning, on one glorious afternoon at Haydock Park, eleven miles out of Liverpool. It was a little handicap named after the nearby village of Hermitage Green, but Chalk Stream won it by two lengths at 3–1. Robert and Christine and all of the entourage, including, of course, a massively relieved Nick Robinson, had the most wonderful celebration.

Then Cousins worked the magic again, sending Chalk Stream to victory at the old Manchester Racecourse in early October. It was quite a competitive little contest, its prize money sponsored by a local dog-food firm, and afterwards Eric Cousins announced that he would now prepare Chalk Stream for a shot at a big race, the Liverpool Autumn Cup, to be run on the flat at Aintree, almost opposite the Vernons Pools offices, on a Friday afternoon in the dying days of the flat race season, 4 November. The prize money was about £1000 to the winning owner.

Robert had rarely known such overpowering elation (not since Tiny hit the deck, anyway) as he experienced in the days leading up to that great North Country handicap. Just to have a chance. Just to be in there with a horse. To be at the local racecourse with all of his friends. What a day it was going to be.

The weights were announced. Chalk Stream was in with seven stone two pounds. 'Is that good?' asked Robert. 'That's very adequate,' replied Cousins, which Robert took to mean: 'We're in with a real shout here.' He proceeded to have what was the biggest bet of his life, £100 on the nose. Chalk Stream to win. 'I'll take 9–1.' They all went in, some of them with ten bob, Nick with £25.

As the field of eleven went down to post on a cool, windy afternoon at Aintree, Robert and his men gathered in the owners' little stand with a good view down the course. Eric Cousins had decided the horse was better over distances of beyond the mile of the Lincoln, and today's test would be over an extended ten furlongs. The trainer mentioned to Robert before they went off that the start was the problem. Chalk Stream hated 'jumping off' and was apt to 'dwell' making up his mind whether to run. This split-second indecision had cost him his chance in the Lincoln, but today Eric Cousins fervently hoped he would break fast with the rest of the field.

But this time luck was against him. They came under starter's orders in a good line, but as the tapes flew up, only ten horses rushed forward. Chalk Stream had done it again. Eric Cousins's whispered oath was not heard by Mrs Sangster, but they all saw Chalk Stream hesitate and finally break several lengths behind the field. 'Is he out of it?' asked Robert. 'Not yet,' replied his trainer, but the field was racing towards the home turn with Chalk Stream very definitely last with a great deal of ground to make up. His rider, the five-pound-claiming apprentice Brian Lee, was sitting very still and then, halfway round the turn Chalk Stream began to improve. The commentator was calling out the leaders, 'Royal Chief, Windy Edge, Laird of Montrose, Tompion, the favourite Chino improving . . .'

Chalk Stream was in the middle of the pack as they came off the turn. Lee switched him off the rails and the big gelding set off gamely down the outside. They hit the two-furlong pole. Chino struck the front, chased hard by Chalk Stream still with two lengths to find. The Liverpool crowd roared as Lee went to the whip and Chalk Stream quickened

again. As they hit the furlong pole he burst clear of the field and then
drew right away to win by three lengths from Tompion, with Chino the
same distance back in third. Robert Edmund Sangster nearly died of
excitement. Forget Tiny, this was the biggest moment of his life. To
this day he says, 'I will never forget the Liverpool Autumn Cup. Not if
I live for a hundred years.'

   Robert ordered the finest champagne for the celebration. Dinner
went on into the small hours. 'I wish', he told his friends late that night,
'that this day would never end.' And in a sense, it never did. Robert
Sangster had taken the very first steps towards becoming, one day, the
most powerful owner and breeder of thoroughbred horses in the entire
two-hundred-year modern history of the Sport of Kings.

2

A Glimpse of
the Green

Robert Sangster learned, before the 1961 racing season even opened, what it was like to be hit hard by the Jockey Club handicapper. For the Liverpool Spring Cup, Chalk Stream was put up nine pounds in the weights. In addition, on the day of the race, he behaved very mulishly at the start, finally condescended to run, and trailed in ninth of thirteen. Fortunately Eric Cousins, liking neither the weights nor Chalk Stream's general attitude, had told Robert on no account to have a bet. The weight was a problem, but the real trouble was in Chalk Stream's mind. In Cousins's opinion he may have been one of those horses which carry for a long time bad memories of a race. They remember the whip and the aching that all athletes experience in the final stages of a hard struggle. Chalk Stream had had a tough one at Liverpool in November and he did not really want to line up at the start ever again.

But he had an easy time in the Spring Cup – the jockey did not drive him out when defeat was inevitable – and Eric again tested him in mid April, and he finished second at Wolverhampton coming with a strong, steady run from two furlongs out. Again it was a not hard race, nothing like the great battle he had fought in November, coming from far back to victory when the money was down. Eric Cousins decided the time was right to bring Chalk Stream to a fever pitch of fitness and send him out to try and win the Great Jubilee Handicap worth nearly £3000 (probably £30,000 in today's currency) on the fast, flat course of Kempton Park to the south-west of London.

Naturally Robert and his team, who would be making the two-hundred-mile journey south for the race, wanted to know two things: was he going to run well, and did they have a bet. For once Eric Cousins was cautious. He told Robert very carefully, 'In a handicap like this he cannot afford to throw it away at the start. If he is difficult and gives them an eight- or ten-length lead before they start, he will not win. But we are in with only seven stone five, and if he runs like he did at Liverpool he might just make it.'

The situation was not only forked, it was double-edged. To bet or not to bet? Chalk Stream's two defeats in 1961 had got four pounds off his back, his apprentice jockey would claim three more. But this race would sway with the weights. Chalk Stream must carry three more pounds than he did when he last won. That three extra represented one and a half lengths – the distance that separated the first four in last year's Lincoln. Could Chalk Stream deliver again? Would he break fast at the start? Would Robert dare to go in with another £100 bet? The conundrum preoccupied Robert almost to the exclusion of all else. He loved the academic aspect of this sport, measuring risk against hard cash. Trying to make a sound decision without giving away £100 to Major Ronnie Upex, the rails layer for the big bookmakers Heathorns with whom Robert had a fluctuating credit account.

Robert did not just like the world of racing, he was rapidly becoming addicted to it. He and Eric Cousins would sit for hours over at the Tarporley stables discussing their problems over a few glasses of champagne. Finally, one evening, Eric came up with a master plan, based on the fact that Robert would not put the money down until they knew the horse was racing with the rest of them. It would take split-second timing, but it *was* possible, of that Eric had no doubt.

On the day of the race, the scrum of the Birkenhead Park second team was sorely depleted, as its tight-head prop forward headed for the owners' stand at Kempton Park. Two other members of the pack were also going to be at Kempton and there was an atmosphere of tense excitement as Robert and Christine flew down the old A34 road towards Oxford in that 100mph Mercedes sports car of his. Nick Robinson was actually going the other way, speeding one hundred miles cross-country to Worcester to join his grandfather who had a runner there. But the Great Jubilee would be on national radio and Nick was already tuned in. He had already taken his chance and placed a credit bet of £25 on Chalk Stream to win at starting price. It was a quieter, less restricted time in England – only about one-fifth of the cars of today were being driven. There were no speed limits on fast country roads, the breathalyzer had not been invented, and it was indeed a privileged time for young men like Robert Sangster and Nick Robinson.

The horses came into the Kempton paddock and Robert and Christine watched Chalk Stream walk round. Eric thought he looked a bit on his toes, a bit restless. The trainer spoke tersely to his young jockey,

Brian Lee, instructing him not to leave things too late, to set off for home two furlongs out with a steady run, and then to drive him to the line, if necessary under the whip.

The runners left to go down to the start and Christine and Eric headed to a high point in the grandstand while Robert walked down the sloping lawn towards the bookmakers. He located Heathorns' pitch and strolled up to look at the prices. Chalk Stream was fluctuating between 7–1 and 9–1, drifting in the market, if anything. There was a big crowd and he stood unnoticed, as the throng hustled and bustled to place their bets.

'They're at the post!' called the racecourse announcer. And within a couple of minutes Eric Cousins had his binoculars trained on the green and blue colours of Chalk Stream and Brian Lee far out across the course. Robert edged nearer to Heathorns, keeping his back to Major Ronnie Upex and his eyes on the grandstand, from which Eric was watching from the pre-planned spot.

The starter called the horses in. Chalk Stream moved up with the rest of them. Robert edged back further. 'They're under starter's orders!' – Chalk Stream was standing still – 'And they're off!' Chalk Stream suddenly rushed forward, racing away with the leaders. Eric Cousins's hat flew from his head and he held it aloft for his young owner to see. Robert whipped round and shouted, '£100 to win Chalk Stream, please, Major. I'll take the 8–1.'

'Eight hundred pounds to one, down to Mr Sangster,' said Major Upex to his clerk, and even as he spoke the field was already through the first furlong galloping fast down the back straight with a little over a mile to run. It was a very hot race. The favourite was Nerograph, who had already won the prestigious City and Suburban Handicap this season, and he was carrying only two pounds more than Chalk Stream. The great Australian jockey Scobie Breasley was on Thames Trader who would go on to win the Bessborough Stakes at Royal Ascot, and then there was Alec Head's horse, Sallymount, who had come over from France and carried top weight, twenty-eight pounds more than Chalk Stream. All the great English jockeys were riding: young Lester Piggott, Joe Mercer, the Queen's jockey Harry Carr, Bill Rickaby and the ultra-stylist Jimmy Lindley.

Robert struggled his way to higher ground. Now they had only five furlongs to run and he could see the favourite Nerograph was out in front with Optimistic on his inside, these two tracked by Powder Rock and Midsummer Night. Chalk Stream was racing about eighth of the sixteen. They swung for home with a little more than two furlongs to run. The grandstand erupted with a deafening roar as the French horse Sallymount went for home first, coming to challenge Nerograph as they raced towards the furlong pole. The commentator called out: 'It's Sallymount for France on the outside, Nerograph on the inside, Thames Trader improving.'

Then he added the words which sent a dagger-like shiver down Robert's spine: '*Chalk Stream coming with a run along the rails.*' And the crowd was on its feet to a man, shouting with excitement as Chalk Stream came to challenge Sallymount in the lead. Now Neville Sellwood went for his whip as he fought to hold the Sangster horse at bay. Chalk Stream was at his boot straps, and Sallymount fought with every ounce of strength he had, carrying his huge weight with immense courage. The ground was running out for both of them, and the post loomed in front. The two horses were locked together with fifty yards to run, and again Lee went to the whip. Chalk Stream gave it his all, running on with the utmost gallantry, and on the line he had it. By only a head, but he had it. Robert Sangster's face was a photographer's study in pure joy.

The rest of the day passed in a kind of glorious glow which turned to a bit of a blur, courtesy of Rheims finest. Robert had had a truly sensational start to his career as a racehorse owner, or at least Christine had. But for Robert the entire horse-racing scene represented something far deeper. He knew at Kempton Park on that sunlit spring afternoon in 1961 that he was hopelessly in love with the sport, that he would never stray far from the thunder of the hooves across the turf – win, lose or draw. He loved the sight of the horses, their beauty, and their courage. He loved the planning, the scheming, the second guessing the bookies and the handicappers. And today's highly profitable endeavour against Major Upex? Well, Robert went for that in a major way. The sheer mischief of it appealed to him hugely. As well it might. Because mischief is a word which is very fitting to Robert Sangster. He has a mischievous face and a mischievous turn of mind, and he laughed about it for years afterwards.

Eric Cousins, by the way, wondered whether Chalk Stream would ever volunteer to run like that again. It had been another very tough race and the gelding had shown many signs of worry in his career so far. Privately, Eric thought that the horse had probably had enough of flat racing and that he would decline to enter for another battle such as the one he had just fought, and so bravely won. And Eric was right.

Chalk Stream never won again. Chalk Stream actually never finished in the first three again. Very broadly, Chalk Stream had made an announcement, which, expressed in human terms, was simple: 'Forget that. I have no intention of ever trying that hard again. I'm strictly here for the exercise.' All through that season Eric Cousins tried to make him cast that ordeal from his mind. They ran him five times and they traipsed all over the north of England watching him. But he would not try again. The year which had begun with such sparkling promise, rather petered out for Robert.

In his very first season, Robert received a thorough grounding in the joys and agonies of racehorse ownership. He really was put through the mill, with enormous highs, culminating in the most dreadful anti-climax. He learned a million lessons about the wily ways of the thoroughbred racehorse. And he learned one lesson which would last him for all of his life: accept the greatest victory as if you are used to it, and accept the most awful defeat as if it does not matter. For Robert, the season ended officially on 11 November in the traditional English big-race finale, the Manchester November Handicap. Twenty-nine runners took part. Chalk Stream beat three. But now, as Robert and Christine drove home to the Wirral, there was no air of despondency. Robert's eyes were on the future. He wanted more racehorses. Maybe quite of lot of them. He and Eric Cousins were not finished yet. Not by a long way.

In fact Eric was already regarded as a 'hot' trainer. Earlier that season he had won the 1961 Lincolnshire Handicap with a lightly weighted runner called Johns Court from a massive field of thirty-seven horses. Lee rode him and the horse won by three lengths at 25–1. Johns Court was sensationally fit that day, but he never won again all season. Not that this troubled Eric much. He also won the 1962 Lincolnshire with a different horse, Hill Royal, which also carried about seven and a half stone in a field of forty. Robert's victory at Kempton was the start of a quite remarkable rampage in this race by Eric Cousins. He was to win it for the next three years in succession. Everybody was talking about Eric Cousins. Bookmakers were griping and moaning, handicappers were furious with him, and the Stewards of the Jockey Club were beginning to get very beady. How the devil could this ex-fighter pilot keep on producing horses so superbly fit on the day, never with as much as one pound too much on the handicap, invariably at a whacking great price?

Robert, of course, was by now right in the thick of it. He had prised loose some family cash and now had half a dozen horses in training –

all bought by Eric at the sales, all judged by him to be capable of 'improvement'. And as he improved them the Stewards became crosser. They usually have a short unwritten 'hit list' of trainers they believe are being devious in the extreme, losing races when it suits them, and then flying to victory with light weights and big bets. To suggest Eric Cousins was on this 'hit list' of trainers who might be called in to face the Disciplinary Committee would be childish in the extreme. He was at the top of it. And everyone knew the Stewards were watching his every move.

The phrase 'Cousins and Sangster' was being heard in high places, as the pair of them toured the North Country and Scottish tracks having what Robert recalls as 'some of the most wonderful days of my life'. The racing was very much 'bush league' but to the young heir to Vernons Pools those races might have been the Derby. Every one of them gave him a charge of adrenalin. He never gave a thought to the beckoning glory of great classic races, with hugely expensive horses and massive prizes. For him, every race in which he had a runner *was* the Derby, especially when Eric told them to 'get on'. Robert just loved the local courses, and he loved to drive up to Scotland with his golf clubs, playing nine holes in the long summer evenings after the races, then dining sumptuously with his close friends, preparing to face the enemy (the bookmakers) once more on the morrow.

In those years of the 60s, he and Eric had some mighty 'touches'. They also had some diabolical strokes of ill-fortune which were just another part of the game, but which the Stewards neither knew nor cared about. Goodwood Racecourse, set high in the glorious Sussex Downs with a long southerly view to Chichester Cathedral and the Isle of Wight, was the scene of perhaps their most spectacular catastrophe. It occurred in 1963. Nick Robinson, by now almost a 'blood brother' to Robert, was heavily involved. In fact Nick's grandfather, the redoubtable Sir Foster, former captain and wicket-keeper for Gloucestershire County Cricket Club, fly fisherman and occasional punter, could be said to have been the instigator of the entire disaster. The race was the 120-year-old Stewards Cup, a six-furlong sprint handicap which was traditionally run on the opening day of Goodwood's July Meeting. It is always an enormous betting race, a regular target for 'hot' trainers with lightly weighted horses. It provides also one of the most spectacular sights in all of English racing as a big Stewards Cup field thunders to the top of the hill, the silks stark against the horizon, and then hurtles line abreast down the steep dip towards the grandstand.

Old Sir Foster had actually lost this race three years in a row, finishing second every time with a very fast horse called Deer Leap. The distances were, hideously, a neck and two short heads. Each time Nick and Robert, not to mention Sir Foster, had had a good bet. Each time they lost – in 1961 to the great Skymaster. The Stewards Cup was not much short of a bug-bear to all of them. Now, as the 1963 season headed towards midsummer, Eric Cousins imparted the nerve-jangling news that Robert's horse Highroy was just about fast enough to avenge Sir Foster. In fact the horse's entire preparation would be for the Stewards Cup, and he, Eric, believed he would win it. This possessed enormous appeal to the Robin Hood of Vernons. He, Robert, now had the means to win them back all of their lost money. For weeks before the race, they plunged the cash onto Highroy, as if defeat was out of the question.

However, when the overnight declarations came up, there was bad news. The venerable Newmarket trainer Jack Jarvis had unexpectedly decided to run Lord Rosebery's sprinter Creole, and naturally summoned his stylish stable jockey Peter Robinson to ride – the same Peter Robinson Eric had booked for Highroy. This was a serious blow. Eric hustled around and booked Paul Tulk for Highroy, a capable jockey but not his first choice. The race was, as usual, run at a ferocious pace and on the line Creole beat Highroy a short head. Robert and Nick *could not believe* their luck. Eric was very fed up too. But he had a plan. Three days later on the Friday there was another Goodwood sprint, the Chichester Stakes, and in his view Highroy would have recovered sufficiently to run and win. 'The competition is not so hot,' he said. 'And Jarvis does not have a runner. Peter Robinson will ride for us.'

Once more Robert and Nick plunged into the bookmakers, and once more they stood, gripped by nerves, high in the County Stand, their fingers white-knuckled on their binoculars. This was getting expensive. And once more Highroy got beat in a photo-finish, by a short head.

'Christ!' said Robert. 'Can you *believe* that could happen? Can you *believe* that?'

'Not easily,' said Nick. 'By the way, did you see who rode the winner?'

'If you say Paul Tulk I'll probably commit suicide.'

'Don't do it, Robert,' said Nick, shaking his head gravely. 'Let's go and have a drink.'

This was not the only time in 1963 when Robert felt the need for a drink. It was an awful season for him. Not one of his horses won anywhere. But this seemed only to spur him on to greater ambitions, to own more horses, to go racing more often, and to study formlines and breeding lines even more assiduously.

Curiously it had been a powerful owner-breeder and member of the Jockey Club who had inspired him to lose so much money on those Goodwood sprints. And now it would be the same senior establishment figure who would get it all back for him and more. Sir Foster Robinson had a two-year-old filly who had not yet won a race. She was bright chestnut in colour and rather lean and athletic in conformation. Her name was Homeward Bound. It was her ancestry which intrigued Robert: she was a half-sister to Chalk Stream, his very first horse, both of them being out of Sir Foster's mare Sabie River. When Nick imparted the news that his grandfather's trainer, John Oxley, thought she would win the Oaks, England's premier mile-and-a-half classic for fillies, run at Epsom three days after the Derby in June, Robert could scarcely locate a bookmaker fast enough.

On the day of the race the bookmakers were still offering 100–7 against Homeward Bound winning the Oaks. They who handled the accounts of N. J. F. Robinson and R. Sangster lived, however, to rue their careless and uncharacteristic generosity. On a wet afternoon on Epsom Downs, Homeward Bound came with a tremendous run down the middle to win the 1964 Oaks by two lengths from Windmill Girl (the future dam of Arthur Budgett's two Derby winners). It was the finest moment in all of his years of racing for Sir Foster Robinson, now aged eighty-four. It was not half bad for his grandson and his sidekick either.

The victory of Homeward Bound did not spur Robert Sangster on towards the upper reaches of thoroughbred racing – with thoughts of perhaps one day owning an Oaks winner of his own, or perhaps even a Derby winner, or any other classic winner. But rather it seemed to concentrate his mind on the intricacies of breeding racehorses, as indeed the subject has captured men of similar thoughtful and ambitious disposition down the years. He had loved the electric atmosphere of the big summer occasion on Epsom Downs, but what really fascinated him was the fact that Homeward Bound was from the same mare as Chalk Stream. He worked out that the basic shape and conformation of the two horses was from the dam. He also considered that their similar will-to-win must spring from the same genes. But Homeward Bound's superior class, and her ability to run over a longer distance, and to keep running on strongly, uphill to the finish, must surely have come from her sire, the great staying horse and champion stallion, Alycidon. Robert immersed himself in books about the subject, poring over long-forgotten pedigrees, tracing bloodlines to famous stallions, trying to formulate patterns of breeding, which stallion lines worked best with which female lines.

But these were his evening preoccupations. His day-to-day dramas on the racecourse were still conducted around the northern tracks, and the one he loved most of all was the modest Scottish course which sits on the south Ayrshire coast on the shores of the Firth of Clyde. The two big meetings at Ayr Racecourse, in June and the Western Meeting in September, represented for Robert something approximately between Christmas and Mardi Gras. Or at least he was apt to turn the occasions into those qualities of celebration. He would arrive on the evening before the racing began, by now sweeping up the drive to the Turnberry Hotel in a new Rolls Royce, and within the hour he would report to one of the greatest golf links in the world. Turnberry, a 7000-yard championship test, spreads along the shoreline, guarded by a magnificent lighthouse. In terms of difficulty it compares very favourably with Robert's home links of Hoylake, and like Royal Liverpool has been the scene of a titanic and historic battle for the British Open – in 1977 Tom Watson and Jack Nicklaus burst ten strokes clear of the field before Watson's 65 beat Jack's last-round 66. Its views out towards the Irish Sea are as romantic as those from the Wirral. In the near distance you can see the granite dome of the island of Ailsa Craig, and beyond that the Mull of Kintyre. On very clear days, you can see the distant shores of County Antrim in the north-east of Ireland. With the possible exception of the winner's enclosure at the nearby racecourse, Robert's favourite place on all of this earth may very well be the ninth hole at Turnberry, the tee of which sits on a rocky pinnacle out to sea.

Nick Robinson recalls one glorious summer evening here, just as the sun was turning the far reaches of the ocean to the colour of spent fire as it sunk behind the waves. Robert was about to hit when someone carelessly asked him, in the middle of his backswing, 'Does that lighthouse work?'

'Only when it's dark,' replied Robert breezily as he struck a long drive out over the in-running tide and over the cliffs towards the fairway, and the green, set hard by the great nautical light.

Only truly diabolical weather ever prevented him playing nine holes after a day at the races. And nothing ever prevented him playing eighteen before he went to the races.

Win, lose or draw, he and his friends – plus of course Eric Cousins

– dined sumptuously at the Turnberry Hotel every night, not, incidentally, at his expense, although he would usually insist on standing the party two or three bottles of decent champagne by way of an overture. Sometimes the party was overshadowed by a particularly grim loss to the bookmakers, but not for long. And certainly not on the occasions when his chestnut colt Shy Boy (by Alycidon) – bought for 2300 guineas at the autumn sales – won twice at the Ayr June meeting over a mile and a half. Definitely not when his bay gelding Endorsement – bought for only 1000 guineas from Jack Jarvis – won the Ayrshire Handicap by a neck from Night Star. Words can barely describe the fun and games which broke out after Robert's lovely chestnut filly Brief Star got up on the line to win the major race of the Western Meeting, the Ayr Gold Cup.

However, no race in Eric Cousins's relatively short but meteoric career as a trainer ever matched that Gold Cup for such personal tensions and feelings of rivalry inside his own stable. It had all begun back in the days of the old Kardomah lunch club. Robert had introduced two of his friends to Eric. They were David Freeman who ran an upmarket meat canning business (Gold Dish Ox-Tongues), and Leo McParland, whose family owned a major cattle importing business, bringing the beasts in from Ireland presumably in order to help fill the Freeman cans. These two old friends also went in together and bought a couple of racehorses, but one of them was a very useful filly named Ludham, and when she finished third in the Oaks, having finished second in the Cheshire Oaks, Robert felt slightly aggrieved at the sheer quality of their filly – better than any horse he had ever owned. Then Ludham came out and won the Doonside Cup at Ayr and they all thought Robert's nose was really out of joint, though he said nothing.

But now things were rather different. David Freeman and Leo McParland had another good racehorse, a very fast but moderately bred gelding called Salan. They very much wanted him to run in the Ayr Gold Cup where Robert's own filly was bidding for glory. In addition everyone knew Robert had a massive wager on the race. He would never say precisely how much but Nick Robinson thought it was a £100 double – Intermezzo to win the St Leger at 7–1 and Brief Star for the Gold Cup at 33–1. When Intermezzo won the St Leger the entire situation became rather serious.

Robert turned up at the Turnberry Hotel, at the usual time, and took a surreptitious glance at the wine list, which was reputed to be the best in Scotland. After the traditional twilight nine holes, he changed and prepared for dinner with four of his closest friends – Nick; Bobby McAlpine, heir to the large northern-based construction company Sir Alfred McAlpine Ltd; Tim Holland, proprietor of the legendary London gaming club, Crockford's (whose faithful caddy Mullins sat alone at a nearby table); and Tim Kitson, the young Yorkshire politician who was to become Parliamentary Private Secretary to the future Tory Prime Minister Edward Heath. Eric Cousins joined them an hour later. By now the dining room was full of racing's major personalities, as it always was for this meeting: the champion jockey Lester Piggott, the professional gambler Alec Bird with his guest Phil Bull, the red-bearded publisher of racing's 'Bible' *Timeform*, leading northern owner Guy Reed, trainers Geoff Wragg, Peter Easterby, Sam Hall and Harry Thompson Jones, and others.

All through dinner Robert kept going on about the presence of Salan in *his* race. Eric was, naturally, in a very awkward position. He owed loyalty to all of his owners, and Freeman and McParland were insisting on running their horse. Robert kept muttering darkly about the consequences of Salan beating Brief Star. And as Robert kept looking at the form, Eric was clearly looking at the sack from his old friend and principal owner. He tried to explain his position, but Robert continued to grumble. He was still grumbling the following day when the starter sent the field away. And he was beside himself when Salan hit the front coming to the final furlong. But Brief Star was still there, running fiercely in the middle of the pack. Suddenly she made her break, on the outside, and flew over the closing yards, to nail Salan right on the line, winning by a neck.

Robert, fighting back his overpowering joy, turned to Nick and said cheerfully: 'Well, that wasn't much trouble, was it?' And then to Eric, he said, with a smile of absolute calm, 'Of course, you knew I was only kidding, didn't you?'

There was another occasion at Ayr a few years later when Eric Cousins advised Robert to have a bet on yet another chestnut filly of his, Solo Stream, in Ayr's big race of the day, the five-furlong Bass Special sprint. However, before they went to post, Robert had spent half an hour chatting to the great Irish trainer Mick O'Toole, who could be damned if he could see anything beating his horse in the race. Robert changed his mind and backed the Irish horse instead of his own. He watched the race with Nick Robinson and, with a couple of hundred yards to run, Robert cried in exasperation: '*Damn!* We're beat.'

Nick, who had stuck to his original bet on Robert's Solo Stream, replied: 'Yes, very boring for you. But you've just bloody well won the race!'

'Who's won the race?'

'*You* have! Solo Stream, your horse, remember?' replied his long-time cohort. 'I suppose we had better get down to the winner's enclosure to meet Eric.' And they bolted down the grandstand back stairs, chuckling as they had done for so many years, like two dreadful schoolboys, who had nearly got caught, but not quite.

By the end of the 1960s Eric Cousins had won Robert fifty races, including a few over the jumps, including the Midlands Grand National at Uttoxeter. He had also won at Newmarket, the headquarters of English racing. This was with his grey colt Hang On in a contest named the Crawfurd Handicap, about three weeks before the Jockey Club had blackballed Christopher Soames, just down the road at The Rooms. At precisely that time, Robert had become so engrossed with the challenge of actually breeding his own racehorses that he bought himself a stud farm in Cheshire, or at least he bought himself a rather decrepit two-hundred-acre farm in Cheshire with a view to turning it into a stud farm. It was called Swettenham Hall and it was situated in the most lonely part of the countryside to the north of Congleton. Basically, the only serious landmark in the entire area was the giant inter-planetary telescope at Jodrell Bank which you could just see from some of the paddocks. Its privacy, its good, damp, green land and its calcium soil seemed potentially perfect for rearing horses.

Robert attacked the entire project with immense style. He sought expert advice on the quality of the land, and then he ploughed up the paddocks which they judged were in a flood-plain to the River Dane, and he laid down a complete drainage system. He had top architects design his barns, the paddocks were all newly fenced with post-and-rail. He studied the National Stud's operation at Newmarket, copied what he liked best, instructed his builders to renovate the great archway into the courtyard which supported the grand clock tower. There was a beautiful lawn set into the middle of the yard with a wide gravel path around its perimeter. With his normal brutal adherence to 'the numbers' and carefully advised by his father, Robert brought the stud farm up to scratch 'right on budget'.

When it was finished, the Swettenham Stud looked as if it had been there for ever. As a matter of fact, so did Robert, elegantly tailored as usual, with a Rolls Royce purring in the background as he chatted to his new stud groom Joe French. All around the property the staff addressed him with the courteous familiarity of the more feudal reaches of the English countryside, "Morning, Mr Robert . . .', 'By the way, Mr Robert, would that filly have a bit of a chance at Haydock on Friday?'

He renovated the turreted seventeenth-century manor house, re-painting its stucco exterior gleaming white. Flower beds were planted, new trees set around the grounds, while Christine began re-decorating the interior. Robert began to fill the new paddocks with the broodmares he had collected in his few years of ownership. There was Audrey Joan, a sprinting filly he had bought after she had won the Portland Handicap with a smashing victory over Close Call and Forlorn River and who would later produce him four stakes winners. There was his lovely grey filly Flying By, a top-class sprinter who had cost him more than 9000 guineas at the December sales. Soon there would be his extremely tough brown filly Tora Santa, who was by the 1964 Derby winner Santa Claus, and who had won for Robert a big twenty-two-runner maiden at Ascot. Pride of place in the main paddock would go to his beloved Brief Star, heroine of the Ayr Gold Cup.

By the time Robert and Christine moved in, their first son Guy was seven years old and, with his two younger brothers, Ben and Adam, a new and enlarged Sangster dynasty was already in the making. Sur-rounded by his family, his broodmares and his paddocks and staff, Robert felt for the first time in his life that he had truly come home. Here at last was the environment he loved, far from the daily hassle and hustle that all young businessmen cope with as they take on more and more responsibility from their fathers.

Robert, at thirty-one, was now the kingpin at the Vernon Organiz-ation, relied upon by Sangster Senior to ensure the day-to-day running of their empire. But even he was unable to put into profit the division which handled credit betting on horseracing. Robert tried. He even tried to steer some of the more chancy bets of his own through the firm, on the basis that if he was to lose, he may as well lose it to the company. But, being Robert, there was something of *quid pro quo* to his thoughtfulness. Nick Robinson says it was simple really. Robert only bet with Vernons if it was a real long-shot which probably would not win. He would call Nick in the morning and say, for instance, 'Put £25 on for me this afternoon, would you? On your Vernons account, Bright Hopes at Newmarket this afternoon, see if he will give you 16–1.'

Nick would telephone Vernons sometime before the race and ask for the odds, only to be told, 'I'm sorry, Mr Robinson, we cannot give you better than 100–8 on that horse.'

'Oh, you could do a bit better than that, I'm an old customer. Ask the manager for me, would you?'

Nick would then hear a rustling and someone call: 'Er, Mr Robert. I've got Mr Robinson on the line. He wants 16–1 about Bright Hopes. She's only 100–8 on our board.' And then, in the distance: 'Oh, that'll be all right, Joe, give him the 16s.'

Of course they nearly always lost, so it never did anyone any harm, but Robert's instincts were sound: if I lose, the family firm gets the money; if I win, I do better with Vernons than I would anywhere else. Very, very neat. Very, very Sangster. His father might almost have approved. But only just.

By the start of the 1970s Robert's organization was well-established in sponsoring a major race at the local Haydock Park, the Vernons Sprint Cup. It was run at the October Meeting with a big prize and some very good horses had won it. But in 1971 there was a particular sense of drama. The outstanding sprinter Green God, who had finished first five times in a row that season, was a very questionable favourite because in his last race Green God had managed to get left at the start in France, and lost to Fireside Chat. Most good judges, including Robert, believed that Green God was the fastest horse in England, but in the Vernons he would face two other pretenders to the sprint championship, Sweet Revenge, who had won two big races in France demolishing Fireside Chat both times, and Apollo Nine, who had shouldered a massive weight of nine stone five pounds to win the Stewards Cup at Goodwood in August. The whole of England was talking about the ensuing six-furlong battle at Haydock Park which would surely decide the fastest horse in the country. Robert, by now a director of the race-course, was as ever heavily into the 'crack' in the members' bar, talking to trainers, owners, breeders and, on this day, managers of stud farms, the stallion masters who would be watching for the horse who might make a top sire. And the horse they were all watching was Green God.

On the day before the big sprint, there was a large gathering in the members' bar discussing the day's events, but more particularly discussing the forthcoming clash between Green God, Sweet Revenge and Apollo Nine. Robert was with a group of Irish bloodstock agents, everyone talking to everyone, whether they knew each other or not, as is the general form on such occasions. Robert was talking to his old friend Jack Doyle who pointed out that the tall, dark-haired young Irishman 'across the way' had settled terms with Green God's owner David Robinson. The horse would be sold this evening for £160,000 and the

deal would stand no matter what happened in the race. Green God
would run in the colours of Mr Robinson for the last time tomorrow,
leased back to his owner just for the day, and then he would leave
England to take up stud duties at Castle Hyde in Tipperary.

How, precisely, did they arrive at that figure? That was what Robert
wanted to know. What if Green God gets beaten?

'Well,' said Jack, 'that's where they start. The buyers' syndicate
assumes he will get beat. If that should be the case, I would think they
would hope to stand him at perhaps £1000 to cover a mare, which they
plan to do about forty times a year. That's £120,000 in three years.
That means each share will cost £3000, because there are always forty
shareholders. So he's got to cover another forty mares during his first
three years to get all the shareholders out clean on their investment.
Well, he may not quite do that, but I don't think an extra thirty would
be asking a lot. And then they are out very little in terms of cash.'

'But', said Robert, 'what if he wins?'

'Now you're talking,' said Jack. 'That's what that syndicate is fervently
hoping. Then, as Champion Sprinter, Green God will probably stand
at £1500, and forty mares will earn £60,000 in a season. In three seasons
he will have earned £180,000. And, if he covers a few extras for the
farm and perhaps six or eight for the syndicate members, there'll be
another £15,000 in the pot each year. In three years that's £65,000
profit, less the cost of his keep. If he is successful, which we won't really
know until his fifth year, there will be a serious amount of cash around
for these brave fellows who have just risked £160,000.'

'Christ!' said Robert thoughtfully. He looked across at the young
Irishman. He seemed such a countryman and here he was representing
a group of Irish breeders risking phone numbers on the purchase of a
racehorse. As far as Robert could see they had a long-term bet of nearly
£100,000 riding on this race tomorrow. Now that was serious. Suddenly
all that he had done in racing, all the fun and laughter and betting he
had done in partnership with Eric Cousins seemed of little consequence.
These Irishmen were playing a major game and Robert felt a weird
compulsion to be part of it. He had just received a crash course in how
modern thinkers were basing their judgments on the syndications of
stallions. Forty shareholders, putting up three times the cost of one
covering for a share. You 'get out' in three years, after that you are on
the gravy train. It was new, but it already made rock-solid financial
sense to Robert, and he could not stop thinking about it, through all of
the hours that led up to the running of the fifth Vernons Sprint Cup.

The following afternoon when the runners came belting out of the stalls Robert could not take his eyes off Green God. He watched Lester Piggott try to straighten him out after a bad break, saw the horse keep hanging to his left in the middle of the pack, as Apollo Nine and Sweet Revenge fought it out in the lead. Then he saw Lester ask him to quicken, stared enthralled as Green God came to deliver his challenge at the furlong, felt his heart leap as Sweet Revenge swerved violently. And he stood rapt in admiration as Piggott kept his mount straight and drove Green God past the post almost a length to the good. Sweet Revenge was second, Apollo Nine two and a half lengths further back in third place.

Robert reckoned he had seen two great professionals in action in the past twenty-four hours: Lester Piggott, who had ridden this fiery son of the equally fiery Red God to victory; and the young Irishman, who had staked so much money on a six-furlong sprint for the championship of England. Late that afternoon, back in the members' bar, everyone was talking about Green God, his pedigree and his prospects as a stallion. Robert walked over to talk to Jack Doyle who was deep in conversation with the young Irish purchaser. 'Hello, Robert,' said Jack. 'Will you have a drink with us? I don't believe you two have met have you.'

'Well, I know of course who you are, sir,' said the Irishman. And he leaned forward to shake the hand of Robert Sangster. It was a handshake which would begin a lifelong friendship, a friendship which would change the world of bloodstock breeding for ever, would send prices for young racehorses to heights never before contemplated. 'I'm John Magnier,' he said.

3

Facing
the Almighty Dollar

John Magnier was twenty-three years old on the day he first shook hands with Robert Sangster. Thus he was eight years junior to the heir to Vernons Pools. In terms of birth, that is. In terms of horses, John was about one hundred and forty-eight years older, since the Magnier family of Fermoy, County Cork, traces its roots in the serious business of breeding racehorses to at least 1800 and probably back into the previous century.

John's father Michael Magnier stood the great steeple-chasing stallion Cottage at the family's Grange Stud on the outskirts of the town. Cottage it was who sired three Grand National winners including Sheila's Cottage and Lovely Cottage in 1946 and 1948. He also sired the immortal Cottage Rake, trained by Vincent O'Brien to win those *three* Cheltenham Gold Cups in succession 1948–50, while R. Sangster was grappling with elementary French a few miles to the north at the Leas Preparatory School. John's grandfather Thomas Magnier owned the fine Irish stallion Edlington who won fourteen races in the 1880s and was then occupied in the traditional way as a 'travelling stallion', being ridden along the lovely valley of the River Blackwater beyond Fermoy and covering the racing mares of the local Irish farmers. Like John Magnier himself, old Edlington had a firm sense of place in this world and spent many weeks on an annual sojourn at the Duke of Devonshire's great estates surrounding the castle of Lismore.

Home to Edlington was nonetheless Fermoy. As was the Grange Stud to Cottage. Green God would live about four miles away at Castle Hyde Stud, which had been purchased by John Magnier a few months previously. Green God was a lucky horse because in this deep, quiet Irish country grooms and stud owners alike understand the high-mettled racer perhaps as no other breed of men on earth. To the uninitiated, a thoroughbred stallion can look very fearsome, standing glaring in a paddock, his breath coming in short snorts, perhaps pawing the ground, irritated at being disturbed. Some farms in Kentucky and Australia carry the stark warning: STALLIONS BITE. BEWARE. It is thus a source of absolute wonder to watch a gentle Irish groom unlatch the gate, close it quietly behind him and stroll out to the beast, muttering softly: 'Will you come over here now? And stop your showing off. I'm not planning to chase you ... Come here now.' It is even more amazing to watch apparent anger fall from the stallion. To see him dip his head, almost as an apology and then walk sheepishly up to his man, his head held low like an old dog. John Magnier can charm a stallion like that. If Robert Sangster lived to be a thousand years old he could never learn it. Nor could most people. You have to be born in Ireland to achieve that degree of harmony with a fighting-fit stallion of the blood.

Even the language of the two men, that late afternoon at Haydock Park, was different. Robert is always inclined to talk in terms of great victories, courage, jockeys, bets and values. John Magnier is much more of the horse. His judgments are punctuated by the phrases of the horse-man: 'If you look at him in a certain light he can really fill your eye', 'For a sprinter he stands over a lot of ground', 'For a son of Red God he has quite a kind look to him, but at a certain angle you can see a touch of the devil in his eye'. Those are the timeless words of the stallion master, bred into the man as profoundly and surely as the speed, gallantry and temperament is bred into the horse. In John Magnier's case, it was bred into him for just as many years. When he stands and looks at a racehorse going into action, he is not looking entirely at him. He is looking, in his own mind, at the foals of a future generation: 'Will I always be looking for mares with better knees than he has?', 'Will he want medium to small mares given his own imposing height?', 'He was sweating when he went to post – is there more of Red God's temper about him than I can see? Will I spend half the year looking for mares of a quiet, calm temperament for him?'

Always a thousand questions. Usually considerably fewer answers. He and Robert Sangster had many things to say to each other but largely in a different language. And yet there was a quick and early bond between them. That bond was money. Robert, having inherited his first one-third of the Vernons empire, had a considerable amount of it. John had long had far-reaching plans to make a considerable amount of it but, in broad terms, it occurred to him that he could go further, faster, with some serious Sangster money behind him. In turn, Robert did not care how far John went in the stallion business, nor how rich he became in the riveting business of syndicating expensive stallions, just as long as he took him, Robert, along with him. Great partnerships have thrived on less worthy premises. This one was destined to go every step of the way.

The two men talked for a long time at Haydock and, aside from the Irishman's enormous knowledge of breeding, he demonstrated to Robert an equally grand knowledge of the actual racing. John Magnier's family stronghold of Fermoy was a mere twenty-eight miles across the Cork–Tipperary border from the south of Ballydoyle, the sprawling training complex which was home to two of the last four Derby winners, Sir Ivor and Nijinsky. It was also the home of Robert's boyhood hero, Vincent O'Brien, who had prepared them both for glory. The Magniers and the O'Briens, both originally Cork families, had known each other for generations. Indeed John's mother was matron of honour at Vincent O'Brien's wedding. John's keenly observed views on the various merits of the two Irish-based Derby winners were completely absorbing to Robert. John's words were glossed by the fact that here was a man who was not simply fiddling about trying to win a sprint handicap at Haydock. Here was a man to whom racing at the very highest classic level was the principal arena in which he intended to participate.

There are many owners and breeders who have a fairly shrewd idea of what is going on in a training stable, but John Magnier possessed insights which no one had ever expounded to Robert before. He had, perhaps, only a vicarious proximity to racing's Hall of Fame, but he had talked with the natural authority of a young man who knew the O'Brien family and nothing seemed to intimidate him. He would, he said, given half a chance, have dived at the opportunity to stand the great Nijinsky at stud in Ireland. As he mentioned on that afternoon, 'Jesus, Robert, he was sold to an American syndicate for $5·5 million, which is only about 2·2 million Irish punts. With 40 shareholders, that's only £55,000 a share. That seems like a lot of money, but it's not. I'm laying you dollars to doughnuts right now that Nijinsky's first-sale yearlings, on the market in Kentucky in 1973, will fetch $100,000 *each*. I would not be that surprised if they fetched up to $200,000 each. How the devil can £55,000 be expensive when your first yearling will – at least in my view – damned nearly get you out of your investment? After that you can breed to him every year for the rest of his life. Free.'

Robert Sangster has never forgotten that conversation. Magnier's cool belief that he should actually have *bought* the great Nijinsky from the platinum billionaire Charles Engelhard and run his stud career in

County Cork was tantamount, in Robert's view, to calling the Queen and asking her how she felt about raffling the Crown Jewels. Top stallions, Robert believed, went to Kentucky, where the big dollars lived. That was the modern pattern. There was not enough money in Ireland to buy a leg in most of them, never mind the entire horse. In addition, things looked like growing worse because, in John Magnier's view, there were signs of a serious upswing in world bloodstock prices which were being driven by a run of star racehorses: aside from the recent US-bred English Derby winners Sir Ivor, Nijinsky and Mill Reef, there was the crack English 2000 Guineas winner Brigadier Gerard, who had never been beaten. In the United States yearlings by sires such as Buckpasser, Raise a Native, Dr Fager and Northern Dancer had all gone close to $200,000. What bothered John Magnier was that Ireland, and England, might be left behind in the world bloodstock league. This would be something of a mortal blow to him, since he envisioned himself at the top of that league, not in some halfway house.

Magnier's view of the future, his slightly roguish charm, his deep, conspiratorial Irish voice, the muttered tones whenever he mentioned specific amounts of money – all of this appealed enormously to Robert. Because this was a man who was not just nattering about the industry, this was a man who had just laid a king's ransom on the line for a horse called Green God. Robert had watched it, comprehended the risk and admired from afar as Magnier and his friends had somehow bounced out on top, with the best of the deal. When they parted in the early part of the evening, he and John shook hands again, resolving to stay in touch and to talk more. Neither one of them, however, had the remotest idea of the ferocity of the financial rollercoaster ride upon which they would ultimately embark.

Through the following spring the whole of Ireland was discussing the chances of Vincent O'Brien winning a third Derby in five years with his American-bred bay-colt Roberto, owned by the Ohio construction millionaire John Galbreath. John Magnier told Robert all about it, how fast, though slightly unpredictable, Roberto was. But, generally, they all thought he would get home at Epsom. On Derby day they were proved right, Roberto made it by a short head, ridden by Lester Piggott.

That same day Robert said on the telephone, only half jocularly, that he supposed John would be out there trying to *buy* Roberto for God knows how many millions, but the Irishman replied very seriously:

'I'll give you several reasons why not. Firstly, Mr Galbreath has just a little bit more money than Croesus and he never sells anything, far less his first English Derby winner. Secondly, he has already announced the fact that the horse will stand at his own Darby Dan Farm in Lexington, Kentucky. And thirdly, there's just a little bit too much fire in Roberto's make-up for me. I think he might produce a lot of very hot horses which might be difficult to train.'

In the same phone conversation, however, Robert agreed to make the trip to the Keeneland Sales in Kentucky in July, where he would team up with John Magnier's Irish friends and have a proper look at the world market. There was now little doubt that Robert was determined to enter the breeding industry in a major way. Before he went to Keeneland he talked the entire subject through with his father, who affirmed what Robert had always known: that he would support financially his hard-working son and heir in all of his serious business ventures. Robert was already making a success of his Swettenham Stud breeding operation and Vernon was wisely of the opinion that he would not interfere until the former heavyweight champion of the Berlin Brigade made a mistake of unreasonable magnitude.

Robert arrived at the Keeneland Sales as a near-total stranger. There were one or two English trainers and bloodstock agents who knew him, but as far as the big buyers and sellers were concerned, the name 'Sangster' was not poised on the lips of the mighty. John Magnier casually introduced him to Vincent O'Brien which was much more of a thrill than Robert ever admits, and he also fell into conversation with the big English owner-breeder Charles St George. The upshot of that morning's discussions was that Robert ended up taking a share in a yearling Vincent was buying for St George and which would subsequently be named Cellini. The colt was by the great American stallion Round Table, from one of the finest families in the American Stud Book, his dam being the brilliant racemare Gamely, a US National Champion and winner of sixteen races. The second dam – the yearling's grandma – was Gambetta, granddam also of another great American racer Drumtop. Gambetta was also a half-sister to the stallion Ridan, and to the Champion Two-Year-Old filly Moccasin, and to the dam of Vincent's current best two-year-old Thatch. There are no better families than that in the entire world.

The yearling was a strongly-made individual and Vincent was very taken with him. Robert conferred with John Magnier who became, he recalls, just a tad poetic. 'I think it was Damon Runyan who said, Robert, that the race is not always to the swift, nor the battle to the strong. But that's the way to bet! And Vincent wants to bet. Get in.'

Robert got in. Vincent was forced to $240,000 against determined bidding from the English trainer Bernard Van Cutsem and the French trainer Alec Head.

'Christ!' said Robert as the bidding spiralled.

'Don't worry about it,' said John Magnier. 'He's a very tough-looking individual and the pedigree is outstanding. The horse is a sound investment, I'm sure of that. He'd be cheap if he could win a decent race. Vincent knows that's a real stallion's pedigree.'

Robert was enthralled by all of this. He understood the economics with total clarity. He knew his father would approve, because this horse was already the property of a syndicate: he, Robert, was in for a share; St George was in; and Captain Tim Rogers, another Irish stallion master, was also in. The risk was already spread. What do you want, a third of a potential classic racehorse and future stallion perhaps to be valued in millions or three prospective handicappers at Ayr? Robert was very certain of the answer. Ayr had been fun, but he had, irrevocably, moved on. As he and John Magnier talked long into the night after that first day at the Keeneland Sales, they both knew with immense sureness that the answer to *all* of the thoroughbred breeding conundrums rested with the business of syndication. Big partners, with big money, going for the best horses together. And, in the opinion of John Magnier, Robert was the man to head it up, to become the international salesman.

But to this, Robert had a rather uncharacteristic reaction. He felt, still, that he was just too much of a new boy. All the discussions he had had over so many countless hours with John Magnier had underlined, in his own mind, how much he had to learn. With Magnier he often felt as he had once felt with Nick Robinson – 'Bloody ignorant, since you mention it!' – and he was uncertain of his credentials.

'How could I, for instance, telephone some Greek shipping billionaire and suggest he throws in a couple of million dollars and buys into half a dozen yearlings with us? Who am I? Robert Sangster, football pools operator, won a few handicaps at Haydock and Ayr . . . flattened Tiny Davies! Ask yourself, John, who am I? I mean, Vincent could call them and everyone would know he was the greatest horse trainer in the world. But I am nothing like qualified. I lack horse credentials. They would not even bother to talk to me.'

Magnier pondered the problem. Robert, he thought, had a point. His Liverpool-based friend had big money, tons of charm, a gambler's instinct and a top-class business brain. He also had considerable experience now in the racehorse business. But he was not a born and bred racing man. And it might show. 'Perhaps', he suggested, 'Vincent could get you elected Honorary President of Ireland or something. You need to be at least that important!'

For a few weeks in the latter half of 1972 they shelved their plans for an international syndicate, while they concentrated on the racing. Their attention was caught for the time being by a potential stallion for which John Magnier had an obdurate, unreasonable obsession. The word 'interest' could not even remotely convey his passion for the slightly disappointing chestnut sprinter Deep Diver, owned, like Green God, by David Robinson. A brilliant two-year-old winner at Royal Ascot, Deep Diver had run well a few times, but had not hit the jackpot at three. John Magnier was sure he would improve and he tried to get in and buy him before anyone agreed with him about the horse's potential. He approached David Robinson who would not sell yet. Nor would he utter anything other than vague telephone numbers about price. Then Deep Diver came out and won the Nunthorpe Stakes at York, by two lengths from the brilliant filly Stilvi. He ran the feet off a top-class field and smashed the track record while he was about it.

John Magnier did not know whether to say: 'Wonderful. I knew he was that good' or, alternatively, 'Damn it. That'll put the price up to £250,000.' Robert says he settled for the latter. Again John Magnier enquired about buying the horse, but David Robinson would not deal until after the running of the Prix de l'Abbaye, the top sprint race in France run at Longchamp in Paris in early October. There Deep Diver would face the reigning European sprint champion Home Guard on ground perhaps faster and drier than he really enjoyed. But the race turned out to be literally 'no contest'. Deep Diver burst out of the starting stalls like a howitzer and opened up such a massive early lead nothing ever got near him. Home Guard was four lengths away at the finish.

Now John Magnier went into serious negotiation. He was determined to buy Deep Diver and determined to raise the money. He called Robert again, told him they may have to go to £400,000, but it was still cheap. 'This is the fastest horse in Europe,' he said. 'And he's the fastest by a very long way. His sire Gulf Pearl was fast, and tough enough to win the Chester Vase. Deep Diver himself ran eleven times as a two-year-old. No one can say if a horse will make a stallion, but at £400,000 we will either make serious money or at worse get out with a small profit. I'll fill him at £3500 a cover.'

Robert knew how to do the sums now. With forty-five mares to the horse in each of his first three seasons at £3500, there would be a grand total of £472,500. That would more than cover purchase price, keep and insurance. There would be a few bonus breeding rights for the main shareholders, perhaps five a year, and, if the stallion hit with a couple of fast horses in his first 'crop', the shareholders would all be on the gravy train. If none of Deep Diver's offspring could run by the end of year five, well, he would be sold to Japan for a song. But for a profitable song.

Robert laid out a business plan and went to his father. Vernon grasped the facts extremely swiftly and agreed on the strategy. Robert could put up the original money and, as the paymaster, have a strong say in the sale of both shares and one-time breeding seasons. Two weeks later John Magnier agreed terms with David Robinson. Deep Diver, purchased for £400,000, would never run again. He would report for duty at Castle Hyde Stud in County Cork. Robert Sangster's money and John Magnier's vision had combined for the first time.

Meanwhile on the other side of the Atlantic a further phenomenon was in the process of breaking out. It came in shades of bright, burnished copper, and it went by the name of Secretariat, a colt already considered by all of the top judges to be the fastest two-year-old seen in the United States since Native Dancer twenty years before. By the time John Magnier had bought Deep Diver, Secretariat had won seven races in four months, including three at Saratoga, and two more Stakes at Belmont Park. He was already the hottest favourite for the 1973 American Triple Crown in living memory.

In the November of the year, John Magnier told Robert Sangster on the telephone from Ireland that if Secretariat should triumph in all three American classics next summer, the US public would go berserk over the first Triple Crown winner since Citation in 1948. 'There will', he said, 'be a massive upsurge in interest in horseracing.' They both knew that seven weeks after the final leg of the Triple Crown – the Belmont Stakes in New York – the first yearlings by the English Triple Crown winner Nijinsky would come under the hammer at Keeneland. 'I am telling you', said John, with some alarm, 'that prices will go higher and higher. Christ! I've just paid a one hundred per cent premium for Deep Diver against what I paid for Green God one year ago. Do you have any idea what could happen in this industry in the next few years?'

Robert did not. But he caught the drift. He was becoming aware of the great fear of John Magnier: that in five years' time it will be impossible either to buy, or even retain for breeding, a top-class American-bred stallion in southern Ireland, or even England.

'They'll freeze us out,' said John. 'The sheer weight of their dollars will dominate the industry. Big prices for yearlings *always* mean big prices for stallions. Over here we will find ourselves looking at second-line stallions, and they in turn will produce second-line racers, which will in turn make third-line stallions. In this business you have to get the best, and breed the best to the best. There is no other way. And I am afraid the Americans could cause us to become strictly a third-rate power in the bloodstock business.'

Once more Robert and John reconvened in southern Ireland. They spent time going to visit Deep Diver and Green God at Castle Hyde, and they went over the list of shareholders. The entire business was sound, and again they talked long into the night, once more agreeing that the answer was to form powerful syndicates that could take on the Americans financially at the breeding end of the industry. But like all major business reviews, they were apt to simplify what was already easy, and complicate what was already confusing. The issue was the same. Robert remained the obvious man to head up the sales operation to the big potential investors. But he needed credentials. Four weeks later, from a rather unexpected quarter, he got them.

At the conclusion of their meeting in Portman Square on 11 December 1972, the Jockey Club announced the election of three new members. The first was the tall Old Etonian Champion Amateur Steeplechase rider Christopher Collins, heir to the Goya perfume business; the second was David Alan Bethell, the fifth Baron Westbury MC (confidant of the Royal Family, former Captain in the Scots Guards, twice wounded, North African campaign); the third was the Cheshire Regiment's former private soldier and scourge of the rails bookmakers, Robert E. Sangster KO (Heavyweight Campaign, Berlin). Proposed by the local Liverpool peer, the Earl of Derby, and seconded by the third Viscount Leverhulme, a near-neighbour from the Wirral, Robert was elected, unopposed, for basically the same reasons as Chris Collins. After the nasty scare the Members had received over Christopher Soames's blackballing five years previously, the Club had agreed to bring in new blood, young men of vision, who were important investors in bloodstock and seemed likely to show an interest in the administration of racing in Great Britain in the coming years. Under this new post-Soames regime, the Jockey Club had recruited several racehorse owners and breeders who had demonstrated outstanding abilities beyond the paddocks: Sir Robert McAlpine of the giant construction company; the stockbroker John U. Baillie; the Midlands industrialist Brian Jenks; the De Beers Consolidated Mines (diamonds) director Sir Philip Oppenheimer; the electronics mogul Sir Michael Sobell. And now they had Robert Sangster, untitled, uncommissioned, unconnected and unpretentious – embryo bloodstock adventurer *par excellence*.

Robert did in fact know dimly, somewhere in the back of his mind, that his fellow stewards at Haydock Park were planning to propose him for membership, but since everyone knew – post-Soames – that you were unlikely to be thrown out these days once proposed and seconded by persons of high rank, he never gave it much thought. News of his election came as rather a surprise to him. But he and John Magnier knew simultaneously that their number one problem was solved. In the world bloodstock business, there is no higher form of credential than to be recognized as a Member of the English Jockey Club. This remains true in all racing countries from Tokyo to Longchamp, from the Antipodes to Santa Anita. Membership denotes total respectability, total honesty, total uprightness. Besides, a meeting with such a man might secure you an invitation to the Jockey Club Room at Newmarket, or Epsom, or perhaps even Royal Ascot. Members of the English Jockey Club are well received everywhere, and in Australia and the United States they are quite often feted.

What the Members did not however fully appreciate was Robert's former close association with a bookmaker – his own family credit account division which Robert shut down before it became a total embarrassment both financially and socially. And nor were they fully appraised of his most recent venture which saw him as the owner of a financially doomed bloodstock agency in Newmarket which was currently acting as a paper-thin shield for a pile of debts that stretched from Deauville to Saratoga. In the fullness of time, Robert would describe his involvement in this absurdity as: 'A bit hasty!'

The Newmarket Bloodstock Agency was its name and it was presided over by the tall, balding Richard Galpin, a man whose charm and relentless salesmanship hid a business brain which was apt to function in a rather unorthodox manner. His personal memoirs might easily have been entitled, *What They Would Never Dream of Teaching You at the Harvard Business School*. Within a few weeks of his Jockey Club membership being finalized, Robert had bought up the shares vacated by Richard's cousin and become, in effect, the owner of this most shaky enterprise. His decision to become the head of a bloodstock agency was probably encouraged by the fact that his old friend Nick Robinson had elected to part from his family firm, following the death of his grandfather Sir Foster. Robert decided that he and Nick had better run the bloodstock business between them and Nick was duly appointed chairman.

'It was', Nick recalls, 'one of the most nerve-racking periods of my life. Five minutes on the phone with Richard would give me an instant headache. And if I hung up on him, he'd ring right back and keep on talking as if nothing had happened!'

Within a few days of taking over, Nick Robinson reported to Robert that all was not absolutely ideal with the new agency. Because, not only did he own the company, he also owned twenty horses in Australia which Galpin had bought speculatively the previous year. Unsold by the Agency, they were currently in training, at high cost, now at Robert's expense. 'Worse yet,' Nick added, 'Galpin wants to go back to Australia and buy some more!' Robert replied in rather colourful language, which meant, broadly, that perhaps Richard should rethink his Antipodean strategy.

The ensuing few weeks were full of rancour. Nick had decided to go to the upcoming Fasig Tipton Sales of two-year-olds-in-training held annually at Hialeah, in Miami. No expert in the subtleties of conformation himself, he received a five-minute lesson in a bloodstock agent's technique from Galpin. 'Feel his legs, like this. Then get up and say something, like "Well, they're not perfect, but neither were his father's, and that didn't stop him running, did it?"' Without any huge confidence Nick departed for Miami, with a local trainer, Ian Walker, leaving Galpin in charge of the office. Over the next few days he would ponder long and hard as to why the normally shrewd and sure-footed Sangster was fooling around in this chaotic enterprise anyway.

Nick arrived at the sales in Florida and reported immediately to the Fasig Tipton office in order to establish his credentials, as the new chairman of the Newmarket Bloodstock Agency. His reception was inordinately frosty and he was told that the head of the sales company, the rather pompous John Finney wanted to see him. Nick was taken to the back row of the empty sales ring and asked precisely when the Newmarket Bloodstock Agency intended to pay for their purchases at the Saratoga Sale in New York the previous August. It was the first indication Nick had received of any debt problem Robert might have inherited from the previous owners: problems with unsold horses were one thing, but these debts were completely unaccounted for. A thousand little red lights started to flash before Nick's eyes.

He called Robert immediately, direct from Finney's office, and recounted the problem as succinctly as he could. The facts were relatively simple. Galpin had bought a very expensive horse for the tight-fisted London electrical tycoon Sir Jules Thorn, a man notorious for claiming a six-month credit line to anyone to whom he owed money. That included industrial suppliers, accountants, trainers and definitely bloodstock agencies. Sir Jules was famous for it. In this case however his reluctance to pay Galpin had been almost fatal because Galpin had bought in dollars and billed Sir Jules in English pounds. During the six-month suspension of payment, the dollar had firmed and the pounds with which Sir Jules had paid Galpin had not covered the dollar amount owed to Fasig Tipton. The shortfall ran into several thousands. Galpin had pleaded with him, but Sir Jules had not grown as rich as he was by listening to the bleatings of penniless agents. Unsurprisingly, he informed Galpin the problem was not his. Thus, in the usual way of such men, he had no further interest in it and would not pay another cent.

Robert's options were narrow. Either he could pay Finney and allow Newmarket to continue to trade in bloodstock, or he could request Nick to return home and wind up the company, and try to sue Sir Jules for the loss. Robert bit the bullet and paid. And Nick, slightly shaken by the experience, settled down to inspect the two-year-olds, and perhaps buy a couple for an English client. His peaceful perusal of the barns and their expensive occupants was, however, short lived. In the middle of the sales that evening, the tannoy system suddenly paged him: 'Mr Nick Robinson of the Newmarket Bloodstock Agency to the office, please.'

Nick, who was becoming increasingly underwhelmed by the entire exercise, duly presented himself at the office where he was confronted by one Monsieur Olivier Victor Thomas of the French sales company, Office du Pur Sang. This particular Frenchman was not merely angry. He was shaking with rage.

'*You!*' he yelled. 'You represent *l'organisation des criminels*.'

'Who me?' said Nick.

'Newmarket Bloodstock! Ha! I spit on Newmarket Bloodstock!'

'Oh Christ,' said Nick, and added that he would prefer to discuss anything of this rather disagreeable nature somewhere less proximate to the officials of Fasig Tipton. They retreated to a little office above the open-air bar where most of the English bloodstock agents had congregated. 'Newmarket Bloodstock is a disgrace,' bawled the Frenchman.

'Sssshhhhhhh,' said Nick, acutely conscious that all eyes were now upturned from the bar below as he and Monsieur Thomas gave a passable imitation of Romeo and Juliet having their first row. '*Monsieur Robinson!*' thundered the Frenchman. 'We do not like people who do not pay for their horses. Your organization is a disgrace and you will be blackballed from French racing. Not one of your bills from the August Sale at Deauville has been paid.'

Down below a few sniggers had turned into full-scale laughter. The agents and trainers were falling about at the plight of the rookie bloodstock agency chairman, even though they all knew the debts were obviously Galpin's not Nick's, nor, clearly, Robert's. The grandson of Sir Foster Robinson sighed the sigh of the profoundly depressed and headed for the second time that day to a telephone to call Robert. Then he realized it was three o'clock in the morning in Liverpool, and instead booked the call from his hotel for three a.m. Miami time. Robert took the news with immense irritation. 'Jesus Christ' was his precise phrase. Nick told him glumly that he knew Galpin was a bloody fool all along. But once more Robert agreed to pay the debt and to call the Paris office of Pur Sang to guarantee the credit of Newmarket Bloodstock.

When the chairman arrived home he called a meeting in Newmarket with Galpin and informed him that these kind of amateur dramatics were going to have to stop. Galpin pleaded to be allowed to attend the sales in Sydney where he believed he could make the kind of buys that could get the agency back on an even keel. Robert weighed up the cost and decided he either had to let Galpin try again or close the place down. Once again he was tolerant and agreed that Galpin could go as long as Nick was informed as to his precise activities in the sales ring. On that Nick was crystal clear.

'If you sell all of the Australian horses we have in training you may buy *one*,' said Nick. 'That's all. Not two, not three, just one.'

With that Galpin set off for the Land Down Under. All was calm for three days. Then one evening Nick was still poring over the office accounts at 10 p.m. when the telex machine in the corner began to rattle. 'Guess who?' sighed Nick to himself and, walking over to the noisy modern communicator, read to his utter horror the following words: 'From Richard Galpin. This is a list of the yearlings I have purchased at Sydney today ... Lot 21 ... Lot 57 ... Lot 102 ...' There were about ten purchases in all, but to Nick they looked like five hundred. He simply could not believe it. He let out a yell of anger that might almost have been heard in Sydney, grabbed the phone, called Robert, and then called Galpin instructing him to return home forthwith, if not slightly sooner.

This really was the end. Nick called Lester Piggott's wife Susan, who was fast making a name for herself as an extremely efficient bloodstock agent, and offered her Galpin's job. Robert, appalled at this opening venture as the owner of a Newmarket bloodstock agency, called a meeting at his London office. Present were Galpin, his wife Vivien, Derek Lucie-Smith, the company's accountant, a director Keith Tamlin, Sangster and Robinson. Galpin opened with a rambling account of the great opportunities in Australian bloodstock. Robert, furious at the way his money was pouring in, and out, of this enterprise, demanded to know why Galpin had not carried out the very clear instructions given to him. Galpin rambled on some more, finally suggesting, with a marketing flourish, that Robert invest in six massive billboards to be erected at regular ten-mile intervals all along the London–Newmarket road. 'That will increase our business,' he declared.

Robert's eyes rolled heavenward and his right foot shot out and slammed Nick in the shins. 'For Christ's sake, put the boot in, old friend,' he groaned. 'I think this man is crazy.'

Nick did his best to force Galpin to resign, but to no avail. Then Galpin went berserk, shouting and screaming, waving his arms, threatening Nick, threatening Robert with law suits. Nick was pretty angry himself, and his shin still hurt. But Robert went ice-cold silent and he stared hard into the eyes of Richard Galpin, who continued to rant and rave. There was no one to inform him that blind fury was not a good way to subdue R. Sangster and, in the regrettable absence of Tiny Davies, he kept yelling. When he finally subsided, Robert told him quietly: 'Don't shout at me again, Richard. You're fired.'

The terms of his departure took many weeks to be settled and in the end he agreed to buy out Robert on a pay-back guarantee of £100,000 to cover the debts Robert had paid for him and the shares. It would take several years, but Robert was happy to cut loose from the agency. As they left the final meeting together Nick said quietly, 'I never thought I'd see you that tough and that determined. But I shouldn't hold your breath for your money.'

Robert grinned and said, 'Don't worry about Galpin. I know he's a bit unusual, but there's a touch of genius about the man in selecting horses. Remember he bought Solo Stream for me. And I have a lot of patience. He won't owe me £100,000 for ever. That I can promise you.'

Richard Galpin never paid any of the money back, but in 1979 he had a two-year-old colt in training with Ron Sheather named Flash N Thunder. It won its maiden by four lengths and then finished a close second in the Prix Eclipse at St Cloud to earn a nine-stone rating in the Free Handicap. Flash N Thunder was thus valued at around £100,000 – and from out of the blue Robert claimed the colt from Galpin in settlement of the old debt. He relocated this fast three-year-old in Lambourn with Barry Hills who sent him out to win the Duke of York Stakes at the York May meeting. He was placed at both Royal Ascot and Goodwood, and Robert finally got his money in full when Flash N Thunder was sold to stand as a stallion in Greece. Eight years later the Newmarket Bloodstock Agency Ltd was declared insolvent in the Royal Courts of Justice in London, and compulsorily wound up.

With the Agency now out of the way, Robert began to concentrate more on the purchase of yearlings. His relationship with Eric Cousins was now on the wane, despite Eric training for him a first Royal Ascot winner with Cade's County in the Norfolk Stakes in 1972. Eric's principal talent and interest was the improvement of handicap-class horses from other trainers. At this he was supreme, but it was a policy guaranteed to keep him permanently in Division Two, where Robert no longer wanted to reside. And when Cellini began to please Vincent O'Brien in his early work at Ballydoyle, the die was cast for Robert. He was definitely going to stay in the Irish camp and moreover he was going to the Keeneland July Sales with his Irish friends in the summer of 1973 – and he was going to get involved in something big.

In the spring of the year, Secretariat did what no American racehorse had done for twenty-five years, winning the Triple Crown – the Kentucky Derby, the Preakness and the Belmont – with three track-record-breaking performances, the latter by an unprecedented thirty-one lengths. In one week Secretariat appeared on the front cover of *Time* Magazine, *Newsweek*, and *Sports Illustrated*. He even made the centrefold in *Vogue*. No one could remember such adulation ever being lavished upon a racehorse – not for Man O' War, not for Equipoise, not for Citation, not for Native Dancer, nor for Kelso. Not even for Secretariat's own father Bold Ruler. With the row over Watergate threatening to dislodge President Nixon, it was as if this nearly unbeatable big chestnut colt had come along to provide a hero when everyone felt they needed one. All over New York there were even blue bumper stickers demanding: 'Secretariat for President!'

When Robert, John Magnier and Vincent O'Brien met up at Keeneland they found themselves in the bull market to end all bull markets. Prices for yearling racehorses were rocketing as owners, trainers and agents battled it out in the ring for the next Secretariat. As John Magnier had forecast, yearlings by Nijinsky fetched huge amounts, two of them selling for around $200,000. A Northern Dancer yearling fetched $200,000, with four more making well over $100,000. Two by Raise a Native made around $200,000, with two more above $100,000. But the colt everyone wanted was one of the last sons of the late Bold Ruler, from the French mare Iskra. Tom Cooper of the Irish branch of the British Bloodstock Agency considered the colt the best-looking horse in the sale, and Vincent O'Brien agreed with him. Robert asked John Magnier what he would cost and the Irish stallion man replied, 'I would say it'll take a half million dollars to buy him.'

'Is that a lot?' said Robert.

'No,' said Magnier.

Robert told Vincent they would go to $500,000 for the son of Bold Ruler. And, further, Robert had a plan to blow all other bidders out of the water: he would cut them off before their prime with one massive bid which would, hopefully, frighten them all to death.

The usual procedure for auctioneers is to start off by saying something like: 'Now here's a top-class colt, as you can all see. Who'll gimme a half-million for him ... all right, what about $300,000 ... OK $200,000 ... $100,000 ... start him at $50,000 ... and $50,000 I have!' But on this particular evening Robert Sangster planned to curtail that little scenario. The auctioneer had no sooner demanded 'Who'll gimme a half-million for the son of Bold Ruler ...?' when Robert upped and bid the full amount. The auctioneer could hardly believe his eyes. He hesitated and then said quietly: '$500,000 I have.'

This bid was only $10,000 short of the all-time Keeneland record and Robert, not absolutely certain how they were going to raise the $500,000 at this point, sat and waited for the shock waves to subside. He watched the auctioneer demanding a higher bid and was stunned when suddenly he got it. Jim Scully, bidding for the Japanese syndicate headed by Zenya Yoshida, replied with a devastating bid of $600,000. Vincent moved over towards Robert and John Magnier and urged them to try one more. 'Jesus,' said Vincent, 'he's the most beautiful colt. Let's go higher.' But Robert was very, very nervous. He sat with his head well down, saying nothing, refusing even to look up, as Scully landed the fine bay son of Bold Ruler for the greatest amount of money ever bid at Keeneland.

Secretly he was extremely relieved, but Vincent O'Brien was disappointed. John Magnier was very much within himself, turning the problems over in his mind. Late that evening he told Robert, 'This sale is running thirty-three per cent up on last year. Secretariat has driven everyone mad. You can already see that Nijinsky was syndicated cheaply at $5·5 million. Personally, I think the Bold Ruler was cheap. Look, bull markets tend to run for quite a while. Here we had two of the best judges of a racehorse in the world Vincent and Tom Cooper *telling* us to buy. When we come here again, we have to be much more serious, much more organized. We have to come with several million raised from a syndicate so that *nothing* frightens us off. We must be in a position to back our judgment.'

Robert too was thoughtful. He resolved to look carefully into the fates of the big-priced Kentucky yearlings, to see what they were really worth at the end of their careers, and how many people actually made money from them. In his heart he believed in the philosophy of John Magnier – that you have to back the judgment of your team. Otherwise, why bother to come? And in the next twenty-four months he would have much time to ruminate upon the night they failed to buy the Bold Ruler yearling. The Japanese named him Wajima, and he won *nine* races, beating the Kentucky Derby winner Foolish Pleasure twice. Once he beat the immortal Forego, in a head-and-head stretch-battle for the Marlboro Cup at Belmont Park. Wajima won nearly $600,000 in prize money alone. He was syndicated as a stallion in 1975 for $7·2 million.

Back in England, Robert was delighted to hear that Cellini was in great form at home. In the next few weeks he won his first two races in Ireland. In Vincent's view he was one of the two best colts in the country – and that judgment was proved to be sound when Cellini came out and won the 1973 Dewhurst Stakes at Newmarket, England's premier two-year-old championship, in October. Whether or not he ever won another race, this tough son of Round Table had to be worth $1 million as a sire back in Kentucky. Whichever way you looked at it, Vincent had been right to pay $240,000 for him. And John Magnier's advice to Robert had been correct: with his first major share in a top-class expensive American yearling, Robert had quadrupled his money.

The following eighteen months was a period of consolidation, during which time Vincent O'Brien, John Magnier and Robert Sangster formulated a serious game plan. It was John Magnier's opinion that top

American-bred stallions were already beyond their reach. He pointed out over and over again, 'You cannot buy such a horse after his career in the States because they all go to Kentucky for huge amounts of money which we could never pay. And if they race here in Europe and win at the highest class, the Americans quite simply buy them back. They can *always* pay more, because their stallion fees are so much higher. Any well-bred yearling in America is worth more than his counterpart here because he can win so much money in the States. We do not have the prize-money structure to copy them. They will always have too much cash.'

As the 1974 season wore on, a mood of resignation was beginning to set in. John Magnier and Vincent were deeply unimpressed with the current crop of horses running in Europe, with the possible exception of Dahlia, the brilliant French filly who was superior to all other horses of both sexes, but was unlikely to make much of a stallion. John Magnier also liked the tenaciously tough Ascot Gold Cup winner Sagaro, who he thought one day would sire some good national hunt horses. Basically, he thought the entire answer to the breeding of fast horses over the next two decades rested very firmly in America. The problem was, how to get his hands on them.

Robert Sangster recalls with total clarity the moment Magnier solved the puzzle. He and John were having a quiet drink at Goodwood, right after a tough-looking American-bred colt by Vaguely Noble named Ace of Aces, owned by Nelson Bunker Hunt, had humbled the best milers in England to win the Sussex Stakes.

'Look at that,' said Magnier. 'You could have bought him as a yearling for $30,000. Now he'll probably be syndicated for upwards of $2 million to go back to Kentucky. I'm wondering if that might not be the answer: to raid the sales in the United States for yearlings, which cost one-twentieth of the price of stallions and hope to get it right once every four or five times. That way we'd *own* the stallions before they retired – and *no one* could get them away from us.'

He may have said something like it before, and he certainly refined the raw intellect of the thought many times again, but Robert Sangster says that was the moment, the moment when both he and John Magnier knew that at last they had a strategy to take the world of thoroughbred breeding by its neck and shake loose the key of gold. Robert recalls vividly the warm glow he felt as he pondered John's words, the warm glow every businessman knows when he has been presented with a winning idea.

'I poured myself a generous glass of Roederer Cristal,' says Robert, 'and I inhaled it as if it was draft lager, and I kept on saying over and over, "I like it, John, I like it, I *really* like it."'

'Baby stallions, Robert,' said Magnier. 'That's what we're after. The trick is to be absolutely professional about it. And remember, professionalism is about the total elimination of mistakes. It has nothing to do with money.'

Robert did venture the opinion that it would not be much fun if none of them could run. 'We'll have good times, and we'll have a few bad times,' replied John memorably. 'But the good times will finance the bad. The trick is really very simple. We gut the catalogues from Keeneland and Saratoga as if they were fresh haddock. We'll fillet out *only* those yearlings whose pedigrees are those of a stallion. There will be good racehorses out there in which we have no interest. We will not even bother to look at yearlings which do not have an unmistakable stallions' pedigree. With Vincent, we have not only the finest classic trainer in the world, we also have the finest selector of a yearling, the man who bought Nijinsky among others. We also have the best possible advisors, Irishmen of the blood, who will spot faults, help Vincent, rally round to help us get it done. And when we go in to buy, we *buy*, never mind Yoshida, Scully or anyone else.'

Robert felt all of the old sense of adventure and gamble welling inside him. This was going to be nearly as good as Chalk Stream winning the Liverpool Autumn Handicap. He returned to Liverpool, to the office and to his breeding books. All through the winter of 1974–75 he studied the fates of the ten highest-priced yearlings of the past ten years, one hundred in all. He studied their racing careers and their stud values, and he reviewed some truly spectacular disasters, yearlings which had cost fortunes and could not run a yard. There were many which were not quite good enough but did not lose money, but there were also some spectacular successes.

His chart was huge and the permutations many. But however often Robert returned to the drawing board, there was one single conclusion which could not be diminished: the only man who could have made real money from buying such yearlings would have been the *man who had bought them all*.

4

The Raiders from Tipperary

The fields around it stand soft, silent and green in their innocence. They are swept by the sodden westerly winds of the Golden Vale of Tipperary, but not by the cares and the monstrous decisions made each year upon these ancient grasslands set to the south of St Patrick's Rock. This is Ballydoyle, the training grounds of Michael Vincent O'Brien, upon whose slender shoulders the grandiose plans of John Magnier and Robert Sangster would ultimately rest. Here in this private six-hundred-acre domain, five miles down the road from the historic town of Cashel, he has laid down perhaps the finest racing gallops in the world: some flat, some uphill, some dead straight like Newmarket, some curved like Epsom. But they are all perfectly cut grass tracks, white-railed as neatly as Ascot or Belmont Park, each stretch designed for the happiness and comfort of young horses, but ultimately designed to reveal them in all of their power and all of their vulnerability. Down towards the bottom end of the grounds stands one lonely ruin of a greystone Norman castle, a sentinel of another age and, in a way, a terrible reminder of the tolerance this land has for suffering.

This is not so much a training centre as a kingdom. And Vincent O'Brien is its ruler. On the mornings when the horses work, ridden steadily through their easy paces by men with timeless Irish names like Gallagher, Murphy, Rossiter and Doyle, the great trainer watches from his private little grandstand, alert to every nuance of the galloping race-horse. The twitching of ears which may signify worry, the slashing of a tail which may foretell temper or discomfort, the slight swerve to the left or right – 'Is he still feeling that tendon?' – the sound of their breath upon the morning air – 'Is the chestnut horse clear in his wind?' – and 'Why did the big bay horse drop behind? Is he still too weak? Will he want another six weeks on the "easy list"?'

No conductor of any symphony orchestra requires more sensitivity, more powers of observation, more finely tuned instincts, more passionate desires for perfection than the great classic racehorse trainer. If Maestro O'Brien has a critic, I feel certain even that critic would nonetheless grant him one enduring and undisputed accolade: 'Vincent misses *nothing*.'

He is a Cork man by birth, originally from a little village named Churchtown, forty miles south-west of Cashel, beyond the Galtee mountains, close to the town of Mallow. Vincent himself, like all Irish boys from that corner of the country, knew that a short distance to the south were the vast waters of Cork Harbour, which flow for almost thirteen miles from the Atlantic to the City docks. Cobh, they call it, the Harbour of Tears, the last sight a million Irish people ever had of their homeland, when they fled not only the Great Hunger of the nineteenth century, but also England's shockingly cruel evictions of the people from their tiny tenant farms. Almost every family treasured the memory of relatives who were forced to leave.

Dan O'Brien himself, with his eight children, was very much a member of the Irish farming gentry. He had two hundred acres, deep in this horseman's country. The world's first steeplechase, which finished at the church steeple of Doneraile, was conducted close to the O'Brien land. Dan was greatly respected and in the Directory of Munster, published in 1893, in the section marked 'Churchtown (Clergy and Gentry)', there are seven people listed. One of them is D. O'Brien of Clashganniff House, Vincent's first home. His father kept several mares on his land, and owned and raced horses locally. He regularly bought and sold prospective 'chasers and hunters'.

All of the children were well educated. Vincent himself went away to college, and one of his sisters was sent to school in Paris. Upon Dan's death, however, in 1943, the family suffered their first experience of a shortage of money. Farming in Ireland in the late 1920s and 1930s had been very, very bad. England, as ever, was at the root of their problems, trying to impose tax on these rural farmers. Eamon de Valera, the Brooklyn-born Premier, who had fought in the streets with a machine-gun during the Easter Rising of 1916, not altogether surprisingly refused to pay it. England hit back by refusing to buy Irish produce and there were years of great hardship for the farmers of Cork, and Limerick, and Kerry and Tipperary.

Vincent O'Brien took over the care of the horses, but there was little money when, the following year, he took out a training licence of his own. From these difficult beginnings he emerged from obscurity in the

1940s, when he was famous only locally for the magic he could work on horses, to international acclaim. By 1974 he was, indisputably, the best trainer of a jumping horse ever, with four *Derby* winners to his credit, three of them in the previous seven years – a record which may never be bettered and which carries with it the general accolade among most experts that Vincent is the finest horse trainer this world has ever seen. On the flat, over fences, sprints, marathons, hurdle races, colts or fillies. The beautifully tailored, slightly built Irishman, with his fast eyes, gentle speech and mystical touch with all horses, has proved beyond any doubt the master of the Sport of Kings in all of its facets.

Those who know him best swear he can see into the soul of a young horse. John Magnier says Vincent can look at a yearling and in his mind he can see the horse as it will be two years from now, preparing for a three-year-old classic race. His meticulous mind, his obsession with every tiny detail, has driven generations of assistant trainers mad. When he is preparing two or three top horses for championship races he rarely, if ever, speaks to his assistants. *Everything* is written down in clear, concise memorandums, lest *anyone* should forget *anything*. He once said, 'It is quite difficult to remember everything yourself. To allow someone else to forget something you have already remembered would be rather silly.'

Like all of his family, Vincent is both a devout Irishman and a devout Roman Catholic, attending Mass each week. He has always resisted leaving Tipperary and training horses in England or even America, with their much bigger prize money and their markets for racehorses. His unyielding faith in the devotion and the horsemanship of his Irish stable staff have too strong a hold for that. But modern air transport, enabling him to take horses safely and quickly to the races in England, France and even America, also played a part in his decision to remain close to his beginnings. Above all, he cherished the quality of the land, and indeed of life, in this paradise for countrymen who like to hunt, or shoot, or fish the lovely salmon rivers.

But in Tipperary and in Waterford, Kilkenny and Cork, Kerry and Limerick, memories are long and the folklores are deeply ingrained. All across the sometimes sad, but heartbreakingly beautiful southern counties of southern Ireland there are ruins of great houses, which stand grey-stone frozen in the abyss of a seven-hundred-year-old quarrel with Ireland's rich and imperious neighbours east across the St George's Channel. Indeed, six years after the Easter Rising of 1916, Corkmen and Kerrymen were fighting with fearsome courage, shoulder to shoulder, in guerrilla warfare against England's detested Black and Tans. Families like the O'Briens cannot escape their traditions, and indeed their very roots in this kingdom of saints and scholars. Their love for this land draws them together as children not of a greater God but certainly of J. P. Donleavy's 'Almighty Gaelic God, for whom this land alone is worthy of his blessings'.

'I could never leave here,' Vincent once told me back in 1975 when I was preparing an art book of classic racehorses. He was gazing west at the time, and the sun was crimson as it placed long shadows over the tranquil gallops of Ballydoyle. He stood quietly for a few moments, perhaps recalling the pounding hooves of the flying Nijinsky, or Sir Ivor, or perhaps Roberto. And he stared down at the old Norman tower, one of Ireland's many reminders of conquest. And then I remember him smiling as he turned away and began to walk back towards the house. But he stopped once more, and he turned again towards the distant farmlands from which, down the years, so many had fled. And he was not smiling any more. And he just stood there, a five-foot eight-inch giant among Ireland's patriots and said quietly, 'Never.'

Empire building is not a basic ingredient of the Irish character. As a race they have usually been too busy trying to fight their way out from under England's own historic ambitions to bother with any such delusions of their own. Men like Vincent O'Brien and John Magnier were the exceptions. In this land, the land of W. B. Yeats, Eugene O'Neill, Sean O'Casey, and the Dublin-born writers Oscar Wilde, George Bernard Shaw and Brendan Behan, the pen has usually proved at least as mighty as the sword. All the same, Arthur Wellesley of Maynooth, later the first Duke of Wellington, scored a few points for the warrior classes. The empire of Vincent O'Brien and John Magnier began in 1973 when the master of Ballydoyle bought fifty per cent of the nearby Coolmore Stud Farm, owned at the time by the ex-Battle of Britain pilot and ace international bloodstock agent Tim Vigors. Tim did not particularly wish to manage a major, and growing, stud farm and he readily agreed to Vincent's suggestion that they bring in John Magnier to run it. Within a few months there was an even bigger merger being prepared. Vincent, Tim and John asked Robert Sangster to buy into the partnership and, when he did so, they proceeded to combine Castle Hyde and Coolmore into the strongest thoroughbred-breeding complex in Ireland.

At the time they stood stallions like the milers Home Guard, Thatch, Gala Performance and King Emperor, the sprinters Green God and

Deep Diver, and the winner of the Prix de l'Arc de Triomphe, Rhein-gold. They had also acquired, for a sum not far off £700,000, the miler Sun Prince, who had won at Royal Ascot at two, three and four, but who had been defeated roundly in his last race in 1973 (the Queen Elizabeth II Stakes at Ascot). This had caused many long faces in the Irish bar, particularly those of Robert and John who had signed the deal before the race. Sun Prince, though about seven pounds off top class, was nonetheless outstandingly good-looking and John Magnier thought he would make a sire, given time. Altogether these stallions were a useful, commercial bunch, but they were not world-class, and they were definitely not precisely what the triumvirate of O'Brien, Magnier and Sangster had in mind for the foreseeable future.

They agreed that their opening attack would be on the Keeneland Select Sale in the July of 1975. Each of them had his priorities laid out. Vincent himself, the man who trained them, who watched each day of every horse's development, had some fairly stringent views on stallions which he wanted to be followed. He knew that Nijinsky had sounded a trumpet call for his father, Northern Dancer, the tiny battling Canadian champion who had won the Kentucky Derby by a neck in a record time of two minutes flat in 1964. He believed that the tigerish little Northern Dancer, who was not much bigger than a pony, held the key to world breeding. As a racehorse the Dancer had never been out of the first three in eighteen starts. He had won fourteen of them, including seven wins and two seconds as a two-year-old. These were, in the opinion of O'Brien, the battle honours of a top stallion, because they displayed outstanding early speed at a very young age and they signalled the heart of a lion, which he had already bequeathed to his son Nijinsky. They also suggested soundness, on the basis that weak-legged horses do not run eighteen races in fairly quick succession, far less remain in the firing line for honours in every one of those contests. A testament to the horse's quality was that in Northern Dancer's first six crops of foals, born between 1966 and 1971, nineteen were major stakes winners. In addition to Nijinsky there were: One For All, True North, Franfreluche, Alma North, Minsky (trained by Vincent), Northfields, Lyphard, and Northern Gem.

Vincent was certain of where he stood. 'We must buy the Northern Dancers,' he told John Magnier and Robert. 'We must buy them at all costs. And the same goes for yearlings by Nijinsky. I am telling you. We must have them. I am very certain of that.'

He was fairly certain of several other stallions as well. He had a very

keen eye for any yearling by the lightning-fast American Two- Year-Old
Champion of 1970, Hoist the Flag, a son of Tom Rolfe and thus a
grandson of the immortal, unbeaten Italian stallion Ribot. He also
wished to look extremely carefully at any progeny of the great American
Horse of the Year of 1958, Round Table, son of the Irish stayer
Princequillo, who was born about ten miles from Ballydoyle in County
Tipperary, and became Champion Sire of North America. The other
stallion for whom Vincent carried a constant torch was the ex-
Argentinian Champion, Forli, an American-based grandson of the English Derby-winner Hyperion. This stallion was producing a lot of
winners, several for Vincent, including Home Guard, Thatch and Lisa-
dell. No one could select the Forlis like Vincent O'Brien, and it was
deeply ironic that the fastest, toughest racehorse in the world during
the next *four* seasons, the American, Forego, should actually be running
for a different trainer. However, Forego ran for his breeder Mrs Martha
Gerry in the USA. He had never come up at auction. But if he had
ever done so, he would have ended up at Ballydoyle. No doubt about
that. Vincent would never have missed this big, dark, rather stern son
of Forli.

Vincent O'Brien's one luxury when travelling across the world to buy
horses is shared with many of his fellow countrymen. Vincent is apt to
get homesick when not surrounded very closely by other Irishmen. In
America he liked to be accompanied by his younger brother Phonsie
O'Brien, who was formerly a fearless amateur rider over the fences –
he survived a terrible blunder at the last fence in the 1951 Grand
National, but held Royal Tan together to finish second to Nickel Coin.
Phonsie, a superb judge of any racehorse or hunter, was himself a very
useful trainer of steeplechasers. He also enjoys a towering reputation
in Ireland as a wit, a raconteur, a fisherman and a Chinese cook. He is
as close to Vincent as any brother has ever been to another, and the
years have not mellowed the great trainer's appreciation of Phonsie's
ever-green and always-renewable stories. The younger O'Brien's gift
for words does in fact enjoy a rather wider audience than that locally
based in County Tipperary and its borders, not least in the Oval Office
of the White House in Washington.

President George Bush only has to hear the name 'Phonsie' and that
great Texan grin of his seems to light up his whole face. They go fishing
together almost every year, mostly with Nicholas Brady, Secretary to
the United States Treasury. Their stamping ground is the warm shallow
waters of the Florida Keys, which stretch in a nearly two-hundred-mile-

long archipelago, swerving south-west from the entrance of Biscayne Bay all the way to Key West. The friendship began back in the late 1950s when Nick Brady's father, James Cox Brady, first had horses in training with Vincent – one of them, Long Look, won the Oaks in 1964.

Jimmy Brady, who was Chairman of the New York Racing Association, naturally spent endless hours with Vincent discussing racing and breeding, on his fairly frequent visits to Tipperary. His son Nicholas however was not quite so devoted to the subject of horseracing and Phonsie would take him off to the quiet waters of the Blackwater, or the River Suir, to cast for trout, or perhaps, in season, for salmon. The two men both loved to fish and as the years passed Nick Brady became something approaching an artist among the pools and runs of the Tipperary, Cork and Kilkenny rivers. Sometimes he and Phonsie would go along to the River Nore, near Thomastown, and fish the reach above the great McCalmont estate of Mount Juliet. The fastest racehorse who ever lived, The Tetrarch, is buried here. And the river which flows swiftly past the hallowed ground is paradise for the salmon fisherman.

In turn Nick Brady invited Phonsie to America to fish with one of his oldest friends, George Bush, off the coast of Florida. And there they have gathered almost every year ever since. Their quarry is the fabled grey ghost of the flats, the chromium-coloured eagle-eyed bonefish, which forages in mere inches of water, and goes absolutely berserk upon taking the fly. Also he can swim like The Tetrarch could run. Fishermen, prowling the dappled, sunlit shallows silently in their flat-bottomed boats, are apt to go almost into a trance at the sight of the forked tail of a big bonefish. He is wary, frightened and warrior-brave, all at the same time. The chase is conducted slowly, in utter silence, but George Bush, Nick Brady and Phonsie O'Brien swear there is nothing quite like it when the bonefish hits. The line snaps taut, the fish takes off, racing across the flats in a lunatic trail of bubbles. The two American statesmen and the horseman from Ireland stand riveted by the musical scream of the reel, as stark and as lonely as a Beale Street clarinet.

Relaxing over a drink in the evening President Bush loves the stories of Ireland. Phonsie wishes he was not President because sometimes the pressures of the world's highest office means they must miss their magical fishing trip south together. But they usually find a way and the old friendships stay solid. Vincent O'Brien and President Bush probably share many admirable characteristics, as leaders in every walk of life often do, but one of them is a love of the company of Phonsie O'Brien.

Phonsie would travel to Keeneland as Vincent's trusted confidant.

His word would not be law – if he liked a horse but Vincent liked it less, the horse may not be purchased. Generally speaking, if Phonsie disliked a horse, they all disliked it. Vincent would also take the Curragh veterinarian Bob Griffin, who was probably the best racehorse doctor in Ireland. His speciality was lameness: any faults with tendons, joints, hooves, pasterns, shoulder muscles or the big sweeps of muscle in the quarters. Vincent's association with Bob went back twenty-five years. He hated to buy any horse, even in Ireland, without Bob Griffin, but he would not buy a single one in Keeneland without him.

By the spring of 1975, John Magnier was in residence in Coolmore, slowly preparing a breeding empire in anticipation of the influx of American-bred horses they all hoped would establish themselves under Vincent's patient care. John Magnier had grown up a lot since Robert had first met him four years previously. Now, as master of the new complex, he assumed a new authority, with his ever-present cigars jutting jauntily from his mouth. Tall, handsome and rather rakish-looking with an unmistakable touch of the 'black Irish' about him (the jet-black hair and the dark eyes of the Spanish seamen who were reputed to have swum ashore and settled after the defeat of the Armada by Drake in 1588), John was now always to be seen with cigar, tailored tweed jacket, and a somewhat sartorial cravat at his throat – like a Spanish diplomat on vacation. The mystique of his dashing appearance was only marginally affected by his occasional side-of-the-mouth confidentialities: 'I'm telling you, there's a hell of a fast young "chaser" going in the t'ree o'clock at Limerick tomorrow. He'll be 20–1, but don't let that put you off.' This appearance of being a high-born sophisticate, perhaps more at home on the Champs Elysees or Bond Street, is an inadvertent deception. John Magnier is really a well-born Irish countryman, and he loves jumping horses, coursing greyhounds, golf and, of course, gambling on all of them. But you'd always somehow know he'd never be entirely lost on the Champs Elysees.

By now John was engaged to Susan, one of the three daughters of Vincent O'Brien. No father could have been very much more delighted at the choice his daughter had made. Not only was John a devout Catholic like all of the O'Briens, Vincent believed he was easily the cleverest and most far-sighted stallion master in Europe. Aided by Robert's influx of capital, he was masterminding a programme of improvements for Coolmore, the like of which had rarely, if ever, been seen in Ireland. Stallion boxes were being renovated, new drainage systems dug into the paddocks, great beech hedges planted, paths laid, fences renewed, new staff taken on. The telephone system was completely renewed. Coolmore was on the march before they had even bought the new horses.

Robert Sangster spent the spring trying hard to get his life in order, which was a major challenge. He had reaped a pocketful of cash when they had syndicated Cellini after an adequate but not sensational three-year-old season. But, sadly, his marriage to Christine was in deep trouble. In the past three years Robert had spent an increasing number of months flying around the world in search of broodmares. He now had about one hundred of them, many in residence at Swettenham, but some in Ireland with his new partners. He also had a small racehorse-breeding operation in France, and one in Australia, where he had judged land and horses to be cheap given the sudden upsurge in the world market. Robert had rather a grand plan that somehow a northern-hemisphere breeding business based in Ireland could be married with a southern hemisphere project based in Australia, perhaps using stallions to work two different seasons. Well, it might have been fine for the stallions, but it was not right for Robert, because on one of his several trips to Sydney, he had fallen somewhat recklessly in love with the wife of one of Australia's senior political figures, Andrew Peacock, spokesman for foreign affairs in the Liberal Party and regarded as a possible future Prime Minister. She was Susan Peacock, blonde, vivacious mother of three, with a love of expensive champagne and fast horses which rivalled and occasionally surpassed his own. In fairness, in the spring of 1975 they had not yet embarked upon their passionate and all-consuming affair. But they were about to, before the year was out. Robert knew it. Susan knew it. And Christine would very soon suspect it.

Meanwhile the technicalities of Robert's massive inheritance were all but driving him mad. He had been given his first third of Vernons at the age of thirty in 1966, and had a liability of £1·5 million to pay the government's Capital Gains Tax. In 1971 when Robert was thirty-five, he had received the second thirty-three per cent, and again he had had to borrow – this time £2 million to pay the Capital Gains Tax. When he was forty in 1975 he was scheduled to receive the rest – in Vernons stock – but again the tax was crippling, and the government would only accept cash, not stock, in payment. It was all but impossible to raise the money, and Robert suggested a public issue to raise some cash. Vernon, even at seventy-five, in the autumn of his life, was still an intensely private man with a strong independent streak, and he hated the idea of 'going public'. But Robert's position was clearly terrible: either he would have to sell a substantial share of Vernons in order to pay the government, or he would have to go public prior to receiving the last tranche of his stock. Vernon, with immense reluctance, agreed to the latter course.

He and Robert went to the London merchant bank Hill Samuel and, after weeks of negotiation, it was agreed that the public issue should be made, but that Vernons wide interests in bloodstock ought not to be included. Kenneth Keith, the towering ex-Guards officer and chief executive of the bank, made one formal condition: a financial director had to be appointed. Vernons, anxious for a senior money-manager to strengthen their board, chose Brian Wallis. Hill Samuel set the date for the Vernons flotation, but it was a politically turbulent year. The miners were on strike. Edward Heath's Government was beleaguered, attacked on all sides by the Labour Opposition leader Harold Wilson – a Yorkshire coal miner's son whom many in the nation thought could solve at least some of the problems. Heath, in some desperation, decided to go to the country and called a General Election for the day before the Vernons share issue. With half the British work force on a three-day week, due to chronic shortages of coal and thus electricity, Hill Samuel, concerned about the possibility of a Labour victory, advised Robert and Vernon to cancel the issue.

Hill Samuel were right. Harold Wilson swept to power and, as is predictable upon the arrival of a left-wing government in England, the London Stock Market collapsed. Robert was back to Square One. He had a year to find a solution. And he tried hard. He held meetings with Charles Clore, the chairman of Sears Holdings, which owned the big bookmakers William Hill, and suggested a merger but it could not be made to work. He held meetings with the senior executives of the Hanson Trust, Lord Hanson and Gordon White, but Robert felt they were 'too tough'. He met with Laddie Lucas of the Greyhound Racing Association, and with the Rank Organisation, and with the other big bookmakers Corals. Robert made most progress with Ladbrokes, whose chairman Cyril Stein agreed a deal worth £14 million, which would have made Robert the biggest shareholder in the company, but Vernon and his managing director George Kennerly vetoed the deal.

That was the end of that. Robert, faced once more with crippling taxes on the third tranche of Vernons shares, could borrow no more. Nor could he sell. In addition, the new Labour Government would want ninety-eight per cent of his income from his capital. Robert Sangster had no option but to leave England, and to go into 'tax exile'. He was not alone. The mass exodus of well-heeled, talented, industrious Englishmen did not in any way rival the tragic diaspora which had taken place to the south of Vincent O'Brien's Churchtown family farm in the 1850s, but one principle was the same. Most of them *had* to go for financial reasons, inflicted upon them by an English government. To this day Robert says thoughtfully, 'I was not a voluntary tax exile. I was always perfectly prepared to pay my share of taxes. But the government wanted *all of my income*, and then a bit more. I could not stay. They drove me out. *Anyone* in my position would have had no choice but to do the same.'

Robert and Christine moved out of Swettenham. They rented a house, from the fabulously wealthy Swiss racehorse owner-breeder Countess Margit Batthyany, in Marbella on the southern coast of Spain. It was a terribly upsetting wrench for the entire family. That year, 1975, Vernon Sangster was elected Captain of Royal Liverpool and Robert's mother Peggy was Ladies' Captain at the same time. It was an unprecedented situation in the historic old golf club, and rightly a source of immense pride to them both. The three-time Open Champion Henry Cotton came up to play a few rounds with his old friend Vernon. Greatly though the old gentleman enjoyed it, he was fighting a bitter inner sadness. It nearly broke his heart that he could not play the Hoylake links, just once, as Captain, with his only son.

Despite all of his troubles, Robert pressed on as Syndicate Chief of the O'Brien-Magnier-Sangster partnership. As an established member of the Jockey Club, and a considerably rich one at that, almost all doors were open to him and he recruited accordingly. Charles St George, the immensely wealthy Lloyds insurance broker in whose colours Cellini had run, quickly joined the team.

The next man in was the son of one of England's richest financiers Sir Charles Clore, young Alan Clore, whose inheritance at a very early age had been seven figures, and well over halfway to eight – pounds, that is, not dollars. Alan was extremely keen to break into the top end of the horseracing market and shared the general opinion that Vincent O'Brien was the man to take anyone there who possessed a big enough bank account. Sir Charles himself was an enthusiastic racing man and had owned a winner of the Oaks, Valoris, in 1966 – trained by O'Brien. Alan, who did not have the absolute addiction of his father for big business, was contemplating a career in bloodstock as an owner-breeder which he envisaged being very nearly full-time. But for this he knew he must obtain ownership in world-class stallions. He saw Robert and the team as his way forward.

For his next move towards serious money, Robert chose the aristocracy, casting his sights north to a great Scottish castle set in the Highlands to the west of Inverness, where the ice-cold waters of the Beauly river flow gently into the Moray Firth. Here stands Beaufort Castle, home of the Barons Lovat, a warlike, ruling Scottish family since the fifteenth century. The present lord, and Chief of the Clan Fraser, had served with tremendous gallantry as a commando in the Second World War. He fought both in Dieppe and at the Normandy landings, where he was wounded, and won a Military Cross for his bravery and leadership. His wife Rosamund was the only daughter of Major Sir 'Jock' Delves Broughton, who stood trial for the 'White Mischief' murder of the Earl of Erroll in Kenya's 'Happy Valley' in 1941. It was however their son, Simon Fraser, aged thirty-five, the romantically titled Master of Lovat, who was of interest to Robert Sangster. Simon loved horseracing and, like Charles St George, and Charles and Alan Clore, and indeed Robert, was an owner of Vincent O'Brien's. But it fell to Robert, as the head and chief salesman of the syndicate, to form this diverse group into a fighting unit, prepared to go and do battle at the Keeneland Sales, and to stay in the bidding ring until they came out victorious.

The next member of the syndicate was the steel tycoon Jack Mulcahy, who had left Ireland at the age of twenty and made his fortune in the United States. Jack's brother Dan was the cashier at the Munster and Leinster Bank in Cork, where Vincent had opened his first racing account back in 1943. Having met through Dan, Jack and Vincent became devoted friends over the years – the O'Brien family called him 'Uncle Jack'. He owned the great miler and stallion Thatch and would be a stalwart of the syndicate, ambitious with his money, and firm in his belief that if a horse could run, Vincent could make it run for its life. And that if Vincent could not make it run, then no one could.

The final member of the syndicate was Mr Walter Haefner, the Swiss businessman who had bought the lovely Moyglare Stud in Maynooth a few years previously, and nursed similar quiet but strong ambitions to those of Robert himself – to buy, and one day to breed, champion racehorses.

Between them the partners were prepared to put up something in the order of $3 million to buy yearlings. The arrangements were fairly informal but, in the broadest terms, Vincent would buy fifteen per cent and be given a five per cent share in each horse as a bonus for being the best trainer in the world. John Magnier would then provide fifteen per cent, the shareholders would put up thirty per cent, and Robert would stand up for forty per cent, which may have required of him an investment of $1·2 million, or £800,000. They were not devoted to spending all of this money. But when the chips fell, and they entered the ring to buy, this was their upper limit.

Since the average price of a yearling at Keeneland in 1974 had been a little over $50,000, and horses selling for more than $300,000 were extremely rare, there was likely to be a major impact by the men who came to be known, affectionately, and with immense good humour, as 'The Brethren'. Each of them closely followed the premise that Robert had discovered on his chart: the *only* man who can make money out of buying the best and most expensive yearlings is, in the end, the man who buys them all.

Robert trusted John Magnier and he trusted Vincent, but in the midst of all the activity he felt that he, like them, should have a personal friend and advisor standing with him when decisions of great moment were made. His choice was for a man he had known for only a couple of years but who always impressed him with his uncanny instinct for a good horse. He was Mr Patrick Hogan, of County Limerick, one of the greatest riders to hounds in the whole of Ireland, a horse coper, buyer of foals, and bloodstock agent of legendary dimensions – a man some people still swear is the best judge of a potential young steeplechaser who ever lived. In his day he was a brilliant amateur rider, setting a record in 1942 by kicking home thirty-two winners from only ninety-eight rides. He rode for the great Irish trainers, O'Brien, Tom Dreaper and Paddy Sleator. Once at Punchestown Racecourse he rode five winners and a second from six rides. To this day people still say his nickname, PP, stands for 'Punchestown Pat'.

PP Hogan spent years as the fieldmaster for the great Irish Foxhunt, the Black and Tans. He also hunted for years over the steep banks and ditches of the Limerick country close to his home in the tiny village of Bruff, fifteen miles due west of Tipperary town, to the south-east of the Shannon estuary. This was the foxhunt of the great landowner the Earl of Harrington, and his son Viscount Petersham, each of whom considered PP without peer in pursuit of a fox, and beyond belief in terms of courage and horsemanship. A small wiry little man with the smile and charm of a leprechaun, PP could beguile any man alive with his stories of hunting and racing deep in the green heart of southern Ireland. He could also sell you anything, and after a few glasses of stout you would be well advised to check your wallet. You might just have purchased a share in a seventeen-hand 'chaser' when you were thinking it was all a bit of a joke.

On the other hand you might have found yourself a great steeple-chaser. PP it was who masterminded the purchase of Rheingold with his trainer Barry Hills for 3000 guineas at Newmarket – and then watched with a cheerful smile as the horse won nearly £360,000 in prize money. 'Jesus, it was written all over him, in bloody great letters, from the time he was a yearling, from the second I laid eyes on him', was his characteristic comment. And it may have been. But no one else saw the letters. PP helped Lord Petersham buy the brilliant Royal Ascot winner Highest Trump, and it was calculated that in 1974 PP Hogan had advised in the buying of over two hundred winners. For Robert alone he bought fourteen yearlings, and ten of them won fifteen races, with another two running second. Robert and PP were fast friends. The Irishman was always on the lookout for good, highly bred pedigree mares for the English millionaire. If there was a classy filly for sale, anywhere in Ireland, PP would be certain to hear of it and if he liked her she would be on her way to one of Robert's studs no questions asked. Robert trusted PP, and the little Irishman respected him for it. He never did a bad deal for Robert, and the Englishman swore by his judgment. PP would go to Keeneland with the team, to make his quiet observations, and to protect his friend from any bursts of over-enthusiasm from the partners.

As a matter of fact it was an arrangement which did not terribly please Vincent, who felt he did not require the input of this tough little Lim-erick horseman. But PP cared not a jot what Vincent thought. He was prepared to back his judgment of a yearling against any man alive, including the Master of Ballydoyle, and if Robert wanted his opinion, he, PP Hogan, would ensure that he received it. It was a slightly uneasy arrangement, but, upon reflection, it probably kept everyone ultra-sharp. After all, Robert, as the principal investor, was surely entitled to a private opinion from one man who had no vested interest in the outcome whatsoever, save to ensure that Robert did not spend a lot of money on any horse which did not please the uncanny eye of Mr PP Hogan.

By now Robert was fed up to his back teeth with playing golf in Marbella, which he had been doing intermittently for several months. He was fed up with the constant sun, and he was fed up with life as an expatriate. He considered moving the family to Ireland, but that might have landed him with worse tax problems than he had in England.

Instead he decided to go to America for the sales, and upon his return to take Christine and have a careful look at houses on the Isle of Man, that curious thirty-mile-long island which sits bang in the middle of the Irish Sea, seventy-five miles from both Liverpool and Dublin. He knew the island well having spent numerous childhood holidays there with Vernon and Peggy, who had owned a holiday home there for some years, and he thought that both of his parents would approve of such a move. Before he went to America he called his dad and told him that on a clear day he could probably see the Royal Liverpool links through the telescope of the Royal Douglas Golf Club. 'You'll never know when I might be watching,' he chuckled. 'But I miss playing golf with you, Dad . . .'

It was now May and Vincent had secured the services of the man he regarded as the best bloodstock agent in the world, the former barrister Mr Tom Cooper, who ran the Irish branch of the British Bloodstock Agency. Every year Tom checked out the yearlings in the massive horse-breeding areas of America – Kentucky, Pennsylvania, Virginia and Maryland, a vast area more than double the size of the British Isles, which involved thousands of miles of travelling. He and Vincent had been friends for many years, and Tom had first led him to Larkspur, the first Derby winner to be trained at Ballydoyle in 1962. The task was daunting, and Vincent wanted an exclusive first look at Tom's ratings. He knew how meticulous the agent was, taking with him a small tape recorder, making detailed notes of every well-bred, good-looking horse which took his formidable eye. 'When you are planning to spend the kind of money we have in mind,' said Vincent, 'you want to seize every piece of professional assistance you can, from people whose judgment you can really trust. Tom was going to become "our man".'

Back on the home front, Robert was watching an interesting scenario. He had a horse at Ballydoyle which had been there for almost as long as he could remember. His name was Boone's Cabin, by Forli out of an unraced mare called Stay at Home, which is what her son usually did on big race days. Boone's Cabin was now five years old, a powerful sprinting type and a full-brother to the high-class racehorse and modest stallion Home Guard. In his time Boone's Cabin had won four or five races and run well in a few others, but never in the best company. Robert had wondered at the end of his three-year-old career whether Vincent would say quietly, 'Sell him, Robert,' as he did at other such inauspicious moments. But the trainer felt he had not yet 'got to the horse', and he would like more time to do so.

Nothing much changed when Boone's Cabin was four. He was still below top class and again Robert waited to be told: 'Sell him, now.' But again Vincent was thoughtful. 'I'd like just a little bit more time, Robert,' was all he said. And so Boone's Cabin went into his fifth year and, sure enough, he won a nice little race at the Curragh, and then scrambled home by a short head from a horse called Willy Willy in a four-horse race for the Ballyogan Stakes at Leopardstown. As form goes, it was not bad, but it was not good enough to stand him as a thoroughbred stallion, anywhere outside of a banana republic. Robert privately thought it was about time he cashed his chips and sold Boone's Cabin to the nearest bloodstock agent who represented such a banana republic. The Ballyogan Stakes often amounts to very little, but it was supposed to be Ireland's top sprint and that might just be good enough to get him sold to a moderate foreign power.

Vincent, however, thought differently. 'I'd say he's just about straight now,' he said patiently. 'We'll take him to Royal Ascot and he might just surprise you. I've always thought a lot of him, but he's just taken a little bit of time to come to himself.'

Robert who had been paying training fees for the biggest part of four years now considered that was quite modestly phrased. But to Ascot they went. Boone's Cabin was in the highly competitive six-furlong Wokingham Stakes. Thanks to his victory over Willy Willy, he was shouldering ten stone, one hundred and forty pounds on the handicap, the highest weight it is possible to carry in an English flat race. Not since Trappist in 1878 had any horse carried anything approaching ten stone to victory in the Wokingham. And even Trappist had carried four pounds less than Robert's horse.

Boone's Cabin, ridden by Lester Piggott against nineteen hard-trained rivals, won it by three parts of a length, with a blistering display of speed and courage, striking the front with a furlong to run, and belting home boldly, under his huge weight, in the style of a sprinting champion. It was a very fast time, and represented one of the most stupendous weight-carrying performances seen at Ascot. Robert Sangster could not believe his eyes. 'Some of those Forlis are very fast, you know,' said Vincent chattily as they made their way to the winners' enclosure. 'He's a nice horse. Just needed a little bit of time. I always thought he had a nice race in him.' Boone's Cabin never ran like that again, losing the July Cup to the crack French filly, Lianga, but the Wokingham stamped him as a stallion and he was sold very well to stand in Australia. Robert put another pile of cash into his pocket, and pondered thoughtfully over the indisputable fact that the little genius from Tipperary had done it again.

And now it was back to work. Tom Cooper's report had arrived on Vincent's desk. He called John Magnier instantly. They pored over the pedigrees, marking down those yearlings they must see, those they would get Phonsie to check first, and those they would never see, the ones which did not have the pedigree to justify themselves at stud, even if they won the Derby. They were now working on the opening steps of a ten–fifteen year plan: a plan which must be given time to work and to mature, time to produce the correct fillies and future broodmares, time to put the stallions in place. It takes six years minimum to establish a top sire. Robert thought the earliest their buying programme would finish would be the year 1985 or perhaps 1986.

Then the catalogues arrived from Keeneland. Vincent studied them at all hours of the day and night, like one of Wellington's generals marking up an ordnance survey of the ground beyond the village of Waterloo. He plotted out the families he had trained before, sometimes smiling alone in his study at the memory of a fast colt or a fast filly. Would this new half-brother, full-sister, or even cousin, run with that determination? 'Here's a Northern Dancer we must look at', 'And what about this half-brother to Sham, that very brave horse who chased home Secretariat in two classics?' The list was endless. For the first few days after the catalogues arrived, Vincent tried to discipline himself to go to bed before midnight, because he must be up to supervise the training shortly after 6.30 a.m.

Over at Coolmore John Magnier, too, sometimes worked half the night, staring at pedigrees until he almost went cross-eyed, trying to co-ordinate in his mind the dozens of lessons Vincent had impressed upon him. He knew he was operating as a back-up man for the master, but he still kept searching, for the little sections of type which might signify the precious commodity of speed, which the others might miss in a blue-blooded pedigree which had lain dormant for a while. Vincent had marked many lot numbers off, working against the list that Tom Cooper had provided and dismissing pedigrees in which most of the fast runners were fillies, the classic sign of the non-stallion – the possibly fast, brave horse who will breed nothing. And all the time John kept telling himself never to forget the master plan. 'We are going to buy baby stallions. I have zero interest in anything which might easily win a big race if I do not consider he will make a breeding stallion.'

Robert flew over to visit and to listen to their preliminary plans. He remembers watching the horses work at Ballydoyle on his last morning, when a sudden rainstorm swept down the vale and soaked the land as far as the eye could see. But as the clouds dispersed and the sun fought its way out of the south-east, a glorious rainbow filled the western sky. It arched high above the great mountain of Irish legend, Slievenamon, and it ended casting a beautiful, coloured light over the soft acres of the distant Coolmore.

Vincent called for his wife Jacqueline, whom many people consider to be the best photographer in Ireland, to come immediately to capture the sensational and poetic landscape. She gathered up her camera and a wide-focus lens, but she was not in time, and the rainbow faded, as rainbows will. And Robert observed jauntily that as far as he could tell things were looking very promising at Coolmore, 'Just over there, at the end of the rainbow'. (Jacqueline was not to be defeated and eventually took a brilliant picture of an identical scene four years later, after another rainstorm.)

On Wednesday morning, 16 July 1975, John Magnier swept up the drive of Ballydoyle. Vincent, Jacqueline and Phonsie were waiting, suit-cases packed. They had a hurried cup of coffee and set off for Shannon Airport to pick up the midday flight from Dublin to New York. The vet Bob Griffin would already be on board, his trusty stethoscope packed into his briefcase. At approximately the same time Robert Sangster was boarding the first-class section of a British Overseas Airways flight from London to New York. He would arrive at JFK marginally later than the others. Tom Cooper and PP Hogan were already in Kentucky.

Both flights were quick and uneventful. They gathered as planned at the big New York airport and were escorted with little delay to the private Gulfstream jet which was already on the tarmac with its engines running. Within moments they were airborne again, racing into the setting sun, across Pennsylvania and Ohio down towards Kentucky, which sits to the south of the Ohio river, but east of the Mississippi.

Robert had made all of the last-minute banking arrangements. The three million available dollars were in place. The catalogues of horses for auction had been reduced to around fifty yearlings, of which they would probably buy twelve. They travelled in companionable silence. John Magnier organized a few in-flight drinks, in anticipation of the fact that they were about to spend more money, at this most competitive sale of racehorses, than any man had ever spent before.

At 8.23 p.m. they touched down at Blue Grass Field, Lexington. As they walked from the plane towards the limousine provided by the Hilton

Hotel, Robert peered into the gloom, across the highway from the air-field. He could not quite make out the shape of the big round sales pavilion, now in darkness. But he knew it was out there somewhere. 'We are going to set this place alight sometime in the next week,' he muttered to anyone who happened to be listening. As it happened no one was. There was not a single 'hardboot' in sight to record formally the arrival at Bluegrass Field of the horsetraders from across the Atlantic who would change this town for ever.

5

Empires of Kentucky

All over the horse-breeding country of central Kentucky the lights were going out as Robert Sangster and his men gathered in his suite of rooms at the Hilton Hotel, after a late dinner. They went once more over their plan for the morrow ... listing, finally, the yearlings which Vincent, accompanied by John and Robert, would see immediately, the prime targets whose pedigrees were outstanding, whose sires were admired by the master-trainer, and whose conformation and attitude had caught the eye of Tom Cooper.

They ordered some champagne and shortly before midnight they drank a solemn toast to themselves and their success. John Magnier turned away quickly and crossed himself in the Catholic way, mindful perhaps that a greater power might look more kindly upon them as they sought to place the Irish racehorse industry at the very forefront of the world league. But their responsibilities were awesome, and each one of them knew it. From the twelve horses they would buy, there must be *one* good enough to become a champion. Of the ten thousand horses which go into training each year in the British Isles, the best of them all *must* be one of these twelve if they were to recoup their money. The odds against them were formidable, except for the fact that these Irishmen were the best judges of a potential stallion and racehorse in the world. 'We must not make mistakes, that's all there is to it,' said Vincent quietly.

As he spoke, Kentucky slept, unaware of the impending revolution, unaware of what was about to hit their rather sleepy little horse-breeding industry. The average price of a yearling had not risen by more than around fifteen hundred bucks a year since 1946 – that is, in total, from about $10,000 to $53,000 in 1975. A boom industry it was not. Kentucky however had had a few rarefied moments, mostly involving the big farm out on Ironworks Pike, Spendthrift, home of good ole 'Cousin Leslie'

– Leslie Combs II, the man who had bought the mighty racehorse Nashua in 1955 for the biggest sum ever paid for a stallion ($1,251,230) and put himself, and his farm, on the map, in letters large.

Spendthrift Farm had become a citadel of Kentucky breeding because, although Cousin Leslie was a mere prince among the great horse breeders like Bull Hancock, he was a Czar among salesmen. Year after year he was the leading consignor of yearlings to the Kentucky Sales. In 1967 he offered a chestnut son of the great stallion Raise a Native from a mare named Gay Hostess, and it fetched the staggering, world-record sum for a yearling of $250,000. The colt was named Majestic Prince and won the Kentucky Derby and over $400,000 in prize money. Three years later Cousin Leslie offered the full-brother (Crowned Prince) which fetched $510,000, and went to England to become Champion Two-Year-Old. Leslie Combs II, who now slept in his great white-columned mansion as Robert and his men conferred, was seventy-three years old. And he slept the sleep of the deeply optimistic. For next week he would offer yet another full-brother to his two previous world-record-breaking princes, and the smart money in Kentucky said the world-record price – the $600,000 for Wajima in 1973 – would surely be obliterated, especially as Cousin Leslie knew there were big buyers in place out there, with big money to spend for the son of Raise a Native.

Actually there was a fantastically wealthy first-time buyer interested in this horse, a Minnesota couple who would not be attending the sale but were keen to enter the highly glamorous world of Kentucky horse-breeding. Cousin Leslie had 'heard tell' of this agreeable state of affairs and it pleased him greatly. If there was one thing on all of this earth that Cousin Leslie loved more than anything else – even more than he loved ice cream – it was a first-time buyer with big bucks, the optimism of the inexperienced and the keen desire to be a part of a lifestyle, which he, Cousin Leslie, most surely represented. The mansion at Spendthrift, behind its immense Doric columns, represented the Old South at its most perfect. The atmosphere was of privilege, of calm, gentle voices, beautiful flowers, superbly cooked food, elegance and grace. Beyond the portals of the mansion were manicured paddocks containing famous thoroughbred stallions, and others containing nearly priceless mares and foals. Drinks were served from polished silver trays, carried by courteous black servants. This was Spendthrift in the enduring tradition of Tara. It might have been the inspiration for the formal toast of the Kentucky Colonels: 'A broad door open wide with the welcome of the slow, soft-spoken word, the familiar step of friendship.'

But like old Mr O'Hara, Leslie Combs II, had a rough edge to him which sometimes contrasted sharply with his rich and genteel surroundings. Guests were occasionally surprised to hear him snap, 'Hey! Send that nigger boy over here,' or 'Bring them mint-juleps here, boy!' He had travelled a long road from rather humble beginnings and he was apt to rely on charm and humour, rather than the manners of the high-born. Despite his total adoption of the trappings of the Southern gentleman, he was a real Kentucky 'hard-boot' underneath. Leslie's father, Daniel Swigert Combs, shot himself stone dead through his right temple at eleven o'clock on the morning of Thursday, 28 January 1915. His wife Florence, one-year-old daughter Elizabeth and thirteen-year-old son Leslie were left penniless. It happened one day after Daniel had been fired from his job as manager of a fifteen-thousand-acre cattle farm in Hardeman County, Tennessee. By then, however, young Leslie knew enough to realize that the only important aspect of his family tree was that name Swigert. His great-grandfather was indeed the owner of Elmendorf Farm, Kentucky, the famous racehorse and stallion owner Daniel Swigert, breeder of three winners of the Kentucky Derby in the late nineteenth century.

Shunted around between relatives for most of his formative years, Leslie made his first serious move towards substantial wealth when he married Dorothy Enslow, the heiress to a major fortune founded upon banking, real estate and the Chesapeake and Ohio Railway. She and her family lived in a twenty-seven-room mansion in Huntington, West Virginia, and she became Mrs Leslie Combs within ten years of Daniel Combs's death. Her new husband, who frequently teased her that 'I only married you because you were so rich', was, at the time of the wedding, a teller at Huntington National Bank. Her father had been president until his death in 1917 and now the young couple lived with her mother in the grand mansion house on Third Avenue, attended by a butler and several maids. By the 1930s Leslie had used many of the connections his new family could provide and not only owned an insurance business, but had also turned himself into a high-goal polo player. He developed interests in his old family preoccupation, thoroughbred horses, and was very much in attendance when a group of Lexington businessmen, including his uncle Brownell Combs, founded the Keeneland Association and brought horseracing back to the Bluegrass.

The opening meeting in October 1936 was highlighted by two

dazzling performances by Brownell's great racemare Myrtlewood, who won both the Keeneland Handicap and, forty-eight hours later, the Ashland Handicap. It was a truly sensational performance, but not, however, as sensational as events over in Huntington on the same day as Myrtlewood's second triumph. Mrs Juliette Enslow, mother-in-law of Leslie Combs II, was found beaten and strangled in her bed. The murder absolutely stunned the town. Despite the fact that the victim's son, by her first marriage, was charged with the crime, he was found not guilty and the case was never solved. Leslie Combs, close now to violent death for the second time in his life, said flatly, 'I was down in Lexington the day she got killed, fortunately. Otherwise they'd'a said I did it.' Mrs Enslow's will provided a sizeable fortune for Dorothy, plus automobiles, jewellery, silver, china, furniture and a trust fund for the Combs children's education. To Cousin Leslie she bequeathed only a set of novels by the nineteenth-century French writer Honoré de Balzac, whose books so frequently featured steely-eyed seducers and fortune hunters moving in a world consumed with social prestige.

Within a year Leslie and Dorothy had moved into Kentucky. They bought a hundred-and-twenty-acre farm out on Ironworks Pike in Fayette County. It was on land which had once belonged to Elmendorf, to Leslie's great-grandfather Daniel Swigert. He had often gone out to look at this land, often stood and contemplated the possibility of buying some of it. When the transaction was complete he said thoughtfully, 'One day I'm going to buy *all* of it back. Restore my family to its rightful place.' And he named the new farm after one of Daniel Swigert's great runners, the winner of the 1879 Belmont Stakes and the grandsire of the immortal Fairway, sire of Man O'War. Daniel's horse was named Spendthrift.

Three years later Leslie found one of those people he sought out and feted all of his life: the new convert to thoroughbred racing, with huge amounts of dollars to spend. The name of this particular convert was Elizabeth Arden Graham, owner of the giant cosmetics empire. Cousin Leslie met her and beguiled her in 1940. She knew he was a terrible rascal, and he knew what she wanted from racehorses – the opportunity to parlay her millions into social connections, to rub shoulders with Whitneys and Vanderbilts out there in the Bluegrass, to race great horses in great races. The best way she could see to achieve all of that was to stand right alongside Cousin Leslie and let him do the rest. He became her advisor and racing manager. He bought her horses, handled all of her racing interests, and he took her where she dearly longed to go –

with a horse called Jet Pilot. This gutsy chestnut son of Blenheim II led wire-to-wire in the 1947 Kentucky Derby, winning by a head against the charging Phalanx. Leslie also coaxed into the thoroughbred business the film mogul Louis B. Mayer, the financier Louis E. Wolfson, and the American newspaper baron John S. Knight. Later he would bring into the Spendthrift domain the New York Yankees owner George Steinbrenner.

Leslie Combs was always selling a dream, of glamour and manners, of the romance of the Sport of Kings, and of the endless possibilities of making huge profits from what he would call a 'goddamned running horse'. To the end of his days he would drive around the farm, or indeed around Lexington, with his 'trademark' special horn on the big Lincoln Continental. No beep-beep for the master of Spendthrift: when he hit the horn it blared, loudly, the 'Call To Post', the bugle summons which sounds out at every US racetrack as the horses come out onto the track ... 'DAH DAH DAH, DAH DAH-DAH, DAH DAH-DAH, DAH DAH-DAH, DAAAH!' 'There goes Cousin Leslie.' He could promote his stallions and yearlings when he was all on his own, in his car, waiting at the traffic lights. Everyone knew he was there, still selling, sounding out the gospel of Spendthrift. 'Have I got a horse for you!' And he always had.

Men like Cousin Leslie do not suddenly arrive on the map. They are always on it, marching around, treading on toes, selling, getting talked about, delighting some people, driving others mad. But thoroughbred-breeding farms in the Bluegrass have traditionally needed something major to happen to them. For Spendthrift it was the great racehorse named Nashua. Everything about the deal that brought the champion to Kentucky was slightly bizarre, even the event which caused the sale. Nashua's owner William Woodward Jr, the New York millionaire, was shot dead by his wife, who mistook him for a prowler in their house. Nashua had not only won two American classics, he had also won perhaps the finest match-race ever run in the USA: a $100,000, winner-take-all clash with the superb Kentucky Derby winner Swaps. Nashua beat him over ten furlongs at Washington Park in August 1955 by six lengths. When he retired in 1956 he had won twenty-two races – five of them carrying one hundred and twenty-seven pounds or more. His winnings totalled almost $1·3 million, more than any other horse had ever won, and to the American public he was nothing short of a towering hero. Upon the shocking death of William Woodward, the estate put Nashua up for sale in a sealed-bid auction. Most people thought he might fetch $1 million, which was a colossal sum of money at that time. But Cousin Leslie thought someone might go to a million and a quarter. He thus elected to add the numbers '1-2-3' to his bid and he went in for $1,251,230. Nashua was his, the first stallion ever to be syndicated for such a sum in a deal which made the front page of the *New York Times*.

Spendthrift Farm had joined Cousin Leslie – on the map. In the ensuing years Leslie Combs perfected the art of 'the syndication' and he brought great stallions to his barns. Another of them was Raise a Native, the massively built son of Native Dancer, who may very well have been the fastest two-year-old to race on a US track since the Second World War. Unbeaten in four races, in which no other horse could even race with him, never mind beat him, Raise a Native was breathtaking to watch. Charles Hatton, the chief columnist for the *Daily Racing Form*, once wrote, 'Raise a Native worked five furlongs along the backstretch at Belmont Park this morning. The trees swayed.' At Leslie Combs's farm he would found, literally, a dynasty, based entirely on his own all-American bloodlines. He would sire tough, hard, dirt-track runners who could withstand the test of racing in the USA. In turn these horses would become sires themselves and by the 1990s an entire generation of Raise a Native's sons had made a major mark on the world's Stud Books. There was however a question of whether these fast horses would act on European grass, and Cousin Leslie would spend in the coming years many sleepless nights wondering whether his young stock would attract the attention of the wily Irishmen who could earn you a king's ransom at the sales.

Like every other commodity, the great thoroughbred stallion needs promotion and salesmanship. And it was here that sires like Nashua and Raise a Native had a huge advantage in the sales ring. Leslie Combs II, a pretty good horseman with a pretty good eye, was nothing short of a sensation as a salesman. He could sell electric fires in the Congo Basin. He invented the entire concept of 'high-life' in the Kentucky Bluegrass, throwing spectacular parties for the Derby in the first week in May to attract new clients, and then he would throw sales parties. He would even throw 'syndicate' parties. Bewitched by the aura of Spendthrift, awestruck by the sight of the magnificent stallions, seduced by the promise of the vast riches to be made in the most glamorous of all sports, prospective clients rarely made it off the charming side-porch of the mansion of Spendthrift with their wallets intact. The view from here, down across the paddocks in the early evening, was truly magical, as the mares and foals moved quietly at grass, and the sun slipped down behind the dogwood trees. Somewhere to the north of the house Nashua and Raise a Native were being fed. Down on the porch Cousin Leslie held the key to this mystical world.

'Now, right here I've got this itty-bitty little contract for you to sign . . . and this, sir, is something you are *never* going to regret. I'd say you were about to make one of the smartest judgments of your life. This, sir, is a *running* horse, if ever I saw one. *Yessir.* Hey, *boy!* Bring them mint-juleps here.'

In stark contrast to the well-preserved, five-foot ten-inches tall, balding Leslie Combs, was his son Brownell, born in 1933 and, partly due to an inherited adoration of ice cream, built more on the massive lines of Raise a Native. Brownell, at six foot four inches, sent the scale straight over the three-hundred-pound mark without giving it too much prior thought. In 1975 Cousin Leslie was preparing to hand over the operational running of his empire to Brownell, which many people thought was unusual, since the senior Combs had spent much of his life abusing his only son in a way which was heartbreaking to Brownell, and at times cringe-makingly embarrassing to colleagues and guests.

'Goddamnit, Brownell, you are just never going to amount to nothing, you big dumb sonofabitch.'

He was wrong too. Brownell was never asleep in the horse business. He had an excellent grasp of the technicalities of the big syndication. He knew how to round up partners and shareholders in the stallions. And he knew how to bring all the pieces together. In this he was assisted by his wife Linda, a lady who was extremely adroit at bringing clients to Spendthrift. Brownell's problem was Leslie and, perhaps to make up for his lack of parental affection – Dorothy Combs had died in 1968 – the heir to Spendthrift farm developed a penchant for high-living. Real high-living, spending money in a way which would have qualified him to be cast in bronze and placed at the entrance to the farm, as its international symbol and logo.

Linda too had a problem. And its name was also 'Leslie'. He never appreciated her, and he would belittle her in front of the staff for wearing trousers in the office. Cousin Leslie did not approve of ladies wearing trousers. He had an office rule that no female member of the staff was allowed to wear trousers. And when he saw Linda wearing jeans, he would yell out his anger and order her out of the office, reducing her to tears, right in front of everyone. Brownell, who still called his father 'Sir' to his face and 'Mr Combs' to everyone else, felt helpless to intervene, confronted by his all-powerful father who had scarcely ever had a good word to say about either himself or Linda. Senior staff in the Spendthrift executive offices hardly knew where to look when old 'Mr Leslie' shamelessly abused members of his own family. But he was the boss and that was the way things were in this grandiose Kentucky breeding farm, where the horses took precedence over everything. No one ever called Nashua a 'big dumb sonofabitch'.

A few miles away at Claiborne Farm, in the village of Paris, to the west of Lexington, the most famous of all the great horse-breeding families, the Hancocks, conducted their operation with rather less flamboyance than Cousin Leslie. There had however been trouble here in the past few years after the unexpected death of A. B. 'Bull' Hancock, the man who had brought the great ill-tempered Irish stallion Nasrullah to the United States. Bull had two sons, Arthur and Seth, and they were about as different as any two sons could ever be. Big, athletic Arthur, the eldest, was, in his youth, a young man who might generously be described, in the local vernacular, as 'a bit frisky'. He loved, in no particular order, beer, fast cars, girls, country music, playing his guitar, singing, staying out half the night, and general carousing. He had, however, two colossal strengths: one, an ability to fight his way out of bed early in the morning and report for work no matter how utterly shocking he may have felt; two, he was an innate horseman. Arthur *knew* both a racehorse and a stallion, like his father before him. He did not, however, much like being told what to do.

Seth, younger, quieter, perhaps less rash, apparently more sensible, was all any father could hope for, as a calm, careful, reasonable and indeed likeable young manager. Seth could get along fine with just about anyone, and he inspired older men to trust him with the reins of the farm. While Arthur might just buy you a world-beating stallion for a bargain price, he also conveyed the suspicion that he was capable of turning the breeding shed into a recording studio for Ricky Nelson. That may not have been so, but with the dangerously rich older generation which controlled Claiborne, impressions counted for everything.

In 1972, when Bull Hancock died, there was a formidable stallion roster at Claiborne. In addition to the English Derby winners Sir Ivor and Nijinsky, there was Forli, Tom Rolfe, Round Table and Buckpasser. In the recent past there had been Nasrullah, Bold Ruler, Princequillo and Blenheim II. Secretariat himself would be coming to Claiborne, along with the 1972 Kentucky Derby winner Riva Ridge. Bull had thus placed America's greatest stud farm in the hands of executors, and the principal advisors were two of the richest men in America, Mr Ogden Phipps and Mr Bill Haggin Perry. They were of course, as serious horse breeders, the two biggest clients of the farm. The will stipulated that Arthur and Seth should run the farm as joint vice-presidents. But by late 1972 this arrangement was not working. Arthur had had a major row with his executors and advisors over the syndication of a potential stallion named Bold Reasoning. And Mr Phipps had put forth the view that every ship needs a captain, and Claiborne should have a man at the helm: both he and Bill Perry believed that man should be Seth Hancock. They suggested that the boys' mother Mrs Waddell Hancock should be president, with Arthur and Seth vice-presidents, but with Seth in day-to-day command. This was never going to work with a forceful character like Arthur, and he decided to go.

He told his family that he knew that Mr Perry and Mr Phipps did not want him. He said he also knew that 'my daddy's will said they must be listened to'. As far as he was concerned that was an end to it. On a cold December afternoon in 1972 Arthur B. Hancock III resigned from Claiborne and left the hundred-and-ten-year-old family business for ever. He turned his back on all of the tradition and all of the security, and he drove down the long driveway devastated at what he had done. It almost broke his mother's heart. Close friends say she never got over it. Arthur leased a little stone farmhouse from the estate, and swore to himself that one day he would breed and race a Kentucky Derby winner, and he would have a farm *bigger* than Claiborne. In the boom years to come he would achieve both of those ambitions, except that he would breed and race *two* Kentucky Derby winners.

Thus the Hancock family split, leaving Seth to continue the Claiborne horse-breeding traditions begun in the last century in Virginia by his great-grandfather Captain Richard Hancock, a Southern officer who fought with incredible gallantry under the command of General Stonewall Jackson in the Civil War. Captain Hancock was with the General when he fell, mortally wounded, at the Battle of Chancellorsville, and was himself hit three times in the murderous Battle of Gettysburg when the South lost twenty thousand men killed or wounded. Arthur still has his letter home – 'I cannot', he wrote, 'see how any of us were saved.'

When Arthur left this great Southern family to begin life anew, he took with him one valuable, loyal ally, Mr Nelson Bunker Hunt, the Texan oil tycoon and, at the time, the biggest man in bloodstock breeding in the world. Bunker really believed in Arthur, as did several of the staff of Claiborne who also went with him. Among those who stuck by the son who was most like his father was Ann Worwick who had once been Bull Hancock's secretary. 'All kinds of people came up to Stone Farm to help out in the early days,' she recalls. 'Most everyone I know has a real soft spot for Arthur.' By 1975, when Robert Sangster and his men arrived in force, Arthur was increasing his acreage to between three and four hundred and, assisted by Bunker, was trying to build his own roster of stallions, in addition to the mares and foals. He was always trading horses, always borrowing from the bank, always buying, selling and repaying loans. Bunker Hunt was a great financial backer and would enable Arthur to strike hard and often in the world league of breeding stallions.

Bunker himself, the son of the Texan tycoon H. L. Hunt, had built for himself a huge financial empire in oil, silver, land and cattle. He had been taught by his father the rudiments of thoroughbred racing and by 1975 had made a major impact on the world's thoroughbred breeding markets. He had bought a controlling interest in the winner of the 1968 Prix de l'Arc de Triomphe, Vaguely Noble, and was busily establishing both himself and his stallion as the pre-eminent players in the global scene. The owner of some two thousand five hundred acres of central Kentucky, comprising several spreads, all under the banner of Bluegrass Farm, Bunker was building up a band of the most fashionable broodmares in the world. There was one of the greatest racing fillies of this century, Vaguely Noble's home-bred daughter Dahlia, winner of Ascot's King George VI and Queen Elizabeth Stakes in 1973 and 1974 (the only horse ever to win it twice); there was Goofed, the dam of the classic racehorse and stallion Lyphard; there was the dual French classic winner Gazala; there was Nobiliary who had just finished runner-up to Grundy in the 1975 English Derby; and there was Charming Alibi, the dam of Dahlia. There was even Homeward Bound, Sir Foster Robinson's Oaks winner whom Bunker bought at the dispersal of the estate. Already in training in France was Gazala's son, Youth, who would win the 1976 French Derby, and another son of Vaguely Noble, Empery, who would win the 1976 English Derby. Bunker was in a position which might reasonably have been described as impregnable. He had seventy-five mares at his various Kentucky locations, anything he sold fetched a very good price, and he had an uncanny knack of keeping and racing his best colts and fillies.

He was extremely popular in the Bluegrass and he was well-respected as a man not to be trifled with. He shared with the great Kentucky breeders an inordinate love of money and he was not prone to squander any of the millions he had already accumulated. One of his most endearing little idiosyncrasies was that he would *never* travel first-class on a commercial aircraft. Bunker sat at the back with everyone else. If he was in a hurry he would hire a plane, maybe fly the Atlantic in private, but he would not buy himself a first-class ticket. It was probably a character trait he had picked up from his father, Old HL, who used to have a private box at the big races which cost him thousands. But to the end of his days he never dined expensively at the racetrack. He always took sandwiches, in a brown paper bag.

Across the other side of town stood another of the world-famous Kentucky nurseries. This was Darby Dan Farm, owned by the Ohio construction tycoon John Galbreath, himself the owner of Roberto, the colt Vincent O'Brien trained to win the 1972 English Derby, and who now lived at Darby Dan. In 1975 Darby Dan was managed by the seventy-five-year-old Olin Gentry, the doyen of the Kentucky breeders, a man who had been in the business for sixty-one years and who, during that time, had personally raised five Kentucky Derby winners, five horses which finished second, four winners of the Preakness, and four winners of the Belmont Stakes. For all but two of these, Olin Gentry had personally selected the matings. Mr Gentry was fabled around Lexington. Everyone knew who he was and when he spoke about a horse, or a horse race, it was a very hasty man who did not wish to listen. Like most great horsemen he treasured a few massive biases, the most prominent of which was a powerful belief that the greatest racehorse he ever saw was the 1966 three-year-old son of Ribot, Graustark. 'You can mention Man O'War, Native Dancer, Citation, Swaps or even Secretariat,' he said. 'But Graustark would have pulled away from all of them. Of that I am quite certain, because they were just racehorses. He was a locomotive.'

There was something extremely 'proper' about Mr Gentry, who died in the late 1980s. He was always well-dressed, and a bit outspoken, but he was thoughtful and temperate. It was always a great pleasure to meet and talk to him, and always a source of unending mystery how he, with his impeccable judgment of bloodlines, could possibly have bred a son like Tom Gentry, the opposite of his father in so many ways. Tommy Gentry was a salesman in the Leslie Combs mould. He was short in stature with the widest grin in all of the Bluegrass. He had a two-hundred-acre farm out along the Paris Pike, and he may not have bred the string of classic winners that stood alongside the name of his father, but, boy, could he spot a commercial yearling. Of all the incredible salesmen of the Lexington area Tommy Gentry stood right up there

with Cousin Leslie and the best of them. That Keeneland sales ring
was to Tommy what the three big rings at Madison Square Garden
were to P. T. Barnum. And as for sales parties, Tommy could probably
have issued a few lessons to the late film mogul Mike Todd.

In a more sedate setting stood the most legendary of all the Kentucky
farms. Painted in its own livery of devil's red out near the airport stood
the gracious Kentucky mansion of Calumet Farm, which had for half
a century set the standard for the racing and breeding of racehorses.
This was the birthplace of Whirlaway, Citation and six other Kentucky
Derby winners. It was founded upon a vast fortune made by the Wright
family in the baking-powder business in the early part of the century.
Calumet Baking Powder was sold for $32 million in 1928. William
Monroe Wright bought the Kentucky farm in order to raise trotting
horses, but his son Warren Wright Sr converted it into a nursery for
thoroughbreds in the 1930s. No farm ever had success like Calumet
and Warren Wright lived to see his Triple Crown Champion Citation
achieve what no other racehorse had ever done: win $1 million on the
track. When he had done so, he was retired to Calumet.

A few months later, Warren Wright died, leaving the farm essentially
to his wife, the former Lucille Parker, who was already established, and
would remain so until her death, as the 'Grande Dame' of central
Kentucky. In 1952 Lucille remarried to Admiral Gene Markey, a novel-
ist and bon vivant who had three times been married to Hollywood
beauties. Admiral Gene was liked in Kentucky and he added to the
high-society image of Calumet. However, the farm went into a long
decline after Warren Wright died and few top horses carried the famous
devil's red and blue to victory in the late 1960s and early 1970s, though
Forward Pass did land the Kentucky Derby after the disqualification of
the winner Dancer's Image in 1968. In general terms Calumet was
never a major seller in the yearling markets, preferring to stay with
Warren Wright's old maxim of breeding to race, and keeping their
yearlings to do battle on the American tracks. But times were changing.
Mrs Markey yearned for the old glory days of Calumet and she frankly
dreaded the prospect of her myopic and somewhat dim-witted son
Warren Jr taking over the place. 'If there was one way in all of this
world I could keep him from having Calumet, I would,' she once said.

Lexington was a turbulent place in the mid-70s, often rife with family
jealousies, frequently short of cash, fighting to keep up the great façade
of gentle Southern living among the most noble of all of God's creatures,
the high-bred thoroughbred racer. Even John Gaines, heir to one of

America's largest dog-food fortunes, occasionally found it a tough selling job to keep his magnificent Gainesway Farm, out on the Paris Pike, in the forefront of the stallion syndication game. But there were better times to come, and those better times were already here in July 1975. Their names were Vincent, John, Robert, Bob, PP, Phonsie and Tom.

At 9 a.m. on Saturday 20 July Robert Sangster and his men drove into the Keeneland Sales complex out near Bluegrass Field airport. Their catalogues were marked, the barn numbers logged and they headed as a team, falling in behind Vincent and John, towards the boxes which housed the yearlings submitted by Windfields Farm, of Chesapeake City, Maryland, one thousand miles away on the eastern coast, close by the estuary of the Delaware river. This was the two-thousand-acre spread purchased four years ago by the Canadian brewing magnate, E. P. Taylor. It was sprawling, flat horse country, next door to Mrs Allaire Du Pont's farm which housed the now-retired, but still mighty American champion, Kelso. Windfields, by comparison with some of the Kentucky breeding establishments, was in some ways rather unprepossessing. But for Vincent O'Brien it represented something close to Valhalla. This was the home of Northern Dancer, sire of Nijinsky.

There would be several other farms offering yearlings by the Dancer, but Windfields was the first stop for Vincent. The catalogue told him they were offering two, plus another by his sire, Nearctic, and another by Nijinsky himself. They had all been driven out to Kentucky, half-way across the continent, in the big Windfields horse transporter with its yellow livery, to match the racing silks of Eddie Taylor. They would all be offered for sale as the final consignment late on Tuesday afternoon.

It was quiet at the barns in the morning, but there was a groom in attendance when Phonsie O'Brien asked, not unpredictably, to see Northern Dancer's son from a mare named Fleur, a daughter of Mr Taylor's Canadian stallion Victoria Park. It was the female line which interested Vincent. Fleur was from Flaming Page, the dam of Nijinsky. Thus the yearling was a three-parts brother to Ballydoyle's big, bold, temperamental Triple Crown Champion of 1970. But when the yearling marched out into the early morning sunlight, he provided a bit of a shock, principally because he was everything Vincent assumed he would not be. For a start he was tiny, a characteristic summed up by Phonsie thus: 'Jesus! I've got a labrador who's only a bit bigger!' Nijinsky was a hard bay, the yearling was chestnut. Nijinsky looked like a big stern racehorse. The yearling was flashy, with four white stockings, and a big white blaze.

'Hmmm. He's not very big, is he?' said Bob Griffin.

Vincent said nothing. He stared quietly into the yearling's eye. And the little horse stood stock still, staring right back. Vincent smiled at him, pulled his ear gently, ran his hand down the horse's neck. Then he moved along his flanks, to get an accurate fix on his height. 'He's more than 14·1 hands,' he said. 'But not much. He could just be big enough, but only just.' He asked the groom to walk the horse for thirty yards or so, and he stood directly behind him, watching the confident swing of the quarters, the long, almost flaxen tail flicking at the end, rhythmically, first left, then right. He then stood head-on as the horse walked back towards him, noting the occasional flick of the ears, but noting more than anything the bold firm walk, the way the little horse slapped his front hooves down.

The master-trainer said nothing, almost as if he was trying to sort out the unspoken conundrum that Nijinsky was so big, and this little chap was so small. But then Northern Dancer was also small, and so were several others of his sons and daughters. The Windfields chief of operations Joe Thomas always swore it was due to the Dancer's grandma, Nearctic's dam Lady Angela. She was herself a daughter of the pony-sized winner of the 1933 English Derby Hyperion, champion racehorse, champion sire.

'Anyway,' said Phonsie helpfully, 'if size had anything to do with speed, a cow'd outrun a rabbit.'

Robert chuckled, and whispered to Phonsie, 'Do you like him?'

The Irishman's reply was definitive: 'I bloody love him,' he said.

The other major strike against the chestnut yearling was all that white. The four stockings represented a near-taboo for a horseman. There is an old saying which goes, in various forms:

> One white foot, buy a horse,
> Two white feet try a horse,
> Three white feet, look well about him,
> Four white feet, do well without him.

Vincent O'Brien was inclined to subscribe to this, not because of a belief in some daft old wives' tale, but because he suspected that white about the hoof signified weakness, and perhaps a proneness to injury, or even quarter cracks (the horse's 'athlete's foot'). This, plus the general feeling that the chestnut colour is the equivalent of the quick-tempered equine redhead, and he had much to ponder over with this self-assured son of Northern Dancer. Of course there have been great chestnut racehorses, but they also have a reputation for petulance and there is always a suspicion that in the heat of battle they might give up the struggle.

Vincent stood for a few more minutes with the horse, and then he asked Bob Griffin to go over him carefully. They left the Irish vet checking him over, the knees, the ankle joints, the heart, the lungs and all of the rest. Robert remembers that Vincent said not a word for about ten minutes afterwards. 'That little horse was on his mind,' he said. 'Really on his mind.' But they had much to do, miles to walk before they slept, and they spent another forty-five minutes with the Windfields yearlings, inspecting the other Northern Dancer, a filly, which Vincent did not like, and the colt by Nearctic, which he liked even less. For the rest of the day they moved methodically along the barns, marking the catalogues, noting the ones they would see again, drawing a line through the pages of those in whom they had no further interest. At the end of the afternoon, Robert was talking to Vincent, everyone was tired, most of them were dying for a drink and a bath, and they had found only about four yearlings which Vincent really liked.

The trainer excused himself and said he would be back in twenty minutes. Phonsie O'Brien, watching his brother walk swiftly out into the fading light, said, 'I can tell you where he's going. He's going back to have another look at the little Northern Dancer.'

For the following two days they patrolled the barns. They went over to see Leslie Combs's yearling full-brother to Majestic Prince, the one everyone thought might top the sale. Vincent quite liked him, but the horse 'did not speak to him', and they crossed him from their list. He did like a very tough-looking colt being offered by Seth Hancock's Claiborne Farm, by Round Table out of the American Two-Year-Old Champion Moccasin. This made him a full-brother to Appalache, Vincent's 1973 Champion Two-Year-Old in England and Ireland – same family as Cellini. He also loved a chestnut colt consigned by Gainesway Farm, by Prince John out of Hornpipe II, which made him a half-brother to the American Two-Year-Old Champion of 1973. Like Seth Hancock's father, Vincent believed devoutly in the speed of very young horses and he rarely bought from a family without it.

There was another elegant colt by Round Table out of Stylish Pattern which he liked and two more by Bunker Hunt's Vaguely Noble. Every one of them, if they could run, would make a valuable stallion. But John Magnier was very within himself through the entire operation, worrying about the pedigrees, praying that he had not made a mistake, even that he had not missed something. Phonsie kept them all smiling, and he was a great encouragement to Vincent, confirming opinions, generally agreeing with the master's judgment, occasionally mentioning something which would turn his brother's head very quickly, and sometimes elicit a quiet nod from PP Hogan, who basically confined his opinions to Robert. There was not much discrepancy however. Vincent's opinions were always solid, and sometimes inspired. But he needed his close-knit team around him – no man's nerves could stand the strain of making the kind of decisions he was saddled with, all alone.

The opening day of the sale held only marginal interest for the Irishmen, but early in the evening Vincent instructed Tom Cooper to go in and buy the colt by Round Table from Stylish Pattern. It cost them $110,000. They studiously ignored a rather fractious youngster by Hoist the Flag from Princess Pout which failed to make its reserve, but four lots later they bought a colt by Crowned Prince, inexpensively. They watched dispassionately as the new owners from Minnesota, Mr and Mrs Franklin Groves, plunged into the thoroughbred industry with a gigantic, world-record bid of $715,000 for Cousin Leslie's Raise a Native, via their agent Mrs Anne Trimble. But Vincent bought the last colt consigned by Spendthrift, a strong-looking bay Northern Dancer, for only $45,000. On Tuesday afternoon he went to $172,000 to secure a filly by Hoist the Flag out of Sir Foster's former champion Homeward Bound, half-sister to Chalk Stream. And then Vincent vanished again. When he returned he was in conference with Bob Griffin who had pronounced the little one 'sound as a brass bell'. And then he spoke to Tom Cooper. 'I think we'll go for the Northern Dancer out of Fleur,' he said. 'He's small, and he may not fetch a lot, but I like him a lot and I think he'll grow enough.'

The bloodstock agent was pensive. 'There are other Europeans here,' he said. 'You'll remember perhaps how small Lyphard was when he went through the ring at Newmarket in 1970 – turned out to be one of the best milers in France. You could have serious opposition in the ring. He could go for a quarter of a million dollars. Maybe even more. There's a buzz about Northern Dancers from fashionable families. Will you give me a limit to bid?'

Vincent said nothing. And Tom remembered him standing there, once more lost in thought, wondering whether he could possibly be right about the little horse, with the wrong colour, the wrong markings, who 'spoke to him' so boldly. The Irish trainer let the information filter

Above: The Minstrel, on the outside, hard under the whip of Lester Piggott, gets home in the 1977 Derby at Epsom in the final stride and changes the world for Robert and Vincent

Right: Robert with Vincent O'Brien, pictured at Newmarket shortly after the summer rampage of The Minstrel – right after the little chestnut warrior scrambled onto the last plane to Maryland

Left: Pat Hogan, of Limerick, one of Ireland's finest riders to hounds, Robert's personal sage, the man who found the champion filly Detroit

Below left: Phonsie O'Brien, brother of Vincent, fishing companion of President Bush, Chinese cook and advisor to the team

Below: The training grounds at Ballydoyle, carved from the green heart of County Tipperary – the home gallops of Nijinsky, The Minstrel, Storm Bird, Golden Fleece, Caerleon, Lomond and Royal Academy

Above: Eric Cousins, Robert's first trainer, beneath the hat that hit the bookmakers at Kempton Park

Right: John Magnier, the most daring of the Irish stallion masters – married to Vincent O'Brien's daughter – 'John is probably the best master of a thoroughbred stud farm there has ever been,' says his father-in-law

Above: Bloodstock agent Richard Galpin, a cavalier of the industry, but his debts in France and the USA were too big a surprise for Robert Sangster

Left: George Harris, the Irish agent, who made a stock exchange out of the blood-stock industry

Above: Golden Fleece wins the Derby for Robert Sangster in 1982 – he passed more horses from Tattenham Corner to the wire than any other previous winner of the race

Right: Susan Sangster the First

Above: Joe Thomas, the man who arranged the mating of Neartic and Natalma – sire and dam of the greatest thoroughbred stallion of this century

Below: Northern Dancer – the feisty little winner of the 1964 Kentucky Derby. Vincent O'Brien and Robert Sangster followed his star and changed for ever the world of thoroughbred breeding

Left: In their 'slightly illegal' private spot in front of the Epsom enclosure fence – Robert and Vincent, fraught with nerves, prepare to watch The Minstrel do battle

Above: The two-year-old Storm Bird, racing on the outside, faces the final hill in the 1981 Dewhurst Stakes at Newmarket against To-Agori-Mou – pure class got him home, and a valuation of nearly $30 million

Left: The Sales Ring at Keeneland, Kentucky – the prime marketplace of the thoroughbred racehorse industry – once the private domain of Robert Sangster and Vincent O'Brien, later a battleground when the Sheikhs moved in

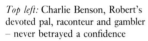

Top left: Charlie Benson, Robert's devoted pal, raconteur and gambler – never betrayed a confidence

Above: Billy McDonald, the less subtle of the epic Benson–McDonald act and the California bloodstock agent who spotted the dam of Sadler's Wells – Fairy Bridge (*above right*), going to post under Tommy Murphy

Right: 'Waltzing Matilda!' Susan Sangster standing on a table at Maxim's in Melbourne, after Robert's Beldale Ball had won the Melbourne Cup. Susan brandishes the Cup and leads the restaurant in a stirring rendition of Australia's anthem of the outback. Robert (*on her left*) and former husband Andrew (*right*) look on

once more through his mind, and he recalled the horse marching along, so confident, only for thirty yards but with the gait of a racehorse twice his size.

He looked up at Tom Cooper, and he said, finally, 'No limit, Tom. Buy him.'

=== 6 ===

The Minstrel's
Battle-song

There were 1,796,000 dollars' worth of baby racehorses settled down in the giant cargo area of the Aer Tura DC8 freighter as it inched its way north-east across the black Atlantic ocean. They were attended every minute by softly spoken Irish grooms, watchful for the flash of temperament or fear, or indeed the flying back-kick, which could cause such panic and danger in this artificial environment hurtling through the stratosphere. The twelve horses in here were heading for Ballydoyle, and as the aircraft banked across the Bay of Tralee and continued high above Listowel racecourse towards the estuary of the River Shannon, the grooms patted necks, rubbed noses and made the soft Irish sounds that have brought comfort to high-bred horses for hundreds of years.

Out now over the river, with the landing wheels stretching out beneath the dawn mist, the DC8 came down swiftly towards the airport, lumbering over the water, flaps down, engine screaming. The most expensive of the horses, the son of Round Table, who had fetched $500,000 for Seth Hancock's operation, was restive and nervous. Next to him stood the third highest priced yearling of the sale, the son of Prince John ($375,000) and he too was very wary of this lunatic contraption with its floor which changed its slope every few minutes. His neck was dark with sweat, and the same applied to the other Round Table colt, from the mare Stylish Pattern.

None of the above applied, however, in any way to the chestnut colt who could only just angle his head over the front of his travelling box to get at his hay-net. There was no sound from him, save for a steady munching. The robust little son of Northern Dancer and Fleur was as confident and indifferent to the fuss going on around him as he had been back at the barn area of the Keeneland sale. Tom Cooper had paid $200,000 for him in the late afternoon of the second day of the sale. Basically they all thought he was something of a bargain, because he alone, of all the yearlings, had 'spoken' to Vincent. There was something about him, and John Magnier thought that if he could run and win a top race he would be the most serious stallion asset Coolmore had ever had. A three-parts brother to Nijinsky, standing in Ireland. This was something close to John Magnier's lifetime dream.

The big horse van from Ballydoyle was awaiting them at Shannon Airport and as the sun rose above the hills of County Limerick they all set off for the picturesque racing complex to the south of Cashel which would be their home for at least two years. They were on the last leg of the four-and-a-half-thousand-mile trail which has bound the horse-breeding areas of Kentucky to Ireland for most of the twentieth century. From Ireland's point of view it had been generally a one-way trail, with much of the best bloodstock being bought up by American breeders and shipped to Kentucky. By the 1950s and 60s the situation was becoming quite serious. Between 1968 and 1972 four of the five winners of the English Derby were American bred, and three of them had Irish grandfathers. One of them, Mill Reef had *two* Irish grandfathers. Indeed, of the dozen hopefuls packed into the Ballydoyle van, nine of them could trace their origins directly to the Emerald Isle – four of them direct descendants of the Tipperary-born stallion Princequillo; three of them descended from the Kildare-born stallion Turn-To; one a grandson of Kildare's Nasrullah, and one the son of the County Meath-born Vaguely Noble. Most of this group were not emigrating from the USA. They were coming home, to the land of their forefathers.

Even the two colts by the Canadian Northern Dancer could find deep Irish blood a few generations back. The Dancer's dam Natalma, was a granddaughter of the Derby winner Mahmoud, who was pure-bred Irish on *his* dam's side through Mah Mahal and Mumtaz Mahal. It is often said that Ireland's greatest export has been her people, and it makes a sad and terrible history. Her second greatest export is a bit more cheerful, but nonetheless carries very wistful overtones. For that export is surely her racehorses. And deep in the back of the minds of Vincent O'Brien and John Magnier was the unspoken thought that somehow they might be manoeuvring themselves into a position to redress the balance, to restock the Irish breeding industry with its traditional blood, which now flowed through the veins of most of the fastest racehorses in the United States.

In the following days, after the arrival of the Kentucky yearlings, Ballydoyle resembled some kind of an Arab market. With an informality native to Ireland, deals were struck, shareholdings allocated between the partners. It was not quite down to the Irish 'tinker' horse-trader's method of a spit in the palm and a solid handshake, but it was close. They had bought every yearling they had wanted and Robert was a major shareholder in almost every one. Vincent was in everything, and so was John. The 'outside' partners were slightly more selective. No sooner were the owners sorted out, and the horses settled into their new homes, when they set sail again, this time for New York State, to the Saratoga Sales. At Keeneland they had been the biggest buyers in the history of thoroughbred breeding. At Saratoga they came essentially for one horse, the full-brother to Sham, first spotted by Tom Cooper at Claiborne. They stuck to their policy, instructing Tom to buy the colt, no limit. He picked him up for $127,000. Another grandson of Princequillo was on his way home to Tipperary.

The only person clearly not on his way home was Robert Sangster. At least not in the permanent sense of the word. The only home he had at present was the one in Marbella, with which he was crashingly bored. And now he prepared to allow the lease to run out on that and to evacuate the family to the Isle of Man, to a pleasant but not grandiose house called, curiously, Derby Haven. This became, albeit briefly, the family headquarters, just over a hundred miles, but in reality more like a million miles, from Christine's beloved Swettenham in which they had all been so happy. Now, however, as 'tax exiles', they were forbidden to re-enter England without Robert being financially wiped out by Harold Wilson's Labour Government.

Christine was busy with her new baby, Kate, and Robert was moving restlessly around his burgeoning bloodstock empire. He had recently bought two more very valuable mares, privately, from the estate of Nijinsky's owner, the late platinum tycoon from New Jersey, Charles Engelhard. One of them was Ribot's daughter Arkadina, a fast-finishing third in the 1972 English Oaks, and the other was Mandera, a well-bred daughter of Vaguely Noble. Both of them were in foal to Nijinsky. Just as Christine Sangster was about to learn how cruel the world could be when your husband falls out of love with you, so Robert was about to learn how harsh the thoroughbred world could be when you have backed big money on the co-operation of nature. With a 100-to-1 piece of bad luck, *both* of Robert's new mares foaled twins, the kiss of death to the breeder. They are always too small, too weak and none of them is ever any good as racehorses. There may be a few exceptions but in nine hundred and ninety-nine cases out of every thousand, twins are diabolical news.

Since the in-foal mares had cost Robert $150,000 each, he felt justified in having a conciliatory chat to the executors of the estate. Robert asked, not unreasonably, whether they might grant him one free service to Nijinsky to make up for his terrible ill-fortune. There is no doubt that Charlie Engelhard would have agreed, since he was an extremely nice man, and anyway it would not have cost him anything. No doubt John Magnier would have reacted the same to any of his clients. So would Arthur Hancock. And so, curiously, would old Cousin Leslie, or Brownell. Those who now represented Mr Engelhard, however, told Robert Sangster to 'get lost'. Robert never got over that. It hardened him. Some people think it really changed his entire attitude to what had become a serious business.

Meanwhile he boarded a flight to Australia, essentially to attend the annual November festival at Flemington Racecourse which culminates with the running of the two-mile Melbourne Cup, founded in 1851 and the Holy Grail to every Aussie owner. The very mention of the race to an Australian conjures up visions of the immortal Phar Lap of 1930 – the horse who won the Melbourne Stakes on 1 November and then, three days later under a record top weight, took the Melbourne Cup by three lengths – and within four days he won two more races at the same meeting! But the phrase 'Melbourne Cup' did not conjure up visions of Phar Lap for Robert Sangster. It conjured up visions of the laughing blonde wife of Australia's Foreign Minister in the new Liberal Government – the thirty-four-year-old Mrs Andrew Peacock. He checked into the Hilton Hotel and swiftly devised a way to see her. It took approximately three minutes before they each knew that all of their initial feelings about each other were not imaginary. This was real. And they embarked on one of the most publicized runaway romances since the young Jimmy Goldsmith took off in 1953 with one of the richest young women in the world, the Bolivian tin heiress Isabel Patino.

Susan Peacock was not rich. But she was not unimportant. Her father Sir John Rossiter was a prominent Victoria State politician, and in 1975 he was the state's Agent-General in London. Susan had worked as a newspaper reporter for the *Melbourne Sun*, on the women's and society pages, but had also written more seriously, and been a current affairs television journalist for Australia's Channel Nine. She was a pretty good journalist, but her career was always overshadowed by her life as one of the most dazzling socialites in the country. Married now for twelve years to Australia's current spokesman for foreign affairs, she was scarcely ever out of the pages of the glossy magazines and the society columns of the newspapers. If Andrew had been publicized half as much as his wife he would probably have been prime minister.

Susan quickly confessed to Robert that she and Andrew were unhappy together, but that he, Robert, was more or less her idea of heaven. Robert, almost vibrating with excitement over the sensuality of this dramatic-looking lady, with the elegant figure and glorious smile, was blind to reason. She asked him point blank, that, if she was prepared to leave Australia's Foreign Ministry temporarily without a chatelaine, would he then marry her? They each understood that this meant he must divest himself of his wife of fifteen years and his young family, Guy, Ben and Adam, plus the new-born Kate. Susan, on her part, also had much to give up. She had three daughters in boarding school, and her husband, while not as rich as Robert, was an extremely handsome man, with a long family interest in racehorses. Also he was considered by most people as a future prime minister of Australia.

Swearing undying love, among other things, Robert flew home. Christine, heartbroken, flew to London with the children, shocked by the drastic step Robert plainly proposed to take. At this time no one beyond Robert, Susan and now Christine and their friends had any idea of the great scandal about to be unleashed upon an unsuspecting Australian public. But it was not long in coming. In January 1976 Robert flew back to Australia and he knew his marriage was over. Susan met him and within days the Australian press had gone wild with excitement over the rather unusual fact that the Foreign Minister's wife had vanished with a football pools promoter from Liverpool. A pom, at that. My bloody oath!

It was slightly difficult for the couple to know quite where to go. Susan, who had left in school her three daughters aged nine, ten and eleven, had to go to London to talk to her mother. Robert for several reasons, not least the government, clearly could not turn up in England, and certainly not with Mrs Peacock. So they set off on an odyssey of several thousand miles, staying together in the Far East, in a suite at the Peninsular Hotel in Hong Kong, and later in the Philippines and Singapore. They tied Susan's trip to London with a journey to Chantilly in France to see some horses, and then they ended up on the French Riviera. Robert arranged to buy a house in Virginia Water, Surrey, for Christine and the children, and was quite glad that he was not allowed back in England to face the wrath of his mother.

Peggy Sangster had been absolutely furious with Nick Robinson when he too had gone through a divorce five years earlier, telling him it was disgraceful that he should leave his wife and that he would live to regret it. Robert knew all about this and the thought of a personal confrontation with the matriarch of the family, Ladies Captain of Royal Liverpool Golf Club, struck something close to terror into his heart. She had told him on the telephone that she was shocked by his childish behaviour and that anyone who could treat the very beautiful, very kind and sensible Christine in this way was only marginally acceptable as her son. 'There are three things we all know about Christine,' she thundered. 'Firstly, she is the mother of all four of my grandchildren. Secondly, she has always been completely loyal to this family. Thirdly, she has never once shown any inclination towards spending too much of your money. If you are intent on betraying her, I shall be interested to see if you ever again meet anyone like her. For my part I will always regard her as my own daughter. I am quite frankly appalled by your behaviour.'

Robert, very shaken, jumped on another plane. This time he headed with Susan to Los Angeles, picked up a message from Nick, who was now on holiday in Nassau, and telephoned him immediately. 'You've been divorced,' he said. 'What's it like?'

'Bloody awful,' said Nick. 'But it gets better in a few years. I bet Peggy is absolutely thrilled.'

Robert shuddered. The trouble was he knew that ultimately he was going to have to come in to land. He could not keep prowling around the world with his mistress, without a home base, despite its obvious advantages in keeping the world's press at bay – a syndrome which was new and a bit uncomfortable for him, but apparently a source of great amusement and interest to his prospective second wife. Derby Haven was strictly a go-between house in preparation for a serious move into a derelict castellated mansion called The Nunnery he had purchased from the Manx government a few months previously. It was an interesting old place, some of it Elizabethan, but the last time he had set foot inside its great front door he discovered a vagrant living there – 'The type of chap who had backed too many beaten favourites' was Robert's precise description – and now he was not quite certain that this was exactly the life-style Susan probably had in mind. He decided to postpone a visit together to the Isle of Man and to linger for a while in the exhilarating company of another Irishman with whom he had become friendly over the past couple of years, the inimitable wag of the bloodstock agents, from Ballynahinch, Billy McDonald, the thirty-one-year-old son of the chairman of the Irish Showjumping Association, James McDonald.

Billy first came to prominence on California's west coast during his tenure as a brilliantly successful Rolls Royce salesman in San Francisco in 1966, when he was shipwrecked on the island of Alcatraz, an incident his detractors may consider to have been delivered by some form of divine providence. However, it was not entirely his fault. The boat concerned was a single-masted forty-footer, which Billy and the blood-stock transport executive Michael 'Lunchtime' O'Sullivan had hired for the afternoon. The basic objective was to impress a couple of attractive local ladies, and both Billy and Michael had regaled them with stories of their ocean-racing exploits.

'I'm not too bad really,' Michael had asserted. 'Not quite up to my dad's standard, but competent.'

Billy told them he traced his sailing experiences back to Ireland. Indeed, according to O'Sullivan, Billy claimed to have been an Olympic helmsman, representing Ulster in the Summer Games. 'Something you never forget, really,' he added, jauntily. And with that, they elected to go for a sail around the bay.

They boarded the yacht, hauled up the mainsail, then the jib, and cast off. Billy, positioned behind the tiller, said cheerfully, 'You wanna take her?'

'No, that's all right, Billy, you press on.'

In that split second it dawned on Billy McDonald that neither of them had ever sailed a yacht in their entire lives. But it was a bit too late to do much about it. The mainsail was flapping in the breeze as they drifted out into open water. Billy, scared by the noisy cracking of the sail in the wind, hauled the mainsheet tight, but, unwittingly, onto a port-tack and they caught a nice stiff westerly gusting in under the Golden Gate Bridge. The boat accelerated forward, and heeled hard to starboard, shouldering her way into San Francisco Bay at about nine knots. Next stop Red China.

'Holy Shit!' yelled Billy.

'Whatsamatter, Bill? You're doing great.'

'*Great?*' bawled Billy. 'I haven't the slightest idea how to turn the bastard round, or how to stop.'

'But I thought you said you could sail?'

'*Jesus Christ!*' yelled Billy. 'I thought you said *you* could!'

By now they were making good speed towards the bridge and the only thought in Bill's mind was to turn round, despite the fact that this course of action would put them on a fast downwind run towards Oakland. Nonetheless, Billy hauled on the tiller, hard. The yacht temporarily slowed and straightened up and then the boom crashed over as he jibbed her across the wind. It flattened Billy and his pal, but since neither of them had loosed off the mainsheet, she tightened again, hard on the wind and headed for the shore at top speed. Billy got up, grabbed the tiller and swung the boat towards the island of Alcatraz. His crewmate tried to loosen the sail to slow them down, but it got away from him and the boom slammed out against the shroud. Their two girlfriends wept continuously with sheer terror.

In a life built on bold decisions, Billy made one of his boldest. '*I'm going for Alcatraz!*' he shouted.

With the sail open wide, the mainsheet flapping loose and his shipmates praying silently on the foredeck, he aimed the boat at the distant beach of the legendary old federal penitentiary from which no man had ever escaped. Faced with the possibility of broaching out in the bay, with its reputed population of sharks, Billy had elected to take his chances. He held a steady course, across the treacherous currents towards cell-block 'A', former home of the Birdman. He finally crashed the yacht into the rocks and thankfully hurled himself over the side onto dry land like a wounded walrus. The Coast Guard later picked them up, to the subsequent delight of the readers of the *San Francisco Examiner*. 'Wasn't bloddy fonny noither,' confirmed Billy. 'I could have lost me focking loif.' The insurance company were not terribly amused either.

In the ensuing years Billy returned to the horse business, helping to set up a stud farm in England for his old boss at the car dealership, Mr Kjell Qvale, who was, coincidentally, the senior stockholder in Golden Gate Fields Racetrack, San Francisco. By 1972 Billy was settled down, back in California as a bloodstock agent of varying reputation. His admirers swore he had a superb eye for a horse, any horse, a foal, a yearling or even a mature racer. His detractors – possibly including some of his seven fiancées (he says he bought rings for only five of them, including the renowned New York television commentator Charlsie Cantey) – consider he has a slightly impetuous side to his nature. Robert says the first time he met Billy was in Lexington in 1972 when the agent had told him, 'I have a horse you *must* see.' Robert says Billy kept him waiting in the hotel foyer for one and a half hours, turned up finally in his socks, popped back upstairs for his shoes and then got them both lost for another hour and a half trying to find the farm out on the Versailles Pike.

'All lies,' says Billy. 'He knew me before that.'

Now they were together again in Los Angeles. Billy had a horse he thought Robert must see, a two-year-old in training, by Hoist the Flag out of a mare called Princess Pout. His name, said Billy, is Alleged. Immediately, Robert thought there was something familiar about this pedigree. Hoist the Flag was a son of Tom Rolfe, an American classic winner whose famous dam, Pocahontas, was from the Princequillo mare How. On his female side, Alleged had more Princequillo blood, Princess Pout being by the Irish stallion's son Prince John. This is known in the trade as 'a 5 X 3 cross to Princequillo', and Robert knew it *must* have attracted the attention of John Magnier and Vincent.

Sure enough Billy confirmed the colt had been led out unsold in front of their very eyes at Keeneland with only $34,000 bid. He had been apparently 'presented' very moderately and he was a gangling, unfurnished sort of a horse, who looked a bit tricky to boot. Billy knew precisely why Vincent had rejected him, but he spoke to Robert darkly now, from the left-hand side of his mouth, 'Jesus, Robert, I'm telling you, this is a damn nice horse. You have to see him.'

Despite his near-total preoccupation with his own 'elopement', Robert decided the show must go on and, with Billy and Susan, he went off to see the colt, now in training at Monty and Pat Roberts's Flag Is Up Farm, but scheduled to go to the next California two-year-old sale. Billy was close to the Robertses, who owned Alleged, and he had watched the steady improvement in the colt all winter. What Robert now saw was a big fine horse, with a wonderful head, broad between the eyes and a magnificent racehorse's shoulder. His weakness was his knees, which Billy knew. He told Robert, 'Let me get into that sale ring and buy him for you. Then take him home to Ireland, away from these dirt tracks. Vincent will turn him into a champion. I've got a real feeling about this horse.'

Billy also had another arrow in his quiver: he was a friend of Bob Fluor, the chairman of one of the six biggest private corporations in the United States. He knew that Bob would come into the horse as a partner, and in the end they bought him privately before the sale for $120,000. Later that day a trainer named Hoss Inman from Hot Springs, Arkansas, offered Billy a substantial profit on the horse. Robert said he'd sell for $200,000. Billy ambitiously asked $225,000 and Mr Inman walked away, right back to Hot Springs, without the horse that would one day be a champion. They agreed to ship Alleged immediately to the soft grassland of Ballydoyle, which they all knew would be far more suitable than the hard dirt tracks of California around which he was already working.

That bit of business concluded, Robert bit the bullet and headed back with Susan for the Isle of Man, and The Nunnery, hoping fervently that neither the tramp nor Mrs Peggy Sangster would be waiting for him. He loved his mother dearly, but when that lady was angry she was a formidable adversary and Robert was certain that she was very angry indeed. But still, he had to get his new life organized with this spectacular blonde Australian socialite. The future beckoned in glorious technicolor. Also he had to prepare his syndicates for the on-rushing Keeneland Sale of 1976, the most difficult sale of all, because no one knew if any of the 1975 purchases could run worth a damn. Also his partners Alan Clore and Simon Fraser were metaphorically in retreat, afraid, as well they might have been, of the great unknown: how Vincent's American two-year-olds would perform when they hit the Irish tracks in the autumn.

Meanwhile Robert had a few weeks to organize The Nunnery, which rested in decaying but historic splendour a short distance from the town of Douglas. The two rivers, the Dou and the Glas, actually join in the grounds of the house, which contains among its great lawns the ruins of the original priory, founded in the sixth century by Saint Bridget when she came to receive the veil of virginity from St Maughold. Robert was not entirely sure that his current activities were bringing much glory upon the pious celebrity of the foundress, but he pressed on with his plans to renovate this, the most elegant and beautiful house on the entire island. Today the building is mainly Victorian. It has six magnificent reception rooms, a marble-pillared hallway and a nearly circular dining room. There are six guest suites and two other bedrooms. The formal gardens and paddocks are spread over eleven acres. For years the house had lain dormant, but one of its former residents was a man cast in much the same mould as Robert. He was Sir George Goldie and his family, smugglers by profession, had presided over the island from this house for several generations. And none of them had terribly much in common with St Maughold.

Like Robert, Sir George was a buccaneer by nature, who had done his fair share of eloping – once with a beautiful Egyptian princess with whom he had taken off into the Sudanese desert for several years, and once, from The Nunnery, with the family governess, with whom he became trapped in Paris when Bismarck put the French capital to siege with his armies in 1870. Sir George Goldie had a great vision of trade in central Africa. He proposed to form a massive trading company in the heart of the southern Sudanese desert, in the burning lands between the White Nile and the fifteen-hundred-mile-distant River Niger. He knew it well, having hobnobbed with the pilgrims on their long journey across this very route towards Mecca while he was besotted by the nubile Egyptian. Against all odds he achieved his goal, forming ultimately the National Africa Company, which made fortunes in palm oil. He died on the Isle of Man in 1925. In the end they printed a special postage stamp of him in front of The Nunnery. Robert bought up *all* of the stamps and had the original artwork blown up and framed, surrounded by hundreds of stamps. 'Not everyone has their house on a stamp,' he says offhandedly. 'Me, Her Majesty, possibly Wellington. I think that's all.'

Besieged by the history of the house, Susan Peacock cast Saint Bridget's veil of virginity from her mind and weighed in with a figure for re-decorating the house which would have financed an entire public issue of the shares of the National Africa Company. In fairness to her, she adored the great mansion and gleefully embarked on an eighteen-month project of fabrics, wallpaper and grand English, French and Italian furniture, which would turn it into a showpiece. If Robert's mother had ever known the cost, she would probably have fainted, particularly as Mrs Peacock was still very much married to the Foreign Minister of Australia. And Robert was plainly still married to Christine. Anyway, life begins at forty and Robert and Susan, after some preliminary work on the main rooms, moved in. Almost immediately Robert had to leave for Ireland and then Kentucky. As he had suspected, Alan Clore and Simon Fraser were out. He needed new partners in a major hurry. And Billy McDonald provided them. He recruited Bob Fluor, in whose colours Alleged would run, to join the syndicate and he brought in a very rich Californian builder, Danny Schwartz, with whom Robert would develop a long friendship.

The newly formed syndicate agreed between them to go in for almost $4 million, if that sum of money was needed to purchase the horses Vincent and John wanted. It was a brave decision, since no one still at this stage had the slightest idea whether they would have *any* success when the new two-year-olds came out to run. Even in Kentucky there was immense consternation as to whether the Irishmen had picked a couple of winners. If they had, they would surely be back and great fortunes would be made in the Bluegrass. If the Irishmen had been wrong, then they would obviously retire hurt and once more people would be saying what they had always said, that it was impossible to make money out of racehorses.

Meanwhile John and Vincent hit the catalogues, just as they had done in 1975. Again they pored over the pedigrees long into the night. And again they all gathered in Lexington, Kentucky, to inspect the yearlings. At the end of their four-day marathon around the barns, Vincent had selected twelve colts and Tom Cooper bought them all, plus three beautifully bred fillies which Robert wanted as future broodmares, at a staggering cost of $2,419,000 – an average of over $150,000 each. There were two by Vaguely Noble, which permitted Seth Hancock and Bunker Hunt to split more or less a $1 million. There were three by Northern Dancer, two of which enriched Eddie Taylor's Windfields Farm by $330,000. And a million dollars worth of other yearlings by the sires of the moment, Nijinsky, Round Table, Mill Reef, Forli and his son Thatch. Thus in two years Sangster's men were out over $4·5 million, with transport, insurance and training fees on top.

'Basically you would have to say we were getting a bit jumpy at this stage,' recalls Robert. 'But something happened at that sale which I'll never forget, and which always makes me laugh. Needless to say it involved guess who?'

The scene was Claiborne Farm. Robert and his men had gone there early to see the yearlings before they went to the sale and Billy McDonald had decided to short-circuit the conventional way of perusing the young horses. Taking the yearling manager aside he pressed a $100 bill into his hand, and said, 'Which one do *you* like best?'

'Oh, I'd go for the little Bold Reason filly every time,' he replied. 'They always race over to this gate from right across the far side of the paddock and that little filly is always yards in front when they arrive. *She* is a racehorse.'

Billy headed back to Robert, confident in his new knowledge. 'We're definitely buying the little one,' he disclosed. 'I have inside information.' Robert grimaced. The filly was even smaller than the son of Fleur had been last year. 'Actually, I'm not here to discuss this,' said Billy. 'I am buying her, and I would like you to come in as partners.' Vincent also thought she was too small, but he was benevolent about it and, in the end Robert, John and Vincent bought in, with Billy holding on to 'a leg'. She had cost $40,000 in the ring.

Next stop was again Saratoga, and once more they plunged in, for the two horses Vincent had selected: a bay colt by Comedy Star from the brilliant racemare Cawston's Pride, and a dark bay filly by Sir Ivor. These cost $75,000 each and helped to push the sale average up by nearly twenty per cent on 1975. As Robert and his men left the old spa town on the last day of the auction there were again breeders from all over Kentucky wondering whether *any* of the horses Robert had purchased would run. They knew that in the autumn Vincent would begin to enter them – and on those distant Irish tracks the fortunes of the entire industry would be decided.

No one had long to wait. In early August the Round Table–Moccasin colt, now named Brahms, ran at Leopardstown and came from far back to win his first race by two and a half lengths. Then, as an odds-on favourite, he had to battle every yard of the way to get up by a short head in the last stride to win the 1976 Railway Stakes at the Curragh. It was good, but not 'classic good'. However, Brahms, showing a classy turn of foot on the Ballydoyle gallops, had been re-syndicated for $1·4 million. The horses from Ballydoyle were on the move and there was a $900,000 profit on the first colt.

Next out was the Northern Dancer–Fleur colt, now named The Minstrel. He was still very stocky in appearance and still very flashy looking with his white socks and face, but Vincent still loved him, and such was his reputation that he started at 9–4 on for his first race at the Curragh, and won it by five lengths in a new course record for six furlongs. This was promising and in his next race, ridden for the first time by Lester Piggott, he came home smoothly to win the Larkspur Stakes at Leopardstown by an easy length. October was better than September. Vincent sent the improving Round Table–Stylish Pattern colt, now named Artaius, out as an odds-on favourite for the Beresford Stakes and he ran very promisingly, in the colours of a new partner Mrs Jacqueline Getty, daughter-in-law of the old oil magnate John Paul. Artaius lost by a couple of lengths after running in a rather immature way.

If there was a crack two-year-old in the yard, thus far it would seem to be The Minstrel, and Vincent sent him over to Newmarket in England to contest the Dewhurst Stakes, the most important juvenile race in the British Isles, worth nearly £40,000 and won in the last few years by both Nijinsky and Mill Reef. The Minstrel bolted home from a surprisingly moderate field to win by four lengths. This made him probably the best two-year-old around, but Vincent was wary because in three races he had had everything his own way, winning over fairly fast ground, which he liked, against opposition which did not challenge him seriously. The question was: would he train on to race and win a classic in 1977?

In the dying days of the season Vincent O'Brien played his last card. He had been extremely pleased with the work of Alleged, and now he entered him in a fifteen-runner maiden at the Curragh in November, in nice, softish autumn going, perfect for the colt's still-immature knees.

Alleged flew to victory by eight lengths in the style of a really classy horse. His win prompted Vincent to observe, 'Well, if The Minstrel is the nicest two-year-old I've seen all season, this fellow would be very nearly the second best.' Robert and John Magnier were ecstatic because it looked as if they had real prospects of recouping all of their money with these two colts, and if either of them could win a big race at three, well, everyone was heavily into profit.

All through the winter The Minstrel continued to please his trainer. His devil-may-care character which had first impressed itself on Vincent back at the sales was unaltered by the harsh demands of his new profession. He was still as sound as a bell and he had none of the temperament of his three-parts brother Nijinsky. Nothing bothered the little chestnut and, as the cold rain and sleet of winter swept through the Golden Vale of Tipperary during January and February, The Minstrel seemed to become even more of a man. He was tough, obedient, sensible and willing. If his rider asked him to quicken through a freezing cold headwind, quicken he would.

The first time there appeared any kind of a chink in his armour happened in his first race of the new season, the 2000 Guineas Trial at Ascot. It had rained for nearly a week around London and the ground was like a bog. The Minstrel struggled through it, won the race by a length and a half from a horse called Gairloch, but it was clear that he hated it and he was exhausted at the end of it. How much that race took out of him no one will ever know, but he was beaten very decisively at Newmarket in the English 2000 Guineas itself, finishing third, two lengths behind the winner Nebbiolo. They were bitterly disappointed in Ireland. But Vincent was faced with a conundrum. The Minstrel was by Northern Dancer whose maximum distance was ten furlongs. His dam, Fleur, was from a sire and a dam who went only ten furlongs in the highest class and thus there was no reason whatsoever to believe The Minstrel would last any further himself. However, neither England nor Ireland has a ten-furlong classic. Therefore, since he may not stay the mile and a half of the English Derby in June, he would have to win his classic over one mile at the Curragh in May. There was no other choice. At Newmarket he had run on very strongly in the closing stages, but he had not much liked the ground which was on the softish side of good, and in the Irish 2000 Guineas it might be a shade wetter if anything. If The Minstrel was going to win a classic it had to be the Irish Guineas, because the distance at Epsom might be too far for him.

Again there was terrible disappointment. The Minstrel was beaten once more, by Pampapaul at the Curragh. Nebbiolo was third and, although he had crashed into The Minstrel a furlong out, defeat was defeat. Great horses find a way to get to the line first. There would be good money for The Minstrel as a stallion, but not great money, not the kind of money Robert and his men were looking for. Everyone was very fed up, and the general atmosphere was characterized by the immense depression of Messrs Clore and Fraser. In the middle of this, Robert suddenly received a message from Lester Piggott and he went immediately to the weighing room. He remembers to this day the sight which greeted him. The room was covered with empty glasses and champagne bottles left over from the Pampapaul celebration. In the middle of it all was Lester, sitting all alone on a bench, still dressed in his riding breeches and a white vest. Robert said he seemed completely lost in thought.

'Oh . . . Hello, Robert. He had a very hard race today.'

'I know he did. What d'you think? Will he go to Epsom?'

'If you run him, I'll ride him. On decent ground, he'll win.'

The miracle of it all was that The Minstrel came out of the battle without a care in the world. He chomped through his usual bowl of power-oats that evening as if nothing had happened and pulled out for a little walk the next day sound as ever, cocky as normal. Everyone liked The Minstrel and everyone knew that his task at Epsom in just over two weeks was very formidable. In France there was a top-class horse, the Aga Khan's Blushing Groom, who had won the French Guineas by three lengths. He was now 9–4 favourite for the Epsom Derby. Vincent O'Brien was worried. From all accounts the French believed that Blushing Groom might be the fastest miler since his own great-grandfather, Tudor Minstrel, back in the 1940s. They also thought he would get home at Epsom on sheer class, regardless of his pedigree. Vincent and John Magnier both knew that a third classic defeat would tarnish The Minstrel for ever, because horses who always find a way to lose are quickly dismissed as faint-hearted. The dread, unspoken question was: were the flashy markings, the bright chestnut coat, the badges of a horse who would not, after all, fight for victory?

Vincent consulted Lester, who thought the precise opposite of the French.

'Blushing Groom won't get the trip at Epsom,' he said flatly. 'He's by Red God. His sons never get a mile and a half. And they're often bloody bad tempered.'

'Well,' said the trainer, 'what do you think?'

Lester repeated, verbatim, what he had said to Robert: 'You run him, I'll ride him and, on decent ground, he'll win.'

That was the conclusion of the discussion. For the next two weeks the sun shone intermittently and the rain stayed away. The ground at Epsom was dry and fast, just as it had been at Leopardstown last October. Lester Piggott remembered the difference in the horse, how he had bounded easily across the dry turf, in stark contrast to the way he had struggled through the mud at Ascot. The jockey thought that today was The Minstrel's day and he grinned cheerfully as Vincent gave him a leg up into the saddle in the crowded paddock before they set off for the parade in front of the stands. As the crowds made their way back up the course to the grandstand, and to the members' lawn, Robert and Vincent hung back and waited. They watched Lester gallop The Minstrel to post and then they set off long after everyone else had left. Vincent's plan was to arrive just as the gate to the stands was shut and then to watch in private with Robert right down on the fence opposite the winning post with a clear view up the course.

The gateman knew of course who they were and turned a blind eye, with the words: 'He's 5–1, sir, a very fair price, and good luck to you.' Vincent nodded and smiled. Both he and Robert were on the edge of their nerves as the starter began to order the runners into the stalls. Even as he did so, dozens of telephone lines from Kentucky to England were open all over the country. Breeders were talking to friends in Newmarket and Berkshire. The fate of the industry in a real sense hung on this race. Joe Thomas of Windfields had persuaded a friend to put the phone on top of the television set so the entire staff at The Minstrel's birthplace could hear the live commentary. It was 10.20 in the morning in both the Bluegrass and in Chesapeake City.

The race was run at its normal fast pace. Milliondollarman led them down to Tattenham Corner, chased by the tough and resilient Hot Grove. Caporello, Nebbiolo, The Minstrel and Blushing Groom were right behind the leading pair and, as they swung around the steepest part of the left-hand, downhill turn, Lester moved almost imperceptibly on the outside into third place. He knew the battle would be joined in the next five seconds and, as they whipped past the three-furlong pole, Willie Carson, riding Hot Grove hard and straight, kicked for home, racing past Milliondollarman. Piggott had to go. Through his binoculars Vincent saw The Minstrel set off after him. This was the moment of truth. Now would the little son of Northern Dancer fight?

Lester shook him up asked him to quicken and The Minstrel's action seemed to flatten out. His head went forward and he tried desperately to catch Hot Grove. They were on the outside, but making no impression, and coming to the quarter pole Lester drew his whip. The crowd packed eight-deep on the rail heard the two cracks, like gunshots, as Lester hit him. Right behind he could hear another horse gaining rapidly and he guessed correctly it was Blushing Groom.

There were now less than two furlongs to run and The Minstrel still had not cut back one inch of Hot Grove's lead. Behind him Lester heard the other horse falter and again he guessed correctly – the favourite had gone. Once more he went to the whip, cracking The Minstrel twice, and then he hit him five times in quick succession and still there was a length between them as they hit the furlong pole.

But The Minstrel was running for his life. He was racing with heart-stopping courage, straining with every ounce of strength and speed he had. Lester raised his whip again, now slashing four times rhythmically as his little partner's white feet thumped into the turf. The fact was The Minstrel was running for the whip as few horses ever will. And this was a straight fight for the English Derby. The huge crowd of over two hundred and fifty thousand roared with excitement as Piggott gunned him up the hill towards the finish.

Whose heart was the biggest? Which horse was the stronger? Together they raced into the final hundred yards. Hot Grove still had it, but still The Minstrel would not give up the chase. He fought his way over the ground with a fury that few of the spectators had ever witnessed. And just as he seemed doomed to defeat, The Minstrel found, from somewhere deep within, another stride. His white face was at Carson's boot straps. Now he was level. Piggott cracked him again, and the crowd let out a deafening roar as the white-faced son of Northern Dancer struck the front ten feet from home and belted past the post a neck to the good.

Vincent O'Brien admits he was trembling with emotion as he watched them flash across the line. There were tears streaming down his wife's face at the sheer unending courage of the little horse. Robert was in shock and grown men, some of whom had fought in two world wars, gave each other those very British, tight-lipped, curt little nods in recognition of a battle won with outstanding valour. Some people just stood there, still gripping the rail, long after the race was over.

Lester Piggott steered the little horse back to the winners' enclosure amid roars of applause. The Minstrel was awash with sweat, quivering from his ordeal, his flanks heaving, his breath coming in long bursts through nostrils flared pink now, like anemones. Hundreds of people were packed around the enclosure as Piggott took off the saddle. He stood for a few moments grinning at Vincent. No one said much, except for 'Well done!' There was nothing else to say. But as he walked away, Lester stopped suddenly and he looked back at The Minstrel, and he shook his head, and he smiled at him. Many of those in the crowd caught the gesture, and the cheering and the clapping began all over again. It was a great explosion of joy.

But it may not have been so great an explosion as that caused by the whoops and yells of, '*Go get 'em, Lester baby!*' which were echoing down the transatlantic telephone lines from the great horse-breeding farms of the good ole US of A.

7

Bonanza in the Bluegrass

Sixteen years and eight months had passed since Robert Sangster had stood, awe-struck, in the winners' enclosure at Haydock Park, stroking the dark velvet nose of his beloved Chalk Stream. He was an outsider then, among the belted earls who ran the sport of horse racing. But today, at Epsom, standing on that hallowed piece of enclosed circular lawn, this time stroking a whiter and faster velvet nose, he was a member of racing's inner circle. If he had had his wife with him rather than his Australian mistress, he might even have been considered a member of the establishment. In any event he possessed the easy charm and sportsmanship of one who was. As they led The Minstrel away, trailing clouds of glory, Robert walked quietly over to Viscount Leverhulme, the owner of the defeated Hot Grove, and he held out his hand and said: 'I am so sorry, Philip. Sorry that it had to be you.' Lord Leverhulme, a fellow Jockey Club Steward at Haydock, smiled at the victor, to whom he had been something of a father-figure for many years, and replied, 'Treasure this day, Robert. They don't happen often. If it could not have been me, then I'm delighted it was you.'

They shook hands, old friends now, and Robert proceeded to make his way, alone, up the stairs to the Royal Box where he would take tea with the Queen of England and the Royal family, the traditional privilege of owners of the winner of the Derby. As he climbed the stairs he found himself suddenly assailed by a fleeting sadness, that he was not doing so in the company of Christine, who would have been so shyly proud of him, and who had travelled so far with him on the journey to this pinnacle. For a moment his thoughts began to cascade. He imagined for a few seconds of how perfectly mannered she would have been in the Royal presence, and how together they had raced Chalk Stream and then built up the Swettenham Stud. Now, that was all in ruins, and in some insane way he would not see her again, and it was all of his own doing. Many of his friends, not to mention his mother, were absolutely shocked at his decision. For a further few seconds he wondered if he might be losing his grip on reality.

But it was too late now. Downstairs Susan Peacock was cheerfully facing a battery of press photographers, there were new friends crowding in from the wings. One of them, the droll and urbane Old Etonian racing correspondent of the *Daily Express*, Charles Benson, was already on the line to Annabel's, the Berkeley Square nightclub, taking over the private dining room from the Aga Khan (who had thought Blushing Groom would win), and transferring it to the account of Robert Sangster.

'Get rid of the red carnations,' Charles was instructing Louis, the club's renowned maître d'. 'And replace them with something blue. Robert's colours are green and blue. What? Well, there must be blue flowers somewhere. What about pansies? No, forget that, forget pansies, they wouldn't be Robert's kind of flowers. What about those big things, pointed at the top. No, I can't remember their name. Christ! Call a florist.'

Things were moving apace as Robert was presented to Queen Elizabeth II. He and his monarch chatted amiably for some time little knowing how each would be thrown into combat against the other during this tumultuous racing season – and how in two of the principal contests, Her Majesty would best him.

As twilight fell over London that evening Robert's joyful gathering moved into Annabel's. In addition to Robert and John Magnier, there was Vincent O'Brien, who had just won his fifth Derby, and Lester Piggott, who had just won his eighth. Susan Peacock, who had rushed to the gate to lead in 'her' first Derby winner, despite not being related to any one of the owners, now assumed the role of hostess. The group of well-wishers in attendance included the Aga Khan, who was full of good sportsmanship, despite his bitter disappointment that Blushing Groom had not stayed the mile-and-a-half. His English wife Sally thought her old friend Charles Benson had looked after the flower arrangements 'extremely skilfully'. In the small hours, Susan Peacock surprised the late-night regulars by standing on the table and singing that anthem of the Outback, 'Waltzing Matilda'.

As the clock moved passed midnight, Vincent for the first time voiced his concern over the fact that The Minstrel's victory had been earned after one of the most brutal battles through the home straight ever seen at Epsom. 'I cannot think', he said, 'that it will not affect him in some way, possibly in his mind. Not many horses have a race as hard as that and come out unscathed.'

But perhaps the most significant words about the race were being uttered not in London at all, but three and a half thousand miles away in the flat horse country beyond Chesapeake City, where Joe Thomas, the great horseman who had arranged the mating which had produced The Minstrel, was wrestling that evening with an awesome set of numbers. 'I'd have to stand him at over $60,000 a service,' he was muttering. 'And that'd mean a $200,000 share. With thirty-six shares, like his daddy, he'd have a book value of $7·2 million. Jesus! I'm not sure Mr Taylor will stand up for that. But I want that beautiful little sonofabitch *back*. It's going to cost us a lot of money ... but I know he's just doubled the price of Northern Dancer's yearlings. I have to get him *back* to stand as a stallion right here, where he belongs, next to his daddy. The question is, will they sell?'

In the following six weeks The Minstrel did everything he could to make life even more difficult for Windfields Farm. First of all, he came out of the race not much more tired than he normally was after a good work. Then he won the Irish Derby by a length and a half against rather moderate opposition. It was his fifth tough race in twelve weeks. And he was not finished yet. Late in July he went to Ascot to face his elders for the first time, in the King George VI and Queen Elizabeth Stakes. This race represents the summer championship of Europe where the three- and four-year-olds from England, France and Ireland are apt to clash. In fact this race forms the last leg of the modern Triple Crown – since the mid-sixties the very best middle-distance horses generally try to win the two Derbys, and then the King George VI. Nijinsky did it, and so did Grundy in 1975. And on a sunlit afternoon, after a sensational battle, no less hard than that at Epsom, The Minstrel also achieved it, racing home hard under Piggott's whip to win by a short head from Orange Bay, with Bunker Hunt's Exceller third, and the French Derby winner Crystal Palace fourth.

John Magnier had, several weeks previously, joined Joe Thomas, in a manner of speaking. The two of them, three and a half thousand miles apart, were each trying to force the numbers into a format which would allow The Minstrel to stand at their respective farms. John desperately wanted the little horse to stay in Tipperary and to begin his stallion career at Coolmore, but he could not match Joe's stud fee. The big American, born, like Judy Garland in 'A Star Is Born', in Pocatella, Idaho, was working on a fee of around $60,000 which was too rich for

John in Ireland. The breeders who supported Coolmore could not pay that much money. Windfields's opening offer was $7·2 million, on the basis that Robert and his men would keep some of the shares. John Magnier and Robert felt that it was not enough – that it *had* been the right price for him after the Derby, but that it no longer applied, not after his two other world-class victories.

Joe thought he might have to go to $10 million, which scared him to death. In the end he agreed to value The Minstrel at $9 million, and to buy one half of him for $4·5 million. This would take the new stallion to Windfields, but would allow Robert and the team to send their mares to be bred to him, perhaps as many as ten, and then have eight more to sell on the American market for around $60,000 each, for at least four to five years. Joe Thomas, faced now with shares which must be sold for $250,000 each, decided to spread the risk over four years and to place a $65,000 price on the breeding rights. He had a glittering list of clients and almost every one of the breeders who were getting so well paid for their Northern Dancer shareholdings jumped at the opportunity to go in as shareholders in the heroic little winner of the big three summer races in the British Isles.

The Minstrel arrived in Maryland a lot quicker than most people thought he would. All plans for future racing were scrapped upon the outbreak of Contagious Equine Metritus in the USA. A ban on European horses would go into effect in September and The Minstrel was rushed away from Ireland in a big jet freighter to beat the deadline by just a few hours. Everyone connected with the horse was in a collective panic in the days preceding his departure – to miss the deadline would have been enormously expensive – but the pressure never got to The Minstrel, who was, after all, a veteran at leaving matters of high importance to the very last second. John Magnier watched him go with great sorrow. But he realized they must think of their own massive cash flow and that here was a chance to pay themselves back for the enormous risks that they had taken. Still, it irked him that he could not raise the money in Ireland and England to stand such a stallion at Coolmore. Sometimes he lay awake at night, turning the problem over in his mind, trying to find a way to beat off the American offers that would surely come flooding in, every single time Vincent sent in one of their highly bred American purchases to win a European classic.

In the midst of all of this excitement of 1977, Robert and his Irishmen had struck again at the sales. They went to Keeneland and spent $2,272,000 on just nine yearlings which Vincent and his back-up men had selected. They broke the world-record price, paying $725,000 for a son of Secretariat from one of Windfields's best Victoria Park bloodlines. They also bought colts by Northern Dancer and Graustark from the same farm for $290,000 the pair. They were easily the biggest spenders at the sale, paying out three times more than the second-biggest and four times more than the third. They pushed the average price for a yearling up nearly thirty per cent on the previous year, and sixty per cent on 1975. At the Saratoga Yearling Sales during the first week in August they spent another $1,271,000, nearly four times more than any other buying operation. They pushed the average here up by nearly thirty per cent on the previous year and brought their spending at the two sales to a little over $3·5 million. For this they picked up the two sales toppers, both from Kentucky, both by Northern Dancer. The one out of Bamboozle cost $375,000, the one from the Nashua mare, Fun Palace, $340,000.

It is difficult to turn back the clock to recreate the world situation in 1977 and to realize what huge sums of money these were. Even the American publication, *The Bloodhorse*, the bible of the US thoroughbred breeders, was completely mystified by this rush of money from Ireland to America. 'Why is this?' wondered the editor of the magazine, Kent Hollingsworth. 'Whence the demand for well-bred yearlings ... Whence the money?' Even as the Dow Jones index slid down nearly twelve per cent from its 1976 average, Sangster's men were in there bidding, driving prices up in a way which was apparently without foundation.

Little did the industry realize that they had not even begun to fight. For back home on the racetracks of England and Ireland, Vincent O'Brien was having possibly the greatest year ever recorded by any horse trainer in history. In addition to the victories of The Minstrel, he had sent out one of the Sir Ivor fillies purchased at Keeneland in 1975, now named Lady Capulet, to win the 1977 Irish classic 1000 Guineas in her first appearance on a racecourse. He sent out Artaius, the Round Table colt from Stylish Pattern, to lead wire-to-wire in both the Eclipse Stakes at Sandown and the Sussex Stakes at Goodwood, having been runner-up in the French Derby. He sent out the Prince John–Hornpipe II colt, Transworld, to win the classic Irish St Leger by four lengths at the Curragh. He and Robert and John went out and paid £300,000 for the fast grey three-year-old sprinter Godswalk, and Vincent trained him to win the King's Stand Stakes at Royal Ascot before syndicating him for £500,000 to stand at Coolmore.

Vincent sent out Meneval to win the Hardwicke Stakes at Royal Ascot, and a Northern Dancer colt, Be My Guest, to win the Waterford Crystal Mile at Goodwood. The two-year-old Comedy Star colt they had bought at Saratoga was named Solinus and won the top two-year-old race, the Coventry Stakes, at the Royal Meeting. And Fairy Bridge, named for a little river-crossing on the Isle of Man, the tiny filly which had cost Billy McDonald a $100 bill at Claiborne, won two good races in Ireland – one by five lengths – to be the top-rated filly on the Irish Free Handicap and the fifth highest of both sexes. Second-highest rated was Solinus and third was a colt named Octavo, by Roberto, which they had picked up for $18,000 in Kentucky as a yearling in 1976. Octavo, running in Robert's colours, gave weight and a beating to nine rivals in the Ashford Castle Stakes over a mile at the Curragh.

The full-brother to Sham, by Pretense, named Leonato, had been a brilliant selection by Vincent and John and failed by inches to make them a huge profit. Like his esteemed father, who had been so gallant in his pursuit of Secretariat, Leonato was just a stride or two short of the top class. He went down half a length in the King Edward VII Stakes at Royal Ascot and then finished second in the Princess of Wales Stakes at Newmarket.

The jewel in Robert's 1976 shopping basket was the beautifully bred Northern Dancer colt, from an unraced mare by Buckpasser, named Sex Appeal. This was a pedigree which John Magnier had been unable to resist. Sex Appeal's dam, Best In Show, had won five races including the Comely Stakes. Her second dam Stolen Hour had won six races and bred seven winners. Her third dam, a champion US Handicap mare of the early 1930s, had won twenty-one races in one hundred and twelve starts! John Magnier, whose own family had been involved for several generations in the breeding of hard Irish 'chasers', loved tough, sound mares, who ran and won. This American family had been bequeathing such qualities to its offspring for nearly half a century. Sex Appeal's mating to Northern Dancer was plainly important to students of the breed and Vincent O'Brien himself had loved the conformation and attitude of the yearling. Now he was named Try My Best and Vincent sent him out to race in the September of this phenomenal year.

He chose the Whitechurch Stakes over five furlongs at Phoenix Park and Try My Best burst clear halfway up the straight and won it by six lengths. He did something very similar three weeks later in the Larkspur Stakes over seven furlongs at Leopardstown against some of the fastest two-year-olds in Ireland. At this point there was only one target for the colt: the Dewhurst Stakes in England, the championship two-year-old race which The Minstrel had won with such authority one year ago. But this year it was much tougher. Sexton Blake, a colt which had beaten Solinus, was running. So was Camden Town, the runaway winner of the Duke of Edinburgh Stakes at Ascot. So was Tannenberg, who had won top races at York and Goodwood; and Labienus who had been placed in both the Champagne Stakes and the Middle Park. But Try My Best treated them all with total disdain, storming clear of the field in just a few strides and running on to win by an easy length and a half.

Top of the English Free Handicap, top of the Irish Free Handicap, Try My Best was the best two-year-old in Europe. The sixteen-month buying spree by Vincent O'Brien, John Magnier and the Irish magicians, which had started in July 1975 and gone through until the autumn of 1976, must surely have been the greatest exercise in selecting yearlings to race ever accomplished in the entire modern history of bloodstock auctions (about two hundred years).

Thus far, however, the story has been recounted without mention of another saga, in a season of sagas, which may very well have been the greatest success of them all. Remember Alleged? From California? The one they missed at the Keeneland Sales just before they bought The Minstrel, and who ran such a cracking race in his only start at two? Well, after a couple of easy victories in Ireland in the spring of 1977, he was beginning to look superb. He still had knees which no top trainer would want to risk on very firm ground, but he was able to work with The Minstrel, and his owner Robert Fluor wanted him to run in the Irish Derby. As the head of his gigantic corporation, Mr Fluor was unused to being argued with. As a matter of fact he was not all that accustomed even to being interrupted. In this instance, however, he had serious opposition. It was Vincent O'Brien's opinion that the colt ought not to race at the Curragh in late June because the ground was hard and fast. Robert Sangster, who owned forty per cent of the horse, had been brought up to agree with Vincent's thoughts – 'Otherwise you're telling Mohammed Ali how to throw a left jab!'

But now Mr Fluor was very determined. He sent a message that he was coming from California to the Curragh, with family, with fellow partner the American millionairess Shirley Taylor and with other friends, to watch Alleged try to win the Irish Derby. 'Looking forward to it, Vincent. It's gonna be a great day for all of us.'

'Not', thought the Irishman, 'if Alleged gets beat on the ground – which he will. And particularly not if he gets so jarred up I cannot get him ready for the autumn.' But, being Vincent, he kept his own counsel. He brooded on the problem, looking with mounting dismay at the clear sunny skies which had made the ground fast at Epsom, perfect for The Minstrel, but now so dangerous for Alleged. Actually, the problem really got him down and he did not quite know what to do. Here in the stable he had a colt in The Minstrel who would cheerfully have run up the Dublin Road on his iron legs and sprung-steel joints. Alleged needed 'give' in the ground, because he did not have The Minstrel's conformation. He was taller, with a powerful shoulder, and he would not stand the pounding, especially coming downhill at the Curragh at the entrance to the home straight. Also Vincent wanted to give him more time to develop.

The insistence of the American turned a routine decision into an agonizing question for Vincent. But what to do? It was Robert who noticed something was bothering his friend and trainer. 'Vincent,' he said, 'what's the matter? You have something on your mind. I can tell you have. Is there anything I can do to help?'

So the master of Ballydoyle unburdened his soul and he told Robert all of his fears about running Alleged at the Curragh. Robert said briskly, 'Oh, I'll soon fix that.' He contacted Bob Fluor, as the senior partner, and broke the news that it would not be sensible to overrule the trainer and that Alleged was being withdrawn from the Irish Derby. This is basically why The Minstrel was allowed to go and win it and why Bob Fluor spent much of the summer and half of the autumn being very brassed off indeed at his colleagues in the Sangster syndicate.

Meanwhile Vincent pressed quietly on with the preparation of Alleged. His general target was the great autumn race in Paris, the Prix de l'Arc de Triomphe and he produced the colt to run in the Great Voltigeur at York, a race in which he would be opposed by the runner-up in the English Derby, Hot Grove, and all three of the horses which chased The Minstrel home in the Irish Derby, Lucky Sovereign, Classic Example and Orchestra. They may as well not have turned up. Alleged pulverized them, racing clear with three furlongs to go, and drawing right away to win by seven lengths. Here was a colt of true brilliance, not the kind of blood-and-guts battler that characterized The Minstrel. This was a colt who belonged in the peerless realm. He had fantastic acceleration, as all of the great ones do. He could end a race with a burst of speed that no other horse could match. They say Joe Louis could knock a man cold with a punch that travelled a mere ten inches. Alleged could end a horse race in a matter of a few strides, over a mere twenty-five yards.

Vincent aimed him first for the St Leger, over a mile and three-quarters at Doncaster, and then for the Arc, over a mile and a half in Paris. He lost the first one, beaten by the Queen's Oaks-winning filly Dunfermline, probably due to lack of experience against opponents of this quality. Alleged looked a bit bewildered as the powerful daughter of the Derby winner Royal Palace blew past on the outside and bolted for the line under the Royal colours. He had, after all, been used to having things all his own way for a long time now and this was a test of character for which he was basically unprepared. Something very similar might also have been true of his owner, Robert Fluor, who had been beside himself with excitement after the great victory in the Voltigeur, but now sat glumly with Robert and Susan, staring into a glass of flat champagne, with the look of a lovesick bloodhound etched upon his face.

Alleged had lost his only classic. In Robert Fluor's opinion he should have run in the Irish Derby. He had beaten the second-, third- and fourth-placed runners this season, and therefore he would have won. In his mind there stood the question, do this crowd of Irishmen actually know what they are doing? Since the doubt was great, and the American's gloom was even greater, Robert stepped in and offered to buy him out. He never would say the price, but it was around $250,000 for most of Robert Fluor's shareholding.

The Californian returned home with a nice profit, but not quite like that which accrued to his fellow shareholders when Alleged flew home in the Arc, defeating the Italian champion Balmerino, the French Derby winner Crystal Palace, and Dunfermline. Somewhere back in the pack was Orange Bay who had run The Minstrel to a short-head in the King George VI. Alleged carried the colours of Robert Sangster in Paris that day and he won something like £130,000. Which was interesting, but not as interesting as the $7 million valuation there was now placed upon the son of Hoist the Flag.

Billy McDonald was so impressed with his own brilliance he insisted on buying bottles of Krug for everyone, breezily telling Robert to keep his money in his pocket. This, he said, was an academic triumph for a great bloodstock agent (W. McDonald) and should be respected as such. He was not far wrong either. Another of his discoveries, little Fairy Bridge, was now on her way to stud and three years from now she would foal possibly the best of all Northern Dancer's stallion sons, the brilliant Sadler's Wells.

The balance sheet was looking, after two years in operation, extremely sound. They had spent $8 million at the summer sales of 1975 to 1978 in America. They had also paid out $1·4 million to buy Be My Guest for Coolmore from Mrs Diana Manning, the sixty-six-year-old sister of Ambassador Raymond Guest, owner of the 1968 Derby winner Sir Ivor. There had been other yearling purchases, plus of course the $320,000 Alleged had cost Robert, and the $500,000 Godswalk had cost as a three-year-old. In broad terms, in search of stallions, they had probably spent close to $11 million. In today's terms that might be something like $50 million.

On the credit side there was $4·5 million for The Minstrel; $1 million for Transworld; Alleged was clearly worth $7 million to go back to Kentucky; Artaius was being sold for a book value of $4 million to stand at Tim Rogers's Airlie Stud, in Kildare; Solinus was worth $1 million; Godswalk almost $1 million; Try My Best $3 million; plus there was money for other fairly good runners like Leonato, and one of the Vaguely Noble colts. Add in the value of the fillies as potential broodmares – Lady Capulet and Fairy Bridge – and by any yardstick you would have to conclude that Robert and his men had doubled their money, with a couple of million to spare. In addition there was in Vincent's yard a future sprinter, aged two, who at four would become the fastest horse in Europe running in the blue and green silks of Robert Sangster. His name was Thatching.

There had of course been disappointments for Robert, even in a season as glorious as this one. The filly Sookera, running in the colours of Uncle Jack Mulcahy was beaten in the 1000 Guineas, at the same meeting that The Minstrel went down to Nebbiolo. And another filly, Durtal, who was trained for Robert in England by Barry Hills of Lambourn, made a near-catastrophic mess of her attack on the Oaks. She had been a brilliant two-year-old winning three of her five races, and at three she had won the Fred Darling Stakes by five lengths and dead-heated for second place in the French 1000 Guineas behind the unbeaten Madelia. At the Oaks however she became tremendously upset, broke free before the start and charged down the course. Her saddle slipped and Lester Piggott hit the ground hard, before being dragged along for several yards. The filly crashed into the rails and cut herself so badly she had to be withdrawn. She was a heavily backed favourite for the Oaks, which was a blow to the massed ranks of British punters. Not, however, as great a blow as it would have been if she had managed to end the life of England's greatest jockey, which she came pretty close to doing.

One way and another, however, 1977 was a season for which Robert, and all those who sailed with him, should be profoundly thankful. As Viscount Leverhulme had warned in the winner's circle at Epsom, they do not happen often.

Spring of 1978 crept slowly north and reached the Isle of Man in the early part of March. Daffodils bloomed in profusion all over the former garden of the great romantic Sir George Goldie. Beneath the vast slate roof of The Nunnery, Robert and Susan were settled into a cheerful kind of champagne-sipping, sexy bliss. But within a few weeks of the season of re-birth, two events happened which were to cost the owner of Vernons a great deal of money. The first was that Try My Best failed to train on as a three-year-old and trailed in last of nineteen in the first English classic, the 2000 Guineas, at Newmarket. The second was that with the divorces finalized, he married the free-spending, photogenic siren of the Antipodes, Susan Rossiter Peacock.

One other person also lost a huge packet of money on Try My Best. His name was Patrick Gallagher, a twenty-seven-year-old Irish property developer and horse owner. Intoxicated with the glamour and charisma which surrounded Sangster's operation, he decided to join them and paid them £750,000 for a quarter share in the winner of the Dewhurst Stakes. Defeat in the Guineas was catastrophic for him. His investment crashed in a matter of seconds and he almost went into shock at the racetrack. Robert tried to steady him with a quarter bottle of brandy, but within days Gallagher decided to cut his losses and he sold his share back to them for a sum believed to have been £250,000. The winner of that Guineas, Roland Gardens, cost £3200.

Try My Best, with his outstanding bloodlines, was easy to syndicate as a stallion. A son of the great Northern Dancer, he had shown blinding speed as a two-year-old, finishing his season as the undisputed Champion of Europe. He was from a tough, running American family, which was being bred to the best, all of the time, and his potential as a commercial stallion was considerable. John Magnier still liked him immensely. He was a superb-looking horse and he had possessed the magic ingredient of tremendous speed and class at a very young age. Arthur Hancock's father Bull Hancock had always sworn that the most important racing 'form' of stallions was that of their two-year-old career. Northern Dancer was a good two-year-old, so was Nijinsky. Three of the great contemporary American sires, Graustark, Raise a Native, and Hoist the Flag (sire of Alleged) never won classics: almost their entire racing reputations were built at a young age. Try My Best went to Coolmore with high credentials. He stood for £20,000, with a share costing £60,000. This gave him a book value of £2·4 million, which was a very sporting profit on the $185,000 he had cost as a yearling.

The new Mrs Sangster had a propensity to tip the balance sheet the other way, given her great love of parties, designer clothes, expensive properties (she lost little time in persuading Robert to invest in a massive $6 million house on the waterfront of Sydney), five-star hotels and first-class air tickets. She also had great *joie de vivre* and she brought a lot of fun and laughter into Robert's life. Susan was a 'no-bullshit' Aussie, who cared nothing for English customs and the unwritten rules of etiquette which have always taken precedence at golf clubs and in the 'members areas' of the great racecourses.

On one memorable Saturday afternoon, in the members' dining room at Newbury in Berkshire, she listened to Nick Robinson laughingly suggesting that a horse of his might beat Robert's runner in the Prix de l'Arc de Triomphe, and then she picked up a three-quarters-full ice bucket and poured the entire contents over him. About half a gallon of water, ice and champagne corks hit him over the head, soaking his suit, drenching the person next to him, the American jockey Steve Cauthen, and flooding the table. Steve, who had been dieting for three days, saw the final smoked salmon sandwich sitting in half an inch of water.

'Christ! Susan!' he yelled. 'I haven't had anything to eat since Thursday. And I'm riding light tomorrow. That was my goddamned supper.'

Robert's oldest friend was furious. But he said nothing, as other racegoers gazed aghast at the extraordinary scene taking place in the corner of the room. Nick counted to ten . . . and then laughed. Four waiters rushed forward with arms full of tablecloths to dry the dripping guests off. Nick, less wet and with the chairs scrubbed dry, tipped the waiters and told them it had been an accident. Someone began to sing the first line of a little Australian song: 'I love to have a drink with Susan, Love to have a drink with Sue . . .' It broke the tension and it saved Robert from further embarrassment, but it also illuminated the gigantic clash of cultures between Susan and some of Robert's most loyal friends, some of whom would begin to play a far less prominent role in his life.

The wedding day, 10 March 1978, was a very fair example of how his life would change with Susan as chatelaine of The Nunnery. The Anglican bishop had denied them permission to marry in St Bridget's Chapel in the grounds of the great house because they had both been divorced, so they had to settle for the local registry office. Representatives of the national press invaded the island, but Robert rather cunningly had told them the wrong day and by the time they arrived he and Susan were already married. A local photographer did get a couple of shots of Susan arriving in a gleaming dark blue Rolls Royce Corniche and they snapped another shot after the ceremony, but no one caught even a glimpse of a blessing which took place the following day, in the Chapel of St Bridget, in which nearly fourteen centuries ago the saint had received the veil of virginity. At the reception at The Nunnery, Susan was finally in the heaven that she had always believed her new husband represented. With a huge budget to back her up, she provided a wedding banquet fit for the Queen of Sheba, a lady to whose life-style some people thought she aspired.

The on-rushing racing season would have been something close to ecstatic for any other owner in the world, but for Robert it did not produce the new beautifully bred stallion for which they ceaselessly searched. By normal standards, however, they had spectacular success. For a start, they bought a half share in a colt by Sham named Jaazeiro who had been a very good two-year-old in France. Vincent took over his training and sent him out to win the first Irish classic the 2000 Guineas, then he won the St James's Palace Stakes at Royal Ascot, then the Sussex Stakes at Goodwood. He was a good racehorse, perhaps the best British miler, but he did not possess the superlative blood sought by Vincent O'Brien and John Magnier. At the end of the season they sold him for around £1 million to stand as a stallion at Ballylynch Stud, in County Kilkenny, where his distant ancestor The Tetrarch is buried.

Solinus won three top sprints including the King's Stand Stakes at Royal Ascot, and Alleged stayed in training to win his second Arc de Triomphe, thus placing a value on him of $16 million. Robert owned a very good racehorse named Hawaiian Sound, in training with Barry Hills, who very nearly won both the English and Irish Derbys. They brought Bill Shoemaker over from America to ride him and he was beaten a head in the first to Shirley Heights, and a head and a neck in the second to the same horse, with the Irish-bred Exdirectory second. He was also second in the King George VI and Queen Elizabeth Stakes to Ile de Bourbon, but in mid August he won the Benson and Hedges Gold Cup, probably the best mile and a quarter race in Europe. Hawaiian Sound, like Jaazeiro, did not have the blood they sought and he was sold to America.

In Ireland they had a very useful and very special two-year-old filly named Solar, who was by the brilliant Windfields stallion Halo, out of Sex Appeal. A half-sister to Try My Best, they had purchased her two months before big brother ran, which was more a reflection on John Magnier's opinion of the family than anything else.

The real drama of the season took place at the 1978 Keeneland Sales, where Robert and his men spent $5,490,000 on sixteen colts and two fillies. This represented nearly fourteen per cent of the entire sale and helped to push the average price for a yearling up by 45·2 *per cent* to $125,751. The gross take for the sale rocketed from $26,769,000 to $40,366,000. In the twelve months before the sale, America's inflation, measured by the Consumer Price Index, was 10·9 per cent for all commodities and services, which should have put the average price for a yearling at $96,000. But Sangster's men were in there with a vengeance, and they cared nothing for Consumer Price Indices. They knew what a horse was worth and the Irishmen thought they knew which of them would run. They spent $1·5 million for two colts from Bunker Hunt's Bluegrass Farms, helping him to become the sale's leading consignor with sales of almost $5 million for eighteen yearlings. They spent $600,000 for a son of Hoist the Flag offered by Tom Gentry. They spent $375,000 on one colt from Cousin Leslie. A sister to Sex Appeal set them back another $300,000.

But it was the one they did not buy which caused the biggest fuss. This was a small, but rather elegant colt by Northern Dancer out of a mare by Forli, named Special. She was the dam of little Fairy Bridge, and a full-sister to Thatch. She was also a half-sister to King Pellinore and Marinsky, both of whom Vincent had trained with conspicuous success. This was a family which was not merely spending time in County Tipperary, it was putting down roots. Vincent and John wanted the colt, and Phonsie was very keen on him. Robert thought he might cost them $400,000, maybe more. But they had a policy, based on Robert's own research – that they must buy *every* colt they wanted. It was not a scrap of use backing down, because that would be to buck their own system. The only man who could possibly make money out of expensive yearlings would have been the man who bought them all. They had now been here for four years, and they had *never* backed down if the yearling was on Vincent's prime list.

Special's colt was, therefore, one they must have and he was in the Tuesday night consignment of Seth Hancock's Claiborne Farm. Because of the colt's size, the bidding opened very sluggishly at only $20,000 and, with many different bidders, it ground its way slowly up to $200,000, then $400,000, then on to $500,000, then $600,000. Right here things became serious. Joss Collins of the British Bloodstock Agency in London went to $625,000. A challenge from the far side sent the price higher. Collins held sway until well over $800,000 and Vincent signalled for Phonsie to join the fray. The Irish fisherman bid $860,000. Collins went to $880,000. Phonsie bid $900,000. Joss Collins bid again. Phonsie shook his head and left his seat, moving quickly to the back of the pavilion to caucus with Vincent, Tom Cooper and Robert.

Vincent wanted to go on, no matter what the price. The others were cautious. Robert thought the money behind Collins was from the Greek shipping magnate Stavros Niarchos. This could be expensive. Collins bid $960,000, but a new man came in at $975,000 up behind the auctioneer. Robert urged his men on. But Collins was back in and he bid $1 million, only the second time in history such a sum had been offered for a baby racehorse. The man behind the auctioneer raised it by $25,000. Joss Collins said $1,050,000. Tom Cooper now countered for Robert bidding $1,100,000.

Two fast $25,000 bids followed, and then Collins went to $1,200,000 for the son of Northern Dancer. 'One million two I have,' called Tom Caldwell, the auctioneer. 'Will you gimme a million and a quarter?' Robert and Tom Cooper both nodded. Caldwell then shouted, 'OK. Let's deal in round numbers. Gimme one three.'

Joss Collins nodded. Robert spun round to Vincent. Tom Cooper spoke to each of them briefly. No one was sure quite what to do. Now Caldwell was demanding, 'One million four, will you go to one million four.' Tom Cooper, trying to interpret his clients' wishes, looked and up and shook his head. 'Was that a "No"?' asked Caldwell. No one answered. Robert moved further back with Vincent to talk for one last time. But Caldwell was anxious. 'Is that an emphatic "no"?' he asked again. Vincent stopped, looked up. And as he did so the hammer crashed down. They had lost, to Stavros Niarchos, Nureyev, a truly brilliant racehorse and a sire who would one day be valued at $40 million.

Vincent, recalls Robert, was not pleased. He summoned the team around him for what turned out to be a military debriefing. He said he was certain they had made a mistake. 'We should have gone to two million for him if necessary,' he said. 'That is supposed to be our policy. We *never* back down if a yearling is on our "A" list.'

But back down they had and it would cost them dear. Robert puts the problem down to the fact that they originally thought the price was in the $500,000 range, maximum. It was the dramatic leap in price which had thrown them. They had not made a contingency for such an event. Also the fact that Vincent obviously wanted the colt – his own brother was doing the bidding – was giving other bidders confidence. Robert was certain that they were going to have to be a great deal more devious in the ring in future, placing unexpected bidders strategically around the auditorium, anything to put rivals off the scent – to blind them to the fact that a yearling colt or filly was very definitely wanted by the master of Ballydoyle.

No such timidity was in the air when they arrived at Saratoga two weeks later. Vincent's prime list totalled just four: three colts and one filly. And they bought them all. One of the colts was a half-brother to Alleged and it was Billy McDonald who bid. He landed the yearling for $700,000, the biggest price they paid in their total of $1,635,000. Saratoga's average price for a yearling now obliterated last year's record: it went from $57,000 in 1978 to $80,000, a colossal increase of almost forty per cent. And again the American trade press were demanding to know how and why this could possibly be happening. Horse breeders all over Kentucky and the equine hinterlands were wandering around with ludicrous grins on their faces. No one quite knew why it was happening, but it sure felt good. Real good. 'Yessir, Mr Sangster, 'preee-shiate it.'

In total Sangster's men had spent over $7 million at the two American sales, but the money they knew Alleged would be worth when he won the Arc – when, not if – would pay for the lot. Vincent was right. On a bright October day in Paris, Alleged bolted past a couple of very high-quality French fillies, Trillion and Dancing Maid, and won in the style of an outstanding four-year-old racehorse. They agreed to sell him back to Kentucky. And they got $16 million for him. Paid for all of this year's purchases and all of last year's with some change.

Everyone was cleaning house. There was money all over the place. Banks, institutions and investors were taking serious notice all over Ireland and United States. The potential for profit seemed to be without limit. All you seemed to need to start was a filly who could run a bit, from a decent family. Then breed her to some fancy stallion and head right on down to the sales with the yearling. It used to be known as a licence to steal, but right now it was going close to the horseman's nirvana, known colloquially in the Bluegrass as 'Hog Heaven'.

In addition to the world-record breaking figures being recorded at the principal American sales, there were dramas breaking out on the racetracks which were proving to be nothing short of riveting to the

American public. The previous year, 1977, had seen another winner of the US Triple Crown. A big, dark, brooding sort of a colt named Seattle Slew had won all three American classics without having lost a race in between. His very sporting owners had decided to keep him in training as a four-year-old and, after a long illness, he was preparing for an autumn campaign.

The next year yet another Triple Crown was won, the third in five years, after only one in twenty-five years. This new champion was Affirmed and he had won the three classics after a series of knock-down-drag-out battles with the Calumet colt Alydar. In the Kentucky Derby they were separated by a length and a half, in the Preakness there was just a neck in it, and in the Belmont Stakes, over one and a half miles, Affirmed won by a neck after one of the most sensational head-to-head struggles ever seen at Belmont Park between three-year-olds.

This Belmont Stakes was the ninth time they had met (the score was 4–2 to Affirmed as two-year-olds), and it was the race in which the eighteen-year-old Steve Cauthen burst into the world league of race-riders. At Belmont Park Affirmed was not as well as he had been at Churchill Downs, and he faltered in the stretch. Alydar drew level at the three-sixteenth pole. The great, packed stadium rose to its feet as one to roar home the beloved, battle-hardened underdog Alydar. Cauthen went after Affirmed, driving him on, asking him the supreme question, one last terrible call on the remnants of his courage. But Affirmed was giving his all and he could find no more. Steve Cauthen, with the greatest reluctance, and with the Triple Crown slipping away from him, drew his whip and he hit Affirmed for the first time in his life. Somehow, from somewhere, Affirmed dredged up the final ounces of his strength and he fought his way over the dying yards of the race to win by a neck. Both horses had run to within an inch of their lives. It was hard to find anyone in New York City who was *not* talking about the titanic struggle for the 1978 American Triple Crown.

In the autumn, things grew, if anything, hotter. Seattle Slew made his comeback and beat Affirmed in the Marlboro Cup. Then he beat Exceller, Bunker Hunt's great European stayer in the Woodward Stakes. Then in the Jockey Club Gold Cup a huge New York crowd saw one of the finest races of all time. Seattle Slew, out in the lead on a track awash with rain, was collared and passed by Exceller deep in the home stretch after Bill Shoemaker had brought Bunker Hunt's horse from twenty-five lengths back. Exceller had more than a half-length advantage and they charged to the wire together, with Slew fighting back, gaining with every stride. On the line he lost by a head. In defeat, Slew found, perhaps, his finest hour.

Watching all of this with a maniacal smile on his face was Cousin Leslie, who had agreed terms with Slew's owners to stand the champion at Spendthrift in a syndication worth $12 million. In addition, he also had Affirmed lined up. After one more season of racing at four, Affirmed would join Slew, 'Chez Cousin Leslie', at a similar price, because he was pure Spendthrift blood, being by Exclusive Native, who in turn was by Raise a Native. All of them were Spendthrift stallions and that autumn there were more parties out along the Ironworks Pike in Cousin Leslie's mansion than anyone could ever remember. The mood was close to ecstatic. Everyone was trying to buy into the syndications. Prices were soaring. Profits were beyond belief. Cousin Leslie and Brownell were looking real carefully at the private jet aircraft brochures.

'*Hot damn!* Ain't this beautiful?'

'*Hey, boy!* Y'all fetch them mint-*juleps* right here!'

Back on the racetracks of Europe nothing even remotely as dramatic was happening. And Robert and his partners were having a moderate 1979. Thatching emerged as a top sprinter and a filly by Sir Ivor, named Godetia, won the Irish Oaks, but the mood was not terribly optimistic. Certainly the money for Alleged meant that they were well into profit and they owned a lot of relatively valuable horses. But the big stallion with the Northern Dancer blood that they all wanted had not materialized yet. In fact they had not succeeded yet in keeping one of their own top racehorses to stand at Coolmore. The offers from the States were always too high to resist.

The truth was, a lot of the American-bred runners did not seem to act that well on European turf. In addition, Secretariat had not come through as a stallion for them. Neither had Vaguely Noble. Nor, with the exception of Alleged, had Hoist the Flag. Northern Dancer had given them The Minstrel but not much else. What they needed was a big hit at the sales, a new Nijinsky. The best Northern Dancer sire at the moment appeared to be Lyphard, who had just gone from France to Gainesway in Kentucky, after a string of very good stakes winners. Robert moved in fast and bought eight nominations to him for $80,000 a piece.

The men from Tipperary thus hit Keeneland in 1979 in determined mood, but they showed no interest in the sale-topper. A colt by Hoist the Flag from Royal Dowry, submitted by Tom Gentry, fetched the unfathomable price of $1·6 million. A year previously a half-brother by

Protagonist had fetched only $15,000! Maybe it was the magic of Alleged in Paris which had suddenly made Hoist the Flag all the rage again. But Tom Gentry nearly died of excitement when the Japanese breeder secured the colt for the biggest price ever paid for a yearling at auction. He leapt to his feet and whipped the brightly coloured sports coat off his back and *gave* it to the startled buyer, who held it high above his head to roars of applause, which caused the colt to rear up in terror on the podium.

Robert, Vincent and John were basically on a mission. They knew the two they had come for and, as ever, they instructed Tom Cooper, 'No limit. Buy them both.' Thus the Irish agent went to $1·4 million for a Nijinsky colt out of Secretariat's half-sister Syrian Sea; and he went to a round $1 million to buy Northern Dancer's son from the Windfields mare South Ocean. The latter would make them possibly the biggest fortune ever created by a single racehorse. They took him home to Ireland and named him Storm Bird.

In addition they bought sixteen others at a cost of $8,885,000. The average price at Keeneland went up by nearly thirty per cent from the 1978 figure, to $160,111 each. Coolmore team's average price was nearly $500,000 a piece, almost *twenty per cent* of the entire sale. Then they moved on to Saratoga, spending $2,335,000 on six colts, sending that average price up by another twenty-two and a half per cent. Breeders of thoroughbred horses simply could not believe their luck. Fortunes were being made all over the Bluegrass. Stallion shares were going crazy in the market place, some changing hands for up to $600,000.

Right now there was only one name on the lips of the Kentucky stallion masters and that was Robert Sangster. He was, indisputably, the first big buyer in the history of the sport ever to make it work financially. Here he was actually smashing aside every theory, publicly making serious money out of this lunatic lottery, which had, for generations, consistently failed to do so for some of the world's richest and shrewdest men. There was now, thanks to Robert, Vincent and John, quite literally a stampede to get into the horse business, because it appeared to be the only business on earth which was immune to any fluctuations of any other markets. Consumer price indices, the New York Stock Exchange, the Bond market, the Commodity Market, a volatile dollar – *nothing* seemed to have any effect on the horse market. What mattered here were the flying whips and fearless riding of Lester Piggott, Steve Cauthen and Angel Cordero. This market was governed by stout hearts and photo-finishes, by the stick of wood with the circle on top which marks the finishing line, and by the determination of the powerful syndicates headed by Robert Sangster. 'A top racehorse, or a top stallion is an international commodity,' said Robert to a breathless press conference. 'He has a major value anywhere. He can be moved instantly to where he is most valued. Better still, he never answers back.'

But what no one yet knew, in this bold, greedy and somewhat naive industry, was that the real battle for the best racing blood had not even begun; that the men who would ultimately dominate the world market, and who would make everyone rich beyond even their wildest expectations, had not yet played their opening hand.

8

The Soft Steps of
the Bedouin

Less than one hundred and twenty miles south of the Gulf seaport of Dubai, across one of the wildest and toughest deserts on earth, there is an unseen border in the drifting sands which marks the northern-eastern extent of the vast Kingdom of Saudi Arabia. Beyond here, six hundred miles wide, stretches a boundless level of barren land, split by the occasional mountain. The face of this desert, without shade or shelter, is scorched by the terrible rays of a tropical sun. The hot wind from the south-west, whirling in a monstrous circle of choking air currents, has been known to bury entire armies. This is the Rub' al-Khali, the Empty Quarter, a place entirely destitute of navigable rivers, where all of the water which sometimes rushes in torrents down the mountainside is swallowed by the hot, arid sands, where the only treasures are the tiny springs and wells that occur only hundreds of miles apart. As late as 1945 no pilot of any aircraft had ever dared to fly through the cloudless skies above this awesome place, for it is truly a desert within a desert. Survival in such heat would be measured in hours rather than days. By the 1970s only two Europeans had ever crossed it, the explorer Bertram Thomas and the great traveller and Arabist, Wilfred Thesiger.

Upon the blistered face of this wilderness there is only one human being who can possibly survive for very long. He has lived along its borders for untold centuries. He has taken joy from the endless suffering, he has tolerated its fearsome climate, and taken pleasure from a life of forced abstinence. He has mastered perhaps the cruellest of all the earth's environments. And for fifteen centuries he has journeyed as a pilgrim right across the Rub' al-Khali, swaying to the tireless but fragile rhythm of his camels, along the highway to his God, in Mecca. He is, of course, the Bedouin tribesman.

Such a man was Sheikh Rashid bin Said-Al Maktoum, the Ruler of the desert Sheikhdom of Dubai, which stands on the southern shore of the Persian Gulf. To the north is the headland of Hormuz which juts out into this inland seaway to form the precious, narrow Straits, gateway to the trading ports of the vast twentieth-century oilfields. Sheikh Rashid was born of a centuries-old family of desert warriors, with deep roots in the most royal blood of the northern tribes of the Saudis. He died at a very great age in 1991, beloved of his people, for he had been a wise, liberal and a benevolent ruler, as well as enjoying a reputation as possibly the shrewdest trader along all of the Gulf ports. Neither was he a man to be trifled with. Shortly after he became Ruler in 1943 there was a vicious attempt upon his life. He had the culprits hunted down and, personally, inflicted upon them the most terrible revenge, under the law, stating simply, 'It is unwise to play games with the Ruler of Dubai.'

Disputes over his sand-swept, hazy borders were greeted with similar hostility. Challenged by the next-door Ruler of Abu Dhabi, Sheikh Shakhbut in 1946, he summoned his men to arms and led them fearlessly into a fierce and bloody war, driving his horses and, on occasion, his camels into battle. To the end of his long life he preferred to sit with his advisors in the shadow of his tent, holding his counsels on a great carpet beneath the pitiless sun. Warrior, deal-maker, statesman, ruler, dispenser of timeless wisdom, recounter of history and lover of all things English, especially racehorses, Sheikh Rashid was, to his people, the Winston Churchill of the desert. But with all of his great dignity, he would quite often utter the phrase that proclaims the plain, unbending pride of all such Arabian tribal chiefs. It was simple and it bespoke a thousand words. He would look you hard in the eye, the traditional mark of contact in the desert, and he would say softly, 'I am Sheikh Rashid. I am a Bedouin.'

Such pride encompasses the natural superiority of the desert Arab over the city Arab. For here is a man who can survive for seven days without food or water in the burning wilderness of his homeland. He is able to live easily without any of the comforts of life. He has no permanent home and the ground is stony. His soul is stripped bare of the need for aesthetics. He does not crave refinement. The desert cannot burn him, and even in the bitterly cold nights, huddled under the lee of his camel, the desert cannot freeze him, though it can kill infant members of his family and deliver upon him the most dreadful deprivations. However, only the collapse of his camels can signify, to him, certain death. The Bedouin stands, to the end, unbowed.

After his murderous journey by camel across the Empty Quarter, Wilfred Thesiger, a man who was schooled at Eton and won a boxing

Blue at Oxford, wrote a heartfelt tribute to the desert nomad, citing 'his generosity, his courage, his endurance, his patience and his light-hearted gallantry'. 'Among no other people', wrote Thesiger, 'have I felt the same sense of personal inferiority.'

Sheikh Rashid's kingdom, for most of his rule, was dependent upon trade. It has been ever thus. For people have lived and traded around the port of Dubai since two thousand years before Christ. Dubai was one of the old Arabian Pirate Coast ports which specialized in smuggling, especially gold. The old British India Steam Navigation Company, owned by P&O, ran a service for years between Bombay and Dubai, principally bringing in Indians to purchase gold for their dowries, trade in the precious metal being illegal in their own country.

In the latter twenty years of his life the Sheikh presided over one of the great deep-water harbours in the Gulf. He led the way in the Arab Emirates in installing phone lines and a reliable postal service. He listened to his trusted English advisors, some of whom had stayed on after the Gulf States became independent, and the result was tremendous commercial activity. Sheikh Rashid could grasp the most complex aspects of modern life. He could sit and deal with rooms full of engineers, oil magnates, salesmen for airports, hotels, dry docks, and never demonstrate the slightest sign of confusion. Robert Gibbons, the London solicitor who for many years advised Sheikh Rashid, says the Ruler's uncanny ability to grapple with deeply complicated matters has always impressed those who came to do business with him, whether financial or political.

He was a modern ruler and few modern advantages in commerce and development escaped him. He had four sons, Maktoum al-Maktoum, Hamdan, Mohammed and Ahmed. Sheikh Rashid not only ensured they received an entirely modern education, he also taught them the old ways of the Bedouin, of the unswerving principles of Islamic justice, far beyond anything political; of the first requirement of justice in the Arab mind – to restore rights to those who have lost their rights. He taught them that the duty of wealth is to assist, first brothers, and then friends. He taught them the history of their country, telling them the old Arab fables of the terrible battles along the Pirate Coast, where fearless buccaneers would ransack the precious pearl banks. He explained to them how England had restored order, first with the famous Truce between the little emirates in 1835, and then establishing the modern United Arab Emirates in 1970. In one of her final pieces of colonial legislation, England ordered the Saudis to stay south of the border, permanently. Sheikh Rashid impressed upon his sons that they owed their existence to London and that, without the Government of the Queen of England, they would be a mere part of Saudi Arabia.

The old laws of desert warfare represent a curious chivalry in a land possessed of a bloodthirsty turn of mind. But Sheikh Rashid impressed them upon his sons, whom he believed may one day have to fight, and he ensured that they too grew up to be excellent horsemen and hunters. He explained that if your enemy falls from his horse, you may not attack him; that it is regarded as 'murder' to shoot and kill a horseman from the ground; that any Sheikh, fallen in battle, must be treated with honour; and that, in the requirement of a ransom, his word is sufficient to free him. Each of the old Sheikh's sons was blessed with the natural gift of all great families of hereditary rulers, that of natural courtesy. But among their own close advisors and friends, like their father, they grew up to expect no sign of deference or concession. These men dwell in a society of brothers. Much was given to the young Sheikhs, but in difficult times much would be expected of them by their people.

Sheikh Rashid throughout his rule held several times a week a *majlis*, the traditional democratic gathering at which he would welcome his people in the most informal way to hear their problems individually, to try to solve them, and to dispense wisdom and justice. It was said of him that he never once in all of those years turned anyone away. People came from miles afar to seek his help, some from out of the desert, others down the Gulf in the sailing dhows which slide along the waters like great sea birds from another millennium. At the majlis there would be the *gawa* (coffee), tea and food, with plates of dates being handed, ceremoniously, around. On these frequent occasions, Sheikh Rashid's home was 'open' in an Arabian custom which has survived for thousands of years. 'As salam Alaikum' (peace be upon you) was his greeting. No four sons were ever more exquisitely taught the ancient and trusted ways of one of the wisest of the modern desert rulers.

As young men, all four of the brothers were tutored in the skills of political responsibility and, in Sheikh Rashid's opinion, it was essential that one of them, at least, became expert in the arts of war and soldiering. For he too, like his father, may one day be obliged to lead his people in battle against an invading enemy. For this he chose his third son, the young Sheikh Mohammed, the one who was perhaps most like the old Sheikh as a young man. From an early age this slim, hard-eyed Arab prince, carried himself with the natural upright bearing of the Bedouin. Even among his own people he stood out as a potential military leader.

He walked with none of that innate deference common to some of his countrymen. But rather he held his head slightly back, his clipped black beard casting upon him the imprint of the desert and the unmistakable air of a prince of the blood from those harsh, dry lands, east of the Mediterranean.

Sheikh Rashid sent him to Mons, the British officer training school, in Aldershot Barracks, home of the British Army. The college was named after the great First World War battle of Mons in Belgium in 1914 – the first battle fought by the British on the continent of Europe since 1815. There the young Sheikh was taught the rudiments of war. He was drilled ceaselessly, instructed in tactics, in gunnery, artillery, in the skills of manoeuvres and the transporting of a great army. Already an excellent horseman, Sheikh Mohammed emerged as a thoughtful, qualified Army officer, smartly dressed and perfectly mannered.

From Mons he was sent on to study with the Royal Air Force at their training school in Perth. There he learned to fly jet fighter aircraft and he studied the principles of low-level bombing and the new science of air-launched missiles. His father had long planned that his third son should serve as his country's Minister of Defence and he trusted only the British to prepare him for that great responsibility. As his forefathers had been drilled to fight with two-handed swords and rifles, so Sheikh Mohammed would be schooled in the more lethal, more scientific advances of modern defensive systems.

Meanwhile Sheikh Rashid had visited Royal Ascot with Robert Gibbons. It was slightly unorthodox in that the lawyer's father had always held a reserved table in the upstairs restaurant which looks west across the lawn to the paddock where the horses are saddled. This is a sizeable room where lunch, drinks and tea are served for most of the day. It is situated just outside the Royal Enclosure, above what is known generally as the 'Irish Bar'. Here is the great meeting place of Irish horsemen – owners, trainers, bloodstock agents and major punters. As the afternoon wears on, with hot favourites being defeated and bets going astray, the occasional drunk is not entirely unknown. In moments of high excitement late in the day, the strains of an Irish tenor, with suitable backing from the gathering, has often been heard . . . 'The Pale moon was rising above the green mountains . . .' It is not a place where one might catch a glimpse of Her Majesty, nor indeed any of her immediate family.

Sheikh Rashid loved it in the restaurant, on the occasion of his first and only visit to the Berkshire course. In fact, once settled he would not leave. At one point during the day, Lord Leverhulme, the Senior

Steward of the English Jockey Club, passed on a message that Queen Elizabeth II would be delighted to take tea in the Royal Box with Sheikh Rashid of the Sheikhdom of Dubai. With deferential politeness, that of one Ruler to another, the great man declined, preferring to remain with the 'crack', and to talk about the horses. For a few minutes before each race, he would stand up with an enormous pair of binoculars and stare down at the paddock at the runners. But then he would sit down again, and sip his black coffee and chuckle endlessly at the diabolically inaccurate stories being bandied around. He never went outside to watch a race. He listened to the racecourse commentary, but basically, he just stayed where he was, resplendent in his national dress, talking, listening and laughing. Not even the Queen of England could drag him away.

In time, after Robert Gibbons 'inherited' his father's regular table, Sheikh Rashid's sons too would learn the ways of the English and Irish horsemen. Sheikh Mohammed was also sent by his father to a language school at Cambridge in order to become fluent in the tongue of the cool, green land which his father adored. And this devotion to his British friends ought not to be underestimated. One of Sheikh Rashid's most grandiose and successful schemes was to build one of the largest desalination plants in the world to provide, for the first time in thousands of years, all the fresh water the people of Dubai could ever need.

For him it was a project which ranked on the scale of Gamal Abdel Nasser's Aswan Dam across the Nile. In the end there were two major bidders short-listed for the desalination project: a giant German company and the Scottish engineers, Weirs of Glasgow. Sheikh Rashid listened to the arguments, and it was clear that the Germans had an edge. They were more efficient and thus quicker, and, above all, they were cheaper. But the situation in Glasgow was very moderate at the time. Thousands of jobs were on the line at Weirs and the contract to build the plant meant everything to them. The situation was explained carefully to him and Sheikh Rashid calmly awarded the contract to Weirs of Glasgow. His ministers were slightly amazed and during the ensuing discussions, in which it was pointed out that business is after all business, the Sheikh was asked why he had not appointed the German engineers to build his plant.

The old desert ruler, looked up, with a quizzical smile upon his face, and then he said gently, 'Because I like the British more.'

But, in the normal way, he was the very soul of democratic discussion. He and his leading men would sit for hours, in the Arabian way, and pay attention to every point of view. In the end the decisions of Sheikh

Rashid were essentially a consensus of the opinions of his most trusted advisors. Only rarely was it said of him that he was perfectly prepared to sit democratically, indefinitely, until everyone was too tired *not* to agree with him.

For much of the 1970s the Maktoums of Dubai were wealthy but not truly rich in the manner of some of their neighbours. Their cash came from trading and from some offshore oil, but they lacked the massive profits being gathered in places like Abu Dhabi, Kuwait and Saudi Arabia. However, the American petroleum giant ARCO (the Atlantic-Richfield Corporation) was drilling hard some fifty miles south-east of the port of Dubai. Their geologists and executives were certain there was oil down there beneath the ancient sands and they persistently informed Sheikh Rashid that a strike could not be far away. By 1977 they had not however located any worthwhile reserves, though in this year the young Sheikh Mohammed made a strike of his own: with his father's blessing he had purchased a racehorse in England, a 6200-guinea filly in training with John Dunlop in the lovely precincts of Arundel Castle in Sussex.

On a hot, dry afternoon at Goodwood in August, she won the Molecombe Stakes, sprinting clean away from the heavily odds-on favourite Amaranda. It was Hatta's fourth victory in a row and she beat the brilliant Amaranda by two and a half lengths. It was the biggest upset of the entire meeting – the same one at which the big race, the Sussex Stakes, was won for Sangster's men themselves by Artaius. This was the season in which Robert and his men carried all before them. Even at Goodwood, at that time a very English, understated, summer gathering of racing people, with none of the ceremony of Royal Ascot, Robert Sangster was beyond doubt the dominant personality among the major owners.

It was, in retrospect, a deep irony that the quietly spoken young Arab prince, thrilled beyond belief at his success in the two-year-old fillies race, should have remained utterly unnoticed. On that afternoon, his path had crossed for the first time that of Robert and Vincent, but he had not left the mighty footprints of a man who would become within eight years the major financial force in racing history, and their biggest enemy in the sales rings of the world. But rather he had passed by with only the soft step of the Bedouin. And he left behind prints which would soon be obscured, and which had made no sound, because of the sand.

Sheik Mohammed's victory had fired him with enthusiasm for the sport, and his brother Hamdan too was keenly interested and planned to begin a racing stable with the Newmarket trainer Tom Jones. But 1978 was the year in which another Arabian owner, Mr Khalid Abdullah, moved to the forefront of the bloodstock industry, though he too entered with the quiet tread of the Bedouin. His wish was to be styled very formally as 'Mr Khalid Abdullah', but this represents perhaps an understatement of his importance. His correct name is Prince Khalid ibn Abdullah, and he is the son of Abdullah ibn Abdul Rahman. Thus his father was the brother of the mighty King Abdul Aziz, 'Ibn Saud', the founder of modern Saudi Arabia and also the father of four Kings of that massive desert kingdom which has dominated the Arab Peninsula for this entire century.

Prince Khalid is married to a sister of King Fahad, to whom he has always been an extremely close friend and trusted advisor. He dines with the King on a weekly basis, but beyond the Kingdom he has extensive business interests both at home and in Chicago. In 1978 he attended the Keeneland Sales with his English trainer, Jeremy Tree, and his bloodstock agent, the former Newmarket trainer Humphrey Cottrill, and they bought just one horse, a dark bay colt by In Reality. He cost them $225,000, which was a bold move for a newcomer to thoroughbred racing. Bold, but cheap, because the colt turned out to be one of the toughest milers in Europe.

Returning to the Houghton Sales at Newmarket Prince Khalid bought the top two lots, one of them costing 264,000 guineas. In the end this selective buying was dwarfed by the activities of Robert Sangster and his men, but it did signify the start of the colossal involvement in racing the men from the Middle East were planning. Even in the following year, 1979, while Vincent and John Magnier were grappling in Keeneland to buy the young Storm Bird, the Maktoum brothers, led by Sheikh Mohammed, were planning a major hit at the forthcoming Houghton Sales, at Newmarket. They paid an all-time-record European price of 625,000 guineas for a colt by Lyphard from a Habitat mare. They would name him Ghaadeer, and Sheikh Mohammed wanted him to run in the colours of his elder brother Sheikh Hamdan, Dubai's great expert in the oil market and Sheikh Rashid's representative at OPEC.

As the 1979 racing season drew to a close the principal players in Europe took stock of their situation. Robert and his team had, yet again, the champion two-year-old on the Free Handicap. He was called Monteverdi, another one by Lyphard out of an extremely well-bred mare, Janina. He won the National Stakes at the Curragh, and another Dewhurst Stakes for his trainer Vincent O'Brien. Perhaps even more importantly, the Prix de l'Arc de Triomphe in October, a couple of weeks before the Dewhurst, had been won by a brilliant filly named Three Troikas, by Lyphard. This little stallion was by now the most fashionable sire in the world – with the exception of his own father Northern Dancer – and, if his son Monteverdi could possibly get home in an English classic in 1980, Robert and the boys would have made up for a relatively lean few months in one mighty strike. They stared at the oncoming decade of the 1980s with glorious enthusiasm.

In France, there was high competition for the top spot on the two-year-old handicap. But Nureyev, the Northern Dancer colt which Mr Stavros Niarchos snatched from under Vincent's nose at the previous year's sale, was right up there, in joint-second position, having won the Prix Thomas Byron at St Cloud in the November mud. In this rather hot, late-season contest he faced eleven winners and treated them with derision, winning by six increasing lengths. Stavros Niarchos and his advisors also knew that if Nureyev could get home in a classic in 1980 he too would pay for a lot of failures by other slower horses.

In third place on the English Free Handicap was Prince Khalid Abdullah's colt by In Reality. He was now named Known Fact and he had run extremely well, winning once at Newbury in May, and then coming with a gallant late run to win the prestigious Middle Park Stakes at Newmarket in the autumn. Like Sangster's team, like Stavros Niarchos, the Saudi prince had much to which he could look forward in 1980.

Meanwhile Sheikh Mohammed bided his time. He bought a stud farm at Aston Upthorpe in Berkshire and contemplated the possibility of a major hit at forthcoming sales at both Keeneland and Newmarket. His military career had brought him into contact with many of England's toughest and best-mannered soldiers, several of them sportsmen, and he was as sure as he could be that he wanted to be a part of the English horse-racing world. Throughout the 1970s he and his brothers had regularly spent a few days shooting in Scotland on the estate of Robert Gibbons. And there Mohammed would listen, as all Arabs love to listen, to stories told by the lawyer's great friend Colonel Bill Stirling, whose brother David had founded the SAS. Bill himself had commanded the Second SAS, accomplishing the most lethal work far behind the German lines, and Sheikh Mohammed was fascinated to hear of the Second World War exploits of the British Army's most daring regiment. But most of all he loved to hear about the exploits of Colonel Bill's immortal sprinter Sing Sing and the great wagers they had on him as he rampaged

unbeaten through six two-year-old races in 1959. The story ended like
a Greek tragedy. Sing Sing, carrying the hopes of thousands of punters
and an enormous amount of the Colonel's cash, was beaten a neck in
the King's Stand Stakes at Royal Ascot. No one who was there ever
forgot the sight of Colonel Bill, turning away in horror as Sound Track
got up on the line to beat his pride and joy. Sheikh Mohammed never
forgot that either and he vowed never to become involved in gambling
on *any* horse, on that scale.

Another of the British Army's daredevil soldiers was Dick Warden,
a director of the Curragh Bloodstock Agency. Aside from the fact that
he once rode in the Grand National wearing his spectacles, Dick served
his country in a dark and mysterious way. When the Second World War
began he was working in France at the stables of Jack Cunnington and
he fled before the advancing German army, making his way cross-
country to the port of Bordeaux. There he boarded the last boat home
to England, arrived unshaven, looking like a tramp, and enlisted in the
Intelligence Corps as a private soldier. Within a few months he was
given the routine commission always awarded to a man who will serve
behind enemy lines in the SOE (Special Operations Europe) and he
left once more for France. Dick would never discuss what he did, or
how he did it, at least not in public. Suffice, perhaps, to record that he
worked often alone, in situations of the utmost danger, a long way
behind enemy lines, and he came home a lieut-colonel. He met Sheikh
Mohammed on a military matter in Dubai and the two remained friends.
Now the young Arab would ask him to act as his agent in the buying
of bloodstock at the biggest sales in the world. They did not have so
much to anticipate on the track as Messrs Sangster, Niarchos and
Abdullah, but they intended to make their presence known before the
end of the Islamic month of Rabbia Thami, which covers the period
between mid October and mid November.

Meanwhile the new season got under way with a defeat for Monteverdi in a classic trial at Phoenix Park. There followed, however, a truly
stunning defeat in the Greenham Stakes behind Final Straw at Newbury. There were no excuses and some observers felt that the son of
Lyphard had not really given his all. This was a horse with a six-million-
dollar reputation to defend and it does not get very much more sensitive
than that around Tipperary way. The English 2000 Guineas classic was
out of the question, so Vincent elected to try for the Irish 2000 Guineas
to redeem the colt's tumbling fortunes. They put blinkers on him, in
an attempt to concentrate his entire mind on his job, but he still finished

fifth. The mood among Sangster's men was very despondent and it was not much helped by Lester Piggott who uttered the word 'useless' at his little press conference in the unsaddling enclosure. In fact that one word infuriated everyone so much it signified the end of the great partnership between O'Brien and England's greatest ever classic race-rider.

The 2000 Guineas was thus run at Newmarket without Robert's two-year-old champion. But he still had a chance, because Vincent decided to run a very nice Nijinsky colt Night Alert, whom they had bought as a yearling in the United States for $190,000 and who had won the Houghton Stakes at Newmarket as a two-year-old. The mere fact that Vincent was entering this horse and bringing him over from Ballydoyle caused a rush of money to pour into the betting offices. But everyone at Ballydoyle knew it would take a hell of a horse to lower the colours of the French favourite, the dreaded Nureyev, in the colours of Stavros Niarchos. There were other good horses in the field too. John Dunlop fielded Posse, owned by the chairman of the New York Racing Association, Dinny Phipps, son of Ogden, guardian of Claiborne. Prince Khalid ran his Keeneland purchase Known Fact. Final Straw, conqueror of Monteverdi was in, and there was money for a big fine staying type, Tyrnavos. Altogether, including the very fast Taufan, there were *seven* future stallions in this race.

The Newmarket grandstand was packed on 3 May 1980, with hundreds more massed on the lawns and along the rails, preparing to watch this field of fourteen fight it out over the arrow-straight runway of the Rowley Mile. The big horse-breeders of central Kentucky, Chesapeake City, Virginia, even Florida, were once again hanging on to phone lines connected to England and Ireland to hear the commentary of the one-mile classic. Everyone had a vested interest in the outcome. Everyone was hoping against all hope that the lunatic bonanza in the selling of baby racehorses was going to continue indefinitely.

Joe Thomas at Windfields had his usual arrangement with a telephone on top of a television set in Berkshire. He of course wanted Northern Dancer's son Nureyev to win, since this would increase the legend of his stallion and encourage Mr Niarchos to buy more at Keeneland. Joe would also have been happy with a victory for Robert Sangster's Night Alert, a grandson of the Dancer, owned by his biggest customer. Over at Claiborne they were rooting for Mr Phipps's Posse, but would have liked Prince Khalid's Known Fact to win because he was by the Florida-based all-American stallion In Reality, a descendant on both sides of his pedigree of Man O'War. In Reality was also the sire of one of Claiborne's new stallions, Believe It, whose thankless task it had been to chase home Affirmed and Alydar two years previously in two classics. Cousin Leslie had more of an open mind. Basically he had not been so successful as some in selling to the Europeans, but they had driven up all prices so stupendously he was making a fortune out of the home market. Deep down he would have liked to buy that 'itty bitty son of Northern Dancer owned by Mr Niarchos'. Leslie could develop some real serious plans for a man as rich as that.

The 2000 Guineas started four minutes late, which added a bit to a few transatlantic phone bills, and right from the start, unusual in England, they went off at a fierce pace. The French jockey Paquet elected to ride Nureyev from the back, with a plan to battle his way through the middle of the pack as they spread out across the track coming away from Bushes Hill. As plans go, this one was eccentric since Nureyev had plenty of speed and certainly could have laid up right behind the leaders, or alternately come late on the outside. As it was he raced through four or five tiring horses as they ran towards the quarter-pole, but, just as Paquet balanced him and asked him to run for his life, all gaps closed. Paquet kept going forward, trying to bull his way through and Nureyev crashed hard, at high speed, into Posse, almost bringing this chestnut son of Forli to his knees. Paquet drew his whip and drove Nureyev on. Posse, recovering his stride, swerved and crashed into Taufan. Known Fact hit the front inside the final furlong, but Nureyev was flying now, and he was being hotly pursued by a plainly infuriated Posse. Night Alert, slightly outpaced, was struggling on gamely.

Known Fact kept running with the utmost bravery, but Nureyev had just a touch more class on this day, and he passed Prince Khalid's horse decisively and hung on to win by a neck. Posse was three quarters of a length further back, with Night Alert three lengths away in fourth. 'Nureyev's won it!' yelled the commentator. 'The favourite's won it. Nureyev, another son of Northern Dancer, owned by Mr Stavros Niarchos, trained in Chantilly by François Boutin, ridden by Philippe Paquet, has won the 2000 Guineas, from Mr Khalid Abdullah's Known Fact trained by Jeremy Tree in Marlborough, and ridden by Willie Carson.'

But before the phones in the USA could be replaced, before the horses had even made their way off the racecourse, the sinister tones of the track announcer rang out over Newmarket Heath. And they were the words of the Angel of Death for the connections of Nureyev . . .

'*Stewards' enquiry*'. They meant, beyond doubt, that the beady-eyed English Stewards had seen the bumping and barging that had taken place three furlongs out, when a horse was almost brought down. They had seen the excitable Frenchman batter his way through a gap that was not there. They could be considering any one of a litany of crimes – rough or reckless riding, undue aggression, failing to keep a straight course, intimidating tactics, any one of which would conclude with instant disqualification.

The Stewards were faced with a momentous decision. No horse had ever been disqualified from the 2000 Guineas since its first running in 1809. It was sixty years since *any* horse had been disqualified from *any* English classic. Nureyev was the favourite and he was the best horse in the race. His owner was a most loyal supporter of English racing. Nonetheless, Nureyev's route to the winning line was unacceptable by any standards. If every jockey rode as Paquet had done there would probably be half a dozen deaths a week in the sport of racing. The Jockey Club's Stewards were having none of it. And they disqualified Nureyev, promoting Prince Khalid Abdullah's Known Fact to first place, with Posse second and Night Alert third.

On the face of it, that might have seemed especially bad news for everyone. In truth it was wonderful, particularly in Kentucky, because the race now had *two* winners. Nureyev's future promotional material would always say: 'Finished first in the English 2000 Guineas'. Stavros Niarchos was too rich to care about the prize money (£57,000) but the inherent millions of dollars which accrue to the future value of a classic-winning stallion were still there. Niarchos would be back to Keeneland, no doubt of that. So would Prince Khalid, who had bought a classic winner with his only purchase from Keeneland 1978. Even Robert Sangster's Night Alert, well beaten into fourth place, would always carry the promotional phrase: 'Placed third, behind Nureyev, in the English 2000 Guineas'.

By now it was 11 a.m. in the Bluegrass and, wearing beaming smiles, they all headed south from Lexington for the Kentucky Derby, which would be run that afternoon in Louisville for the hundred and sixth time. The big winner here would be Cousin Leslie, because the winner of the race was the chestnut filly Genuine Risk and she was by his champion stallion Exclusive Native, sire of Affirmed, and that spelt *good* news for the owners of Spendthrift farm. '*Hey boy!* Where *is* that private jet?'

Cousin Leslie could hear the sound of some distant auctioneer's voice in his mind: 'And here, ladies and gentlemen, we have yet another superlative yearling from Spendthrift Farm ... He is by the great Exclusive Native, sire of two of the last three winners of the Kentucky Derby ... Will ya gimme two million dollars for him?'

'DAH DAH DAH, DAH DAH-DAH, DAH DAH-DAH, DAH DAH-DAH DAAAAAH!'

Seth Hancock too was very pleased with the result in England. Mr and Mrs Bertram Firestone, who owned Genuine Risk – only the second filly ever to win the Derby – were good clients of Claiborne Farm's and victories like this always made good clients, better clients. If Mr Firestone had a real mind to get really rich out of this he had one shining option: take Genuine Risk and put her in foal to either Northern Dancer, Lyphard or Nijinsky II and *sell* her for what would surely be the biggest price ever paid for a broodmare. As they say in the Bluegrass, 'We're talking several mill right here.'

And so, once more, with the opening classics over on both sides of the Atlantic, the stallion men began to think carefully about the next bloodstock sales. There would be a slight variation at Keeneland because Nelson Bunker Hunt had now decided to sell his yearlings at his own private sale at Bluegrass Farm – thus saving the commission. Such was the strength of his broodmare band that he knew everyone would turn up on the Sunday afternoon, before the Select Sale began along the road.

He was right about that. Everyone did, and the bidding was fierce. Robert and his men had come specifically for a filly, a daughter of Goofed, dam of the ultra-fashionable Lyphard. The yearling was by the fast, resolute Bold Forbes, whom Arthur Hancock had snatched from under the noses of the big breeders after the colt had won the Kentucky Derby and the Belmont Stakes in 1976. Robert and John Magnier thought they might have to go to a half million dollars to buy her, but it was more expensive than that. Robert hauled up the white flag at $750,000, and the filly finally went for $800,000.

It was, if anything, an omen. With Bob Hope leading the cabaret at Tom Gentry's sales party, the Keeneland Sale began with a ferocity in the bidding which had never been seen before. And there were now *four* European camps all trying to do what Robert and his cohorts had been doing almost on their own for the past five years. They were all in search of the best. Representing Khalid Abdullah, the Saudi prince, was Humphrey Cottrill; representing Sheikh Mohammed's Aston Upthorpe Stud was Colonel Dick Warden, working as usual behind

enemy lines, along the barns; representing Stavros Niarchos was Sir
Philip Payne-Gallwey. In addition there was a new client of Cousin
Leslie's, Mrs Dolly Green, a daughter of Burton Green, whose Belridge
Oil Corporation had just been sold to Shell for more than three and a
half billion dollars. 'Christ!' said Robert. 'She's got more money than
all of us put together!'

The battle for a Lyphard colt, from Stylish Genie (a half-sister to
Artaius) was the highlight of the sale. Needless to say Vincent O'Brien
was determined to get him. So, unfortunately, was Sir Philip Payne-
Gallwey on behalf of the Greek ship-owner Niarchos. And they were
prepared to go very much higher than the Irishmen. The Sangster team
called it a day at $1,650,000. Sir Philip immediately bid $1·7 million
and the colt was his, for the highest amount of money ever paid for a
yearling.

Competition for a Northern Dancer colt out of Mr Prospector's dam
Gold Digger, by Nashua, was equally tough. Robert and his men were
still in there at $1,350,000 but they would go no higher, and Dolly
Green swooped with a bid of $1·4 million which got him. She swooped
four more times on that particular evening spending more than $2·2
million. Cousin Leslie had briefed her well. All five of her purchases
came from Spendthrift.

Two other yearlings fetched more than a million dollars at the sale
and Robert bought both of them, a full-brother to The Minstrel from
Windfields, which cost $1·25 million and a colt by Hoist the Flag out
of Princessnesian for $1,050,000. This was a tremendous producing
family, containing at least two Coolmore stallions, Home Guard and
Fordham, not to mention Robert's Ascot-winner Boone's Cabin. The
mare herself had won the Hollywood Gold Cup against the colts and
was a half-sister to Boldnesian, the grandsire of Seattle Slew. Vincent
swore her colt yearling by Hoist the Flag would run.

Altogether they bought thirteen yearlings for a total of $5,755,000.
Stavros Niarchos bought eight for a little over $4 million. Colonel War-
den had spent $2,425,000 on behalf of Sheik Mohammed, for eight
yearlings, including a Northern Dancer colt from Tappahannock.
Humphrey Cottrill spent $1·66 million on two colts and two fillies for
Prince Khalid. Forty-three per cent of all the money spent at Keeneland
came from outside North America. It totalled over $25 million, and $14
million of that was from Sangster, Niarchos, Mohammed and Khalid.
The average price for a Keeneland yearling was over $200,000 each,
as opposed to $53,000 in 1975 when Robert and his men made their

opening attack, an overall rise of four hundred per cent. That would be tantamount to a five-year New York Stock Market rise from 2600 points, which it hit in 1987, to 10,400 in 1992 (in fact, on Kentucky Derby day '92, it stood at around 3340, as a fair barometer of the general progress of the world economy over a normal five-year period).

Top among the consignors was the package of sixteen yearlings submitted by Warner L. Jones, of Hermitage Farm down at Goshen, along the route to Louisville. Now here was a real Kentucky 'hardboot'. In his prime he could drink more bourbon whiskey than most people and when riled threw a very fair right hook. His left wasn't too bad either. Warner had been in the horse business all of his life, made almost all of his own money, and now owned a lot of land. Warner counted up the dollars from Keeneland '80 and they came to $4,482,000, the second highest amount of money ever collected by one man at one sale. 'I'm pleased with everything,' he said. 'Matter of fact, if I wasn't "on the wagon" I might have just jumped into a tall glass of good bourbon.'

Warner was mainly delighted with the prices the fillies were fetching. His consignment had more of them than most of the other big farms and they all brought a lot of money, a trend which was reflected throughout the sale and which many breeders put down to the remarkable interest shown in the Derby victory of Genuine Risk. But the truth was that everyone wanted to get into the horse business and, whereas anyone could find a stallion to breed to, the acquisition of a racing filly who could run, and thus become a sought-after broodmare who might breed a champion, was considerably more tricky. The most expensive yearling from Warner's consignment was however a colt, and he really enjoyed selling this one, by the royally bred L'Enjoleur out of Native Street. A short while before the sale he had received a visit from Humphrey Cottrill who was prowling the Bluegrass on behalf of Prince Khalid. They walked down to the paddocks to see the yearlings and Humphrey immediately picked out the one by L'Enjoleur, a stallion who is himself by Buckpasser out of Franfreluche, the champion Canadian mare by Northern Dancer. That is a truly beautiful pedigree and the yearling reflected his sire's superlative looks. 'I do believe that is the nicest colt we have ever bred here,' said the master of Hermitage. And he really meant it.

Later, over dinner, they began to talk about golf and Humphrey told Warner how much he loved to play when he had time. Warner refilled the Englishman's glass, slipped out of the room and phoned his local pro, the tournament player Frank Beard. He ordered a brand new set of his finest clubs and told Frank, 'Get 'em up to the farm real quick and put 'em in the trunk of the blue hire car outside my front door.' Humphrey never even discovered them until late that evening and he nearly died of happiness when he did. A week or so later, at the Tuesday night session, they led in hip number 275, the colt by L'Enjoleur, and Warner watched with interest as the big guns of the sale ring went into action. At the end there was a sudden final bid of $850,000. The hammer crashed down. The winning bid was from Mr Humphrey Cottrill. Warner grinned the grin of the master salesman.

His was not the only grin. Cousin Leslie sold eighteen for $4,379,000. Seth Hancock sold fourteen for $3,384,000. Windfields sold ten for $3,302,000. And in fifth place was a rather surprising name. It was that of North Ridge Farm, owned by Mr and Mrs Franklin Groves, Cousin Leslie's new buyers back in 1975, when the world was young, and their bid of $715,000 had set a world record, for a full-brother to Majestic Prince. Since then their involvement in the bloodstock business had mushroomed. Now they had a huge new farm called North Ridge and here they were sending up twelve yearlings to Keeneland which had sold for $2.7 million.

Cousin Leslie's only complaint was that he thought his Northern Dancer–Gold Digger colt might have fetched $2 million, and Mrs Green 'had been pretty lucky to get him for just $1.4 million'. But he was not too put out by that, on account of there was a nice chestnut colt by Exclusive Native out of a winning Canadian daughter of Nijinsky II he was taking to the sale at Saratoga. Robert and his men did not attend this sale. Nor was Humphrey Cottrill in evidence. Nor Colonel Warden. They missed one of the great sights in all of the thoroughbred industry – Cousin Leslie trying to wring the last dollar out of horse he is selling.

Certainly he had primed two major buyers about the running potential of this colt. Louis Wolfson, who had raced Raise a Native and Exclusive Native, and indeed Affirmed, three generations, really wanted this yearling, since he looked very like his 1978 Triple Crown winner. On the other hand, so did Mr Aaron U. Jones, the Oregon lumberman, who had just raced and syndicated another chestnut son of Exclusive Native named Valdez. This colt had won $500,000 and his syndication price in this heady market was a staggering $8 million. He had won in California, but on the east coast, where it counts just about treble the importance, he had won a couple of handicaps at the Meadowlands track and now they thought he was worth nearly as much as The Minstrel. But in this present climate, very nearly anything goes, especially money, and

Mr Jones thought the new Exclusive Native colt looked very like Valdez and he was determined to buy him.

The bidding opened at $50,000 and two calls of $25,000 took it to $100,000. Then Lou Wolfson's trainer Laz Barrera bid $200,000. Aaron Jones said, '$300,000.' This went on all the way to $900,000 when the man from Oregon hesitated for the first time. The auctioneer Laddie Dance waited for a few seconds, and then he said, 'Well, are y'all through? . . . Then I'm going to have to sell him . . .'

But a new figure now entered the fray. Leslie Combs rose from his seat in the third row and told the auctioneer he thought he should give both the contestants a little more time.

'If I listened to you, Mr Combs,' said Laddie, 'I guess we'd be here all night. Now . . . and who'll gimme a million for him? Will ya gimme a million for him? Will ya gimme a million?'

Laz Barrera grinned and nodded. Aaron Jones said, '$1·1 million.' Barrera nodded at $1·2. Aaron said, '$1·3.' '$1·4,' said Laz. '$1·5,' said Aaron. Barrera immediately bid $1·6 million for the son of Exclusive Native.

Laddie Dance pleaded for the $1·7 million which would equal the record set at Keeneland. The man from Oregon responded but slowly. He raised his hand into the air, and turned his thumb to aim at the floor. It was over. Lou Wolfson had him. For double the price ever paid for a Saratoga yearling.

Perhaps the record might have gone if the big European legions had been in evidence, but no one need have worried about the future of the bloodstock-selling industry in the USA. This summer there had been a major development on the other side of the world, to be precise in the kingdom of Dubai, about fifty miles south-east of the port. For several weeks the sand had been turning blacker and slimier around the big ARCO drilling rig which was grinding its way deep into the floor of the desert. Men sweated and cursed in the terrible heat as they listened to the encouraging reports of the geologists. Everyone knew a strike was close. And one August day, in a temperature of nearly 125°F, they hit, a black gusher bursting out of the ground. It was the moment they had been awaiting for four years.

Sheikh Rashid had always been pretty rich. Now he was to become unbelievably rich. And so of course were his sons. Upon hearing the news of their forthcoming great wealth, the light of battle gleamed in the deep, dark eyes of Sheikh Mohammed. For within the soul of every Bedouin there is an unspoken whisper, that he must conquer. For the great Arabian chiefs, like Ibn Saud and Sheikh Rashid, the joy of conquest came in battle. For most Bedouins it was merely the joy of conquering their environment, in the pleasure of knowing that no other breed of man could possibly survive it. These robed nomads could beat the desert and the steel of their being was irrevocably bound in that self-awareness. No Bedouin will easily give best in any confrontation because his soul will not permit it. Sheikh Mohammed bin Rashid al-Maktoum was born of the desert. It has always summoned him back to its burning heart, to hunt with his falcons, to sit beneath its stars, to talk and to listen, in one of the earth's most silent places.

The spell of that wilderness was upon Sheikh Mohammed from the moment he rode his first camel as a boy. And it was the Bedouin's spell, the ancient creed of victory or death. The young Sheikh's battleground would become the bloodstock sales arenas and the great racetracks of Europe and America. Here he would buy and race the thoroughbred horse, the breed which had, after all, emanated from his own desert two centuries ago. And nothing, after 1980, in the world of horseracing, would ever be the same.

9

'Would You Sell Him
for $30 Million?'

On 5 October 1980 Robert Sangster's famous green and blue silks
were carried to victory yet again before a thunderous Parisian crowd in
the Prix de l'Arc de Triomphe. A dark, elegant filly with the most
beautiful 'dished' white face, she was named Detroit and she had run
clean away from the best horses in Europe, including the English champion Ela Mana Mou and the previous year's winner Three Troikas.
Second in the race was the French-trained Argument who would go
on to win the Washington International in five weeks' time. This was a
superlative performance from a brilliant filly and there was a look of
sheer rapture upon the face of Susan Sangster as she rushed to lead
the filly into the winners' enclosure – an awkward and slightly embarrassing chore which most senior owners, including Robert, visibly shrink
from, but which the former Susan Peacock seemed to view as her
God-given duty on a race-by-race basis.

It had been, no doubt, a wonderful run, and if Detroit could ever
produce such breathtaking speed again she would doubtless win for
Robert another $200,000 in prize money. The irony was that if she had
been a colt, she would now be worth possibly $9 million. Her owner
looked rather thoughtful in the enclosure, at once delighted but, in a
sense, deprived. Questioned by the press, he said, absent-mindedly, 'I
wish she had been a colt.' In those seven words were encapsulated all
of the worries that were disturbing the sleep of every one of Sangster's
men as 1980 drew to its close. Not that this put any kind of a damper
on the celebration that evening in the elegant old Hotel George Cinq
in Paris, but there were worries, serious worries, policy worries, and the
victory of this French filly had heightened them. She had been bought
privately by Robert as a foal, and stayed in France to be trained by
Oliver Douieb.

The following morning Robert and his entourage resembled, in spirit, a group of stragglers from Napoleon's army on its way home from Moscow. Robert himself had felt worse, but not, he disclosed, 'in living memory'. They were attempting to regroup on this bright Monday morning on the Champs Elysées. Robert was trying to organize a luncheon, trying to remember who had already been invited the night before, trying to draw up a list of those who ought to be invited this morning and trying to forget those who did not need invitations because they would show up anyway. In the middle of this, David O'Brien, Vincent's son, who was just embarking on his own training career, next door to his father, arrived from Ireland to go to the Goffs Paris Sale that afternoon. He was planning to buy a horse for Robert which he had picked out in a paddock several weeks before at the Moyglare Stud, in Kildare. Robert's great Irish confidant, PP Hogan, was threatening to go with him. 'The hell with the sale,' said Robert. 'Who needs more horses? I've got 'em all over the place. Let's just have lunch.'

David, who had not done an international head-count recently on Robert's horses (if he had he would have discovered two hundred and seventy-nine of them in training, owned either entirely or in partnership with thirty-six trainers in six different countries), was, however, insistent. 'This is a damned nice horse,' said the young O'Brien. 'I really like him and I don't think he'll fetch much. I think Pat and I ought to go and see him.'

Robert, his competitive fires slightly dimmed by the night's festivities, gave in. 'Oh, well, go then. Clear off to the sales. Abandon me, see if I care. And don't go above fifty thousand quid for that bloody horse, whoever he is, or I won't pay. And don't be late at the airport. Five o'clock sharp, or I'll go home without you.'

The lunch party, somehow, gathered and went ahead. David bought the colt, a nice bay, with a white blaze and three white feet, by Be My Guest from a mare named Irish Bird. They all fought their way to the airport on time and Robert was delighted that the young Irishman had paid only £16,000 at the sale. He absolutely knew the horse was special, because PP confirmed young David's opinion. PP rarely made those kind of mistakes. Indeed PP had found and bought Detroit for him. Now Robert could tell he was very excited about this new purchase and with an utterly characteristic burst of goodwill he *gave* each of them ten per cent of the colt. Thus are millionaires created. Thus are champions acquired – with salutations such as 'Go on, then, clear off . . . see if I care'.

Back in the Isle of Man Robert had much to ponder, because several rather inescapable facts were becoming clear. The first was that this was the lowest point they had ever reached. He and his men had, since 1975, spent something in excess of $40 million in their quest to buy, create and stand at Coolmore American-bred stallions, of the Northern Dancer line. In this they had failed, if not catastrophically, then certainly resoundingly. They had found only one championship-class runner of Northern Dancer's blood, in six years, and they had been forced to sell half of him to Windfields Farm to recoup some cash. They had missed Alleged as a yearling, picked him up inexpensively as a two-year-old and been forced to take a $16 million profit on him, after his two victories in the Arc, by selling him back to Kentucky. Hence, a top-class colt *must* win either the Derby, the King George VI or the Arc in order to be worth a multi-million-dollar price. In an age of milers and mile-and-a-quarter specialists, the financial clout of the runner who could go twelve furlongs remained unchallenged. *All* of the great ones on both sides of the Atlantic who had commanded massive syndication prices had gone the mile and a half in a classic or a championship – Nijinsky, Secretariat, Seattle Slew, The Minstrel, Affirmed and Alleged. The other thing they had in common was that they were *all* in America. Coolmore Stud in Tipperary had reaped scarcely any benefit whatsoever from the highly publicized efforts of Vincent, Robert and John Magnier. The place was stacked with the blood of the Argentinian Forli. There was Fordham, Gay Fandango, Home Guard, the incoming Last Fandango and Thatch, every one of them not much better than average.

As far as Northern Dancer was concerned there was the failed three-year-old Try My Best with whom there were fertility problems. There was Be My Guest, whom they had had to buy from Mrs Manning after a racing career in which he just got up by a short head to win the Group III Waterford Crystal Mile at Goodwood. There was Northfields, an American runner they had bought from Sean Collins's Corbally Stud in County Kildare. There was London Bells, a big Nijinsky horse of Robert's, who never won a top race and had a diabolical temperament. There was Hello Gorgeous, a fractious Mr Prospector colt who had been bought after his racing career; and there were the sprinters Godswalk and Thatching. Where were the great Northern Dancer runners and stallions they had set out to find with such optimism six long years ago? Well, one of them, Nureyev, was on his way to Walmac-Wanerton International in Kentucky, which was especially dreary since Vincent O'Brien had always sworn by his 'bottom line' – he was out of the Forli mare Special. The rest were all over the place, but they were not at Coolmore.

The truth was, the surging market in thoroughbred horseflesh was the principal factor keeping the operation prosperous. Yearling prices were driving up stallion prices, which were driving up broodmare prices. The second critical factor in the equation was that prize money in the United States was superior to that in England and Ireland. Thus a good racehorse was, by mathematical definition, more valuable standing at JFK International Airport, New York, than he had been nine hours before at Heathrow or Shannon. And that is how Vincent had kept everyone in such good shape financially. There were several decent runners which he had trained perfectly and which had fallen just short of the high pinnacles he had selected for them. These he then sold for excellent money to the States. They were never going to be quite good enough to make stallions in Ireland, but they were often good enough to win three or four races in the USA, some worth $100,000, before going off to stand as stallions somewhere in that vast country. These kind of beautifully bred American horses, which had just missed Vincent's highest standards, were eagerly sought after by the American agents. There were indeed some American agents who had based their entire businesses on buying high-quality 'cast-offs' from Vincent O'Brien, and occasionally from other English and Irish trainers who had such runners for sale.

Even with the huge amount of money Sangster's men had spent, no one was much out of pocket so far. But Vincent's three-year-olds of 1980 were disappointing by his standards and, in the days following the Arc de Triomphe, there were facts to be faced. The first was that 1978, 1979 and 1980 had lacked a new American mile-and-a-half star at Ballydoyle. Indeed there had not been an American-bred winner of the English Derby since 1977, and nor would there be one in 1981. The second home-truth was that pure-bred milers and sprinters do not show a huge syndication profit. Nor do two-year-old champions which fail to 'train on' and win a classic. All of this now put immeasurable pressure on Vincent. He knew, better than any of them, the magnitude of his task. If they went four years without a major middle-distance champion, the financial hole might just be too big to escape. They were spending at such a rate, $10 and $11 million a year, on yearlings and now they had reached the point where that big syndication was becoming ever more crucial to survival. Vincent smiled his soft smile and nodded wisely, but behind his gently spoken words he had many concerns, and they were all unsaid, some of them not even to himself. 'What if I should miss something?' 'What if I should misjudge a horse, ask too much of him?' 'What if I should mistake fear for bloody-mindedness – or a tiny injury for cowardice?' 'My God, what if I should let everyone down?' These were the subconscious thoughts of the master-trainer and they were never far away. And every day, often on the very edge of his own nerves, he grappled with the fragile psyches of forty young racehorses. And he tried, as ever, to miss nothing.

The weekend after the Arc, they gathered in Tipperary for a council of war. Late on the Saturday night they sat in the big drawing room at Coolmore to assess the situation at the stud and to listen to Vincent's quiet observations of encouragement. They all knew they had not yet achieved their target – of buying a yearling to turn into a great Coolmore sire – and they all knew that the pressure to sell back to America, once they had landed one, would be enormous.

The one with most to lose was of course Robert and, in fairness to him, he never lost his nerve in this, the most nerve-racking of all business ventures. He believed profoundly that Vincent was the best. He had never changed his opinion about the brilliance of John Magnier, and he had faith in their system – that if the 'magic Irishmen' continued to make their selections carefully, looking *only* at the great pedigrees, then Vincent must, by all the laws of the universe, train in the very near future a new Nijinsky. They had, after all, been very close on about a dozen occasions, with horses just a stride or two short of the top of the mountain. And they had amassed some superb fillies. They had breeding rights to The Minstrel, to Northern Dancer, to Alleged, to Artaius, and they had access to the lightning-fast blood of Godswalk and Thatching. In Robert's view, all they needed was a touch of luck and they would come out on top, smelling like the Garden of Eden in the spring.

The trouble was they could scarcely afford a fourth season without a new star. Somewhere back at Ballydoyle there had to be a champion, worth millions and millions. Somewhere on this cool autumn night with the leaves turning to gold all over the Vale of Tipperary, there had to be an answer. Robert knew they were due for a 'big horse' – so did John. Vincent knew he had colts of the highest quality preparing to run. What none of them knew, as they conferred on this somewhat unfestive night, was that seven miles away at Ballydoyle, across the moonlit fields, asleep in their warm boxes, were *four* colts whose inestimable brilliance would net them, in the fullness of time, something close to *$84 million*.

Their little post-mortem did not last for long, however, because all three of them possessed the natural soaring spirit of the born optimist. Actually, anyone at the high end of this game needs that quality because the alternative to massive success is, quite frequently, ruin. These three, however, even in a world where steel nerves are commonplace, were pretty special. They had now fought a hundred battles together and each trusted the other. And soon the gloomy thoughts of impending failure were cast from their minds as John refilled their glasses and they waited for Vincent to expound a little more on the two-year-old he thought might be a champion.

This was the colt by Northern Dancer out of the Windfields mare South Ocean, which they had bought for a million dollars at Keeneland the previous year. South Ocean was a very tough mare. She had won the Canadian Oaks (beating Franfreluche) and she was the dam of Northernette, the Canadian champion filly who had not only won thirteen races, she had journeyed south into America at the age of four and paralysed the field in the Grade I Top Flight Handicap at Aqueduct, New York. This was the kind of pedigree John Magnier loved – because it contained recent, tough, hard runners who had stood the test of fire in New York. The new colt was named Storm Bird and he was completely different from The Minstrel, with none of the obvious small characteristics of Northern Dancer. This one was a tall, deep bay like Nijinsky, with a classical head, a slim white blaze, and two white socks on his near side. He had the boldest eye and, better yet, he had won four races in Ireland. Like Nijinsky eleven years before, he had won the Erne Maiden Plate first time out and then won the Anglesey Stakes. Like The Minstrel and Try My Best he had also won the Larkspur, and like all of them, Vincent was preparing him to make the journey to Newmarket for the Dewhurst Stakes, the two-year-old championship which had sent Nijinsky and The Minstrel on their way to the sound of trumpets, but had sent Try My Best and Monteverdi away, to total obscurity.

An added worry was that, unlike all of the previous four, Storm Bird was to face a *real* racehorse, a big, dark, hard runner from Guy Harwood's Sussex stable, whom the trainer thought was the best juvenile in Europe. His name was To-Agori-Mou. After losing his maiden race by three-quarters of a length at Newmarket, this grand-looking individual had won three off the reel, including the Solario Stakes at Sandown by two lengths. The questions were: had Northern Dancer bequeathed to the son of South Ocean his own tigerish heart, which had got him home in the 1964 Kentucky Derby by a neck, in record time? Would the unbeaten Storm Bird slog it out all the way to the line, like Nijinsky and The Minstrel, and indeed his sister Northernette? Or would he fold under the pressure, decline the battle, once he looked into the deep, warlike eye of To-Agori-Mou? Victory would mean a value of perhaps $6 million for Storm Bird, and Vincent said quietly, 'He'll fight for it.'

And so once more to Newmarket. Friday afternoon, 17 October, fourth race, £36,676 to the winner. The rain had cleared up, but the official going was 'soft'. Five horses were entered for this year's Dewhurst Stakes and they could all run. In addition to To-Agori, there was a French raider, Miswaki, an expensive son of Mr Prospector who had already won the Group I Prix de la Salamandre. There was Kirtling who would show as one of the best ten-furlong horses in England in 1981, and there was a highly promising full-brother to the 1975 English Derby winner Grundy, named Centurius. Storm Bird would be ridden by Vincent's brilliant new contract jockey Pat Eddery, another Irishman of the blood, whose family he had known for three generations. It was impossible not to look with some awe at the strapping figure of To-Agori as he swaggered around the paddock in front of the more relaxed, elegant-looking challenger from Ballydoyle. The big crowd however knew who usually won this race and they sent Vincent's million-dollar colt away as odds-on favourite with To-Agori 4–1 against.

Halfway down this straight seven furlongs, the little field was still tightly bunched and the pace was hot as they pounded over the soft, holding ground. Storm Bird, galloping easily on the outside, just held the lead as they raced up the hill towards the Bushes, that mysterious windswept clump which has stood as an eerie little landmark for battling racehorses for three hundred years. But now the heat was really on for the handsome raider from Ballydoyle and, as they raced down into the Dip, To-Agori-Mou, the toughest young horse in England, came at him, the aggressive Greville Starkey driving him almost level. Storm Bird answered the challenge instinctively and in a split second the two colts came bursting away from the other three – Centurius found it just too much, Kirtling tired badly on the soft ground and Miswaki, still game, but a picture of dejection, found nothing beneath Lester Piggott's whip.

Six lengths clear the two leaders raced and now there was nothing in it. Both colts were giving it everything and back in the stand Vincent, Robert and John gripped their binoculars with milk-white knuckles. You could have heard the roar of the crowd in Newmarket High Street a mile and a half away as Storm Bird and To-Agori hit the rising ground three hundred yards from home, travelling absolutely flat out. Starkey drew his whip first and the English horse was matching strides as they fought their way up the hill, their breath now coming in short, angry bursts, with wet clods of mud flying back from their hooves, each jockey now with his foot flat to the boards.

Now Eddery went to the whip and he cracked the son of Northern Dancer three times. This was the moment of truth and back in the stands Vincent visibly flinched as Eddery laid into the horse. But Storm Bird responded valiantly. He lowered his head and he laid back his ears and he raced with every last ounce of strength he had. The pace over this ground was killing for both of them, but with one hundred yards to go the Irish horse had clawed back that half-length lead. Starkey again whacked To-Agori, hard, right-handed, but his horse had nothing more to give. And Storm Bird, with the light of victory in his eye, flashed across the line, with the green and blue colours of Robert Sangster still a half length in front.

That may have been the best performance seen in the Dewhurst Stakes since the great Crepello beat Her Majesty's Doutelle, three-quarters of a length, in 1956. Storm Bird was the champion of Europe, no doubt of that. So, you might say, had been Try My Best and Monteverdi after their Dewhurst victories, but racing men know instinctively. This had been a battle between two major gladiators, a monstrous struggle over testing conditions. Storm Bird was very tired and the gallant To-Agori, his flanks heaving, was also trembling slightly, the sure mark of a colt who has given his all.

Storm Bird flew home to Tipperary immediately in a small private freighter (Vincent hated his horses to drink anything but water which had been distilled through the soft limestone springs of the Golden Vale). The racing world awaited their next battle, clearly to be the 2000 Guineas, in April, over the same ground, but one furlong longer. But, alas, this would never take place. On one dark winter night, a disgruntled stable lad, fired from Ballydoyle, crept back into the yard, found the peerless Storm Bird and hacked off his mane and most of his tail. It was a truly terrible thing to have done to any horse, never mind the Warrior Prince of Newmarket Heath. The trauma shook Storm Bird badly and he was very down in the dumps for a few weeks. He lost his sparkle on the gallops and then he contracted a virus, which caused him to be withdrawn from both the English and Irish 2000 Guineas.

In a way the attack on the horse had finished him. He was 'wrong' all summer. Vincent tried hard to bring him back, attempting every trick he knew to rekindle Storm Bird's interest in racing. But the delicate mental system of the great thoroughbred still holds untold mysteries, and Storm Bird's was badly hurt. He ran only once more, very moderately in France, and was retired. Meanwhile To-Agori-Mou came out and stamped a golden seal on that Dewhurst battle when he won the English 2000 Guineas. Then he lost the Irish 2000 by a neck, but won the St James's Palace Stakes, the Waterford Crystal Mile, and the Queen Elizabeth II Stakes at Ascot. He lost the Sussex Stakes by a head. He was a lion of a racehorse, very fast and a ferocious competitor, but on the only occasion they ever met, Storm Bird had outgunned him for speed and matched him for bravery.

This brings us back to the July sales at Keeneland, where the big players were once more gathered in full fighting force, booted and spurred for the ensuing jousts in the sales ring. The entire place was just about unrecognizable from the busy but genteel little arena it had been back in 1975. Now the atmosphere more resembled that of a world heavyweight championship fight. The atmosphere was electric as the Europeans patrolled the barns. Guards were on duty outside the boxes that held the precious consignment of Windfields Farm – five colts by Northern Dancer, the most important two being the one from South Ocean, Storm Bird's brother; and the one from Sweet Alliance, the beautifully bred winner of the Kentucky Oaks and a daughter herself of Sir Ivor and Mrs Peterkin. North Ridge Farm too had a very well-bred colt by Northern Dancer from Bernie Bird, dam of the 1977 Marlboro Cup winner, Proud Birdie. When Mr and Mrs Groves's mare had been bred to Northern Dancer for this 1979 mating, he had 'stood' for $125,000. Today his price was $250,000 (no guaranteed foal), and rising. All over Kentucky stallion prices were going berserk. A share in Nijinsky II had fetched $1 million. A share in The Minstrel had traded for $1 million. Nominations to Nijinsky were heading towards $200,000, no guarantee.

And all this inflation had occurred before any serious involvement by Sheikh Rashid's three sons, Maktoum, Hamdan and Mohammed. This year, at the 1981 Keeneland Select Sale, all the big battalions were in place. Parked out on the runway of Bluegrass Field stood the Boeing 727 of the United Arab Emirates, property of Sheikh Rashid al-Maktoum. Its passengers, the three brothers and their entourage, were extremely important and many people were talking about them, and what they would do in the ring. But it was the three sons of Northern Dancer who attracted most attention.

The first of them entered the ring on the opening Monday night sale and Robert knew that Sheikh Mohammed would go after him. In his heart Robert felt, irrationally he knew, slightly aggrieved, for surely the colt out of South Ocean belonged to them, after all of Vincent's brilliance with Storm Bird. But that sales arena can be a harsh and unforgiving place and sure enough Colonel Warden, bidding on behalf of Sheikh Mohammed, was in from the start in an attempt to land Storm Bird's brother. The old world-record yearling price of $1·7 million was obliterated without even a mention as Warden locked horns with Tom Cooper.

Colonel Warden nodded at $2 million. Tom came back matching them bid for bid to $2·9 million. The Arabs caucused. Sheikh Mohammed nodded and Colonel Dick bid $3 million dollars for this son of Northern Dancer. The crowd gasped. No one had ever seen anything like this. Tom Cooper turned to Vincent, who whispered something back and then the Irishman bid $3·1 million. 'Three two,' said Colonel Warden. 'Will ya go three three?' called the auctioneer. Tom Cooper nodded. And again the Arabs caucused. The auctioneer called: 'Have y'all done with him?' And then Dick Warden bid $3·4 million for the colt.

Immediately Tom hit back and confirmed his Irish clients would pay $3·5 million for Storm Bird's brother – more than double the amount ever paid for any yearling in history. And the men from the Gulf finally retreated. Colonel Warden turned away, Sheikh Mohammed, seething, spoke quietly to his men. Robert showed the first signs of strain anyone could ever remember from him at such moments. Instead of his usual cheerful responses to journalists, he snapped without a smile: 'When we come to buy, we buy.'

Sheikh Mohammed, however, was not to be humiliated a second time. When the Northern Dancer–Mrs Peterkin colt came in, a rather cheeky, cocky little bay horse, with an inquisitive eye, Sheikh Mohammed ordered Colonel Warden to buy, no matter what. And the royal family of Dubai saw off the immensely rich Texan Will Farrish III at $3·3 million. The last of the Big Three, the one from Bernie Bird, went for $2·95 million to Stavros Niarchos, spending in advance some of the riches he would surely gain from the stud career of Nureyev. Between them, Northern Dancer's three sons had brought a new dimension to the word inflation. They had fetched a total of $9,750,000 and the $3·5 million Robert had paid was over a million dollars more than Northern Dancer himself had cost when he was syndicated in 1970.

During the course of this year his twelve yearlings would bring $14,385,000, an average of $1,198,750. At Keeneland alone Windfields collected over $10 million for twelve yearlings. The average for the sale rocketed to $240,000 each, up another twenty per cent.

The Ballydoyle syndicate, having spent $9 million on their usual haul of summer-sale yearlings, retired to the Hyatt, battered but uncrushed by their wars with the men from Dubai. But on their way to the elevators, an old friend from Limerick made a somewhat spectacular reappearance in their lives. His name was George Harris, the tall, elegantly dressed nephew of Lieutenant-General Sir Ian Harris, owner of the Ballykisteen Stud, former Commander of the Royal Ulster Rifles (North West Frontier of India and all that). George was a lifelong breeding-farm horseman. In addition to the old family stud at Ballykisteen, his father Percy Harris owned the Athassel House Stud and George was born in the Golden Vale of Tipperary on Christmas Day 1942. Everyone knew that unusual fact about him, and everyone also knew that he was one of the smartest money-men in the industry. He took a Bachelor of Arts degree in economics and a Bachelor of Science degree in agriculture at Trinity College, Dublin, before managing various stud farms in Ireland, in California (for Hastings Harcourt of Harcourt Brace Jovanovich, the publishers) and in Maryland.

By 1981 he had become the first thoroughbred-racing stockbroker. He had an office on the fifteenth floor of a 54th Street high-rise off Lexington Avenue, New York, and there he traded stallion shares, nominations, broodmares and syndications. He knew more about finances at the highest level of the bloodstock industry than almost anyone in the country. Certainly more than anyone in England or Ireland. When George, with all of his native charm and eloquence, started to talk money, that was basically the time to sit bolt upright and pay attention. Right now, in the bar of the Hyatt Hotel, Lexington, Kentucky, George Harris was talking money. Major money. And Robert Sangster was listening very carefully.

'Robert, now let me ask you a question. Would you ever consider an offer for Storm Bird?'

Robert grinned. 'We might, but it would have to be realistic. If the price was somewhere near agreeable, I don't think you would find me terribly difficult to deal with. But you'd be talking something well in excess of $15 million.'

George nodded. Just then John Magnier and Phonsie entered the bar to join Robert. George, who had known both of them all of his life, said, 'Hello, boys,' and then returned to his table on the other side of the room, leaving Robert to confer with his men.

This was a matter of the utmost seriousness. Because George Harris advised two of the biggest hitters in the game – Hilary J. Boone Jr, owner of the impressive Wimbledon Farm out on Walnut Tree Pike, and Mr Robert Hefner, the Oklahoma oil man who had made a huge fortune in the 1970s by drilling extremely deep and then finding a huge demand for his product during America's problems with the Middle East. Robert Hefner, in partnership with one of the best judges of bloodstock in central Kentucky, Dr Bill Lockeridge, owned the magnificent Ashford Stud. They had already bought the winner of this year's French 2000 Guineas, Recitation. And in the last couple of days they had been turned down, with an offer of $28 million, for the Aga Khan's sensational 1981 star Shergar, winner already of the English and Irish Derbys in not much more than a common canter.

Robert imparted the news that they were interested in Storm Bird and John ran the figures through his mind very quickly. He had little time because George popped over again, just before leaving, and said to him quietly, 'John, would you give me your valuation on him?'

The master of Coolmore mused for a bit and then he said: 'Well, To-Agori-Mou has made him look pretty special, wouldn't you think? Even Kirtling who was nine lengths back in that race has won the Dee Stakes at Chester.'

'That's more or less the reason we're having this little chat,' said George, smoothly, but with a smile.

'Well now, George, you're asking me something now. And I wouldn't want to value him off the top of my head, if you know what I mean.'

George knew precisely what he meant: that he was about to value the horse right off the top of his head.

'Well,' said John, 'I'd say he wouldn't be worth a penny less than $20 million, not with his pedigree and his proven ability. Jesus, his unraced brother fetched three and a half last night.'

George said softly, 'John, I think we might be able to do a bit of business here. Will you arrange a meeting? I'd say the sooner the better. Like in the next hour. Will you call me in my room?'

John hit the elevator button as if it was an ejector seat. And twenty-five seconds later he and Robert and Phonsie were searching for Vincent, who had gone shopping. Phonsie rushed out to round him up and they gathered in Robert's suite. There the trainer heard the news that it was entirely possible that they were going to receive a gigantic offer for Storm Bird to stand as a stallion at Ashford Stud, Lexington.

'What did give them as a guide price?' asked Vincent. 'Ten million?'

'Twenty,' said John.

'Mother of Mary!' replied Vincent.

'In this market they'll end up standing him for $150,000. That's where The Minstrel's going this season, and this horse is better looking and, if anything, better bred.'

'Yes,' said Robert, 'but The Minstrel won the three biggest Group I summer races in Europe.'

'I know,' said John, 'but he never beat a horse like To-Agori-Mou. Neither did Nijinsky, for that matter. That Dewhurst set Storm Bird apart, you can trust me on that. I know his value. I want him for Coolmore and if someone thinks they are going to get him away from us, it's going to be one of the most expensive sales in history.'

Robert ordered three bottles of Dom Perignon champagne. John called George who insisted that the meeting take place only with all three of the principal owners in the room. He would not deal if there was a possibility of an agreement being scuppered because either Vincent or Robert was not there and might then object later. John understood George's innocent-sounding but shrewd request. He chortled to himself, and then said to Robert, 'Don't worry about their problems. They'll spread the nomination price out over five years and market him for $750,000 a share which will give them a take of $30 million. Leave this to me.'

George, Bill Lockeridge and Robert Hefner arrived. The oil man immediately took a seat with his back to the setting sun, the old poker-player's trick which makes it hard for your opponents to see your face in the glaring light. Then he said calmly, 'George tells me you might consider selling Storm Bird for around $20 million.'

But he knew not with whom he was playing poker. '*Sell him?*' said John incredulously. 'Oh no, I said nothing about selling him. I only said where I valued him. And $20 million is what I think he's worth. To us. Selling him would be entirely a different sort of a matter.'

George Harris rolled his eyes heavenwards, suppressing a chuckle. There was no end to Magnier's sheer iron nerve. For all he knew, Robert Hefner would get up and say, 'Thank you very much, a mere misunderstanding,' and leave.

But he did not do so. As John Magnier knew he would not. Instead he said, 'Well, let me ask you this. Would you sell him for $30 million?'

'I would.'

George Harris spoke for the first time. 'Well, if you'd sell him for thirty you'd probably sell him for twenty-eight?'

'Well, I'd have to have a little private chat with my partners about that,' replied John, and he signalled them to leave the room with him for a few minutes.

Robert recalls the moment. The three of them stood outside, not quite knowing whether to laugh or cry. They had set their hearts on standing Storm Bird at Coolmore, but everything has its price in this business. Robert remembers Vincent, a huge smile on his face, suddenly breaking into a little Irish jig, kicking up and clicking his heels together, with two sharp snaps. And then he put on his normal thoughtful face and they returned, deadly serious now, to the main room. They sold Storm Bird to Mr Robert Hefner for the biggest sum of money ever asked for a thoroughbred stallion: $28 million. Neither Robert Hefner, nor Bill Lockeridge, nor George Harris had ever laid eyes on the horse.

The terms of the sale took several days of negotiation. They were concluded in Ireland, during a flying visit by Dr Lockeridge and George. Mr Hefner suggested a four-year pay-out. John insisted on three. John also wanted an option to hang on to ten shares, so profound was his belief in the future of this stallion. He also insisted on a very tough penalty clause – that if, after the first $7 million payment, Mr Hefner should subsequently default, he would still owe them the money on that payment, but the stallion would then be returned to the ownership of the original partners with the final payment waived. In short, if Robert Hefner failed to meet his obligations under the terms of the sale, he would lose Storm Bird, plus $14 million.

John Magnier's position was simple. The most critical years of a stallion's life are often his first two and his future is dependent upon the quality of the mares he receives. 'If you are going to take that out of my control,' he said, 'and then let me down over the money with which we have been compensated, then we will expect the highest form of reparations. We want the horse back, plus, in time, the money you owe on the second payment. The same also applies should there be a default on the third payment.' Since there was no question anyway of a default, Robert Hefner agreed the terms. He also agreed that Vincent should try to bring Storm Bird back to race in the autumn; but win, lose or draw, the stallion would cover his first book of mares in the winter of 1982 at the palatial new Ashford Stud out at Versailles (pronounced locally Ver-sales) to the west of Lexington.

The tense and legally complicated transaction completed, Robert and the Irishmen prepared to face a different kind of heat on the racetracks of England and Ireland where the world market was being intensely shaken up. As soon as they returned, Shergar set the seal on his summer by winning the King George VI and Queen Elizabeth Stakes at Ascot, thus winning him the same Triple Crown as Nijinsky and The Minstrel. John Magnier immediately wanted to launch a new attempt to buy the horse from the Aga Khan for Coolmore, but so did everyone else, and in the end the Aga insisted on keeping him for his own Irish stud at Ballymany, on the Curragh, with a syndication value of around $18 million.

Four days after the King George VI John and Robert went south to Goodwood to see the culmination of a saga which had been going on all season. It involved the mighty To-Agori-Mou and a bold-looking son of Nijinsky named Kings Lake. He was out of Fish Bar, the dam of the flying filly Cloonlara, and he was trained by Vincent for Robert and his men in the colours of one of the partners, Madame J. P. Binet of France. Kings Lake had gone through two races against Guy Harwood's champion which would have levelled a less resilient colt. The first came in the Irish 2000 Guineas, when, after a desperate struggle through the last quarter mile, Kings Lake got home by a neck. But the Stewards disqualified him for crashing into To-Agori two furlongs out. The whole of Southern Ireland was stunned. An Irish horse, trained by an Irishman, ridden by a Irishman, disqualified from an Irish classic in favour of the English! Never mind the rights and wrongs, this was terrible. Actually, the right and wrongs were a bit confusing and in the end the Irish Jockey Club reinstated Kings Lake, and there was a collective howl of protest from the English.

At Royal Ascot in June the two of them had clashed again in the St James's Palace Stakes and there was another barnstorming battle up the straight with To-Agori getting home by a neck. The winning jockey Greville Starkey, perhaps inspired by the roar of applause from the top-hatted English crowd, offered a slightly inelegant little signal to Pat Eddery as they thundered across the line and was given a dressing-down by the Stewards for vulgarity right in front of Prince Charles's young wife-to-be.

Now they were to meet for a third time, in the Sussex Stakes over one mile at Goodwood, and the huge English crowd was out in force to cheer home their undoubted champion. Up in the stand the Irishmen seemed to gather together in little cliques in the face of the massed superiority of the supporters of To-Agori-Mou. Kings Lake was not as big as Harwood's horse, nor was he as imposing, but this son of Nijinsky was a real scrapper and he had a heart like Brian Boru. He might be beaten, but he would never give in. It would not be too rash an assumption to suggest that every Irishman between the River Shannon and Chichester Cathedral had backed Kings Lake fearlessly. At least every Irishman with a romantic soul and an interest in racehorses, had – which includes just about everyone.

For Robert and his men this was a very serious matter. To-Agori-Mou had already 'made' Storm Bird and, if Kings Lake could win this, John Magnier thought he would have a book value of £8 million. 'If he beats the English horse, I could fill him at fifty thousand Irish pounds a service,' said John, adding in burning anticipation, 'payable 1 October, if the mare's in foal.'

The trouble was, this was a very high-class field. It contained the Ascot winner Belmont Bay, plus the Aga Khan's stakes winner Dalsaan, and In Fijar from France. It also contained Last Fandango, ridden by Brian Rouse, and trained by Vincent. He was in to set the pace for Kings Lake, which was just as well because things went badly wrong for him as they ran towards the two-furlong mark. To-Agori made a run for it on the outside, and Lester Piggott, riding Belmont Bay, went with him. Now the gaps closed along the fence and the Irish raider was trapped. Desperately Eddery yelled for room and Brian Rouse, glancing round and seeing the situation, veered left, leaving a gap, through which Kings Lake charged as if his tail were on fire.

But was it too late? Back in the stands the blood-lust of the English county set was up and they were baying for the victory of To-Agori-Mou, here on his local racecourse. And now Pat Eddery asked the son of Nijinsky to run as he had never asked him before. Driving him forward he sliced into the English colt's lead and they thundered into the last furlong, with To-Agori on the outside, neck and neck with Belmont Bay. Eddery waited split seconds for them to drift apart and suddenly To-Agori started to veer left off a true line. The Irish jockey raised his whip and slashed Kings Lake into the gap. Now it was all or nothing. Eddery hit him again, and again, and again, and Kings Lake came crashing through, between the two horses, but without touching. In the little Irish section of the stands there was pandemonium as they roared him home. Kings Lake struck the front twenty yards out and, with heart-stopping resolution, flew over the line a head in front. John Magnier was surprised to find himself standing in the middle of all these people, with his right hand raised high above his head, his fist clenched tight, in a silent personal salute to the indomitable little hero from Ballydoyle, now worth £8 million of anybody's money.

The race took a severe toll on both of the colts, but they nonetheless raced each other once more, at the Deauville meeting in France, and they were again separated by a nose. However, the brilliant French miler Northjet finished five lengths in front of the pair of them, which may have been considered something of an anti-climax. John Magnier, however, did not care tuppence. Northjet was by the Coolmore stallion Northfields (by Northern Dancer) and, whatever else happened, no one could ever take away from Kings Lake that he had twice defeated To-Agori-Mou in Group I races, one of them a classic.

Within a few days Vincent and John had agreed with Robert that Kings Lake should stand at Coolmore for £50,000 (Irish), payable 1 October if the mare is in foal. The shares were based on a four-year earn-out, which made them worth £200,000 each. There were forty in the syndicate which put a formal book value of £8 million on the robust son of Nijinsky. The dollar rate was very favourable at the time, which made his worth in American currency around $15 million. Add that to the $28 million for Storm Bird and it is not hard to imagine the warm feeling being experienced by certain horsemen in Tipperary's Golden Vale.

A few weeks after the Deauville race, and with the syndication more or less settled – there was a stampede to buy shares in this horse – Vincent judged Kings Lake might just be at his peak again. He brought him back to the races, for one try at a mile-and-a-quarter, in the Joe McGrath Memorial Stakes at Leopardstown. Kings Lake raced to his third Group I victory, being just hand-ridden to beat Erin's Isle, the subsequent winner of *five* Group I races.

On a smaller scale, Vincent had exercised enormous patience with a horse which ran in Robert's colours named Magesterial. He was a $250,000 yearling from the 1978 Keeneland Sale – by Northern Dancer from Courting Days from the family of the Arc de Triomphe winner Allez France. Vincent had taken him over to the stamping ground of Robert's youth, Ayr, in July and Magesterial had won the Land O' Burns Stakes by a length. Now back in Ireland, Vincent sent him out once more to win the Blandford Stakes (Group II) at the Curragh, by two heads from Old Oak Tree and Dance Bid. Then he beat Dance Bid again in the Whitehall Stakes at Phoenix Park. This was one of those horses – not good enough to win a major race, but a high-class runner with a nice Northern Dancer pedigree. Vincent sold him to

Cousin Leslie for $5 million, $125,000 a share in the syndicate (nearly as much as Secretariat had fetched less than ten years ago, and he could have given Magesterial two hundred yards' start and beaten him). In this market it was hard to go very far wrong, particularly if you happened to be swamped with cash and you had a mystic for a trainer, a visionary for a stud manager and a group of inspired leprechauns to make doubly sure you didn't make a fool of yourself – 'pickin' the roight harrses'.

Now, as the wondrous season of 1981 drew to its close, Vincent began to unleash his best two-year-olds on to the Irish tracks. But this was not just a procession of expensive, highly bred American yearlings parading in moderate races. This was an onslaught upon the senses of every racegoer in Ireland. Out came the expensive Hoist the Flag colt (the $1,050,000 purchase out of Princessnesian). Now named Lords, he started at 2–1 on in a twenty-runner maiden at Leopardstown and cruised home by two and a half lengths.

Next came The Minstrel's brother who had cost them $1,250,000 at Keeneland. He was named Pilgrim, and he bolted home in an eleven-runner maiden at the Curragh, by three lengths. The Derby winner Grundy's half-brother, named Chronicle, who had cost them $220,000, won a fifteen-runner event at Naas by a hard-fought three-quarters of a length. Achieved, who had cost 162,000 guineas at the Houghton Sale at Newmarket (by Thatch out of Last Call) won a Group I race in Ireland, then beat the English in the Champagne Stakes at Doncaster. Gay Fandango's three-parts brother, by Forli, had cost them $185,000. Now he was named Punctilio and he charged home by four lengths in a sixteen-runner maiden at the Curragh.

The highlight of the late season came in a two-year-old maiden at Leopardstown when Vincent fielded for the first time the big imposing Nijinsky colt Golden Fleece, out of the American mare Exotic Treat. He had cost them $775,000 at Keeneland, one of the most expensive ten horses sold in the world in 1981, and now he would have to take on Assert, the £16,000 pick-up David O'Brien and PP Hogan had bought at the sale in Paris ('Go on then, clear off . . .' and all that). Both colts would run in Robert's colours and young David had an immensely high regard for Assert. Everyone wished him well, because Assert was by the Coolmore stallion Be My Guest and thus a grandson of Northern Dancer. But the race was a formality. The big powerful Golden Fleece took a while to get rolling, but one flick of Pat Eddery's whip sent him away at the top of the stretch and he accelerated clear of the field, bounding over the line to win by four lengths.

Vincent waited for a while, watching carefully as Assert, with his lovely ground-devouring action, finished very fast but made no impression on the winner. 'I don't really understand that,' he said to himself. 'Assert ran very well. I liked him very much. I just don't know how he could be so far behind Golden Fleece ... unless ...' But the temptation to make optimistic theories was too great, and Vincent cast the thoughts from his mind.

Three weeks later Assert came out and won the Beresford Stakes, a major Group II race, by four lengths. At around the same time the horse which had finished third behind Golden Fleece and Assert at Leopardstown (beaten by eight lengths) came out and won his maiden decisively. Then the horse which had finished fourth came out and beat twenty-seven rivals at the Curragh. The form could no longer be ignored.

Vincent watched Golden Fleece work very carefully the following week. He saw how he could quicken up. It took him a few strides, but when he went, it was not much short of awesome. He had true power, and a pedigree to suggest it was no fluke. Golden Fleece's dam Exotic Treat was the granddaughter of Rare Perfume, the dam of the mighty Jaipur. Exotic Treat's own dam ran one hundred and one times, winning among other races the Ladies Handicap over a mile and half at Belmont Park. Exotic Treat's daughter, What A Treat, was the Champion US Filly in 1965, winner of the Beldame Stakes and herself a proven runner over a mile and a half. She was also the dam of Be My Guest. Which, broadly, meant that Golden Fleece's sister was Assert's grandma!

The pedigree was wonderful and the form of Golden Fleece's only race was spectacular. Vincent talked to John confidentially about what every sixth sense was telling him: that in this big strapping son of Nijinsky they might have one of the best racehorses in the world. 'I know it's early. I know a thousand things can go wrong, but this fellow is very special. I'm not sure I've ever seen the horse who I might back to beat him.'

John Magnier called Robert that night on the basis that Vincent did not often talk that way about a horse. He had never heard him talk that way about a horse, at least not since Nijinsky. He tried to speak to Robert without betraying too much excitement, but then he blurted it out with a dash of Irish phraseology worthy of O'Casey himself:

'Jesus, Robert,' he yelled down the phone, 'we might just have one of the ones.'

10

Three Derbys

The rumbling bedlam of Lexington Avenue, the narrowest of all New York's one-way downtown highways, has few equals for sheer bloody-mindedness of spirit during the high summer of the year. As it grinds its dead-straight route through the mid-town area, there is usually a mighty jam at Bloomingdales, as cabs and limousines jockey for position. Trying to bisect Lexington in precisely this area is 59th Street, which, all day and half the night, projects a growling convoy of trucks, auto-mobiles and taxis through the lights and over the bridge into the Borough of Queens. A quarter of a mile further on, lining the left-hand side, is a group of hotels. Here doormen with piercing whistles flag down cabs, jamming those about to leave against the sidewalk, holding up two of the three lanes of traffic. Tempers shorten. Drivers yell. Hooters blare incessantly (though none like Cousin Leslie's). Cops shout, 'C'maaahn, you guys, *move it!*' And all the time the traffic backs up, jamming the entrance to the 59th Street Bridge. Often the temperature hovers around 100°F, the steam from a million air conditioners joining the exhaust fumes from those big twelve-miles-to-the-gallon General Motors cylin-ders, choking the atmosphere. It is the earth's diametric opposite to the Rub' al-Khali, but just as hot and utterly unsuitable for normal human life to survive.

Fifteen floors above this rhapsody in traffic warfare, there is an oasis, as far removed from New York and all of its unending frenzy as it could possibly be. Upon the door, at the end of a cool, silent corridor, are the words: 'George I. E. Harris, Bloodstock Associates'. And behind this door, in deep-carpeted, air-conditioned isolation, sits the man who arranged the sale of Storm Bird.

It is the late summer of 1981. Around the walls are pictures of great thoroughbred champions, the backgrounds usually verdant, cool pad-docks, trees and white fences. The photographs on the desk show

George with his American wife Kitty pictured next to a great lake on her family's sprawling country estate in Vermont. There are books about Ireland, Irish horse breeding, and the old stallions of his homeland. There is nothing about mid-town New York in here. But the angry, non-stop ringing of the phone, the painful clattering of the telex machine, the numbers being spoken into the phones were the phrases of finance: 'I'm not sure we can get that done at eight mill . . . Oh, I think we could find $250,000 for that . . . Jesus, it'll cost you a million . . . Well, I could probably come up with a cheaper share, but it wouldn't have the potential . . . They're asking $400,000 but we could try an offer . . . Well, I have a man who might buy it for $200,000 but I don't think he'd go higher . . .'

This place was strictly Wall Street. It was a brokerage in everything but name. And George Harris was the *only* no-nonsense stockbroker in the entire industry of thoroughbred bloodstock trading. There were pretenders, part-timers, and agents who might dabble in anything. But there was no one who was at his desk at 8.30 every morning and who traded stocks in racehorses and stallions all day long, taking a quick sandwich at his desk, and working until after 7 p.m. in order to accommodate clients in California. Except for the man who was born on Christmas Day, George I. E. Harris. By 1981 he had been involved in some of the biggest syndications of stallions in the USA. He had helped Bunker Hunt market the shares in the world-record $12 million syndication of his two Derby winners Empery and Youth. He had bought Appalache for John Gaines, he had even purchased for a client, Virtuous, the dam of Genuine Risk, two weeks before the Kentucky Derby.

He made only rare appearances at yearling sales, because he did not regard that as his business. His place was at his desk, in his office, and in his filing cabinets he held portfolios of stallion shares and nominations for literally dozens of clients. When a new stallion came on the market he was usually in 'on the ground floor' – calling the investors, suggesting a purchase, recommending the sale of a share or a nomination, often to another of his own clients. By 1981 George was single-handedly trading stallion shares to the tune of $25 million a year. And as each year went by there were more and more of them. Spectacular Bid, an outstanding racehorse who had won two classics, had been syndicated for $22 million by Seth Hancock. This despite the fact that he ran on drugs – legal in most American states – and had been beaten in the only two twelve-furlong races he ever faced at drug-free Belmont Park New York.

Spendthrift had raised $8 million for a new stallion named State

Dinner, Gainesway had spent $7·2 million on Private Account, Wimbledon Farm had gone to $7 million for Relaunch, and Arthur Hancock had syndicated Northern Baby, winner of England's Champion Stakes, for $12 million. Right there in those horses alone are two hundred shares, not one of them costing less than $175,000. At the conclusion of the 1981 season there would be more – in addition to forty each for Storm Bird, and in Ireland, Shergar, there would be a $15 million syndication of Northjet going to Brereton Jones's Airdrie Stud near Midway, Kentucky; a $12 million Kentucky syndicate for the Derby winner Pleasant Colony; a $12 million syndicate for the Californian Flying Paster; another $12 million syndication for Mr Prospector's son Fappiano; the Belmont Stakes winner, Summing, was being syndicated for $8 million, Fairway Phantom to Spendthrift for $6 million. That's another three hundred and twenty shares – making over five hundred in twenty-four months. There was no end in sight to this bonanza.

George Harris was in constant touch with dozens of farms all week, but there were so many shares being 'floated' that a situation was arising where many breeders had more shares than mares. There were nominations available to stallions all over the country and, as 1982 approached, there were legions of outsiders being drawn towards this amazingly glamorous way of making money. These were people who did not own a mare, some of them had never been to a horse race, but they were attracted to it because of the headline-making exploits of Robert Sangster and his men, who had turned Kentucky into a kind of mid-western Klondike. In the coming months some thirty per cent of all George Harris's clients were men with money but no horses, and many of them were from Wall Street. They were in there buying shares and nominations like stocks and bonds. There were men buying a 'service' to a major stallion, hoping to trade it through George's office for a profit a few months later.

George had a list of clients wanting to 'buy into' stallions, some of them prepared to buy a $400,000 share to a stallion standing at, say, $80,000. The terms were always reasonable. 'You make your first instalment of $80,000. Then we sell your nomination for $80,000 and within the five years you are out clean, and you have the stallion share for the rest of his natural life.' And each year Robert and his men came in from Ireland, driving up the yearling prices. Now the Arabs were in there doing the same thing. The astronomical price of yearlings was keeping the stallion fees very high, and therefore every well-bred horse coming off the racecourse had an unheard-of value. And so it would remain, unless the market crashed, which of course no one could allow, especially Robert and the Arabs, because that would devalue their own stocks. Uh-huh.

Investors in thoroughbreds were having a free ride to end all free rides. Little investment groups, often headed by money managers, were popping up all over the place, ready to 'buy in', some of them even to purchase mares and take their chances in the sales ring. There were even banks setting up investment funds in thoroughbred horses, and all the time there were stories of huge profits: '. . . Bought the mare in foal for $150,000. Her previous foal then won a stake at Longchamp, and we got $380,000 for our yearling. The mare was free and we still own her . . . Let's pick up a nomination to The Minstrel for $150,000 . . . Guess we'll put her in foal and sell. Should fetch a mill. Beautiful, right?' Right. Just so long as those yearling prices held up.

The uncanny aspect of this overwhelming *joie de vivre* was that all manner of people who eighteen months ago had never even heard of The Minstrel were chatting about him as if he were an old friend. Men in dark suits with briefcases and button-down collars, who looked as if they had never seen a muddy field in the Bluegrass, were suddenly becoming experts on the thoroughbred, dazzling their friends, and not hesitating to expound cringe-making theories on their bloodstock 'portfolios'. George Harris loved it, kept them in touch with developments, sold them what they wanted, did his best to protect them from doing anything extra rash, and impressed upon them the importance of the European classics, the American Triple Crown, the big fall handicaps in New York, and the yearling sales at Keeneland and Saratoga. All through the year these newcomers had a burning interest in the big races: 'Oh, sure, we think he's gotta big chance in the Derby . . . We own his half-sister of course – got her in foal to Alleged.'

'Who's he?'

'Alleged? Oh, he's a fine stallion, won the . . . er . . . whatsitsname . . . yeah, the Champs Elysée Stakes at Ascot, England, coupla times, back in 1958.'

The brochure put out for the massive operation at Gainesway was more in the nature of an educational supplement, designed for the 'new people'. Inside its front cover it set out the historical evolution of the breed which every life-long thoroughbred horsemen knows as the Pope knows the Lord's Prayer. The Phalaris Line, explained John Gaines (in a reference to the 17th Earl of Derby's fifteen-race sprinter of 1915–16), led to Northern Dancer through Nearctic, it also led to Bold Ruler,

Never Bend and even Blushing Groom through Nasrullah. He gave
selected details of the other great bloodlines, of St Simon, Hyperion,
Tourbillon and Teddy.

'Hey! Don't you just love them babies from the Polaris group?'

'Nasrullah? I'm telling you, he's my main man!'

Meanwhile, back in the Bluegrass, the giant stallion rosters were
growing. Cousin Leslie, now taking something of a backseat to Brownell,
had forty-six stallions at Spendthrift, the biggest number of any stud
farm in history. Some of them came from Europe like J. O. Tobin,
Caro and the incoming Lyphard star from France, Al Nasr. But most
were American. In addition to the big hitters like Raise a Native, Exclusive Native, Affirmed, Wajima, Seattle Slew and Sham, there was a
whole string of sires at all prices, some of whom might be described as
owning racing careers which were, well, somewhat obscure. Over at
Gainesway on the Paris Pike, John Gaines had forty-five stallions –
including Blushing Groom, who had chased home The Minstrel,
Vaguely Noble, and Lyphard, who was on his way to siring forty stakes
winners in his first six crops.

At these two massive breeding farms they were covering just about
five thousand mares between them per year, both farms running three
covering sessions a day from 7 a.m. to 10 p.m. This was tough on the
staff and on the drivers, and sometimes there would be lines and lines
of horse vans, with their engines running for heat, waiting throughout
the night in a fantastic queue for the most costly Lotharios on earth.
Some of the mares were important, but here the thoroughbred stallion
was king of all he surveyed. One night at Spendthrift some of the men
got fed up with Seattle Slew, who was a 'shy' breeder and tended to
take a little time to get warmed up to his task. One of them upbraided
him and yelled about the 'regulation four minutes' the operation is
supposed to take at Spendthrift. Slew lost his temper and became very
difficult, lashing out with his hind hooves. When, on the morrow, the
big, powerful Spendthrift vice-president and chief of operations, Arnold
Kirkpatrick, heard about the incident, he paraded the night staff of the
breeding shed in front of him and he told them, 'You are a bunch of
guys working for essentially the minimum wage. That horse earns about
$1 million a day. If he wants Château-Mouton Rothschild, candles, and
a f–ing violin quartet . . . *get it for him! Do you understand me?*'

Even the smaller farms were loading up with stallions. Brereton Jones
in eight years had built his little three-hundred-and-fifty-acre farm with
eight mares out at Midway, into a two-thousand-acre spread, with nearly

one hundred mares and a stallion band which would hit twenty-six in 1982, including the blindingly fast sprinter Barrera, the Preakness winner Elocutionist, Far North, Northjet and old Kirtling, who had tried to chase home Storm Bird at Newmarket. Even Seth Hancock's Claiborne, the most selective of all the Lexington-area farms, had twenty-seven stallions, their all-time high. Seth's brother Arthur, now with two thousand five hundred acres at Stone Farm, had nine stallions. William duPont III, a young member of a very senior branch of the great Delaware chemical family, had nine second-raters at his Pillar Stud, horses which had never really made the top, like the French middle-distance runner Crow, Dance Bid, the poorly bred but courageous multi-stakes winner Noble Dancer, and the Vincent O'Brien highly bred 'cast-off' (by Lyphard) Euclid. But it was hard even for them to lose money in 1981.

The other huge building operation in central Kentucky was taking place out at North Ridge Farm, which now contained over one thousand acres, six miles east of Lexington on the Leestown Road, opposite the Federal Correctional Institution, later to become home to both Leona Helmsley and Ivan Boesky. The owner of North Ridge, Franklin Groves, is president of the S. J. Groves Company of Minneapolis, Minnesota, one of the largest civil engineering contractors in the world – they were partners in the building of the massive Bonneville Dam on the great, broad Columbia river which divides the states of Washington and Oregon above the Multnomah Falls. This one is something like the Aswan High Dam. Thus, when Franklin Groves said 'build', he meant *build*. And, for a comparative newcomer to the thoroughbred business, he had major ambitions. Starting in 1975 when they bought Cousin Leslie's sale-topper, he and his wife created one of the most beautiful farms ever seen in Kentucky. They grew to house one hundred and fifty mares, and they built possibly the finest stallion barn in the world. It was nothing less than palatial and it contained luxurious accommodation for twenty-eight stallions, devised in such a way that it could be instantly doubled in size to hold fifty-six stallions if and when they became the biggest breeding farm in the state.

No expense was spared. For the magnificently paved courtyard, Mr Groves wanted sixteen carefully spaced pin-oak trees about forty feet high. And he had them shipped in on articulated trucks, one at a time, from Tennessee. They were planted with the aid of a one-hundred-foot crane and they were believed to be the biggest trees ever successfully moved. Franklin Groves thought of everything. He even bought in four 'spares' which he had planted on an outside lawn, just in case any of the courtyard trees died. Altogether he bought and planted fourteen thousand trees. He also imported hundreds of shrubs from Ireland, not to mention Dr Michael Osborne, whom he coaxed away from the Irish National Stud to Kentucky to take charge of what he hoped and believed would one day become the most important breeding farm in the world.

He quickly developed his own theories on breeding and set about revolutionizing the way mares were mated with stallions. He took the linear measurements of all of the great modern runners and he worked out all of the ratios – height to length of stride, length of back to stamina. He brought in experts to develop computer programmes and he computed the input of stamina and speed into various pedigrees. This was a man who was going places, no expense spared. He even had a very good racehorse running in his name, The Bart, who in 1981 ran the tenacious American Champion John Henry to a nose, at level weights, in the world's first $1 million thoroughbred race, the Arlington Million.

The Bart could race a bit on his day. There were some very good horses behind him in The Million, like the English filly Madame Gay, winner of the French Oaks, Argument, winner of the Washington International, and Mrs Penny, another winner of the French Oaks. But The Bart's pedigree was somewhat shaky, being by the 1964 French Derby winner Le Fabuleux from a weak branch of a once-excellent family. Nonetheless he would one day reign in solitary splendour over the finest stallion barn in all the world, the one at North Ridge.

At this particular time, Lexington, Kentucky, and its environs resembled Beverly Hills in the late 1920s and 30s when the film actors paid virtually no tax on their colossal salaries and when the local banks in that self-congratulatory little community did not even know there was any such thing as the Great Depression. Lexington was groaning with money, based on the new but simple modern premise that the high-class racing champion was now worth more than his weight in gold. A four-year-old coming off the track weighs around twelve hundred pounds, which is about twenty thousand ounces. Taking the average gold fix at $400 an ounce, that's about $8 million for a horse made of solid gold bullion. Well, out at Cousin Leslie's they had several like that. Affirmed and Seattle Slew were worth nearly double their weight in gold, and even a new sire like State Dinner, who had won the Metropolitan Handicap and the Suburban in New York, was valued at the equivalent of his weight in solid gold.

Storm Bird was of course worth more than three times his weight in gold. It was scarcely surprising that Kentucky breeders had begun to move swiftly into the advanced stages of neo-megalomania. All of the old trusted rule books had long since been thrown on to the dung-heap. No one ever said any more the traditional statements of syndication: 'This horse could stand reasonably at $25,000 a service, and at that price I could fill him. That makes a share worth $75,000. Multiply that by forty and you have the value of this stallion – $3 million.' Forget that. Nowadays days they believed that this boom would never stop, and that prospective stallions were worth what they said they were worth.

'This horse is a running horse, with a big pedigree. He's gotta to be worth $8 million.'

'Huh?'

'Yup. Eight long ones. That's $200,000 a share. Spread that over five years, and we'll stand him at $40,000. The agents will jump for that one, we'll have him filled in a week.'

The terms were always good. And the farms, with all manner of 'outsiders' rushing to get into the new sires, could just about name their price. The men who bought shares, through George Harris's office, never had a problem selling the nomination each year. And every July they watched these astronomical prices being paid for yearlings. This market was golden, in every possible sense of the word. There were even tax-breaks in the USA, depreciation of mares as each year went by. The buying of stallion shares was treated as a straight business investment. There were Scales of Depreciation of Stallions, drawn up by the Federal Government, fifteen per cent the first year, twenty-two per cent the second, twenty-one per cent for the next three. 'Yessiree, have I got a horse for you!'

The riotous optimism of the industry was given a further sunburst of encouragement in late 1981 when someone bid a rock-solid $40 million for Northern Dancer, the twenty-one-year-old culprit who had turned Lexington into a boom town. The bid was received at Windfields Farm by Joe Thomas from the French bloodstock agency, Horse France, on behalf of the Hungarian-born Normandy veterinarian Dr Laszlo Urban. No one was prepared to divulge the name or names of his backers, but the offer was sufficiently impressive for Joe Thomas to poll all of the shareholders to ask who would consider selling a stake in the great stallion. Somewhat to Joe's surprise, several of them agreed to sell. So concerned was Joe that he set out to find the source of the bid and to find out where they wished to take the reigning little Emperor of

Windfields Farm. To France? To Kentucky? To Ireland? Few answers were forthcoming.

The key to the sale rested with Eddie Taylor, the owner of Windfields who held twelve shares, but was now very sick at his home in Lyford Key. Charles Taylor, his son, new to the central running of a big stud farm, deferred to Joe in these matters and no one knew quite what to do. The syndication contract had no clause to act on a two-thirds majority. Joe Thomas decided on a firm course of action. 'I knew', he said, 'that it would be, to any real decent horseman, an act of cruelty to take the little stallion away from his home at this stage in his life. Northern Dancer had been here for sixteen years and he had known most everyone around here for all of his life. Christ, I bought his dam for Mr Taylor and arranged the mating to Nearctic which produced him. He and I have known each other since the day he was born. I felt close to tears when I realized he might have to go. I don't know what it might have done to him. It might have broken his heart. When horses get down like that they can just fret away and get ill and die. So I decided just to sit still for a few days and wait for someone to get mad. It took four days, and then someone did. Real mad.'

The phone call came from Rokeby, Virginia. It was from one of the richest men in the world, the art collector, philanthropist and racehorse breeder Mr Paul Mellon, and he was literally trembling with fury. 'I have known Mr Mellon for a lot of years,' said Joe. 'But I have *never* known him angry like that. Matter of fact I haven't seen many people in all of my life much more angry than that.'

Mr Mellon said that he had never heard of a more outrageous plan. To take a stallion who had been so good to everyone for so long and to uproot him from his home, and put him on a plane and send him away. 'I would not do that to any horse,' he told Joe. 'Not to any horse, not to a hack nor to a hunter, not to an old pony. The contract does not give anyone or any group of shareholders the right to get together and sell him. And if anyone attempts to do so, I shall call in every lawyer that is necessary, I shall place an injunction on the horse and, if I have to, I will take the matter to the highest court in the state of either Virginia or Maryland and, if necessary, *higher*.'

That, essentially, was that. Joe Thomas, smiling broadly now, just said, 'Yessir, Mr Mellon. Northern Dancer's not going anywhere. Because if you won't have it and I won't have it, the family won't have it, and that's the end of it.'

'Thank you, Joe', said Mr Mellon, but even as he put the phone down he was still muttering, 'Absolutely outrageous . . . I will not tolerate it . . .'

Joe's daughter Lesley remembers the day well. 'Joe called from the office,' (she always called him 'Joe'), 'and he told me that Northern Dancer was staying. But he was late home for lunch and I drove up to the farm to pick him up. I found him standing in the pouring rain, talking to Northern Dancer in his paddock. He was just giving him a couple of carrots, kind of letting him know he was safe. Joe was pretty soft about that stallion. But they seemed to understand each other.'

What Joe did not understand was who was trying to wrest the Dancer away, to keep him privately and to own the monopoly on every one of his yearlings for the remainder of his life. There were speculations that it might have been a group of the new owners from the Middle East, but this was vehemently denied. The most obvious man was Stavros Niarchos, who had the finances to support such an operation and might have been attracted by its Machiavellian nature. He never admitted it and no one ever found out for sure, but Joe always thought it was the clever and occasionally mischievous old Greek ship-owner.

The logic of the bid was plain to see. If, over the next two years, Northern Dancer produced a dozen top-class foals which would fetch between three and four million dollars each, then the rest of the progeny, possibly another thirty-eight yearlings, would be free. Better yet, so would the stallion, for perhaps three more years at stud. The curious aspect of it all was that the entire exercise was being governed in Ireland and England, because most of Northern Dancer's best sons and grandsons were bought to race there, by Robert and now by the Arabs. So, as Spendthrift, Claiborne and Windfields sat cheerfully in the middle of this unprecedented symphony of money, the scene switched inevitably to Ballydoyle, where the spring rain was lashing down the Golden Vale and the gum-booted Vincent O'Brien and his team were out on the chilled, windswept hillsides, working the horses, trying to get them fit and shiny in a prolonged winter which kept their coats woolly and their breath misty on the Tipperary air.

There were several which Vincent was watching with special care, but none more so than the great strapping bay son of Nijinsky, Golden Fleece. This really was a giant of a horse, in every way. On the gallops, even with Pat Eddery flying to Ireland twice a week struggling to keep him 'on the bit', leaning into him as they forged their way up the slight rise of the one-mile gallop, Golden Fleece would pull his way clear. Pat could never hold him.

He was like a powder-keg to deal with, for he would stand no messing about, no gentle slaps on the neck. If he was given too much of a long rein in his slower paces, he might whip round and deposit his rider on the ground. In addition, he was claustrophobic, which might mean he would never be able to travel to the races in Ireland, never mind fly to England. Vincent likes to take horses to other nearby gallops to keep them fresh and interested during the winter, but on the way home from one of these little jaunts, Golden Fleece had suddenly become terrified, kicking and kicking against the travelling horse box. He was bathed in sweat, trembling and cut on his hind legs, and when they finally got him home Vincent knew that this was a major problem. If he would not go into a horse box, how could he ever run in the Derby?

Golden Fleece had demonstrated blind panic and it threatened his entire career. For weeks on end Vincent had him loaded on to a horse box and driven a little way, and then walked out again, and then back in again, and driven more, all along the little highways and byways of Tipperary. At the same time he was trying to overcome a similar dislike of the starting stalls. Like many big horses, Golden Fleece brushed against the sides when he went in and it upset him terribly, bringing on that uncontrollable feeling of panic. Twice a week they worked him from the stalls, which all added to a winter which was for Vincent and his staff fraught with worry. Nijinsky himself had possessed the most fragile temperament and the Irish trainer Michael Kauntze, who had looked after him and travelled with him as Vincent's assistant back in 1970, always said he hated 'wide open spaces', especially those which he had never seen before. This was one of a thousand problems on Vincent's mind. 'If we get him to Epsom, how will he react to the massive grandstand, the wide uphill start? Can his nervous system take all of that, on top of the flight from Ireland?'

Somehow they brought him through the winter in good shape for his opening race at the Curragh, the Ballymoss Stakes in mid April, and Golden Fleece won it in effortless fashion. Next, at the beginning of May, he went a mile and a quarter in the Nijinsky Stakes at Leopardstown, and beat Assert once more, by two and a half lengths. Third in the race was the $1 million yearling Lords, by Hoist the Flag, and fourth another very fast middle-distance horse Stanerra. There were those who thought Assert was tenderly ridden, but it was nonetheless impossible to imagine any horse withstanding the burst of speed Golden Fleece could produce when asked. Halfway up the straight his pacemaker Chronicle, ridden by Vincent's chief work-rider Vincent Rossiter, was flat to the boards and Eddery, trying to ride to orders and to keep Golden Fleece 'on the bridle', yelled at him, '*Go on! Go on!*' But Vincent was going on, and Golden Fleece went past him like a guided missile.

'It's the speed that worries me,' said Vincent O'Brien later. 'How can any horse with speed like that *possibly* stay a mile and a half . . . except for Nijinsky.'

From then on the preparation was a pretty good nightmare. First of all, Golden Fleece whipped round and dropped his rider T. P. Burns on the gallops, breaking his ankle. Loose, he charged across the fields, with everyone aghast in case he crashed through a gate. Most of the staff were Catholic and several silent 'Hail Marys' were delivered. They fanned out to try and catch him, racing across the wet grass to save the headstrong grandson of Northern Dancer from himself. But somehow or another the massive colt found his way home on his own. Then his off-hind hock swelled up, ten days before the Derby. Vincent called in Bob Griffin and he had special shoes made for his hind hooves to help tilt the foot forward, just a fraction, taking the pressure off the hock. Jacqueline O'Brien was in touch with physiotherapists at a big London hospital and they prescribed ice-packs and ultrasonics to take the swelling down. They took him out for a walk twice a day to keep him fit and he missed a serious work, and the clock kept ticking away, and now there were only eight days to the Derby, and Vincent was nearly beside himself with worry, though he disguised it with his shy smile and his quiet, serious voice.

In the last six days before the race Pat Eddery flew to ride work and both times Golden Fleece demolished his colleagues, once leaving Lords half a dozen lengths behind, then leaving Pilgrim, all $1,250,000 of him, ten lengths behind. The journey to Epsom was made on the Saturday. Vincent hired a CL44 from Shannon to Gatwick, and they arranged for Golden Fleece's lead-horse General Custer to travel with him for company. Twice on the Sunday they took him for a walk near the racecourse, just to familiarize him with the territory and to keep him well exercised. On the Monday morning Vincent had special permission to work his colt from the Derby start to the seven-furlong gate and Golden Fleece burned up the track. On the following morning he went with General Custer, ridden by Gerry Gallagher, two furlongs at half speed, before a fast quarter-mile.

Then, as they walked quietly home down Tattenham Hill, the unthinkable happened. Golden Fleece suddenly coughed. Then he coughed again, then again. Twenty-four times he coughed. This is the trainer's sign of trouble, impending flu. In a racing yard the cough is treated very much as an outbreak of cholera might be at Buckingham Palace. Eddery and Gallagher cantered right past the waiting press corps near the winning post and headed for the stables where Vincent was waiting. They called Bob Griffin, who was very philosophical. He knew how Vincent was living on the edge of his nerves, that Golden Fleece was favourite for the race, that he would be worth a clear $30 million if he won it. Also that second place would be no good, that everyone's dreams hung on this brutal contest, to be run on the morrow on this brutal switchback of a racetrack. Bob told Vincent that in his view it was almost certainly the heat which had dehydrated the horse and made him cough. Vincent did not know whether to announce there was a doubt about the Derby favourite or not, but the horse was not sweating, nor was he running a temperature. Bob Griffin advised the master of Ballydoyle to say nothing because he thought everything would probably be fine.

To everyone's relief, Golden Fleece did not cough again, but Vincent did not sleep one wink that night in his darkened room at the nearby RAC Club. The sun rose silently on Wednesday 2 June into a hot and sultry sky. Epsom was sweltering by mid-morning and immediately after lunch there was a torrential rainstorm which soaked everything and somehow made the atmosphere even more humid. Horses were breaking out all over the place and by the time they paraded for the two hundred and third running of the English Derby there were few among the field who looked cool. Jalmood, the colt Sheikh Mohammed had bought for $185,000 at Keeneland in 1980, was second favourite and looked better than most, but Peacetime was awash, and so was the grey French challenger Persepolis, for whom there was some major betting money.

Golden Fleece, who was now very warm, was drifting in the market, from 9−4, to 5−2, now 11−4. But he went to post on the most wonderful stride, easy and fluid, flinging his forelegs well out in front of him, but tossing his head and betraying nerves. Pat Eddery, as he had done for so many months, leaned into him and tried to hold him 'on the bridle'. But by any standards, this one was a real handful. Vincent's instructions to Pat had been wary, because he was still uncertain that Golden Fleece would last out a mile and a half. 'Don't ask him,' he said. 'Don't ask him until well into the straight. Ride a quiet, waiting race.'

Privately Pat thought, 'Ask him? The only thing I've ever asked him is to slow down!' Basically he believed that, with a colt of this blinding speed, the only thing to do was pick your moment, let off the brakes and, metaphorically, hang on to your hat.

But now they were loading the stalls and Pat was hanging towards the back, cautious of Golden Fleece's natural aversion to these starting gates. Finally they led him up and he walked in, but he brushed both sides, bridled, and flung his head back. Pat was ready for him, but Golden Fleece shuddered as the gates slammed tight behind him. He was never still as the last couple were loaded and there was dark sweat down his neck and on the reins. The leathers creaked as the Irish jockey pulled down his goggles, tightened the rein and perfected his balance on the biggest horse in the race. This was a whole long way from the plush chairs at Keeneland, from which rich men signalled bids of a million dollars or more.

The last back door slammed shut. And now the gates crashed open, and all eighteen of them thundered forward to face the twelve furlongs of the world's most famous racecourse. Golden Fleece, now watched by a million eyes, broke fast beneath the bright green and blue silks of Robert Sangster, who was standing with Vincent in their usual marginally illegal spot down by the gate.

Pat quickly settled him on the long swerving run to the top of Tattenham Hill and he could feel the terrific power of the horse as they rolled along in that effortless stride to which he had become so utterly accustomed. The pace was fast, because a 250–1 shot named Florida Sun was running flat out, leading the field on down to the harsh and formidable downhill left-hander of Tattenham Corner. Golden Fleece, in total defiance of every Epsom tradition, was sailing along in fifteenth position. No horse in the entire history of the race had ever been that far behind at the Corner and won.

Down along the rails Robert thought he had gone. For brief seconds Vincent cursed himself and everyone else for ignoring the bout of coughing. Neither man dared to look at the other. The tension was not much short of atomic. The only brightness on the entire horizon of Epsom Downs was that his jockey appeared not to give a damn one way or another where he was positioned. Eddery was sitting very still. Out in front was Norwick, ridden by Greville Starkey, and, behind him, the field streamed around the bend, the riders leaning left as seventy-two hooves fought to keep a hold on the still-wet ground. Derbys are won and lost right here. Now, as they raced towards the two-furlong mark, the pace quickened visibly.

Vincent O'Brien's hands were shaking as he waited for Eddery to make what might amount to a $30 million move, and he could see Golden Fleece easing his way towards the outside. The jockey had him balanced as they came to the quarter-mile mark. And now, with the cold-blooded sureness of the hired assassin, Patrick John Eddery let him go. In that wondrous flicker of time all the greatness in that mighty pedigree that was Golden Fleece – the fabulous acceleration of Nijinsky, the guts of Northern Dancer, the belligerence of Native Dancer, the hard staying power of Vaguely Noble – came together in a fanfare of brilliance.

He came from strictly nowhere, charging from the rear of the field with a power-burst that left most of them standing. He hurtled past the stragglers as if they were traffic bollards, and he did not take that much more trouble with the rest of them. The first nine were simple, then it was ten, then eleven, then twelve horses he flew past. Now there was only Peacetime, Touching Wood and Norwick between Golden Fleece and victory.

The commentators, broadcasting to millions all over the world, were bellowing the same phrase: 'And here comes the favourite with a fantastic run down the outside!' A half a million people, on the Downs and in the stands, were roaring Golden Fleece home.

Pat drew his whip and cracked him just twice, hard, sharp and left-handed, as Robert Sangster's big bay colt faced up to the hill that would win him the Derby. Golden Fleece flattened out his stride for the climb to the finishing post and then he accelerated for the second time, whipping past Norwick and Peacetime, and then Touching Wood. Still under the whip, he drew off to win by three astounding lengths. No English Derby winner had ever overtaken that many opponents on his way through the straight to victory.

Robert and Vincent were each stunned by the drama, each wavering somewhere between cardiac arrest and ecstasy. Unaccountably they shook hands formally, each of them speechless with relief, almost overcome by the power and the unyielding spirit of their colt. Vincent hurried out to meet him, to check that all was well, but as they turned in towards the winners' enclosure, he stopped and turned around, and he gazed back down the slightly damp course over which Golden Fleece had raced with such dazzling determination. It was as if he were reassuring himself that this was indeed the very same historic ground over which his other winners, Nijinsky, Sir Ivor, Larkspur, Roberto and The Minstrel, had also run. The final hill at Epsom has, over two centuries, ruthlessly exposed the stamina limitations of all pretenders to greatness.

It has broken hearts, smashed dreams and cost men fortunes. But it remains the direct route to the exclusive little garrison of the immortals. And Golden Fleece was there – the horse that came from nowhere. It was a Derby which will not easily be forgotten.

Vincent was entitled to his moment of reflection. No man this century ever won six Derbys. And no horse since Mahmoud set the rather suspect hand-timed record in 1936, ever went faster than Golden Fleece. But, as the press crowded in upon the trainer, firing questions at him, his thoughts returned to the dark days of the winter, when everything that could have gone wrong had duly done so. He thought of the hours and hours spent by his men trying to get the horse to board a van, the endless hours they had practised at the starting gate, the care they had all taken to protect his injured hock, poor T. P. Burns's broken ankle, and all of the kindness and devotion they had bestowed upon the high-mettled, tough but vulnerable son of Nijinsky. He treated the questions of the press as if he had not heard them, saying quietly, 'It is hard to explain how much I owe to the care and patience of my staff.'

Meanwhile Susan Sangster, assisted by a stable man and Pat Eddery, had safely delivered Golden Fleece to the winners' enclosure. And the talk was suddenly of money. Will he stay in Ireland at Coolmore? Will the syndication run to $30 million? Has there been an offer from Kentucky? What would you think he'll stand at? Fifty thousand? Sixty thousand? A hundred thousand?

It was Robert Sangster who put a stop to it, for he had not changed all that much in spirit since first he stood in the winners' enclosure at Haydock Park just over twenty years ago. He still gloried in the thrill of it all, basked in the warm tide of victory and could hardly wait to get those corks popping. He rubbed Golden Fleece's nose, who right now was too tired to care, and he thought of the night they had bought him at Keeneland and he tried to remember how the horse had looked as a yearling. But the picture was gone. He turned to the reporters and said, 'This is a very great racehorse. And we have all seen a fantastic race. Don't spoil it for me by talking about money.'

No such sentiment clouded the thoughts of John Magnier. He knew what this horse was worth. In his opinion Golden Fleece could and would stand at Coolmore at 100,000 Irish guineas. A four-year earn-out for the shareholders would give the future stallion a value of some £16 million. On the book this would mean an overall valuation of close to $30 million, except that Robert and the team would keep several shares for themselves, which would give Coolmore the opportunity to sell some

'seasons' and for Robert to breed some of his own mares. The majority
of the shares would be taken up by the world's major breeders. For the
initial 'flotation' John would be talking to Windfields Farm, Claiborne,
Spendthrift, the Moyglare Stud, Tim Roger's Airlie Stud, Bert Firestone, Warner Jones, Paul Mellon, Ogden Phipps, and John Gaines.
The thoroughbred industry has always been an incestuous place and
John Magnier represented the biggest customers the major American
farms had ever had. When he came calling to sell a share in the hottest
stallion in Europe, the champion son of Nijinsky, it was time to co-
operate. '$180,000 a year for four? OK, John. Put us in. We'll send
him a *good* mare.' All of them knew that the moment a big, good-looking
yearling by Golden Fleece came into the sales ring in 1985, having
caught the eye of the Arab legions and possibly Vincent O'Brien, well,
we're basically talking millions for such a colt.

With the sale of Storm Bird and the massive syndication of Kings
Lake, and now the 1982 Epsom Derby, Robert Sangster would have
been forgiven for thinking that his luck must be about to run out, with
a theoretical $72 million on its way into the till over the next few years.
But run out it did not. While all of the trials and tribulations over Golden
Fleece had been going on, young David O'Brien, training privately on
the other side of the Ballydoyle estate, had been preparing Assert to a
peak of condition. He had already won the Gallinule Stakes at the
Curragh by ten lengths, but had elected not to take on Golden Fleece
in the Derby, despite being given full permission by Robert to do so if
he wished. Instead David had elected to go for the Prix du Jockey Club,
the French Derby, run over twelve furlongs at Chantilly four days later.
It was not a very strong field and Assert bolted home by three lengths.
He was the first foreign-trained horse ever to win the race and now the
eagerly awaited clash between Golden Fleece and David O'Brien's horse
seemed certain to take place in the Irish Derby at the Curragh in three
weeks' time.

Unhappily, it never happened. Within seven days, Golden Fleece
went down with a virus, which dragged on for several weeks. Then his
other hock swelled and, essentially, there was no more time left to
prepare him for a big race. That was the end of him. He retired to
Coolmore and the numbers were just as John Magnier had forecast.
One hundred thousand pounds for a service to the spectacular winner
of the 1982 Derby. And as the breeders began to beat down the door
to 'get into' him, Robert no longer felt that his day was being ruined
by talking about money.

They went to the Curragh on 26 June to watch Assert attempt the Irish Derby. It was a marvellous occasion because all of the Irishmen who had done so much to create the great horses were there to see it. Phonsie was there to see his nephew try to win his first classic, Vincent was there to herald the arrival of his own son in the highest ranks of Irish trainers. PP Hogan, who had helped buy the horse, as he had so many others, was there, proud as a peacock. John Magnier was there with the boys from Coolmore, Bobby Lanigan, Tommy Stack, David Magnier, Tom Gaffney and Christy Grassick. There was Eamon Phelan and Redmond Carroll, Niall Power and Bobby McCarthy, the men who cared for Robert's stallions. Every one of them was 'here to see David's horse win the Derby'.

Assert was 7-4 on, but they did not care. They laid the odds. Some of them with £40 to £70, the more daring with four hundred to seven hundred on the basis that it was 'like buying £10 notes half price'. No one even considered the possibility of defeat, despite the presence in the field of the Roberto colt, Silver Hawk, who had finished third, four lengths behind Golden Fleece at Epsom.

And right they were. Assert put on a breathtaking display, winning by an official eight lengths which looked more like ten to many people. As the Irish jockey Christy Roche steered him across the winning line, Robert Sangster became the only man in the entire history of horse racing to have won all three major European Derbys, the English, the French and the Irish, in the same year. The Coolmore team cheered themselves so dry some of them were forced to go and have a drink. But they did not spend their winnings. The drinks were on Robert today, not so much because of the £130,000 prize money, but because of the staggering fact that Assert was now worth something in the region of $15 million. And there did not appear, on the face of it, to be a horse in Europe who could reasonably be backed to beat him. Add to this the fact that he was by the Coolmore stallion Be My Guest, whose value was now in the process of quadrupling, and the sublime grin of pleasure which decorated John Magnier's face was easy to diagnose.

There was another reason too for that grin. When Be My Guest had first entered the stud, John had allowed every small Irish breeder and farmer for miles around to send a mare to the son of Northern Dancer for around £7,000 (Irish). By the time he had finished repaying all of the old debts to people who had supported Coolmore and his own Castle Hyde when times had not been so good, Be My Guest, perhaps with a similar sublime grin on his face, had covered ninety-seven mares!

The press had found out and John Magnier had taken a severe amount of stick for over-breeding the stallion and breaking the guidelines 'followed by breeders for centuries' – no more than fifty-five mares, even in the 1970s, for fear that the breed became 'unbalanced'. John said he was sorry, that he would not do so again, that he had not meant it.

Be My Guest had scored with another classic this year when his daughter On The House had won the English 1000 Guineas seven weeks ago. And now his son Assert had won the Irish Derby. Be My Guest must be ready for immediate re-syndication for millions of pounds. And John was still sorry.

But later in the Turf Club bar at the Curragh he confided in Robert, with a terrible Irish chortle, 'I'll let you into a shocking secret, with which you must go to your grave. If I could live 1978 all over again, I'd still breed Be My Guest to ninety-seven mares!' And they both fell about laughing, before John changed the subject because it was now common knowledge that Robert hated talking about money in his highest moments. And this day, 26 June 1982, represented perhaps the highest ever.

11

Tipperary v. Arabia

By 1982 it was becoming increasingly difficult to find anyone with the necessary qualifications to join the depleted ranks of the little army from eastern Tipperary. There were plenty of rich men who knew nothing about racehorses and the hair-raising risks the game entailed. There were plenty of racing professionals with insufficient money. There were also a few rich racing professionals who did not possess the obligatory iron nerves. Money, knowledge and courage were three pretty scarce commodities to find, all in one fragile human package. But Vincent, Robert and John needed such a man to take a fifteen per cent share in an annual spending plan which might hit $15 million. They could never ignore the old Kentucky adage: 'If you wanna stay in the horse business, you gotta buy horses.'

And there in their midst there was such a man. Rich? He had been one of the biggest builders in California and sold out for a gigantic sum of money to the national conglomerate Boise Cascade. Knowledge? He had owned, in partnership with his best friend Frank Sinatra, a very fast horse named Mr Right, who had won the Santa Anita Handicap, New York's Suburban Handicap, and $700,000 back in the 60s. Nerve? At the age of nineteen, on 8 June 1944, forty-eight hours after the Normandy landings had begun and with three thousand Americans dead beneath the tides, he had driven his jeep through the shallows and straight up the middle of Utah Beach with General George Patton's Third Armoured Division. He had nerve.

His name was Danny Schwartz and he had, for the past few years, been a partner in this massive thoroughbred-buying campaign. The top sprinter Solinus had run in his name when he won the Kings Stand Stakes in 1978, as had Gregorian, a big Graustark colt, which won the Brigadier Gerard Stakes in 1980. But now, with Sheikh Mohammed and his brothers preparing for battle, Robert needed a partner prepared to make a firm commitment for what would inevitably be higher stakes. He needed a man who would stand shoulder to shoulder with him, who would not flinch when the bidding hit the stratosphere, and who would help Robert and Vincent and Tom Cooper to stare down the 'enemy' from the Middle East with solid back-up in hard American dollars. 'When we say, "Come on, chaps, let's go another mill," we mean it,' said Robert.

'Guess I'm your man,' said Danny. 'Let's go all the way and leave the rest to Vincent.'

Robert grinned and used the phrase he always used when the burly, broad-shouldered ex-construction boss made a point, with even a hint of aggression, 'Steady, Patton, I'm on your side.'

Danny Schwartz, in the five years he had known the team from Tipperary, had become a very close friend of the O'Brien family. Vincent and Jacqueline were regular visitors both to his big apartment on San Francisco's Nob Hill and to his house in Palm Springs, next door to Francis Albert. Vincent and Robert also used to rent a house in Palm Springs, at the Thunderbird Country Club, where Robert and Susan first met Frank and Barbara Sinatra. In days past Danny Schwartz, a transplanted New Yorker, had been a fierce gambler, playing the tables at Caesar's Palace and The Sands. Once he is reputed to have won $1 million in one night. He was not an entire stranger in a couple of the bigger casinos in Mayfair either. Danny is married to Natalie and they have two daughters. By 1982 as he headed towards the Big Six O, he had decided to forsake the green baize tables in favour of the more careful and sensible pursuit of racing and breeding horses with Vincent and Robert. Rarely has a man of such proven business acumen made a more esoteric decision.

Within three weeks of Robert's great triumph in the Irish Derby they were back on the rollercoaster again, heading for the 1982 yearling sales at Keeneland. It would be, Robert knew, the hardest struggle they had ever gone into, to buy the horses they wanted. John and Vincent had pored over the catalogue, marking down the Nijinsky colts they *must* see. It was clear to them that the sire of Golden Fleece would be almost as keenly sought after in the ring as Northern Dancer himself.

They all boarded Concorde from London Heathrow on 15 July bound for New York. The aircraft was packed with horsemen and waiting for them at Kennedy Airport were three privately chartered Learjets. One was for Robert and his team, one for Prince Khalid Abdullah and his advisors, and one for Sheikh Maktoum al-Maktoum and his advisors.

They took off one by one and followed each other down to Bluegrass Field, Lexington. There, already parked on the edge of the runway, was the Boeing 727 of Sheikh Mohammed bin Rashid al-Maktoum. Within hours the Boeing 737 owned by Stavros Niarchos touched down beside them.

Central Kentucky was in a frenzy of anticipation. Could this madness go on? Would the $3·5 million record be broken? Could the average price for a Keeneland yearling possibly go higher than the $260,000 it hit last year? Which of the new stallions would make the biggest impact? Affirmed or Alydar, the heroes of the 1978 Triple Crown? Would the Arabs and Irishmen lock horns in the battle for the best-bred sons of Nijinsky?

Sales parties were breaking out all over the Lexington area. Tommy Gentry had hired Ray Charles and his back-up men to entertain the buyers, guests were arriving at and departing from Spendthrift Farm in an endless stream – 'Get them mint-*juleps* over here, boy!' Danny Schwartz arrived from California with Barbara Sinatra as his guest. Up at Stone Farm, Arthur Hancock was still celebrating his sensational victory in the Kentucky Derby with his homebred Gato del Sol, a big, tough stayer by Cougar II, who had cut down the field with a devastating stretch-run. If you wanted a glass of good bourbon and you were happy to stay up half the night, you could even hear the richly talented son of Bull Hancock sing and strum a few bars of Ricky Nelson's, 'You Can't Please Everyone, So You Gotta Please Yourself'. Arthur was looking for a big sale here, since he was selling a Nijinsky colt out of Bendara, a half-sister to Be My Guest, sire of Assert. He considered it highly likely that the colt would end up at Ballydoyle but he hoped the Arabians would be in there to help the price along.

Meanwhile Vincent, Phonsie and John, Danny, PP, and Bob Griffin fought their way around the barns in search of the yearlings which would win the great races and earn back as stallions the huge amount of money they were about to spend. Very early in the catalogue came the prime choice of Vincent O'Brien, another big bay son of Nijinsky from the Hollywood Oaks winner Spearfish, a full-sister to the top California stallion Gummo and the dam of the Windfields stallion King's Bishop. She had also produced the Irish 1000 Guineas winner Gaily. And Vincent loved her yearling son. 'I could not fault him,' said the trainer.

The colt was Lot 30 on the opening Monday afternoon and PP wondered whether they might not be lucky and sneak in there to buy without the Arabs noticing. Robert thought it unlikely since the Arabs had dogged his footsteps pretty closely for three years now. 'Fat chance,' said Danny Schwartz. 'They'll be in there. We'll have a fight on our hands.'

Nonetheless Robert and Vincent plotted their tactics carefully. They positioned Tom Cooper right next to the press box, hemmed in by the crowd but flanked by the powerful figure of Danny Schwartz. Robert himself was outside, behind the closed doors, feigning disinterest. They led in Lot Number 30. The announcer Tom Hammond called out, 'A colt by Nijinsky from a whale of a family.' And Tom Caldwell, the auctioneer, shouted: 'And he kinda matches the pedigree, doesn't he? *Look at this colt*, will ya *look* at this colt.'

Everyone did except Robert who was now shut out in the passage, and Tom Cooper who was turning the pages of his catalogue, apparently unable to contain his indifference. The bidding started low, down at $50,000. But it progressed beyond $1 million and then Tom Cooper looked up and casually jumped it by $250,000 with a short sharp nod to bid-spotter Charlie Richardson. Colonel Dick Warden, standing by the barrier behind the rostrum, on behalf of Sheikh Mohammed, nodded at $2 million. Tom Cooper bid again, raising the stakes by $250,000. Colonel Warden said, 'Two and a half.' Tom went in again, another $250,000. Colonel Warden answered at $3 million. And now the auditorium went stone silent as they realized they were watching a major duel.

Tom bid again: $3,250,000 for the son of Nijinsky. This was Vincent's limit. But Colonel Warden was back in with another raise of $250,000. 'Three and a half I'm bid,' called Tom Caldwell. And now Tom Cooper was losing his nerve. Danny Schwartz whispered, 'C'mon, Tom, one more.' The Irish bloodstock agent held up his hand to stall the bidding, dived out of the door to speak to Robert, who agreed with Danny. He dived right back in again with a bid of $3,750,000. Colonel Warden gazed across the auditorium at Sheikh Mohammed who made no sign of surrender. Now he bid $4 million on behalf of the young Bedouin prince of Dubai. And the audience stood up and cheered.

'Hit 'em again, Tom – *fast*,' snapped Danny Schwartz and Tom Cooper immediately signalled that he would pay $4,250,000 for the colt. Now it was Colonel Warden's turn to take advice. And the auction-eer, sensing a surrender, called out to the bid-spotter: 'I'm counting, Charlie . . .' But it was all over. Colonel Warden shook his head firmly and the son of Nijinsky was on his way home to Tipperary, for the new world-record price paid for a yearling racehorse. Robert Sangster finally walked into the pavilion, patted Danny Schwartz on the back and muttered, 'Go get 'em, Patton.'

The sellers of the colt were very typical of the relatively new people who were now in thoroughbred breeding. Chicago commodity stockbrokers by trade, their names were Myron Rosenthal and Mortin Levy. They had bought their first horse in 1976 and then invested in a small thoroughbred farm in the Bluegrass in 1980, with about one hundred and thirty acres upon which grazed a dozen mares. One of them was Spearfish, whom they had purchased from Will Farrish and Warner Jones in 1978 for $165,000. Their first two Keeneland yearlings from this mare, by Graustark and Vaguely Noble, had fetched $100,000 and $500,000, respectively. Then they purchased a *share* in Nijinsky for $500,000, bred the new world-record breaker from it, kept a new 1982 foal and sold the share for $700,000! This was a bull market to end all bull markets. All you had to do was buy big, at the top end, and then invest in a sack in which to take home the massive profits.

Almost everyone was making them, in particular Cousin Leslie. He consigned the second highest priced yearling, a colt by the new sire Alydar out of the Stakes winner Masked Lady, and again this resulted in a bidding duel between Robert Sangster and Sheikh Mohammed. Robert gave way on this one at $2·2 million. By the end of the two-day sale, Spendthrift Farm had sold seventeen yearlings for almost $9 million. Two of them had gone to his friend Mrs Dolly Green. The stupendous market strength is best illustrated in the fact that *none* of Masked Lady's nine previous foals had ever fetched more than $200,000.

As if this were not enough, there was also fabulous news about Cousin Leslie's new stallion Seattle Slew, who had his first crop of two-year-old runners just now coming on to the track. One of his very early runners, a powerful colt named Slewpy had come flying home at Belmont Park. And then, fourteen days later something even bigger happened: the Hollywood Lassie Stakes over six furlongs on the West Coast was won by twenty-one lengths, the largest victory margin in any stake ever run at Hollywood Park. The time was one minute eight seconds, the fastest ever recorded by a two-year-old at the track. The flying filly who achieved all this was named Landaluce. She was bred by Spendthrift Farm from a Bold Bidder mare named Strip Poker. Her dad was Seattle Slew. Like Alydar, Slew's value as a sire suddenly rocketed. He ended up the fourth leading sales stallion behind Northern Dancer, Alydar and Nijinsky. His nine yearlings were sold for an average of nearly $700,000 each, the most important one to Dolly Green, for $1·6 million – this filly was out of the Spendthrift mare Strip Poker, dam of Landaluce. 'I'm telling you,' said one Kentucky hardboot, 'if Cousin Leslie fell headlong into the biggest goddamned dung-heap in the state, he'd come out smelling of lotus blossom. Hot-*daaamn*, he's a lucky son of a gun.'

Also lucky was Arthur Hancock. As he had forecast, his Nijinsky colt went to Robert Sangster for $2·1 million. The Pools millionaire also paid out $1·8 million for a Northern Dancer colt from Solar, Try My Best's sister whom they had once owned, but, perhaps short-sightedly, sold in foal. But in this game there is no time for regrets, recriminations or contrary decisions. If you've made a mistake, correct it. Quickly. Altogether Robert and his men spent over $14 million on twelve yearlings. Sheikh Mohammed spent $12·75 million on nineteen. He and his brothers dropped a total of $20 million at the sale, while Prince Khalid Abdullah's new man, James Delahooke, spent $3·3 million for six, on behalf of this scion of the Royal family of Saudi Arabia. A total of eighteen yearlings fetched more than $1 million each.

The Keeneland average hit a truly fantastic $337,734, up thirty per cent on the previous year! The gross take for the sale hit $100 million. Right behind Cousin Leslie in the consignors' table came Windfields, whose twelve yearlings fetched $8·5 million; Warner Jones was next with fifteen head for $7·1 million; Franklin Groves's North Ridge sent up sixteen and received $6·25 million for them; and Tommy Gentry, still beating his feet to the rhythm of Ray Charles, the high priest of rock'n'roll, picked up $3 million for *two* yearlings, in a total of $6·2 million for his full consignment of twelve.

Within minutes of the end of the sale the jets were warming up on the runway across at Bluegrass Field. It was over for another year – and the big horse transportation companies were moving in to fly the yearlings back to Ireland and London. More than $56 million had been spent on young horses which would race in Europe. The first aircraft to take off was the 737 of Stavros Niarchos and before he went he confirmed that he would be a partner in three of the Sangster yearlings, which of them he would not say. The three Learjets climbed away over the warm summer fields of central Kentucky, in which were many of the great broodmares, whose babies had set the breeding world alight for forty-eight hours at the Keeneland Sales. It was quiet now in the Bluegrass and the millionaire matrons who grazed peacefully were mostly in foal again already to the great sires of the industry. Robert and his men would not pass this way again for several months. But ahead lay more excitement, England, Ascot and the King George VI and Queen Elizabeth Stakes in which Assert would attempt to crown himself the best racehorse in Europe.

This was one of the biggest days in the racing year, eagerly awaited by everyone associated with the sport because it traditionally throws together, for the first time, the cream of the three-year-olds against their elders and, sometimes, their betters. Assert had something to prove because he had won two Derbys without beating a top-class horse. Here is would be different. He would face the tough four-year-old Kalaglow of Guy Harwood's; the multi-foreign stakes winner Glint of Gold, owned by Paul Mellon; the French Derby winner of 1981, Bikala, his own half-brother; the Queen's classy filly Height of Fashion, and the Royal Ascot winner Critique.

It was a superb race, but a grave disappointment because Assert went down after a terrific struggle with Kalaglow. The distance was only a neck, and the pair of them were three lengths in front of the rest. But the fact was Assert had met a top horse three times in his life – Golden Fleece (twice) and now Kalaglow. Each time he had been beaten. If he was going to maximize his potential as a stallion he was going to have to win a Group I race, against very good horses, or there would always be a question mark against his name.

That very day brought news of great sadness in Kentucky. Mrs Lucille Markey, the elegant and autocratic owner of Calumet Farm, home of Alydar, died in Florida, at the age of eighty-five. It was the end of a long era. Mrs Markey had been the Lady of Calumet for half a century. Eight times she had watched her devil's red and blue colours carried to victory in the Kentucky Derby, starting in 1941 when Whirlaway won it by eight lengths in track-record time. She had not been well enough to take up her usual prominent seat at the Keeneland Sales, but she did know that everyone was captivated by Alydar's first yearlings and that they had fetched prices up to $2·2 million each, which she thought, 'quite frankly, excessive'. Mrs Markey's husband, Admiral Gene, had died two years previously, but her son, whom she had so dreaded acquiring control of the farm, had in fact died two years even before that. Now Calumet passed to his widow, Bertha Wright, a rather plain country woman, and her four children. They were very lucky inheritors. Calumet had no debt and in Alydar they had a stallion whose potential was something in the region of $12 million a year. As president they chose the man who had married Bertha's eldest, Cindy Markey, now thirty-six. He was separated from his wife by now, but had long hoped that he would one day take control of Calumet. His name was J. T. Lundy.

Back in England, of course, none of this rated even a mention in the newspapers, except for the trade press, but the horse breeders of Kentucky, Maryland, and Ireland were preoccupied by two common topics of conversation in the following weeks: 'What's going to happen at Calumet?' and 'What's going to happen to Assert?' The answer to the first one would take ten years to resolve. The answer to the second would be provided when David O'Brien's horse ran in the Benson and Hedges Gold Cup over a mile and a quarter at York in August. This meeting is often described as the Royal Ascot of the north, particularly by those who live in the north of England. It was a very dressy place in the Members' Enclosure. Susan Sangster was in her element here and often invited several glamorous people to join their party. And 1982 was no exception, but the day was dominated by a paralysing victory by Assert, six lengths over another moderate field – but six lengths achieved with such fabulous grace and class that no one much cared who filled the other places.

Assert had probably done sufficient to merit a very high price to stand at stud in America and when the offer came it arrived from a very unexpected quarter. Richard Galpin, the former hero of the old Newmarket Bloodstock Agency which Robert had once owned, turned up from out of the blue and suggested he might have a buyer. The interested party was Joe Thomas of Windfields, which was an equal surprise because Assert was not really his kind of stallion. Joe's general guidelines for a potential sire were simple. He liked what he called 'blood'n'guts'. That meant pedigree of the highest quality and the proven ability, on the racecourse, to scrap it out to the end with the very best runners of a given year. He rarely expressed interest in racehorses which had been 'too different' or 'too brilliant' because, he said, you then enter the science of trying to breed a 'freak' from ordinary mares. He often cited the examples of Citation, Brigadier Gerard and Secretariat as horses who completely out-classed their opponents on the racetrack. The first two were hopeless sires and Secretariat was too often a disappointment, only rarely throughout his career siring a top racehorse. Northern Dancer and The Minstrel were the exact opposite. Both of them were out-and-out scrappers, who won races by heads and necks. Both of them were superbly bred. Assert had breeding to match them, but was he the out-and-out scrapper that Joe was always seeking? Or was he a genius of a racehorse, who often ran with wings on his heels, but might not pass on to his progeny an innate courage and determination?

Whatever, Joe wanted him. And he had huge amounts of money to buy him. He was captivated by the unforgettable bounding action of the horse, and of course he cited the battle with Kalaglow at Ascot as an example of his courage. The Windfields bid of $24 million came just before the Prix de l'Arc de Triomphe. Robert accepted and everyone was very philosophical when Assert was a badly beaten favourite on very soft ground in Paris. 'It would have been a bonus,' said Joe, standing in the rain on the Champs Elysées. 'But he'd done enough to justify his price. I have no problems with the deal financially.'

Well, easy come, easy go. In 1982 horse breeders did not get disappointed. They just called in the favours, syndicated the stallion and sat back for three years before blitzing the yearling market. Vincent was very happy with the arrangement, because he was sure that in Golden Fleece they had kept the best of them for Coolmore and that Joe Thomas might have his work cut out turning Assert into a top stallion. But still, Joe Thomas was the man who had put Northern Dancer, Nijinsky II and The Minstrel on this earth. He had looked after 'Northern Dancer's book' personally for every year of the stallion's life. He was a total master of the bloodlines. If he could not 'make' Assert, then nobody could.

This sale completed the quartet of multi-million dollar syndications which had taken place during the previous sixteen months. In round dollars they now added up to around $96 million – Storm Bird ($28 million), Kings Lake ($16 million), Golden Fleece ($28 million), Assert ($24 million). The figures were of course variable and not all cash, but that was the overall value which accrued to the income column of the men from Coolmore, whether in shares, seasons, to use or to sell, or to trade, or in greenbacks. It was a joyous little group which re-convened in the middle of October for the Houghton Sales at Newmarket.

They were all looking forward to Barbados by now, for they had fought their battles for one year both on the track and in the sales ring. There were a couple of nice horses they wanted to acquire this week, but the 'heavy' part of the season, the classics and Keeneland, were over. At this time of the year Susan Sangster really bloomed. In four and a half years of marriage she had done many things for her husband. She had created the most magnificent home at The Nunnery, she had taught Robert to have the most fun it was possible to have out of any given moment. And she had unquestionably brought him luck on the racecourse. Her propensity to rush out and grab the lead rein of a victorious horse was mentioned by so many people because it happened so often. When Susan showed up for the big races, Robert's horses often won. She was an expensively dressed lucky charm. Another of life's fragile lessons she attempted to instil into the owner of Vernons Pools was that indulging oneself in the company of glamorous people ought to become a way of life for a man of his wealth. And for all of the years of their marriage she sought to surround them both with people of a high public profile, often from the mainstream of show business. Robert went along with all of this, whenever it suited him.

Robert's most loyal old friends like the Harrovians Nick Robinson, Billy Hart and Bobby McAlpine, and the Carthusian politician Sir Timothy Kitson, saw rather less of him these days because Susan preferred the company of another kind of person, the kind of person more likely to turn up in the society pages of newspapers and magazines. Since their marriage, Robert had become increasingly friendly with the *Daily Express* racing writer, Charles Benson. Actually, to describe Charlie as a racing writer would be to describe Sir Winston Churchill as a bricklayer. The great statesman was indeed a member of the Bricklayers Union and was a good craftsman, as was Charlie with his sometimes-inspired tips and his column containing what he often described as 'a succession of absolute little sparklers'.

The fact was Charlie was really a socialite. He was a murderous gambler, prepared to risk fortunes on the roll of a backgammon dice and no big race in England during the past forty years has ever gone off without Charlie having about seventeen different bets in perfectly exquisite combinations. Also he was usually broke – broke, that is, by the standards of those with whom he fraternized. Which was no great disgrace since they included the Aga Khan, Lord Lucan, Jimmy Goldsmith, John Aspinall and now Robert Sangster. Charlie, however, possessed an unshakeable belief that he belonged right there, with the big hitters, and as a consequence his life had a permanently switchback quality to it. It is said that only the very rich understand the difference between themselves and the very poor. Equally, only the very well connected and the very witty understand the precise differences between themselves and the very dull and badly connected.

In the often pedantic and literal-minded upper reaches of the Sport of Kings, Charlie shone out like a slightly overweight beacon. He could be dazzlingly amusing, conjuring jests out of other people's diabolical misfortunes, making light of his own catastrophes in the betting ring, and somehow carrying himself slightly higher than those around him. 'Ah, yes, I understand you have been a frightfully clever little chap,' he once said to a towering peer of the realm who had just backed his own horse to win at Cheltenham. He had an unfailing touch with the spoken word, nurtured at Eton College and never allowed, even for one waking hour, to rest on its many laurels. Charlie on the gloomiest day could make everyone laugh. Susan Sangster loved him.

He introduced Robert to the Aga Khan. He took to hand-picking the 'correct' friends for Robert and Susan. He became not only a close and utterly trusted friend, he became a social consultant. By 1982 he was approaching his peak in this capacity. In the little champagne marquee at Newmarket Susan had gathered around her a rather different crowd from those who had been close to Robert in the days of Christine at Swettenham. There were Mr and Mrs Walter Matthau and Alec Head, the great French trainer and breeder and his wife Madame Ghislaine of the Château du Quesnay in Chantilly. There were Larry Hagman and his Swedish wife Maj. The actors Michael Medwin and Albert Finney were joined later in the afternoon by Marie Helvin, the model and former wife of David Bailey. As the racing ended, the talk in here drifted towards Australia, because Robert and Susan made an annual pilgrimage to her homeland to inspect his massive bloodstock interests there and to attend the Melbourne Cup held annually in early November.

This was the year of the great six-year-old gelding Kingston Town who had won thirty of his first forty races. There was high excitement on the flight from London for Robert and Susan, in company with Charles Benson and Billy McDonald. The race lived up to its billing, with Kingston Town, under top weight of one hundred and thirty pounds, narrowly defeated by Gurner's Way. But the Melbourne Cup was not the only reason they had gone to Australia for this annual holiday. In fact Susan was rather hoping that the visit to her homeland would help to improve their marriage, which had been going through a slightly rocky patch. There was no problem that could be construed as drastic, but Robert was spending an awful lot of time in planes, logging thousands of air-miles while attending to his worldwide bloodstock empire. Often he travelled alone or with one of the Irishmen, and Susan had long since given up trying to match his mileage or his stamina. Indeed she marvelled at his capacity to fly all over the world, living out of a suitcase, and then come home and act as if he had been playing golf all day. He possessed the constitution of an African water-buffalo and at the end of the most gruelling trek around the globe he would turn up cheerful, ready for a good bottle of champagne and as many laughs as were available.

In Australia they were immensely popular. Here Susan could pick up almost where she had left off back in the mid-70s, meeting old friends, attending society parties, often outside in the warm late-spring evenings of November and going to the races. Her photograph was, as ever, prominent in the newspapers from the moment they touched down. Where once she had been feted as the wife of the Foreign Secretary, now she was fawned upon as the wife of Australia's most important racehorse owner and breeder. They had always had wonderful times in the neighbouring great houses which flanked their mansion on the long waters of Sydney Harbour and on this sentimental journey Susan hoped the old, familiar places, where first they had met, would revitalize his affections for her.

Robert kept his horses near the city of Adelaide in south Australia, at the Lindsay Park stud and training complex, owned by the legendary Aussie trainer Colin Hayes. During the previous few years Robert and Colin had been working on a system which would allow stallions either to fly to the Southern Hemisphere for the covering season or alternately to cover mares in Ireland, timed to the Australian breeding season, and then fly the mares out to Adelaide in utero. There had been various technical problems, but over the years Robert and Colin were winning the battle both academically and financially. With twenty horses in training, Robert sometimes collected almost (Aus)$2 million in prize money during the season and Colin had made this Southern Hemisphere racing and breeding operation entirely self-sufficient.

Two years previously in 1980 Colin had trained Robert's handicapper Beldale Ball to win the Melbourne Cup. In 1981 Our Paddy Boy had won the AJC Derby, and now in 1982 Colin had trained for Robert a grey filly named Pure of Heart, who won the Group I Ryder Stakes and was the top-rated three-year-old filly of the year. She was by the Coolmore stallion Godswalk, but when Robert flew to Lindsay Park to see the breeding stock it was not the stallion he particularly wanted to see. It was the dam of Pure of Heart, his own Audrey Joan whom he had purchased sixteen years ago from clients of Eric Cousins after she had won the five-furlong sprint, the Portland Handicap at Doncaster. Audrey Joan had been the foundation mare for the Swettenham Stud, one of the first to arrive in the newly cut and fenced paddocks, out by Jodrell Bank in 1968. And now, here, in this paddock in a distant corner of the world, she was still a celebrity. But for Robert, her field would be, somehow, forever Cheshire.

Robert stood and looked at her for a while, this big chestnut mare with her white blaze and still-bold eye, and he remembered her triumph that afternoon in Yorkshire, when she had gone clear of a field of very fast colts which had included Close Call and Forlorn River. Like him, she had journeyed far and he stroked her soft nose in the evening, before the stars of the Southern Cross rose in the galaxy, and he thought, inevitably, of other times and other places. And he wondered whether all of his decisions had been right, and whether he and this mare might both be, in a way, marooned. Even the giant telescope of Jodrell Bank could no longer locate the strange heavens above Audrey Joan. Robert pretended to be impatient with nostalgia, but, like most romantics, he was ever its captive. He said goodbye to the elderly mare from the lost acres of Swettenham and wondered whether he would ever see her again, and whether she perhaps blamed him for her exile.

His mood rested heavily upon him as he walked back to Colin's house, but awaiting him were the two men who could be guaranteed to lift his spirits, his court jesters, Billy and Charlie. Actually, he had brought them on this trip to ensure that Susan remained happy and to retain an atmosphere of goodwill between them. It was almost impossible to be down at heart when these two were on form, particularly when Billy had a new girlfriend, which was often, and Charlie found endless ways of expressing his amusement – 'Such a passionate little chap'. His was the light sting of the épée. Billy's riposte was usually less subtle – 'Shot op, you fat focker' – but he was no less funny, and the pair of them had a wondrous effect on both Robert and Susan, as indeed they would have on anyone. They really were two of the world's great wits and raconteurs, and Charlie's endless stories of how he managed to keep his job at the *Daily Express*, despite the clashing demands of his social life and his editor, ought one day to be recorded formally. It should also be mentioned that he never once betrayed a friend, no matter how close to the inside story he was. Day after day he wrote his column and sometimes he used the most sacred information. But sometimes he refused to do so. The price of his position of total trust among his peers was the frequent wrath of his superiors – 'Such excitable little fellows'.

He also affected total amazement that bachelor Billy was able to attract any girls, far less the string of quite remarkable beauties he seemed to captivate with his stories of high adventure in the world of the thoroughbred horse. Also Billy was unfailingly generous. If he had a pile of money, he would spend it. If Robert had needed money, Billy would have given him every penny he had and never bothered to ask for it back. Such a man, of such boundless generosity both with himself and with his fluctuating wealth, will always have a following, and some

of them will be great-looking girls. The mystery was how many of them
agreed to marry the wily Casanova from California.

But here there was another tactic, shrewdly delivered, recklessly
assembled and guaranteed to fill with awe any lady with designs on
Billy. There was Billy's 'house on the Isle of Man' (The Nunnery).
There was Billy's 'Irish stud farm' (Coolmore). There was his 'racing
stable' (Ballydoyle); his 'runabout' (Robert's private jet); his 'house on
the beach' (Jane's Harbour, Robert's magnificent house at Sandy Lane,
Barbados). Robert knew perfectly well that Billy frequently claimed his
assets to impress new girlfriends and it caused hours of laughter over
late dinners all over the world. '... Then he told her he had this little
stud farm in Tipperary, where he kept a few stallions . . . !'

Occasionally he stepped slightly beyond the boundaries of Robert's
possessions and breezily mentioned 'the house in Newmarket', which
he used for the sales and the races. This was actually the home of Mr
and Mrs Jeremy Hindley, an historic racing stable named Clarehaven,
along the Bury Road, where Robert and Susan usually stayed when they
came to Newmarket. Jeremy was an old friend and trained a sizeable
stable of seventy to eighty horses. He had also been heir to a sizeable
fortune and his family owned the famous Ribblesdale Stud, near York.
His father was a master of foxhounds up on the Yorkshire–Lancashire
borders and had been Captain of the British Equestrian team in the
1952 Olympics. Jeremy's wife, Sally, was the daughter of the Berkshire
landowner and sportsman Sidney Smart. Her sister was married to the
eminent Home Secretary in Margaret Thatcher's Government (and
future Foreign Secretary), Douglas Hurd. The Hindleys' splendid home
on Bury Road was not too bad a place to 'claim'.

Sally always made Billy welcome and of course she knew that various
girls from California to London believed that Clarehaven was Mr
McDonald's Newmarket residence. Like Robert, she and Jeremy considered it a huge joke, particularly on the occasion when Billy had
solemnly announced his engagement to the very beautiful New York
horsewoman and television personality Charlsie Cantey. News of this
forthcoming marriage absolutely stunned the racing world, because
Charlsie, the former wife of the top trainer Joe Cantey, really was very
special. She had used to ride work for Frank Whiteley and had exercised
both Forego and Ruffian. She was slim, with dark wavy hair and was
known to millions for conducting television interviews from the saddle
at the big New York race meetings.

They arrived in Newmarket together and drove up to the front door

of Clarehaven. Charlsie got out of the car first while Billy struggled with
the luggage, and she rang the bell. Sally opened the door and Charlsie,
assuming her to be Billy's housekeeper, handed her the laundry and said:
'I wonder if you would be kind enough to take care of this.'

Sally, with fifteen house-guests, was slightly thrown, but inquired
politely, 'Are you sure you have the right house?'

'Yes. Clarehaven, Mr McDonald's house.'

Sally sighed the sigh of those who have been here before.

'*Billy!*' she thought. But she went along with it, accepted the laundry
and showed Charlsie to her room. Actually, she went along with Billy's
subterfuge all the way to breakfast on the following day, which she
cooked for the happy couple, a service which was slightly marred when
Charlsie sent her eggs back, for being improperly cooked.

Robert, hearing this altercation, for the only time in his life did the
nose trick with his orange juice and practically had to be given oxygen
to stop himself laughing. Sally, less amused, took the eggs away, with
the somewhat ungracious phrase, for an English housekeeper, 'I'm just
not into sunnyside up, or down, or whatever they're supposed to be.'
Anyway all of their joint efforts to portray Billy as the master of
Clarehaven came to nothing, for the engagement floundered and
Charlsie quite swiftly left him.

The efforts of Benson and McDonald in Australia to keep Robert
and Susan happy were also found wanting, because there was another
disagreement and the three men flew to California, en route to the
breeding stock sales in Kentucky in November, leaving Susan to spend
some time with her parents. It seemed that everyone knew things were
not going terribly well with the Sangsters and back in Tipperary John
Magnier was in a slight quandary trying to complete the Coolmore
stallion brochure for 1983. One of the main pictures in it showed Susan
Sangster holding the English Derby Trophy after Golden Fleece's victory. They agonized for days about what to do. What if Robert was
planning to leave 'The Sheila', as Susan was now known in the idiom
of the Aussie bushwhackers? The last thing anyone needed was the total
embarrassment of their principal partner. Finally it was John Magnier
who resolved the matter with a rapier-like parry of Irish logic. 'Susan
Sangster has never done us a scrap of harm,' he said. 'Run the picture.'
And so the big glossy brochure appeared, and it went around the world
with Susan very firmly on board. This was just as well because within
a few weeks Robert was reconciled with Susan, who behaved in a very
grown-up way and continued to try to keep their marriage steady.

They all went off to Barbados on vacation and spent much of their time discussing the latest, massive syndication of a stallion which had taken place in the USA. The colt was Conquistador Cielo, sired by Mr Prospector and owned by the Polish-American aviator Ricky de Kwiatkowski. Seth Hancock had syndicated this horse for $36 million, the most expensive shares ever sold in a stallion in history. Conquistador was a very good horse, and back in the spring he had not only won the Metropolitan Handicap in the fastest mile ever run in New York, 1:33 flat, he had also won the Belmont Stakes over twelve furlongs *five days later* by fourteen lengths in a truly staggering performance. But $36 mill? That was considered a huge figure for an untried stallion, with shares at $900,000 each.

Back in Ireland, Vincent was preparing the three-year-olds for the opening classics of the year. There was an early disappointment when his outstanding Northern Dancer two-year-old Danzatore, which ran in the colours of Danny Schwartz, failed to train on and had to be withdrawn from the 2000 Guineas at Newmarket. In his place ran one of the most beautifully bred racehorses in the world – a son of Northern Dancer from My Charmer, the dam of the great American champion, and now stallion, Seattle Slew. They had bought him privately from his breeders for an undisclosed fortune – rather than wait for another battle with Sheikh Mohammed in the sales ring. But he was worth every penny. The colt, named Lomond, won the first classic and John Magnier, awed by the quality of that pedigree, booked him for Coolmore, even if he never won another race, which, actually, he never did.

The next star to emerge was Caerleon, a tough compact Nijinsky colt from a sister to the American millionaire gelding Royal Glint. They had bought him for $800,000 at Keeneland in 1981, the sale at which the three Northern Dancers had made nearly $10 million. In fact the $3·5 million top-priced lot which they had bought, was now named Ballydoyle and had been a huge disappointment. Caerleon was however a completely different matter. This fellow could run, and win. He had done so twice as a two-year-old and, in 1983, beautifully trained by Vincent, he won the French Derby for Robert, for the second year in a row. He won it by three lengths over the excellent French colt, L'Emigrant, a son of The Minstrel who had won the French 2000 Guineas. They did not have a Derby colt in the same league as Golden Fleece, but Vincent did have very high hopes for Caerleon in the Irish Derby. There they would run into the powerful winner of the English Derby Teenoso and

Vincent was very confident that the improving Caerleon would deal with him.

The slightly unknown quantity was Michael Stoute's colt Shareef Dancer, which now ran in the colours of Sheikh Maktoum al-Maktoum. This was the second Northern Dancer at that sale in 1981, the one out of Sweet Alliance, purchased by Sheikh Mohammed for $3·3 million, but presented to his eldest brother as a gift. Shareef Dancer was not terribly big and possessed many of the characteristics of his sire, and he had won the King Edward VII Stakes at Royal Ascot. Sheikh Mohammed had named him for the descendants of the Prophet Muhammad – the Hashemite Shareefs who ruled Mecca for many centuries.

Vincent could stand defeat for Caerleon, but all of the shareholders silently and privately prayed that it would not be by Shareef Dancer, because they could surely have faced down the Sheikh at that sale just as they had done for Storm Bird's disappointing brother. Shareef Dancer they all knew *could* have been theirs. But he was not, and, as he bolted clear of Caerleon halfway up the home straight there was a collective groan from Vincent, Robert and John. Shareef Dancer won it by three lengths, with Teenoso a further two lengths back in third, but even the groans of Robert and John could not overshadow the glorious smiles of delight from the men from Dubai, as they won their first Derby.

Robert as ever was the first to become philosophical, and Vincent was quite cheerful. He thought Caerleon had run well, been a bit unlucky, and would improve. John loved his pedigree and was desperately hoping that Vincent could win another big race with him, so that he too, like Lomond, could join the stallion ranks at Coolmore. Thus far it had not been a bad season. They had won two of the principal six European colts' classics, with two different horses, one by Northern Dancer and one by Nijinsky. And Caerleon had beaten two of the other winners. They were almost home on their 1981 yearling investment and they looked to the oncoming Keeneland Sale with great anticipation.

'I suppose this will have inspired the Arabs to take us on even more bloody belligerently,' said Robert belligerently, in the Turf Club afterwards. And not so very far away, Sheikh Mohammed felt within him the ancient Bedouin love of conquest. He knew the Keeneland catalogues would soon be arriving back in England. He had dispatched his men to examine the yearlings early. The oil was flowing in his father's desert Sheikhdom. An even more vast fortune was accruing to him and his brothers and he believed that success in this great European classic horse race would bring honour upon his people and his nation. He knew that the pedigree of Shareef Dancer traced its roots to Arabia and he knew the stallions by which those roots were traced. In Northern Dancer it went back through Nearco to Phalaris, and on back through Bend Or, Stockwell and Whalebone to Eclipse. Sheikh Mohammed knew that the great-grandsire of Eclipse was Bartlett's Childers, the son of the Darley Arabian, the great bay horse with the white blaze and three white feet who was shipped to England from Aleppo, in Syria, in the early years of the seventeenth century.

But, more importantly, he knew that the sire of Sweet Alliance, Sir Ivor, traced to the American champion Man O'War through his third dam. Man O'War's sire line runs back to Australian, then West Australian, through Melbourne and Sorcerer to Matchem, the grandson of the legendary Godolphin Arabian. He too was exported around 1730 from Syria. But the Godolphin Arabian came from the Jilfan blood of the great horsemen of the hostile and forbidden kingdom of the Yemen, on the southern corner of the Arab Peninsula, six hundred miles across the Empty Quarter from Dubai. The Godolphin, like his far-distant descendant, Shareef Dancer, was dark in colour and not very tall, just 14·3 hands, but with a huge crested neck. He was an Arabian classic in appearance and, as the new winner of the Irish Derby had roots in the Yemen, so perhaps did Sheikh Mohammed himself, because it was here, in the south-west, that the true Arabs, the sons of Qahtan, were reputed to have originated, long before the tribes drifted north across the Rub' al-Khali, some reaching Dubai and northern Oman. Every time Sheikh Mohammed gazed at Shareef Dancer, he saw in him the desert and a reflection of the ancient breeds of Arabian horses, the bedrock of the modern thoroughbred bloodlines.

There is a sense of romanticism in the steely soul of the Bedouin. But it blooms in his sense of ancestry and survival and, above all, conquest of that which threatens him. Sheikh Mohammed, staring out from the Curragh at the Irish hills to the south-east, thought ahead to the Keeneland sales ring, in which he must take on the entire racing world the following month. He spoke to himself, silently. 'I will not be beaten this year by Mr Sangster and his men,' he vowed. 'I will do whatever I must to win.' And already the light of battle gleamed in his dark, hard eyes.

12

The $40 Million
Short-head

The avalanche of foreign cash into central Kentucky had brought with it, over the past seven years, many outward signs of prosperity: miles of freshly painted white fences, perfectly constructed new barns resplendent in the livery of their owners' racing colours. The cash had bought for them big cars, Lincolns, Mercedes and Cadillacs, chauffeurs and gardeners. It had also bought them private jet aircraft and huge expense accounts for travel and entertainment. All of this applied in particular to Spendthrift Farm, where the towering Brownell Combs had been working like a Trojan to earn the miserably withheld approval of his own father, the redoubtable octogenarian, Cousin Leslie.

What the cash had not bought any of them, however, was peace. All over the Bluegrass the same petty jealousies, disagreements and traditional feuds continued apace. The uncertainty over the accession of J. T. Lundy at Calumet. The sudden decision of Seth Hancock to withdraw Claiborne from the Keeneland Sales at the height of this bull market and race his own stock. While the outlawed brother Arthur crashed forward, built a farm now *bigger* than Claiborne, won the Kentucky Derby and was out there selling yearlings for upwards of $2 million. The lack of peace applied in particular to the residents of Spendthrift Farm.

On one famous occasion Cousin Leslie had bawled out Brownell in front of about four people and told his son, and corporate president, to 'Get the hell off my damned farm'.

'Yessir, Mr Combs,' replied Brownell. 'Would you just be able to give me time to bring in the big horse van, because I shall be taking Affirmed, Seattle Slew and Wajima right along with me, on account of I syndicated them and all of them are owned by Combs Stallions, which in turn is owned by me.'

'Now, I didn't mean anything by that,' said Cousin Leslie. 'Just a manner of speaking. You, son, are my own flesh and blood. And the job you have been doing has been just fantastic.'

It was said to have been the only time in Brownell's entire life that his father showed him any respect. Which says something about the affable good nature of Brownell, the master syndicator of stallions. And it probably says something else again about Cousin Leslie, made him feel that at last the farm was in good hands after all of his years of devoted tuition.

Another problem that vanished for the great man was Linda Combs's suede pants. Stung by his constant criticism of her, by the way he tried to make her feel an outsider, after all that she had done to help them with the syndicates, she finally packed up, left and divorced Brownell in 1981. She had been a very important part of Spendthrift and they would feel her loss badly. Also she left with a major pay-off, some of it in breeding rights to the stallions and with, of course, young Brownell Jr. A great-looking, very bright lady, it would not be long before she remarried.

There were those in Lexington, however, who thought Linda might have jumped ship at precisely the wrong time. Leslie Combs had now made it possible for Brownell to buy out thirty-eight per cent of his own shareholding in Spendthrift and the two of them, with fifty per cent each, had grandiose plans to make Spendthrift into the biggest commercial money-spinner the bloodstock industry had ever seen. They planned to take the entire assets of the farm, stallions, mares, foals, yearlings and land, and become a public corporation. The first step they took in this direction in the spring of 1983 was to float thirty per cent of the assets of the farm to a group of select private investors at a cost of around $1 million each. This bought each of the thirty-five investors 100,000 shares making a 'book' total of $35 million into the kitty, with father and son still retaining the other seventy per cent.

At this time the assets of Spendthrift included 2000 acres, two training centres, one in Lexington and one in Florida, forty-three stallions (most of which were owned by syndicates, not by Spendthrift) one hundred and seventy-five broodmares, one hundred and thirty-eight sucklings and some eighty horses in training around the world. Seventy-five yearlings were scheduled to go to the American sales this summer. In November the plan was that Spendthrift would go public, with shares trading on one of the American Stock Exchanges. There would be ten million shares out there, a third held by the new investors, with a third each being kept or traded by Cousin Leslie and Brownell. The eighty-one-year-old founder would remain Chairman of the Board, with Brownell continuing as president and chief executive.

The thirty-five investors were in place by July 1983 and they included some extremely diverse characters, one of them being Mrs Andrew Wyeth, the wife of America's foremost painter, the only living artist to have had a one-man exhibition at the Metropolitan Museum of Art in New York. Betsy Wyeth had always held a rather arm's-length view of the world of thoroughbreds although she was surrounded with them close to her home at Chadds Ford, on the edge of the Pennsylvania racehorse-breeding country. She had long been great friends with some of the most important of the local breeders, George Strawbridge, Russell and Ritchie Jones of Walnut Tree Farm, Marshall Jenney of Derry Meeting Farm, and, of course, her son Jamie was married to the former Phyllis Mills, a member of the horse-loving duPont family and herself a keen owner of steeplechasers and breeder of flat-racers. Phyllis was the daughter of Mr and Mrs Jimmy Mills of Hickory Tree Farm, Virginia, next door, and of a similar size, to the estate of Mr Paul Mellon.

More than ten years ago Phyllis's sister, Mimi, who was formerly married to the English racehorse trainer Bernard van Cutsem, had been a major part of the syndicate which purchased for a record price Crowned Prince, Majestic Prince's brother, from Cousin Leslie. And now, here was the most unlikely member of the family, a lady fascinated by art, writing, antiques and culture, handing over another big cheque to the very same farm. The world of thoroughbred breeding moves along through small and sometimes unexpected circles, but when the Grande Dame of Chadds Ford moved in, some people thought it was as if her great friend, the author, art historian and Egyptologist, Thomas Hoving, had bought a baseball club.

Meanwhile, back at Spendthrift, on 14 July, they were preparing their consignment of twenty-one yearlings, without an obvious star lot, for the forthcoming sale. The Learjets were screaming into Bluegrass Field, everyone was in early, but the Boeing 727 already parked near the end of the runway was that of Sheikh Mohammed bin Rashid al-Maktoum. This year Stavros Niarchos had agreed to become a serious partner in Robert Sangster's operation, alongside Danny Schwartz, Vincent and John Magnier. They felt instinctively that this year the prices could go even higher, that the $4·25 million world record set by Robert last year could be beaten, that the average cost of each yearling might even go higher than the $344,000 it had hit last July.

The identity of the probable sale-topper was public knowledge. It would be, of course, by Northern Dancer, but this year there was a colt from a very special mare, My Bupers, whose place in thoroughbred history was earned in the final days of the 1976 New York racing season. On a cool, damp autumn afternoon, they ran the race which often decides the destiny of the Eclipse Award for the American Sprinter of the Year. It is called the Vosburgh Handicap and is run over seven furlongs at Aqueduct – 'sprints' in the States meaning a mile or under rather than the strict five- or six-furlong dashes of England and France. This Eclipse Award is both historic and of enormous importance to breeders, for its winners must have demonstrated fantastic speed over a considerable distance of ground in the full heat of competition. Many of the great ones had won it – Polynesian (the sire of Native Dancer), Tom Fool, Bold Ruler, Dr Fager, Ack Ack and Forego. But among these exalted ranks of speed-kings, there were few fillies.

In 1976 there was one of the best Vosburgh fields for years, including the Kentucky Derby and Belmont Stakes winner Bold Forbes, who was odds-on favourite. There was also the stakes winner Soy Numero Uno; the winner of the Carter Handicap Due Diligence; Our Hero, who had just smashed the seven-furlong record in the Atlantic City Handicap; the multi-stakes winner It's Freezing; and the 9–1 shot, My Juliet. The latter filly was a huge sentimental favourite of the crowd. She had won thirteen races before her fourth birthday, but in the May of the year she had badly fractured a cannon-bone. Now she had won three races off the reel during her October comeback, each time again shading twenty-one seconds flat for the first quarter. The crowd loved this brave, dark bay darling of the home-stretch and in any other race but this Vosburgh she would have been favourite.

But today, against Bold Forbes and the rest of these tearaways, she plainly had no chance. No chance until the starting gates opened, that is, because when they did, My Juliet shot forward like a drag racer and, recording blistering times every panel of the way, she was still in front of Bold Forbes at the wire – by two lengths. There was hardly a dry eye in the house as the filly who had come back from the dead lowered the colours of the duel-classic winner. The Eclipse Award was a mere formality for the daughter of the stallion Gallant Romeo. Her dam was My Bupers.

Now, seven years after that remarkable Vosburgh Stakes, here was a colt from the very same mare, My Juliet's half-brother, sired by the greatest stallion of modern times. He had white socks and a white blaze. Everyone who looked at him saw a near-mirror image of Northern

Dancer himself and everyone who looked at him wondered if he might also have the heart, the resilience and the speed of My Juliet. Such was the excitement about this colt, there were people predicting that bidding for him could go to $5 million, maybe even $6 million, a sum of money no breeder had hitherto dreamed of receiving for any yearling who was ever born.

All through the weekend of 16 and 17 July, and all through the day on Monday, the local radio stations were imploring people not to attend the sales. It was feared that the huge crowds might just swamp the place because it had become not so much a horse auction as pure theatre. At Tommy Gentry's sales party the theme was 'Carnival'. Sergio Mendes sang 'Fool on the Hill', and Dolly Green went for a ride on a fifty-year-old elephant named Myrtle, which practically gave Cousin Leslie a haemorrhage. Robert's table was adjacent to Sheikh Mohammed's and nearby Tom had thoughtfully tethered a thirty-year-old camel named Charlie, 'for atmosphere'. Charlie was from a circus in Atlanta and studiously ignored Sheikh Mohammed, the only man in Kentucky who could have taken him for a sharp five furlongs. Late at night Tommy nodded at the tables of Robert and the Sheikh, and he confirmed: 'That's the heavy-duty spot in this tent – they're mah main men.'

On the sale's opening night, nothing could stop Kentuckians from miles around flocking to the Keeneland arena for both days of the sale to watch the unbelievable dramas taking place in the ring. They packed the grounds, the parking lots were full to overflowing, thousands just stood about watching the big, lit-up numbers boards recording the bids. It was almost impossible for the consignors and vendors to get through the crowds into their reserved seats.

On the first day, eleven yearlings fetched over $1 million. Sheikh Mohammed went to $2·5 million for the Windfields daughter of Northern Dancer and Ballade, making this half-sister to the millionaire champion racemare Glorious Song the most expensive yearling filly in history. Sheikh Mohammed then paid $1·3 million for a daughter of Alydar, $4·1 million for a Nijinsky colt from Belle of Dodge Me, and $2 million more for a colt by Blushing Groom from an unraced daughter of Vaguely Noble. But the Sheikh was stopped in his tracks when the first son of Northern Dancer came up, out of the brilliant racemare Desert Vixen. Robert moved in here, with all of their big guns, and they landed him for the world-record-tying price of $4·25 million.

By now half of Lexington was swarming around the outside of the auditorium. It was impossible to get through the long outside passage which surrounds the selling arena. Calls for the crowds to retreat were hopeless. It was like Madison Square Gardens the night Ali fought Joe Frazier, the same electric atmosphere, different gladiators. And everyone knew the time and place of the main event. Late on Tuesday evening, The Men from Tipperary v. The Royal Family of Dubai, for the Northern Dancer–My Bupers colt, Lot Number 308.

Shortly after 10.45 p.m. the two rival camps began to sort themselves out. Sheikh Mohammed left his seat in the auditorium and moved over to the divided holding area, accompanied by his personal secretary John Leat, the son of his former chauffeur and himself a skilled man behind the wheel of a car. Right behind them stood the Sheikh's stud manager, the Hon. Robert Acton, grandson of Lord Acton, Lord-in-Waiting to two British monarchs, King Edward VII and King George V. Indeed Robert's great-grandfather, the first Lord Acton, was Lord-in-Waiting to Queen Victoria. This is a family of immense distinction, of titled scholars and diplomats, stretching back in an unbroken line to the reign of Charles I, and in a further line to the reign of King Edward III. Robert himself had served his apprenticeship in the thoroughbred industry at Claiborne Farm, Kentucky, and now he prowled the area behind the rostrum, trying as diplomatically as he could to scare off the opposition on the basis that his boss, Sheikh Mohammed, was *going to buy this colt*.

As Colonel Dick Warden took up his position a few steps from Dubai's Minister of Defence, Robert and his men gathered in full strength on the other side of the partition in the holding area. Robert Acton knew that if he could somehow discourage Robert, it might save them several million dollars. And he strolled by with a smile and said: 'There's no use your bidding, actually. We're going to get this colt.' Robert Sangster was undaunted. Stavros Niarchos was in this partnership. Danny Schwartz was in 'for whatever it takes'. Vincent and John were absolutely determined that they were going to buy this yearling. Robert had a good 'spread' here. Even if it cost $6 million that was still only $1·25 million for each of the main investors. They could handle this, and he summoned his men to stay close, in case there was a need to caucus. Joss Collins of the British Bloodstock Agency (London) would do the bidding and he would be accompanied by Sir Philip Payne Gallwey, representing Mr Niarchos.

All of the major players in the world bloodstock league were in place in their usual seats: Joe Thomas with Charles Taylor, Leslie Combs and Brownell, John Gaines, Warner Jones and Arthur Hancock. The consignors of the colt, the owners of Crescent Farm, came in a few minutes before the sale – Mr Don Johnson, a coal-mining man from eastern Kentucky, who had bought My Bupers a few years earlier in partnership with John Gaines. Holding his arm, in anticipation of the tense and bitter contest to come, was his new wife Linda, the former Mrs Brownell Combs. She did not even glance over at the president of Spendthrift and his father, who were having one of their more moderate sales, but still raking in several millions.

Lot Number 308 was led in. Vincent muttered, 'My God, he is the most beautiful mover.' And the announcer was quick to point out that My Bupers had not only produced My Juliet, plus Lyphard's Special, a stakes winner in Europe, but also five other winners. And then he handed over to Scott Caldwell to begin the auction. He spoke three sentences about the colt, and then he shouted, 'All right, *let's go!* Who'll gimme a million for him?'

'*Yeah! Right here,*' called the bid-spotter, flinging his arm skywards.

'Two million, will ya gimme two, gimme two . . . gimme two two?' '*Yeah!!*'

'Three million, will ya gimme three, gimme three, gimme three . . . ?' '*Yeah!!*'

'Do I hear four . . . will ya gimme four . . . four . . . four . . . ?' '*Yeah!!*'

Now Dick Warden was in, bidding against the California trainer D. Wayne Lukas, and the crowd stood up and roared their applause as the tropical-suited English gentleman bid $4·5 million, breaking last year's record. As the bidding cleared $5 million they applauded again, but now Wayne Lukas dropped out. Joss Collins nodded for the first time at $5·3 million on behalf of Robert Sangster. Warden and Collins cracked on, unhesitating with their nods, $100,000 at a time. The bids blazed past $6 million and the auditorium sat hushed almost in disbelief as it hit $7 million.

'And one . . . and fifty . . .'

The audience rippled as Joss Collins low-balled Warden for the first time. But the Colonel matched it. Then Collins bid $7·3 million. But Warden suddenly upped the stakes and said firmly, 'Seven and a half.' The old boy could run on both leads, no doubt about that.

Robert's men caucused. There was tension written on every one of their faces. Robert said he'd increase his stake if necessary. And Joss Collins looked up and bid $7·6 million.

'Seven seven . . . do I have seven seven . . . seven eight . . . seven nine . . . *$8 million* I am bid.'

Again Robert's men caucused. Nerves were beginning to fray. John Magnier thought it was getting a bit ridiculous. And Vincent was no longer so strong. Robert, however, was as determined as Sheikh Mohammed. And he increased his share. He said he would take twenty-five per cent of the horse, thirty, if necessary. 'On that basis let's go to ten,' he said.

Robert Acton, watching them debate the issue, spoke again quietly, 'You're never going to beat us,' he said. 'Why try?' But Robert muttered something which meant, broadly, 'Shut up, for God's sake.' And Joss Collins bid $8·1 million.

It was not that Robert wouldn't stop. He couldn't. Something had taken hold of him. His face was set tight. He believed that Vincent had invented Northern Dancer, that it was Nijinsky and The Minstrel who had made his reputation. And Storm Bird had added to it. This little horse in the ring belonged in County Tipperary and he, Robert, was damned if he was going anywhere else. 'Go to nine,' he told Joss. 'And if that won't do it go to ten.'

'Eight three ... eight four ... eight five ...'

A roar went up at $9 million.

Robert said, 'Go on!' Joss bid up to $9·5 million.

Then Warden, his heart pounding, his hands shaking on his catalogue, swung round to Sheikh Mohammed's secretary John Leat, who nodded firmly. Warden cast his eyes to the heavens, and he muttered: 'Jesus Christ!' Then he bid $9·6 million for the son of Northern Dancer.

Robert called in his men once more. He told them he would not back down. They had to be with him. Every time Warden bid, the memories of the lost Nureyev, and the lost Shareef Dancer, stood before him. He *must* have this horse. In his mind Robert had a plan to blow the Arabs out of the goddamned water. And now the English gambler played his final card. He stood up and he stared down at the bid-spotter and he raised all of his fingers together, to signify a bid of a flat $10 million, raising Sheikh Mohammed by $400,000 in one deathly strike.

The lights went out on the scoreboard because they had run out of numbers. A massive roar of applause ripped into the night air outside the arena, and the crowd inside stood up and cheered the sportsman from the Isle of Man. That was surely the end of it. But Sheikh Mohammed had not moved. His eyes still stared directly in front of him. He too sensed victory with all the instinct bred into him from generations of desert warriors. And then Colonel Dick Warden bid $10·2 million.

Robert turned around helplessly. Phonsie put his hand on his shoulder and said, 'It doesn't make any difference what we do, Robert. They're not going to give up. We're bidding against an entire bloody nation. We're going to lose him.'

Robert looked at the bid-spotter for the last time. He smiled and shook his head, and he walked out of the pavilion, uncertain whether to laugh or cry. Sheikh Mohammed too walked out of the pavilion, straight into his waiting air-conditioned limousine which swept him over to the private Boeing. He and his entourage took off almost immediately. Sheikh Mohammed knew he had gone too far, knew that no baby racehorse is worth that kind of a gamble, and he knew that he had been goaded by the in-built Bedouin instinct of pride – the only master of men which knows no boundaries. He also knew that if it had not been for Robert Sangster the colt would have been his for under $5·5 million.

Back at the barns the former Linda Combs was as happy as she had ever been, sipping champagne with her ecstatic husband and friends. The representative of the shipping company arrived for the colt. He had the right papers, but no lead-shank. 'That is not going to be a problem,' she said, with the calm smile that had so captivated the young Brownell, but had nearly driven his father mad. 'For ten point two million dollars', she added, 'I'm going to include a lead-shank. Yessir.'

And so concluded the greatest thoroughbred horse sale in history. A world-record price and a Keeneland average that now hit $526,000 for each yearling, up by fifty-three per cent on the previous year. The gross was over $147 million, up nearly fifty per cent. The foreign buyers had bought forty-six per cent of the stock (129 yearlings) for $96 million. Twenty-four yearlings fetched over $1 million. Sheikh Mohammed and his brothers, Sheikh Hamdan and Sheikh Maktoum, bought twenty-six yearlings for $43,265,000. Robert Sangster's men bought fourteen yearlings for almost $18 million. Prince Khalid bought nine for $5,770,000.

But this sales ring, which had belonged to Robert for so long, no longer did so. The men from the Middle East had taken over. If Robert, Vincent and John were to remain at the top of the game, they knew they must be cleverer, more careful in their purchases. On the plane home PP Hogan finally broke the tension of the losing battle. 'Actually,' he said, 'I didn't like the bloody horse from the start. I've got a t'ousand that says he won't run a yard.' The footnote to the sale was that PP was right. The horse was taken home to England and trained by John Dunlop. Named Snaafi Dancer, he could not beat a fat man going downhill. Sheikh Mohammed's dreams of Derby glory with this highly bred son of Northern Dancer withered on the vine. A mile and a half at Epsom? Snaafi Dancer could not have got the trip in a horsebox. And as a stallion? He was infertile – a $10·2 million catastrophe, which will live for ever in the folklore of thoroughbred racing.

But that was the Arabs' problem, not Kentucky's. As the jets rumbled out over the Bluegrass, heading east to New York, the big breeders were left counting fantastic profits. Behind Don and Linda Johnson in the consignors' league came North Ridge Farm. Franklin Groves was taking to his home beside the transplanted oaks almost $9 million for the sale of a dozen yearlings. Cousin Leslie had just over $7 million for twenty-one, which was not so good a hitting-average as Linda's $10·2 million for one. Windfields earned nearly $7 million for seven, and Tom Gentry sold thirteen for $6,685,000, which helped pay for Sergio Mendes to perform the cabaret at his buyers' party.

John Magnier, studying the results of the sales, said the best news he could see was the fact that so many of the most expensive fillies were coming to Europe to race for the Arabs. A preliminary glance showed him the Northern Dancer, the expensive Alydar, the Seattle Slew, another Alydar, one by Halo, yet another Alydar, a Roberto, one by Irish River out of the Marchioness of Tavistock's great broodmare Pushy, one by Spectacular Bid, one by Alleged, another by Blushing Groom. All fillies. 'That's the good news,' he muttered. 'That means they are going into breeding in a very big way. And they are going to be compelled to use our best stallions.' Magnier, even when he's been on a losing team, does not often miss a trick.

And so they headed back to Ireland. Vincent's task was to get Caerleon home in a major race, because John Magnier passionately wanted the son of Nijinsky for Coolmore. The French Derby would obviously make him a stallion, as would his defeat of the English Derby winner Teenoso at the Curragh. But another big victory would make him very valuable. They would try him in the King George, but privately Vincent thought his best distance was a mile and a quarter, which meant the Benson and Hedges Gold Cup at York. Could this splendid son of Nijinsky bring home the bacon in the top ten-furlong race in Europe?

Vincent brought him to York, trained to the finest pitch he had ever been. Worked hard through the summer mornings at Ballydoyle Caerleon was ready to run for his life. Vincent knew he may have to lead all or most of the way, that Pat Eddery may have to take him to the front early on, stretch the field out, and then hang on in the lead for victory. This is the hardest way to win any horse race and as they swung off the bend, into the long home straight, Caerleon, sure enough, was in the lead, pursued by Hot Touch, John French and yet another son of Nijinsky, the former champion two-year-old Gorytus. As they raced towards the two-furlong pole it had developed into the kind of battle Kings Lake would have relished and now Caerleon faced up to it with all the courage he had. He fought for victory as perhaps no racehorse had been asked to fight all season. He tried and tried, right down to the wire, hard under Eddery's flashing whip. Inside the last furlong he must surely have had enough. No one thought he could keep up the gallop as Hot Touch came from behind, facing the headwind for the first time. But Caerleon would not give in, and again Eddery whacked him, and he flew over the line a neck to the good. The next four horses were all within three lengths of him. Pat Eddery knew what Caerleon had done, and he said to Vincent afterwards, 'No horse ever tried harder than he did today. No horse.'

John Magnier now had two Nijinsky colts with Group I credentials to consider for the stud, because a few weeks earlier Solford, who had cost them $1·3 million in 1981, had won the Eclipse Stakes at Sandown. But John wanted Caerleon and they syndicated him very quickly. Solford earned his price back with a nice profit and was sold back to Kentucky.

The season ended for the Irishmen when another son of Northern Dancer, named Salmon Leap, bred from Kings Lake's dam Fish Bar, finished powerfully to be fifth in the Prix de l'Arc de Triomphe, only two lengths behind the winning French filly, All Along, the fifth of her sex in succession to win this often unpredictable race, contested so late in the season. But at Ballydoyle at this time of the year there is keener interest in the new two-year-olds, as Vincent brings them out, fit and sharp, to see the racecourse for the first time. This year he had two real fliers, both by Northern Dancer – Sadler's Wells, homebred by Robert out of Fairy Bridge, the little one Billy McDonald had found at Claiborne; and El Gran Senor, another Northern Dancer colt out of Sex Appeal, thus a full-brother to Try My Best.

There was huge interest in these two because of their superior breeding: Fairy Bridge was a half-sister to the brilliant Nureyev, and Sex Appeal's half-sister Blush With Pride had won the Kentucky Oaks. If either of the colts could run, they would be worth huge fortunes as stallions. Also they now owned Sex Appeal. Billy McDonald, who had sold out his share in Fairy Bridge to pay a gambling debt, was nevertheless so excited at seeing her son run he flew from California to the Isle of Man to share with Robert the forthcoming dramas on the track. And all the news was excellent. El Gran Senor won three in Ireland, took Vincent's well-trodden path to Newmarket for the Dewhurst Stakes, and won it by half a length from Prince Khalid's unbeaten Rainbow Quest, a future winner of the Prix de l'Arc de Triomphe. Sadler's Wells won his maiden and then slaughtered the field by six lengths in the Group II Beresford Stakes at the Curragh. Billy and Robert were beside themselves with excitement. Everything was going brilliantly and Robert, with his favourite court jester ensconced at The Nunnery, continued to be amazed at the speed with which his American bloodstock agent could think. 'He's faster on his feet than Sadler's Wells will ever be,' says Robert.

On Billy's second night on the island he decided to pop down to the casino, late, for a drink. Robert elected not to go and when Billy returned in the small hours, he blundered into the house and was immediately joined by Robert's new black labrador, an ex-gun dog which had belonged to the English jockey Brian Taylor. As trained, the dog stuck close to Bill, who instantly fell over him, crashed into a Regency table, smashed the table lamp and was plunged into darkness.

Bill regained his feet, fell over the dog again, hit the big magazine table in the centre of the great hall and tipped the entire thing over. 'Fock!!' yelled Bill, sliding around on copies of *Vogue*, *Harpers*, and the *Bloodhorse*. But, game to the end, he rose once more and found the light switches, and turned them all on – about twenty-five of them. Up the stairs he went but, halfway up, he fell over the dog again, this time bringing down a bronze statue which rolled to the bottom.

Now, he was in sight of victory and, like a latter-day Sherpa Tensing, he pressed on to the summit. However, three steps from the top, he fell over the dog again. He lurched forward and, grabbing at the leg of the Georgian table on the left for balance, he pulled it right over his head and it fell to the first landing taking a large Chinese lamp with it. Even the dog left at this stage. And in the morning Robert was absolutely aghast at what he saw: all the lights on and a trail of uproar from the front door almost to Billy's bedroom. Robert's first thought was that the place had plainly been ransacked by thieves in the night. But then he remembered, as he had done so many times during the career of the mercurial agent . . . *Billy*.

He charged back up the stairs, into the yellow suite occupied by McDonald and shouted: 'Bill . . . Bill . . . Wake up, what the devil's happened?'

Billy's eyes opened, focused painfully, and he snapped, 'D'black dog did it,' a phrase which has subsequently entered the rich and varied tapestry of the folklore of The Nunnery.

'It was not the majesty of the words, or anything,' says Robert. 'Nor even the dimension of the whopper. It was the speed. The pure speed of his brain – Billy, three-quarters asleep, with a hangover, is about twice as quick as most prime ministers at Question Time in the House ... "D'black dog did it!"'

Billy was due to depart on the Monday morning and it was essential that he rose early and made the plane to London, to attend to a deal for Robert. However, they went out to lunch on Sunday, had a few glasses, and went back to The Nunnery for a late-afternoon siesta, before dinner. Billy crashed into his bed and slept the sleep of the heavily refreshed. Robert called him at about eight o'clock in the evening, entering the room in his towelling robe and saying cheerfully, 'Christ! Are you still in bed?'

Billy leapt to his feet and shouted: 'It was not my fault. The plane was full. I couldn't get on it. I had to come back.'

'No, Bill, that's tomorrow,' said Robert patiently. 'Come along down for dinner.'

Again, it was not the whopper. It was the sheer, naked speed of it.

They were together again three weeks later at the Keeneland November Sale for breeding stock and foals. Billy was a bit strapped for cash at the time and he and Robert were sitting in the auditorium when a couple came in and sat down next to them. Within a couple of minutes they were bidding on a foal. Suddenly, to Robert's amazement, Billy started to bid against them.

'Twenty thousand I have,' called the auctioneer.

'Twenty-one,' bid Billy.

'Twenty-two,' signalled the couple.

'Twenty-three thousand,' said Billy.

'Twenty-four,' signalled the couple.

At which point Billy leaned over and whispered to them, 'Either you give me a thousand bucks to stop bidding, or I'll give you a thousand bucks to quit.'

The husband and wife, conferred, and then handed Billy $1000. The colt was theirs.

'Fock this,' said Billy to Robert. 'Let's go and have a drink.'

'Basically,' said Robert, 'when you are in the horse business, it's as well to have a chap like that on your side. He just knew that couple had come to the sale to buy that foal. Let's face it, I love him!'

In the little bar at Keeneland that evening, the talk was all of yet another gigantic syndication in the USA. The new Champion Two-Year-Old, Devil's Bag, winner of the Cowdin Stakes, the Champagne Stakes and the Laurel Futurity, had been bought by Claiborne Farm for yet another $36 million. With Conquistador already in residence, Seth Hancock was getting pretty good at this. Storm Bird was beginning to look cheap. Devil's Bag was yet another very fast horse masterminded by Joe Thomas. He was by the Windfields stallion Halo, whom Joe had bought for Mr Taylor for $1 million. This one was absolutely Joe's kind of stallion, tough, durable and resolute on both dirt and grass, winner of the United Nations Handicap at the age of five, and owner of an enviable pedigree – by Hail To Reason, out of Cosmah, who was herself a half-sister to Northern Dancer's mum, Natalma. The dam of Devil's Bag was Ballade, whom Joe had also bought and who was also the dam of the champion racemare Glorious Song. Devil's Bag had been bought at the sales for $325,000 by Mr and Mrs Jimmy Mills of Hickory Tree Farm, Virginia – they were, of course, the parents of Mrs Jamie Wyeth.

Jimmy Mills took the huge profit he was being offered with commendable dexterity and no sooner was the ink dry on the contract than Joe recommended to the Taylor family that they sell Halo. Half the world was banging down the door to Windfields with offers for him and Joe had plenty of the blood on the farm, so he elected to 'cash out'.

'I got a bit confused early on in the dealings,' he recalls. 'All over my desk were these huge numbers. I finally worked out that the ones with ten digits starting with "60" were Kentucky phone numbers. The ones with only eight starting with "30" were offers for Halo.' The best one, however, was from Seth's brother Arthur, on behalf of the Texan, Tom Tatham. The fourteen-year-old Halo went to Stone Farm for something close to $28 million, a number which had stunned the industry when it was paid for Storm Bird in 1981, but now, a couple of years later, hardly raised an eyebrow.

But all was not carefree that winter. Two of the biggest names in racing went down cruelly, and suddenly, with cancer. The first was Golden Fleece, the giant of 1982, and the second was the man who had changed the face of modern thoroughbred breeding, Joe Thomas himself. Everyone connected with them was devastated. Golden Fleece was not yet five. Joe was only fifty-nine. A team of American surgeons was flown over to Coolmore to operate on the stallion and it had seemed successful. But in February 1984, the cancer came back. Golden Fleece fought it for several weeks, but before the flat race season opened, he was gone.

Joe Thomas flew from Maryland to his home at Oshawa, near Toronto, where he had pencilled into his book the historic mating of Nearctic and Natalma, back in the December 1959. And after his operation, he returned to the house, in which they had made him a 'hospital room', where he would finish his days. It overlooked the paddock where once he had watched the young Northern Dancer, and then the baby Nijinsky, spend their earliest months as weanlings. Joe's journalist daughter Lesley, who had spent months preparing a book on the life of Northern Dancer, called her publisher to postpone it indefinitely. Asked what she planned to do, she said, simply, 'I'm just going to sit right here and hold Joe's hand till he dies.'

The season had a double interest for the six-foot three-inch, affable master of Windfields Farm. Years before, Joe had bought Sex Appeal, had bred Try My Best, and had kept the farm in as a partner when El Gran Senor was born. When he concluded his racing days, there was a signed agreement that this colt would return to Windfields to stand as a sire, hopefully as heir-apparent to his father, Northern Dancer.

Joe's second interest involved another Northern Dancer colt, named Secreto, which had been bought as a yearling at Keeneland '82 for $340,000 by the Venezuelan breeder, Mr Luigi Miglietti. Such a 'trivial' sum of money meant that the world's greatest horsemen did not rate the colt very highly, possibly because he had a truly unmemorable pair of front legs. Joe Thomas, who had bought the dam, Betty's Secret, a big, unraced chestnut mare by Secretariat, had done so under attack from every one of his advisors, because her knees were pretty unattractive too. But Joe loved the pedigree, Betty's Secret being a half-sister to the French Derby winner Caracolero, from a daughter of Gay Hostess, dam of the Kentucky Derby winner Majestic Prince. This was a family which often threw out great brilliance in its stock. Joe reasoned, in his deep, rumbling, mid-western voice, 'Sure, she'll produce a few bad-legged horses in her career. What mare doesn't? But when she gets a good one, we might get a champion from her.'

'Don't do it, Joe,' said his vets.

'I agree with that,' said his broodmare man.

So Joe went out and bought Betty's Secret, grinned that great grin of his, and chuckled, 'Now I'm gonna breed her straight to Northern Dancer.'

When the first-born of Betty's Secret fetched 'only' $340,000, with his terribly straight knees, there was a certain amount of leg-pulling, which Joe accepted with his usual good-nature and a large vodka. 'But judge me not in haste.' he added. 'The sucker might run yet.'

Then Señor Miglietti elected to have the colt trained in Ireland, with David O'Brien, on the far side of Ballydoyle. This made it even more interesting for Joe, who dearly wanted El Gran Senor to win everything and come back to Windfields, but he also wanted Secreto to 'show those sons-of-guns that I occasionally know more or less what I'm doing'.

By the spring of the year, it was apparent that Joe Thomas had not been entirely asleep when he insisted on buying Betty's Secret. Secreto, who had won a race as a two-year-old in his only start, came straight out and collected the Tetrarch Stakes at the Curragh in very useful style. So useful, in fact, that David O'Brien elected to send him out for the Irish 2000 Guineas where he would take on Robert's champion juvenile Sadler's Wells, and the excellent French challenger Procida. It was a terrific race and Secreto started as 6–4 favourite, but the mile up the Curragh was too short for him. Sadler's Wells won it, to the everlasting joy of Robert and Billy. Procida was second and Secreto third. There was only a neck and a half length between them.

David O'Brien announced immediately that Secreto would take his place in the field for the two hundred and fifth running of the English Derby at Epsom on 6 June. But for this race he would most definitely *not* start favourite. That honour would go to Robert's unbeaten El Gran Senor, who had won the English 2000 Guineas in the most magnificent style, beating one of the best fields for years. Strung out behind him at Newmarket were: Chief Singer (by two and a half lengths) the future champion sprinter and winner of the one-mile St James's Palace Stakes and the Sussex Stakes; Lear Fan (by six lengths), the winner of the Craven Stakes and future winner of the Group I Prix Jacques le Marois, in France; Rainbow Quest (by nine lengths) the future winner of the Arc; and Keen (by twelve lengths) a future stallion in Australia, valued at $1 million. By such yardsticks are racehorses measured. Perhaps the minor miracle of it all was that Sadler's Wells, Secreto and El Gran Senor were *all* sons of the twenty-four-year-old Northern Dancer, the latter two having been bred from mares which Joe Thomas had bought.

It was scarcely surprising that the entire breeding world was now trying to acquire a natural successor to the Dancer. Since Nijinsky would *never* leave Claiborne and The Minstrel would never leave Windfields, most people were beginning to look extremely carefully at El Gran Senor, with his fabulous racing action and wonderful pedigree. It was well known that Joe Thomas had sewed up the colt's future as a stallion long before he ever even ran, but he had not sewed up the actual ownership of the horse. Windfields would syndicate El Gran Senor, that much was obvious, and Robert and his men would keep several shares. But many breeders believed it may still have been possible to buy perhaps a half of him. And a group of such men, headed by the Californian Joseph Solomon, a close associate of Vidal Sassoon, banded together and made an offer which amounted to a pre-emptive strike. On their behalf, the bloodstock agent Andy Smith contacted Robert with a flat offer which valued the horse at $80 million. They would buy a minimum of half of the horse for $40 million at the end of the season, *provided* he won the English Derby.

Before doing so, Robert consulted with George Harris who believed that in this market, such a price was *just* viable. They worked out the terms over five years at $2 million a share, which would see El Gran Senor standing at $400,000 a service. They also planned to introduce the 'bonus' scheme, perfected by John Gaines during the past three years, under which each shareholder received one extra 'covering' each four years. This of course meant that for shareholders the covering fee would be $2 million divided now by *six* coverings – $333,000. For the ten members of the syndicate, who would collect their *second* bonus in the fifth year, it would mean that they received *seven* coverings, further reducing each one to $287,000. And all of them would have a chance to sell a yearling for perhaps $5 million, certainly above $1 million.

An offer of $80 million for a racehorse may have sounded akin to lunacy, but in this market it was close to feasible, never mind sane. And within a very short time, with George Harris's help, they had the punters in place. They all knew The Senor would stand at Windfields, and everyone was delighted about that. None of them knew how sick Joe Thomas was.

Robert's plan was to hang on to ten shares, and perhaps sell thirty for $60 million. Actually, he thought, that number had a very nice ring to it. Very nice indeed. They told Joe Thomas by phone to Oshawa that they would probably deal. And Joe, who was of the opinion that the entire thoroughbred breeding world had almost certainly gone off its collective rocker, rumbled down the phone, 'Sounds good to me, boys. You'd better check The Senor's wedding equipment though!'

As for the race, the Derby was regarded as the nearest thing to a formality it had been in living memory. El Gran Senor at 11–8 on was the shortest-priced favourite for thirty-seven years. Defeat was unthinkable. You could get 6–1 about Piggott's mount Alphabatim, who had won two classic trials, 12–1 about the Chester Vase winner Kaytu, 12–1 about Affirmed's son Claude Monet, the winner of the Dante Stakes, and 14–1 about Secreto. There were seventeen in the field and Robert, Vincent and John Magnier were huddled down along the rail by the winning post, awaiting the sight of El Gran Senor's elegant head to come hurtling up the hill about six lengths in front of the field, as the form book 'promised' he surely he must.

Over in Oshawa Joe was very weak now. He could not really speak but he could understand, and he could still chuckle. Lesley had told him all about the Derby field. He knew that he and Northern Dancer had two 'runners' in The Senor and Secreto, but he passionately wanted The Senor to win it for the sake of his beloved Windfields. He often wondered if he would ever be well enough to see the horse arrive 'home'. Meanwhile Lesley was on the phone to England, with the receiver placed on top of the usual Berkshire television.

With half the race gone, the field was very tightly bunched and they streamed down the hill to Tattenham Corner with Sheikh Hamdan's At Talaq out in front. But, as they straightened up for home, Pat Eddery made his move on The Senor. Smoothly changing gear, he cruised up to join the leaders coming to the two-furlong pole and then Eddery sent him on, accelerating away from the rest by two clear lengths.

Well, that's that. It's over. They'll never catch him now. But it was not *quite* over. Tracking The Senor was a colt who had been back in seventh place on the turn, but now he was belting along the outside as if his life depended on it, already hard under the whip of the outstanding Irish jockey Christy Roche. Wait a minute. Who's that horse in the yellow and blue colours on the outside? The chestnut with the three white feet? The grandson of the immortal Secretariat was who it was. He was the grandson of the greatest mile-and-a-half racehorse who ever lived. That's where he got his name. Secreto.

Well, he won't pass the Northern Dancer colt ... Whadya mean? He's by Northern Dancer as well, trained by Vincent O'Brien's son David. And at that moment nothing short of pandemonium erupted in the Epsom Grandstand. Thousands leapt to their feet as Secreto, still under the whip, came to join The Senor. Eddery glanced to his right, a bit cheekily, and asked his colt to quicken. The Senor did so, but so did Secreto. Now he was at The Senor's quarters and Roche went to his whip for the fourth time. Eddery glanced right again and saw to his horror that Secreto was on him.

Instantly he too drew his whip, left handed, and he slashed El Gran Senor, hard, three times, for the first time in his life. For a split second his momentum was gone, but Northern Dancer's number one son responded like the great champion he surely was, bursting back into the lead. The crowd was up and roaring. The noise across the Downs was like thunder, as they hurtled into the final furlong, El Gran Senor on the inside, Secreto on the outside, still coming.

Christy Roche, driving for all he was worth, drew his whip again, fighting to get back the neck he had just lost. There were only one hundred yards left to run and still it looked as if the favourite would hold the son of Betty's Secret. Eddery, desperate now, lashed The Senor again ... one ... two ... three ... across his quarters. But The Senor had no more to give. He just kept fighting his way over the ground, struggling towards the line with his last heart-rending ounces of strength.

And still Secreto kept coming and he nailed The Senor three strides from the line, shoving his head in front as they flashed past the winning post, after one of the truly great Epsom battles. The murderous little short-head by which he had won had knocked $40 million off The Senor's value, and added about $20 million to his own. The $80 million deal was off, in that split second, for the simple reason that the Californian syndicate would *never* be able to proclaim in their stallion promotion: 'El Gran Senor, winner of the Epsom Derby'.

Robert and Vincent were stunned and when the result of the photograph came up it was Jacqueline O'Brien who rushed across to congratulate her son on a truly stupendous piece of training, on the horse with the shaky front legs. The Senor had given his all. In defeat he had shown every last vestige of the requirements Joe Thomas wanted for a stallion – speed, class and unforgettable courage.

Vincent was almost ripped apart by his divided loyalties, uncertain whether his genuine delight at David's triumph had entirely overshadowed the savage blow of The Senor's defeat. He stood there with Robert for a few minutes, almost reeling with the emotion of the photofinish. The questions flashed through his mind: 'Had Eddery got it wrong to be left in front so early?' The situation was not terribly improved by Lester Piggott either, who walked past without breaking stride, muttering the words: 'Miss me?'

Back in Oshawa, Lesley did not quite know how to break the news to him, that The Senor had been beaten. She thought for a while, and then she went into his room and held his hand, and she called him

'Dad' for the first time for years. 'You were first and second, Dad,' she said. And Big Joe smiled and he spoke for the first time for several days. 'That's great,' he said, 'That's just great.' Joe died that night. But Lesley says he was still smiling.

13

Summit in the Desert

It was almost impossible to believe that a man who had shown a Senate Committee $2 billion worth of assets, involving the oil and gas deep below the plains of Oklahoma, could possibly go down in the racehorse business during the biggest bull market in history. Robert Hefner, however, the man who had blithely agreed to pay $21 million for three-quarters of Storm Bird, achieved such a distinction. His was a story of truly spectacular collapse. One bank, the Penn Square in Oklahoma City, crashed with him (shut down by the Feds) and two others, the Continental Illinois and the Seattle First, shuddered under the burden of Mr Hefner's indebtedness. Mobil Oil who had invested $200 million in his drilling operation were wondering where $40 million of it had gone. And natural gas, which Mr Hefner had once valued on his 'asset sheet' as being worth $9·50 per one thousand cubic feet was now priced, in 1984, at $1·50.

Robert Hefner, with two of his payments for Storm Bird still outstanding, had reported debts of $770 million. He did not own the showpiece of Ashford Stud outright, but had bought into a partnership with Texan Dr Bill Lockridge, one of the most popular and inspired horse breeders in the entire central Kentucky area, a man associated with champion runners for years – a student of American bloodlines. But Robert Hefner had pledged Ashford Stud against his debts. Claims against the partnership amounted to $56 million. Bill Lockridge, who had originally owned the farm and its horses in their entirety, now saw his fortune vanish. Before Hefner showed up he had had solid assets of $15 million, with $3 million debt. When he finally walked out at the end of the 1984 breeding season he had nothing, save for $500,000 he had received from Hefner for one of his Storm Bird shares – an almost impossibly small sum with which to acquire even a foothold on the ladder of the thoroughbred business. The fact is, Bill Lockridge considers he was very nearly ruined by Robert Hefner.

Of course, in the gigantic scale of things, no one took much notice of the loss of a Kentucky farm, nor the plight of the famous racehorse veterinarian, since there were those in the government who were actually discussing the collapse of the entire United States banking system at the time. None of which was particularly good news for Robert Sangster and his partners, out now for $14 million, plus their beloved Storm Bird. John Magnier's contract was, however, extremely tough. And extremely valid. If Robert Hefner ever wanted to show his face in the horse business for the rest of his life he was going to have to find a way to honour it. So he elected to settle his debt to Robert and John and Vincent. He *gave* them the Ashford Stud Farm plus most of the shares in the horse in settlement of the debt. This was not, as they are apt to say in Kentucky, too shabby.

Bill Lockridge walked away, to pick up the shattered pieces of his life and to spend nine long years building up another breeding operation, during which time he would repay his original shareholders in the farm every last dollar they were owed. Everybody around Lexington likes Bill Lockridge and he received widespread support as such men usually do.

They loved Hefner in County Tipperary though. Every cent he owed for Storm Bird was, after all, repaid. And now Robert and his men owned the most wonderful new stud farm – a place in which the Queen of England, during a visit, had admired the work of the twenty stone-masons who had created the main buildings. The craftsmanship and splendour of the stallion area would have filled the eye of Louis XIV. The address, Ashford Stud, Versailles, would surely have thrown the Sun King into total confusion.

With his first yearlings due to come up at the 1984 sales, Storm Bird served his third covering season at Ashford, whence he would go to the Pegasus Stud for a year, before returning to Ashford under the auspices of the new Coolmore management. As John Magnier has occasionally said, appreciatively, 'Robert Hefner is one of the most honest men I have ever met.' Talented too. The Secretariat of the borrowing world. A real mover and shaker, with other people's money.

'I do not', said Bill Lockridge, 'wish him well.'

As Storm Bird returned to the Coolmore fold, the reputation of his sire, Northern Dancer, reached heights unmatched since Blandford sired four English Derby winners in seven years between 1929 and 1935. By the time The Brethren – as Robert and his men were now referred to in Ireland – were ready to leave for the 1984 Keeneland Summer Sales, the five principal Group I races in England and Ireland for classic colts had been run – the 2000 Guineas of both countries, the Derbys of both countries, and the Eclipse Stakes at Sandown. Sons of Northern Dancer had won them all, El Gran Senor having dealt with Rainbow Quest in the Irish Derby, and Sadler's Wells getting home from a high-class field in the Eclipse, by two necks.

On the other side of the Atlantic there was a sensational start to the career of Seattle Slew. After the brilliance of Landaluce, there followed Slew O'Gold who had been one neck away from winning all three of the 1983 New York fall handicaps, the Marlboro Cup, the Woodward Stakes and the Jockey Club Gold Cup. Then in the spring of 1984 Claiborne Farm's Swale, another son of Slew's, had won the Kentucky Derby and the Belmont. It was not difficult to forecast the top two sires at the forthcoming sales, nor was it difficult to forecast who would be buying them.

Robert Sangster and his men arrived in Kentucky a day early to pay a visit to the stud farm which would soon be theirs. Within twenty-four hours of the touchdown of their Learjet, Sheikh Mohammed and his entourage had landed. In quick succession Prince Khalid and his team arrived, then Stavros Niarchos. Three days before the sale opened, all of the big players were in position. Sheikh Mohammed was ready for the most awesome financial blitz any one man has ever levelled at the Sport of Kings. But Sangster's syndicate were very determined. Forty-eight hours before the sale started, they received word from Ireland that the Nijinsky–Spearfish colt, for which they had paid $4·25 million in 1982, had won first time out at the Curragh, in the Royal Whip Stakes, flying the colours of their latest major partner, Stavros Niarchos.

When the action began, the entire world of bloodstock breeding went berserk. This was not a horse sale, this was a jamboree. Agents swarmed through the barn areas, there were open phone lines to banks and breeding farms all over the world. Parties were taking place all over the Lexington area. Tommy Gentry had hired hot-air balloons to take potential buyers for a ride. Restaurants were packed. The main hotels were packed. Money was being spent at a rate which central Kentucky had never seen before. Whores were arriving from Las Vegas and ambitious showgirls were flying in, dressed to attract the big foreign buyers and their advisors. One old Kentucky hardboot observed, 'There's more whores in the Hyatt than I've got yearlings on my farm.' One of them chatted up Robert in the elevator, telling him she was on her way home to Los Angeles, having been rejected in a line-up of six girls flown in by certain foreign visitors.

When the bidding started, all sense of moderation went clean out of the door. Robert Sangster went to $8·25 million for a colt by Northern Dancer out of Ballade. Sheikh Mohammed outbid the men from Tipperary for the Northern Dancer colt from Fabuleux Jane at $7·1 million. Then Sheikh Mohammed spent $6·5 million on a colt by Seattle Slew out of Desiree, this one a full-brother to yet another major Stakes winner for Slew, the crack US filly Adored.

The three next-most-expensive yearlings were all by Northern Dancer. Sangster bought the one from Truly Bound for $5·4 million, the Maktoums bought the one from Queen Sucree for $5·1 million, with Robert the underbidder, and then Robert and Stavros Niarchos went to $4·6 million to obtain the colt from Mississippi Mud. Altogether eight yearlings went for $3 million or more and every one of them went to Europe.

There were twelve yearlings by Northern Dancer at the sale and they *averaged* $3,446,667 each . . . $41 million out of the entire sale total of $175 million. The eleven by Seattle Slew averaged $1,771,364 each. Foreign buyers spent over $100 million, of which $46 million came from Sheikh Mohammed and his brothers. Another $36 million was spent by Robert and his boys for twenty-three yearlings. The yearly average went up by fourteen per cent to an unimaginable $601,467 each – as opposed to $160,000 five years previously.

Windfields Farm took home $17·7 million for their consignment of fourteen yearlings, the second-last legacy to the brilliance of Joe Thomas. North Ridge Farm received $12,355,000 for their eleven, Lanes End Farm earned $11,355,000 for thirteen, Spendthrift $8,490,000 for thirteen, and Tommy Gentry $7,855,000 for his thirteen. For Tommy the big parties, the balloons and the star entertainers had paid off in the ring. He sold a Seattle Slew colt for $2·9 million, and one by Alydar for $1·6 million. The fact was, Kentucky was awash in money.

And men from old Bluegrass families were beginning to live their lives in a way which they thought befitted their status as the prime movers in the most glamorous business on earth. Men whose families had struggled for generations to make ends meet in the only business they knew – breeding horses – now found themselves in positions of literally coining money. There was no restriction on how many mares a stallion covered, therefore men who stood a stallion for, say, $50,000

– and there were a lot of them – could just breed to four more mares and put the $200,000 in their own pockets. It was the seller's market to end all seller's markets.

No one was thinking very deeply about what *could* happen if the yearling prices should ever drop. What about all those shareholders out there, counting on their 'seasons' being sold each year to pay for their expensive shares? What if the mare owners should ever take a major bath at the yearling sales and refuse to pay the massive prices for stallion seasons? What would happen if the breeders should tell a big stallion farm, 'I will not pay $100,000 to go to your stallion – I will only pay $40,000. The yearling prices are not good enough'? No one was giving that any thought whatsoever. In fact there were a few major players in this game who were actually beginning to live like Pashas. One of them was undoubtedly Brownell Combs, whose farm had made its projected public issue on the Stock Exchange in November 1983. Within three months there was trouble over the way Brownell was running the business. Some of the directors thought he was still proceeding as if Spendthrift were a private family business as it had been for so long.

There was trouble over his gigantic annual salary of $500,000. There was trouble over the farm leasing a private aircraft from Brownell, which in turn was used by Brownell, occasionally across the Atlantic to Ireland. There was trouble over the limousines, the huge travel and entertainment bills. There was trouble over Spendthrift spending heavily on farm insurance with a company partially owned by Brownell. And there was especial trouble over girlfriends of Brownell buying seasons to stallions like Raise a Native at the 'farm price' of $31,500, and then pocketing the change after Brownell sold them on to clients for $157,500. At Spendthrift there was trouble just about everywhere you looked. With all the cash pouring in the door, Brownell was spending like a maniac. Even his own father Leslie Combs II described his son as 'over-indulgent'. He was not alone in the orgy of spending, not by any means, except that Spendthrift Farm was now a public company and it had stockholders and directors, some of whom wanted to know *precisely* what was happening in this new business which was being run like a fiefdom.

Some of those shareholders had big stakes in the farm, men like Joseph O. Morrissey Jr, a director from St Louis, who had a $1·75 million stake in Spendthrift and expected to have a grown-up running it. He was shocked 'by the excessive salary, and travel and entertainment expenditures by Combs, and his failure to communicate with the board'. Also Mr Morrissey said, 'There was no direction, no corporate plan, nothing in the way of where the company was going.' Joe Morrissey called a meeting of the Spendthrift board's audit committee in the Huntington Sheraton Hotel in Pasadena, California. There they almost ousted the big Kentuckian. On the first vote they planned to force his resignation, but Brownell lobbied, pleaded that such an action would totally disrupt the farm. Finally it was agreed that he should stay on but there must be major changes in attitude.

Over at Calumet, where the son-in-law J. T. Lundy was now in the president's chair, matters were moving towards another serious situation. JT believed in expansion and he wanted to put Calumet into the stallion business in a very much bigger way. There was cash available and he authorized the purchase of Secreto, the winner of the English Derby, a tough and resilient horse with front legs so suspect that he never ran again after his triumph at Epsom. In total, Secreto had covered only four and quarter miles in battle in his entire life. It was not certain, but any breeder would say that the odds against such a stallion producing sound horses were very long indeed. J. T. Lundy paid $20 million for *half* of him. The great mystery was that this price put a valuation on the horse of $40 million, or $1 million a share, but his nominations were changing hands in his first year for $80,000, a rate which would get the shareholders out in thirteen years! J. T. Lundy's mathematics were, at best, eccentric.

He too shared some of Brownell's love of high living, private jets, limousines, first-class travel and entertainment, roaming across the world, buying fillies a˜d mares for Calumet, often buying at high prices, as indeed he had done with Secreto. Away now from the withering eye of the late Lucille Markey, the new president seemed especially happy with his great and historic responsibilities at the most famous thoroughbred nursery in Kentucky.

In 1984, for the first time, it seemed that Bunker Hunt's Bluegrass Farm may be in danger. For years, all through the 70s, Bunker and his brother Herbert had been buying silver, some of it in partnership with the Royal family of Saudi Arabia – between them they had hundreds of millions of ounces of silver. They were in at between $4 and $6 an ounce. They owned twenty-five per cent of all the silver shares on the New York Stock Exchange and they rode the price all the way up to $19 an ounce, trebling their money. This, however, was not good enough. They went out and borrowed a truly fantastic $1·3 billion and ploughed it into silver, driving the price to $49 an ounce. They bought 'on margin' that huge sum of money representing only ten per cent of the actual price of their purchase. They secured their loans with the silver, but when the price began to drop, the margin calls were horrendous. The first one, from the New York investment house Bache Halsey Stuart Shields, was for $135 million. The Hunt brothers could not meet it. Bache ordered them to sell silver to meet the call. Bunker and Herbert cashed 8·5 million ounces, plus oil and gas assets for nearly $400 million. They met with the Federal Government and pointed out the possibility of the crisis which may ensue if they dumped another 63 million ounces on the market. They also named the banks that might go down with them, if the government refused them a loan.

The result was a $1 billion loan to keep the Hunts afloat and they serviced it with income from the Placid Oil Company, and from a trust which owns the Penrod Drilling Company, one of the largest oil rig contractors in the world. In 1984 Penrod lost $100 million and the Hunts were again on the ropes. With oil at $26 a barrel, the Hunts could survive on cash-flow of $300 million a year from Placid, even though half of it had to go to service the silver debt. What no one knew was that oil was shortly to crash to $10 a barrel.

Bluegrass Farm and its superb profits from the thoroughbred-breeding business became increasingly important to Bunker. Here in Kentucky he was a very popular man, with a reputation of being hard but straight. He controlled some of the best bloodlines in the state and his shares in some of the great stallions were, at this stage, almost a licence to print cash. It never occurred to anyone that this sprawling farm, with its billionaire owner and hundreds of blue-blooded occupants, could possibly be in danger. The reality of so many situations was obscured behind the general atmosphere of colossal greed and high-living that characterized the entire industry south of the Ohio river.

Meanwhile, the shareholders in Seattle Slew were hanging on to their hats in anticipation of Slew O'Gold's forthcoming tilt at the three New York fall handicaps. He was the most popular horse and the crowds were terrific as Angel Cordero steered him to victory in all three. No horse had ever done that. And now a single nomination to Seattle Slew changed hands for $1 million. That effectively gave the stallion a book value of $120 million (forty shares at $3 million each, Slew being now ten years old). No one batted an eyelid. Kentucky had turned into a kind of esoteric kingdom of its own, with a set of standards that could not be comprehended by anyone beyond the horse business. If, for instance, you had flown an investment banker into Lexington, taken him to Spendthrift Farm and shown him Seattle Slew, the conversation would doubtless have gone thus:

'See that horse over there, the nearly black one eating grass by the fence?'

'Yep.'

'That horse is worth $120 million.'

'Run that by me one more time?'

'That horse is worth $120 million.'

'You mean, the same sort of price as the Pan-Am Building in New York, or a mile of Palm Beach with thirty mansions, or maybe Finland?'

'That's right.'

'You want me to call a doctor?'

There were other factions of the horse-racing industry which also believed that Kentucky was getting rich so easily and so steadily it was something close to obscene. This group were very powerful and very concerned that so many people were getting rich off their backs. They were the relatively silent, but brutally hard-working minority, the racing trainers and their staffs, their work-riders and their jockeys. This was the business end of the industry, the tough, mean, scheming end, which rises at 5 a.m. every day, summer and winter, which could afford no mistakes, which lived on its merits and expected no mercy. This was the world of *racing* which ultimately dictated which stallions and which mares would earn millions for the Kentucky, Virginia and Maryland breeders. Fortunes swing on the results of races, however narrow the margin. That big white stick of wood which marks the unseen line across the track at the end of a race is the sole barometer of this trade. Reaching it first is all that matters to the men who earn a living at the track, rather than on the gentle hillsides of the Bluegrass.

The difference between the two worlds is that between the occasionally tense but deep-carpeted offices of the boxing promoter and the middle of the prize-ring, with punches being thrown and blood splattering the canvas. All through the winter months, on the freezing backstretch of Belmont Park, New York, America's classic runners are prepared. Hard little men in big jackets and crash helmets with whips jammed into their belts are helped into the saddles of these great half-ton thoroughbreds, their breath like white steam upon the morning air. Instructions are given tersely: 'Take him seven, starting at the mile gate. A half in forty-nine and change, the last three quicker, drive him out.'

Out on the backstretch, often in driving rain or sleet, the work-riders drag down their goggles and set off into the headwind. You can hear them shouting as they pound down the stretch, frozen hands gripping the wet reins. But the horses must be worked and shivering trainers await them, hitting the buttons of the stopwatch, watching for the slightest signs of lameness or injury, later bandaging the cuts, feeling the joints for heat, waiting anxiously for blood reports from the vets. One mistake here and the cost can be incalculable. Great racehorses must be brought up to their highest moments with the steadiness that governs the training of all Olympians. They must be driven forward, their speed must be honed, and their stamina developed. Too little work is death, too much is usually worse, because that may finish the horse for ever.

The trainer operates on a murderous little knife edge, watching for the moment when the work can be increased, wary of misjudging that moment, calling upon the instincts of a lifetime, listening to the words of the riders and the stable men. And then they stand as helpless spectators to their own fate, as the hundred-fifteen-pound iron men, crouched in their bright silks, up on the horses' withers, come flying around the turn at up to forty miles an hour, with the dirt flying, the whips flashing, the field crowding, swerving, fighting, straining, coming out of that no man's land at the top of the stretch where the dust obscures the horizon, and the track and the sky are one, and this race will be won and lost – 'Stay on the inside . . . give him time to change leads . . . steady, Angel . . . now, let him go . . . let him go *now* . . . Goddamnit, let him run . . .'

'*And here comes Slew O'Gold* – on the *out*side, as *down the stretch they come . . .*'

But in the early 80s there was an unmistakable feeling at training establishments all over the USA and Europe that none of this counted as the prime object any more; that breeders were breeding horses for the stud, to breed other horses for the stud; that the only thing that counted was the 'paper', the pedigrees and the yearling sales. Stallions were being sold for astronomical sums without having proved themselves on the track. And the people getting really rich were the owners of mares, of half-sisters to champions, half-sisters to dams of champions, brothers to champions. All the big money was in breeding. The actual sport of horse racing was getting left behind the industry which was supposed to support it.

Men with calloused hands, their jackets marked white on the sleeves with the saliva of an exhausted, sweating, but victorious horse, knew that as a result of months of their care and work some lady far away in Kentucky was going to make maybe $5 million when she sold the half-brother at Keeneland. It was, of course, ever thus. But not for these sums of money. And the wisest heads among the breeders knew that it was time for the breeding industry to shape up and give something back to the battleground on which the actual racing took place. And so was born the Breeders' Cup in 1984, masterminded by the inordinately perceptive John Gaines of Gainesway Farm. In the simplest possible terms they created the biggest afternoon of racing in the entire history of the Turf: $10 million of prize money in three and a half hours, beamed live on television all over the world. The first five races for two-year-olds, then older horses, fillies, colts, over varying distances, dirt and turf, were for around $1 million each. Then came the $2 million twelve-furlong turf race. The last race, the Breeders' Cup Classic, was for $3 million.

They raised the money by imposing a 'tax' on the stallions: every farm had to contribute the cost of one nomination to each sire. This was clearly a huge amount of money, but it was also easy. Most farms in this market just let the stallion cover an extra mare and gave the money to the Breeders' Cup. Did not cost them a penny. No one, of course, could refuse, because to do so meant that the stallion's offspring would not be eligible to run for the richest prizes on earth, which in turn would collapse the prices of his yearlings.

They chose Hollywood Park on the West Coast for the opening Breeders' Cup meeting and the track was packed for the occasion. The usual group of expensively bred descendants of Northern Dancer and Raise a Native won the first four races, but it was the Classic, the $3 million shoot-out, which provided the drama and probably converted millions of fans to the sport of horse racing. The finish involved a desperate battle between Slew O'Gold, the Preakness winner Gate Dancer, and Wild Again, winner of the Oaklawn Handicap and the Meadowlands Cup.

At the head of the stretch Slew O'Gold and Wild Again were locked together, with Gate Dancer charging down the outside. Wild Again, on the rail, banged into Slew O'Gold, then Gate Dancer suddenly veered across, forcing Slew to crash again into Wild Again. Pincay was struggling to straighten out the wayward Gate Dancer, Cordero was trying to straighten Slew O'Gold and Pat Day was trying to stay in the saddle. It was a terribly rough race to the line, but to thunderous cheers from the crowd, Wild Again hung on by a head with Gate Dancer helping to squeeze Slew O'Gold out of it. There was less than a length between

Above: Great Sheikhs – the royal princes of Dubai together – Mohammed (*left*) receives the trophy for the Champion Stakes from his elder brother Hamdan al-Maktoum. Sheikh Mohammed's filly Indian Skimmer, sired by Robert's stallion Storm Bird, had just won the 1988 race

Above: The one that got away – the 1983 yearling by Northern Dancer for which Robert Sangster bid $10 million but failed to answer Sheikh Mohammed who boldly raised the stakes. The horse, later named Snaafi Dancer, could not run a yard

Left: The $40 million short-head – Robert's El Gran Senor (under Pat Eddery, *right*) is defeated by Secreto (Christy Roche) in the 1984 Derby, after one of the most awesome battles ever seen at Epsom

Above: Brownell Combs the heavy-weight stallion master of Spendthrift, who toiled in the long shadow of his father

Above: Lesley Combs II, the immortal racehorse salesman, whose empire could not survive without him

Left: Gateway to glory – the royal road of Spendthrift, once home of Nashua, Raise a Native, Majestic Prince, Seattle Slew and Affirmed

Below: Spendthrift Farm – the white-columned Kentucky stronghold of the Combs family

Left: Lester and his mentor Vincent O'Brien – at the Curragh on the day the great jockey rode four winners in a row for the trainer who coaxed him out of retirement

Below: Lester Piggott, rides a sensational race to get Royal Academy home in a thunderous, rough battle for the 1990 Breeders' Cup Mile in New York – 'I thought he rode him very nicely indeed,' said Vincent O'Brien

Above: Vincent O'Brien (*left*) with Michael Smurfit, one of Ireland's wealthiest men – all of their skill and judgment could not save Classic Thoroughbreds

Below: One of Robert's principal partners Danny Schwartz the multi-millionaire San Francisco builder

Left: John Gaines, master of the huge stallion station Gainesway Farm, in Kentucky, sold his magnificent art collection just as the market began to crash

Above: Franklin Groves, the multi-millionaire industrialist from the midwest, whose grandiose plans ended in ruins

FOR SALE
106 ACRES
With 5 BARNS 74 STALLS
• MAIN HOUSE 4,700 SQ. FT. LIVING SPACE
    WITH 4 CAR GARAGE & APARTMENT
• 2 TENANT HOUSES
• IN GROUND POOL   TENNIS COURT
• 1 BARN WITH INSIDE TRACK
• 1 HOUSE WITH 2,164 SQ. FT. OF OFFICE SPACE
CHARLIE MURPHY REALTOR
277-6195 or 223-4713

Right: Tommy Gentry, the super salesman and breeder, a casualty of the crash in Kentucky

Below: Nelson Bunker Hunt – beset by massive financial problems in the silver market, forced to sell his fabled Bluegrass Farm, he only wanted to know that Dahlia was safe

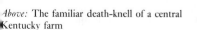

Above: The familiar death-knell of a central Kentucky farm

Left: J T Lundy took over Calumet – presided over bankruptcy

Lester, riding again in Robert's famous green-and-blue silks, steers Rodrigo de Triano into the Newmarket winners' enclosure after the 2000 Guineas in 1992. His very beautiful assistant is Sue Sangster

them at the wire, but the Stewards correctly disqualified Gate Dancer from second place.

With their debt so satisfactorily repaid to the racing industry at virtually no cost to anyone, the breeders got right back down to spending big money. Slew O'Gold was syndicated for around $20 million to stand at Three Chimneys Farm, near Lexington. Then Franklin Groves swooped for a French-trained horse Seattle Song, who had won in France and flown over to win the Washington International in October. He too was a son of Seattle Slew and had in fact been one of the first horses bred by Franklin Groves, who was one of the original investors in Slew when he first became a stallion in 1979. Thus Seattle Song was shipped home to the palatial precincts of North Ridge Farm in the shadow of the new pin-oak trees. He was the second resident of the massive twenty-eight-box stallion barn, hitherto presided over by The Bart, a $17,500 sire whose highest moment had come when he won the Hialeah Turf Cup in record time in 1982. They were a couple of honest racehorses, with adequate blood-lines, but they were scarcely what one might have expected for an emporium such as North Ridge. It was as if the Royal family had rented Buckingham Palace to a couple of local councillors.

Back in Ireland, Sadler's Wells reported to Coolmore Stud for duty in a syndication worth £500,000 a share, making him a £20 million sire. His fee was £125,000, which was a testimony to his looks, his proven courage, his speed and his superlative Northern Dancer pedigree. He was John Magnier's tip to go right to the top. 'This fellow will sire classic winners for years to come,' he told Robert prophetically. 'And that's not said in hope. That's a promise.' It was as well that Sadler's Wells was providing a financial windfall as breeders rushed in to buy shares, because there were two devastating blows currently being aimed at the proprietors of the great Tipperary stud. The first was that there was now a problem over the insurance on Golden Fleece, with Lloyds denying liability and Coolmore saying the insurers were merely trying to avoid their obligations, as they were accused of doing over the kidnap of Shergar. The insurance on Golden Fleece was worth well over £12 million. But there was a far worse scenario brewing in the USA. El Gran Senor, all $40 million of him, was having serious fertility problems at Windfields. The mares were not going in foal and shareholders were growing extremely edgy. The question was whether to declare him infertile and claim the insurance, thus allowing the horse to pass into the ownership of Lloyds; or to hang in there, and hope that things improved.

John Magnier was beginning to look his age, as he dealt on a daily basis with the responsibility of the most important stud operation in Europe.

On the other hand, Robert was sailing along at his philosophical best. He always believed Lloyds would have to settle up on Golden Fleece and that even if The Senor was not terribly fertile, well, they could take him over and try to get some of their own mares in foal to him, and maybe they'd breed one who could run like his dad. 'Tomorrow's always a new day,' said Robert, as he breezed around the world in his private carriage on the Good Life Express. 'You just have to learn to roll with the punches.' Right now he was very preoccupied with the mating plans for two of his outstanding fillies. The first was named Committed, a very fast daughter of the American stallion Hagley. She had just become the European Sprint Champion, carrying the Sangster colours to victory in the Prix de l'Abbaye at Longchamp. The second was named Royal Heroine and she had won one of the first of the million-dollar Breeders' Cup races, for mares, over a mile-and-a-quarter on the dirt.

His other current concern was Mrs Susan Lilley, a slender local blonde from the Isle of Man, whom Robert now planned to marry. This was a complicated situation since Mrs Lilley was still married to Peter, as Robert was very much married to his Australian bride of seven years, Susan. Robert went off to Australia and this time broke the news to his wife that he was leaving her for another. He installed Charles Benson in the Sydney house to provide comfort and support. Then he phoned Sue Lilley, who was at a suite in London, and summoned her to Los Angeles. In the City of Angels there was a brief tryst before they took off for the house in Barbados. Then he returned to the horse sales at Keeneland, Ireland and Newmarket, with the new blonde, twenty years his junior, upon his arm.

Back on the Isle of Man, Susan Sangster was devastated. Unable to face her family, she suffered a nervous collapse at The Nunnery and was attended night and day by a nurse. Her daughters flew from Australia to help look after her and Robert said that he still had a great amount of affection for her and 'knowing what she must be going through', well, the last thing he wanted to do was to cause any unnecessary suffering. In the end, after several months of negotiating, there was a major divorce settlement for Susan. She had named Sue Lilley in her petition, as Robert had been named by Peter.

There were two important assets in the life of Sheikh Mohammed which would have been very handy for Robert. The first of course was his endless money, the second his legal right, under Muslim law, to have four different wives, without battalions of lawyers being involved and everyone demanding cash. There was however something that Sheikh Mohammed sought from Robert: an end to the present ridiculous system which meant they each currently paid double and treble for *any* horse which they both wanted.

The truth was they hardly knew each other. They never spoke before a sale, or during a sale, since they were both trying to play their cards as close to the chest as possible. And at the conclusion of the sale they were both usually reeling from the emotional trauma of the occasion, each knowing that the other had cost him millions. Again, at the races they were invariably in ferocious competition and scarcely wished each other luck. Socially, they moved in rather different circles. Incredible as it may seem, Robert had never spoken to John Leat before the winter of 1984–85, and he could not claim even an acquaintance with Sheikh Mohammed. Although Robert did have horses in England with the Lambourn trainer Barry Hills, the world headquarters of his empire was in County Tipperary, where the racehorses chosen by Vincent lived, where the stallions lived, and where the broodmares lived with their foals. Sheikh Mohammed, however, was creating his empire almost entirely in England.

He had already bought the hundred-and-thirty-acre Dalham Hall Stud on Newmarket's Duchess Drive and the mares which came with it, one of which was Oh So Fair. Dalham was the home of Shergar's sire, Great Nephew, and in its time had been home to Flamingo and Honeyway. The sprinter and stallion Welsh Saint was born here and now Sheikh Mohammed brought in the $1 million-a-share Shareef Dancer. His elder brother Sheikh Maktoum was also becoming heavily involved in breeding. He had made his headquarters the Old Harwood Stud at Woolton Hill, near Newbury, which he now named the Gainsborough Stud, in memory of its first permanent resident, the sire of Hyperion. The big stallion box was still tiled in the pink and white colours which Gainsborough carried to victory in the Derby – the colours of Lady James Douglas, daughter-in-law of the Marquis of Queensberry. Her husband had been the brother of Oscar Wilde's fatal obsession, Lord Alfred Douglas. This was a place steeped in racing's history. For Gainsborough had effectively changed the face of modern thoroughbred breeding by siring not only Hyperion, but also Mah Mahal, the dam of Mahmoud, grandsire of Natalma. The other brother, Sheikh Hamdan, had also purchased Derrinstown Stud in County

Meath, formerly owned by Anne, Duchess of Westminster, and the place where her immortal 'chaser' Arkle ended his days.

The purchase of the studs and the massively expensive renovation work going on in them – comparable in many ways to that of distant North Ridge in Kentucky – signified two very progressive facts. One was that the Arabs were in the British Isles to stay. The other was that they must soon step up their hunt for expensive fillies and mares to fill their sprawling paddocks. The danger was that these priceless equine ladies may soon become too expensive even for the Sheikhs. For as long as Robert and his men wanted precisely the same breeding stock, they were *all* going to cost a fortune. It was quite bad enough paying lunatic prices for colts and the very occasional filly, but if things went on as they had just done in Kentucky, it was going to be a bank-breaking operation to build an army of broodmares. There had been only four which the Sheikhs had particularly wanted at Keeneland, one by Seattle Slew, one by Spectacular Bid, one by Northern Dancer and one by Nijinsky. This little quartet has set them back over $9 million. And they wanted about three hundred of this quality!

Something had to be done. Sheikh Mohammed knew it. And deep in his heart, so did Robert.

It was the Bedouin prince who made the first move. He instructed John Leat to make the contact and to invite Mr Robert Sangster, Mr John Magnier and Mr Vincent O'Brien to visit him in Dubai, to talk and hopefully to become friends. With the new yearlings being broken and 'backed' at Ballydoyle, it was impossible for Vincent to go. But Robert was on his way to Australia and he agreed to go via Dubai, with John. They made the journey in the private Boeing 727, property of the Royal family of Dubai. It seemed strange to Robert and John to be sitting at last in the aircraft which had represented such a nightmarish vision every time they saw it parked at the end of the runway at Bluegrass Field. Its very presence had signified, to them, rivalry, opposition, a new force encroaching on territory which had been theirs for so long. Now they were on board this flying bugbear, hurtling through the warm skies above the Syrian desert, with the Gulf of Iran ahead of them and the mysterious Arab Sheikhdom of Dubai down on the southern shore, beyond the great oil fields of Abu Dhabi.

There were few formalities upon arrival. There was a huge limousine to meet them, with an entourage of courtiers. As they sped through the outskirts of the city, Robert noticed that all the traffic lights were fixed on green. The driver never gave any of them a thought, just sped straight through, heading for the great palace of the ruling family, the palace of the old Bedouin warrior king, Sheikh Rashid al-Maktoum.

They stopped at the Dubai Hyatt, checked in, had a quick shower and change, and jumped right back into the limousine bound for the palace. They were told with simple Arabian courtesy, 'Sheikh Mohammed awaits you.' Three Arabian ministers escorted them through the palace and into a tall, cool, marble-floored room, with European furniture and curtains. They settled down for the long wait that invariably irritates the life out of visitors to the Arabian Royal families. But this was different. Within moments, three other Arab court-iers entered and stood to the side of the door, through which strode, in full flowing Arabian *thobe*, with the red and white *ghutra* headdress, His Highness Sheikh Mohammed bin Rashid al-Maktoum.

He stood before them, sternly, his dark eyes making the hard contact with theirs, in the ancient Bedouin tradition. 'My God!' thought Robert. 'How many times have I seen him look like that in the sale ring – with old Colonel Warden bidding millions of his dollars?' But then the young Sheikh smiled and spread his hands slightly apart, and he said softly: 'As salam Alaikum. Peace be upon you.'

He motioned to them to be seated and formally congratulated them on their very great success during the season with Sadler's Wells and with El Gran Senor. They in turn expressed hope that his outstanding two-year-old filly Oh So Sharp would find a classic success the following year. The talk meandered, as it is always apt to do in the Middle East, neither party wishing to appear too anxious to reduce this mannered, relaxed meeting in the Royal presence into one of negotiation. Sheikh Mohammed had many questions about the selection and training of thoroughbreds. He asked about Vincent and the training of the horses, but to do that is to ask the music-sheet turner how Horowitz plays the piano. It is a subject with no end, a question which could never be answered. At one point the Sheikh mentioned, with enormous charm: 'We have been adversaries for too long a time. I have hopes that we will one day be brothers – rivals on the racecourse, but in friendship and sports-manship, the way I have been brought up to think of the English.'

Servants brought thick dark Arabian coffee and dates, but night was crashing down over the desert. It comes fast and suddenly in this part of the world, bringing with it a swift and embracing chill. Soon Sheikh Mohammed suggested that his visitors must be tired and that they should meet again in the morning, but meanwhile should perhaps return to the hotel for dinner and then sleep.

When they reconvened, the talk was again calm and quiet and it went on for many hours. There were many allusions to the battles in the sales ring, many expressions of regret at what they had done to each other in terms of cost, but by the late afternoon the subject had never been seriously broached. It was clear that the Defence Minister of Dubai wanted a mere exploratory conversation, to become acquainted and to open permanently the channels of communication between them. He invited them to join him in the hall where he would conduct the *majlis* this evening, when he would sit and listen to the problems of his people, as individuals, in the traditions of his father.

Robert was amazed at the number of people who came to seek his guidance. Robert sat on one side of him, with John on the other, and while they were of course unable to comprehend the language, it was clear that Sheikh Mohammed was held in enormous respect by the citizens of Dubai. He knew all of their customs and their innuendoes, and their sense of right and wrong, a code derived from the Koran, the Muslim Holy Book, God's revelation to the Prophet Muhammad set down in the sixth century. Sheikh Mohammed now spoke to them kindly and sometimes firmly, but it was not necessary to understand the actual words to see his compassion and his sense of duty to those he must guide.

They dined together that night on the edge of the desert and they talked more of racehorses. They would leave in the morning, but Sheikh Mohammed wanted to arrange a 'summit' in the desert in the spring, when Mr O'Brien would attend. Sheikh Mohammed wanted them all to bring their wives, which was simple for everyone except Robert of course, since he was on his way to relieve her of further duties and may not have fully wrapped up the formalities with the next one before the proposed gathering in March. But he coped with the situation with his usual shy good nature and these men, who had at times detested each other during several years of furious rivalry, departed the palace of Dubai, on that November evening, as friends.

Sheikh Mohammed had not, however, revealed to them his truly massive plans for his bloodstock empire. John and Robert had no idea of the sheer scale of the operation he planned. Right now the Maktoum brothers had over one thousand horses in training and that did not represent the half of it. The 'summit' in the desert would clarify much for those with the perception to listen carefully to the words of Sheikh Mohammed.

The Boeing 727 contained a cheerful group when it took off from

Heathrow in March. On board were Vincent and Jacqueline, John and Sue Magnier, Robert and Sue Lilley, John Leat and Charles Benson. They left behind them a trade press which was in a state not much short of utter turmoil. News of the summit had somehow leaked out and now the reporters wanted to know if this was some kind of a pact, that the horsetraders from Tipperary led by Robert were going into partnership with Sheikh Mohammed, or alternatively agreeing not to bid each other up any longer.

The reporters had phoned the big consignors in Kentucky and put the fear of God into them with suggestions that the entire market might crash. Those who had ridden this fabled rivalry for so long and grown so rich off its back, went into collective cardiac arrest. 'Jeez! These guys are trying to ruin us. We *need* them out there – paying the big dollars for the y'erlins.' There was talk of an illegal 'ring' – where the buyers band together and agree that no one would pay more than a certain amount for a given item. It had happened before in the world of fine art and antiques between dealers who had teamed up together. But clearly it could not possibly be illegal for a couple of horse buyers to agree to compare lists before the sale and to arrange not to go to war over any single horse, especially since four in five of them couldn't run worth a damn anyway.

The summit was held behind closed doors. The only upshot of it was an announcement that Sheikh Mohammed had taken a share in two horses which Robert had bought at the last sale. One of them was the $8·25 million Northern Dancer–Ballade colt, now being prepared by Vincent. But no word was ever uttered about the essence of the meeting. The Sheikh took everyone out into the desert to see his falcons hunt the *karwan*, a desert stone crow who knows the drill – stay low and run if you can because those peregrine falcons hit you like mortar shells if you take off. But Sheikh Mohammed's men knew how to charge them in the jeeps and force them into the air, which was a great art because the birds are almost impossible to see against the sand. The only European to spot a group of them all day was the hawk-eyed Vincent O'Brien, from about forty paces. Surprised, Sheikh Mohammed paid him the ultimate compliment. 'You have', he said, with a smile, 'the eyes of a Bedouin.'

Then the visitors saw the elegant blue hood taken from the falcon's head and they watched him soar to almost one thousand feet before bulleting down on to the *karwan*. It was at once a cruel and awesome ritual, one that at times had provided the only source of food for the

Bedouin nomads as they traversed the Empty Quarter. The miracle was that the *karwan* survived. And before the falcon returned, Sheikh Mohammed picked up the fallen bird and held it in expert hands while it revived. He then signalled for someone to take it away and place it in one of his bird sanctuaries.

It was a breathtaking look at the old traditions of the desert and, as they stood beneath the hot but sinking sun out now over northern Saudi Arabia, Robert and Vincent came up with the name Imperial Falcon for Sheikh Mohammed's new two-year-old. And on the other side of the world Kentucky still shivered, with fear, not the cold.

And they were correct to do so. Whatever had been decided at the summit, the market *was* about to crash. The Arabs and the Brethren from Coolmore would *not* drive each other up again. The years of craziness were ended, as suddenly and abruptly as they had begun. Kentucky breeders would not need their Brinks trucks to pick up the cash any longer. They needed crash helmets. Nothing, repeat nothing, in the pampered industry of breeding thoroughbred racehorses, would ever be the same again. And the casualties would be legion.

=== 14 ===

The Crash of '86

The 1985 Keeneland Summer Sales catalogue featured a two-page wrap-around cover of an impressionistic painting showing all the seductive high drama of thoroughbred racing: the big fairground in the middle of Epsom Downs, with two horses fighting out the finish of the 1984 Derby ... Secreto and El Gran Senor in their $80 million epic. What drama! What a sight! What fabulous investments for the owners! But one year later things were looking very different. Secreto was worth nothing like the valuation placed upon him of $40 million and breeders fought shy of his price and his shaky knees. The Senor, because of his suspect wedding equipment, was seriously sub-fertile, with only fourteen mares in foal from his first crop of fifty (at $200,000 a stand, that's thirty-six mares not paying, or $7·2 million). That catalogue cover was a stark reminder that all was not precisely what it seemed in the world of thoroughbred racing. And, in the pages between the colour-ful jacket covers, there would be other surprises as well – the main one being that these beautifully printed pedigrees were about to lose their value. This market was about to crash for the first time for over twenty years.

Keeneland still had its show-business glamour, with American soap-opera actors like Larry Hagman and Linda Grey in attendance. But the mighty bidding duels between the Tipperary traders and Sheikh Mohammed were over. The Sheikh was now an owner of Vincent O'Brien's and when his men went in to buy, they did so unopposed by the agents representing the Coolmore team. When Joss Collins stepped forward to buy for the Irishmen, they were not challenged by the men from the Gulf. Which was interesting, since all ten of the Keeneland yearlings which had fetched in excess of $4 million since 1982 had been bought by either Robert or Sheikh Mohammed, usually after a battle with each other. No formal truce or agreement was ever admitted by those who attended the summit in the desert, but there was certainly a better understanding between the two groups. Those massive prices of $10·2 million downwards seemed to be consigned only to memory. The Sheikh had proved himself the heavyweight champion of the Keeneland ring. He knew that. Robert knew it, and so did everyone else in the business. But they had reckoned without the extraordinary resilience and competitiveness of the high-roller from The Nunnery.

The Sale was two-thirds over, with two hundred and fourteen lots through the ring, none of them fetching more than $2·6 million, before something really big broke out. A colt by Nijinsky, out of My Charmer, the dam of both Seattle Slew and Lomond, entered the arena, consigned by Warner L. Jones Jr (he of the giveaway golf clubs) from Hermitage Farm, Goshen, Kentucky. This good-looking bay yearling was clearly the number one choice of the enormously wealthy Californian group led by the trainer, D. Wayne Lukas, and his clients L. R. French, Mel Hatley and Eugene Klein, owner of the football team, the San Diego Chargers. Lukas had done very well for them. He had bought Slew's spectacular daughter, Landaluce, for $650,000 for French, the 1984 Champion US Filly, Life's Magic, for Klein and Hatley, and the winner of this year's Preakness, Tank's Prospect, for Klein. This group were not only on the crest of a wave, they were expanding their racing operations fast, and they had huge amounts of money to spend and they *wanted* this colt.

So did many other people, and the bidding moved very swiftly up to $10 million. The Maktoums were not taking part. But Robert was in there, with Coolmore taking sixty-five per cent, Stavros Niarchos twenty-five per cent, and Danny Schwartz ten per cent. On they went, Lukas against the Irishmen, until the bids hit an unbelievable $12·5 million. There was a short pause as Lukas caucused with his men. The crowd were stunned at this figure, which had been bid just as the sale had been heading south. This was more like it. And back came Wayne with a massive $500,000 raise.

'Thirteen million dollars I have!' shouted the auctioneer.

But Joss Collins of the BBA London, bidding for Robert, immediately went to $13·1 million, and quite suddenly the Californians quit. The hammer crashed down on the biggest price ever paid for a thoroughbred yearling. The crowd leapt to its feet, cheering and shouting their admiration for the fearless gambler from the Isle of Man, who now wore an enormous grin – 'The winnah! And the *new* Heavyweight Champion . . .'

It was a heady moment, but it did not stop the rot. The gross figures for the sale went down seventeen per cent, from $166 million to $137 million. The average plunged from over $600,000 to $537,000. There were twenty-four million-dollar yearlings, as opposed to thirty-three in 1984.

Warner Jones led the consignors' table with nearly $20 million for his eight, but he received less than seven million for seven of them. Tommy Gentry received $12,330,000 for his sixteen, but Sheikh Maktoum's Gainsborough Stud spent $7 million of that for his colt by Nijinsky out of Tom's great mare Crimson Saint. Tom received just over $5 million for fifteen others, many at high stallion fees. Windfields, with their two Northern Dancers and three by The Minstrel, picked up nearly $11 million for sixteen, and North Ridge collected $8·3 for eighteen. The big farm which did badly was the new public corporation, Spendthrift, which grossed less than $2·5 million for six.

It was not as if the big players were absent. They were there all right. Sheikh Mohammed, now operating under the auspices of a company he had named Darley Stud Management, in memory of Arabia's famous stallion, spent over $13·5 million for sixteen head and his brother Sheikh Maktoum spent another $13 million for eight. If it had been 1984 instead of 1985, one could assume perhaps that Sheikh Mohammed would have gone to $14 million for Robert's record colt and this would have brought the Maktoums' total back up to $40 million. They were actually close to spending another $7 or $8 million, on a colt by Northern Dancer out of Native Partner, the dam of the classy English stallion Formidable. This one had been consigned by Bruce Hundley, as agent for Ralph Wilson, owner of another football team, the Buffalo Bills. The Maktoums had bid $7·4 million when someone spotted that the bidder at the other end was Edwin T. Cox, Wilson's attorney. He raised it £100,000 and the Arabs walked out, leaving him with it at $7·5 million, to go home and perhaps to ruminate upon the fact that he was dealing with a Bedouin prince, who, if challenged, would cross the burning Rub' al-Khali on a camel. It is dangerous to tamper with the pride of such men.

It was not that anyone had gone or was not willing to pay a big price. It was just that the Maktoums had decided not to be 'run up' in the ring beyond the horse's value. And this – with the one wild exception involving Robert – meant virtually the end of the lunatic prices to which Lexington had become so accustomed. It was a new situation and it hit the residents of Kentucky as an ice storm might have hit the residents of Tahiti Beach. They were truly shocked. For none of them believed that their Golden Goose would ever fall ill, never mind drop dead. That fall in prices sent a ripple of panic through the big stud farms and none felt it more than Spendthrift whose decline in income from the sale against 1984 was over fifty-four per cent. Brownell Combs was under terrible pressure from his new Board of Directors to get the place into well-managed, steady profit-making, just like the grown-ups do in New York City and Chicago.

The problem was, Brownell had made a classical blunder. He had begun to borrow heavily at a time when the market was softening. The farm had paid out $3·4 million in interest in 1984 and there were still debts outstanding of $18 million *after* the public issue of stock. He borrowed again in 1985 and this year the interest payment was a huge $6·3 million. Brownell negotiated a $28 million line of credit. He also tried a $15 million limited partnership offering for breeding horses, but this failed. For an outfit that had raised only $2·5 million from the world's biggest yearling sale, the numbers were too big, the profits hopeless, the expenditures ridiculous, and the prospects bleak.

There was no question about it. Spendthrift Farm was in deep, deep trouble. Cousin Leslie, aware of Brownell's spending habits, was extremely worried. When the canny old hardboot salesman saw 'them y'erlin' prices going south', he knew, he just *knew* it might be the end of the line. Because they would ultimately drag the stallion prices down with them. No one will pay for a stallion if they believe the yearling will lose money. This meant that Spendthrift's assets were about to shrink, just as the debt was mounting. But with the big line of credit, Brownell still had money to spend and he decided to diversify Spendthrift out of trouble. He had a try at buying Churchill Downs, the big racetrack in Louisville (pronounced, locally, Lewerville). He considered buying a van company, tried to form a thoroughbred club, purchased another training centre. None of this raised enough cash to knock one solitary million off the interest payments. And the debt was rising inexorably. Every month a whacking-great credit-card bill came in from Visa and by the end of 1985 Brownell could hardly pay it. The demand was for $90,000 plus. They had to post some of the farm equipment as collateral against the debt – humiliatingly, this included a fork-lift truck and a skid-loader.

The stock crashed from $12 to under $5. The syndicate which controlled Seattle Slew decided to jump ship and they took the great stallion away, relocating him at Three Chimneys Farm in Woodford County. This was a major loss, because the farm which stands the stallion receives, normally, four free breeding rights. Seattle Slew's price was now $850,000 advertised, and in reality up to $1 million, because the entire top end of the market had been falling over itself backwards to get to him.

Back in Ireland Vincent O'Brien had, by his own exalted standards, rather a moderate 1985. He won the Irish Derby with Law Society, a $2·7 million Keeneland yearling with a terrific turn of foot. But Law Society was well beaten in the English Derby by Slip Anchor and ran in the colours of Stavros Niarchos. But this was the season in Europe when the Arabs began to make serious headway. Robert Sangster was toppled as England's leading owner, a position he had dominated since 1977. Occupying the top place now was Sheikh Mohammed, whose home-bred filly Oh So Sharp had won the 1000 Guineas, the Oaks and St Leger. He also owned another brilliant filly Pebbles who won the Breeders' Cup Turf Championship in New York. Right behind him was Prince Khalid Abdullah, whose Rousillon had won at Royal Ascot, then taken the Sussex Stakes at Goodwood, as well as winning a major race in France. Fourth and sixth were the Sheikhs Hamdan and Mak-toum, who had assisted their younger brother in spending, so far, some $200 million on yearlings during the 1980s.

Robert dropped to seventh place, with prize money of less than £250,000 – somewhat short of Wayne Lukas's final raise of $500,000 on the Nijinsky colt at Keeneland, for which Robert had paid three times the value of the entire prize money available in Ireland for the year. That $13·1 million was a record which would stand for several years, maybe well into the next century. It was also the purchase which finished Danny Schwartz. 'General Patton' had had enough. The iron nerve which took him through the carnage of Utah Beach never wavered. He simply questioned the wisdom of what they were doing. 'There were no properly thought-out, agreed budgets,' he says, 'and I could not continue to be in for an open-ended ten or fifteen per cent. That is pretty scary stuff. When Robert went up over $13 million for that yearling, I was beginning to think seriously that the entire world might be going crazy. And that's a bad attitude for a gambler!'

The problems for Danny were that his partners had a longer-term interest in the horses than he did. 'Vincent O'Brien was basically inter-ested only in being the best trainer in the world,' he says. 'John Magnier was interested in the yearlings as future stallions, from which he would make money for the next twenty years. Robert was a partner in Coolmore and this applied to him too.' Danny Schwartz admits his partnerships at Ballydoyle cost him $10 million. 'But I enjoyed every minute of it and I treasure my friendship with all of them, particularly that with Vincent and Jacqueline and their family.' For years Danny would take his private jet to New York once a month and then pick up the Aer Lingus flight to Shannon, in time for breakfast with Vincent at Ballydoyle. 'They were magical years for me,' he recalls. 'I loved Ireland and the people, and I loved my involvement with the racing in England. I look back on wonderful times. And when I do, I understand that some things are beyond price.'

And if he could live it over again, and know that it would all cost $10 million in the end, would he still have been a prime member of Robert Sangster's Raiders?

'No doubt,' says Danny Schwartz. 'No doubt whatsoever ... God-damnit, you should have been there the night we beat the Sheikhs out for four and a quarter for the Nijinsky colt. That was something!' And he pauses for a minute, recalling the battle, smiling, perhaps hearing the far-lost voice of his Commander-in-Chief, 'Go get 'em, Patton.'

The retirement of Danny Schwartz was a blow to Robert. It came at a time when things were going rather slowly. The massive weight of the Arabian purchases seemed to be taking, inexorably, the Ballydoyle success away. In 1985 there had been a couple of very high-quality two-year-olds – such as the $3 million Mr Prospector colt Woodman, who won three off the reel, but he finished fifth in the Dewhurst and never ran again. There was also a full-brother to Sadler's Wells, another pearl perhaps, from Billy McDonald's favourite little mare Fairy Bridge. He was named Tate Gallery and his Northern Dancer pedigree made him one of the best-bred racehorses in the world. He won the National Stakes at the Curragh at two and all through the winter he was favourite for the 2000 Guineas.

But there were all manner of heart-breaking problems for Vincent at Ballydoyle. Like so many stables, they were hit badly by an equine virus which was almost impossible to detect. This insidious illness was attacking entire yards and only the most modern blood-testing of the 1990s has recently brought it under better control. In the 80s it was the scourge of some of the best trainers in the British Isles. Vincent had to struggle with it along with the rest of them, knowing that if a horse ran unaccountably badly it was not his fault, and that the race had probably finished the horse for ever.

Unaccountably, Tate Gallery finished last in the Guineas at New-market. This was the year of Prince Khalid's Dancing Brave, a Lyphard colt picked up for $200,000 as a yearling by James Delahooke. The colt won a string of Group I races, including the 2000 Guineas, the Eclipse, the King George VI and Queen Elizabeth Stakes, and the Arc. He was beaten by inches in the Derby, after a ride which cost the jockey his job with the Saudi Royal family. The Aga Khan's Nijinsky colt, Shahrastani, won the race and then took the Irish Derby.

These two represented the big syndications of the year. Sheikh Mohammed ordered his men to buy Dancing Brave to stand at Dalham Hall at all costs. They did a deal before the Eclipse at £14 million. Sixteen shares were offered and sold at £350,000 each – nearly $600,000. The remainder of the shares were purchased in bulk by the Maktoum family, with Prince Khalid retaining probably ten. The Aga Khan syndicated Shahrastani for £16 million, retaining a twenty-five per cent interest for himself. The dark forebodings of Kentucky had not yet reached Europe, where optimism remained undimmed, perhaps due to the close proximity of the great Anglophile Sheikh Mohammed. At least the English knew he was here to stay. Some of the Americans were worried they may never see him again.

In fairness, John Magnier was never mad about either of the two great stars of the 1986 season, particularly Dancing Brave with his pronounced 'parrot mouth' – which was the main reason why James Delahooke had been able to snap him up so cheaply at the Fasig Tipton Sale in Kentucky in 1984. Some trainers are less bothered by this pronounced 'overbite', which can lead to digestive problems if it is in any way difficult for the horse to chew. On the other hand, stallion masters are *always* afraid the horse may breed it on to his yearlings.

There was one racehorse during the season which John Magnier coveted. His name was Last Tycoon and he was a son of Try My Best, who still stood at Coolmore having gone some way towards overcoming his fertility problems. He was, of course, a full-brother to El Gran Senor and his son Last Tycoon was a superb-looking bay horse, from a mare by Mill Reef, from the same family as Assert. This fellow could really run. A top French two-year-old trained by Robert Collet in Chantilly, he won two good races in France before coming to Royal Ascot and winning a pulsating battle with Double Schwartz for the King's Stand Stakes. John Magnier watched him win that and he knew that if the colt went on to the sprint championship of Europe he would be a stallion he must have, never mind Dancing Brave, nor Shahrastani. The excellence of Last Tycoon would make Try My Best look better, and one other Coolmore stallion was also coming up trumps for Sangster's men. This was Storm Bird, who was now back under their control and standing at the newly acquired Ashford Stud in Kentucky, alongside El Gran Senor. In his first crop, Storm Bird had sired a fast American two-year-old named Storm Cat, who was beaten only a nose in the Breeders' Cup Juvenile, and there were excellent forecasts about his forthcoming three-year-olds.

Vincent did not have a winner at Royal Ascot in 1986 and they headed for Keeneland at their lowest ebb for many years. The insurance was still not settled on Golden Fleece, which was a huge amount of money outstanding, and El Gran Senor had 'stopped' only twenty-two mares out of his second crop, the price having been slashed in half to $100,000 a nomination. Broadly speaking this meant some thirty mares going home without paying, which was another $3 million down the tubes.

The star of Nijinsky was still bright because he had sired the winner of the Kentucky Derby, Ferdinand, which, with Shahrastani at Epsom, made him the first stallion in history to collect the two Derbys in the same year. This should bring an upward effect on the value of his yearlings and, in the days leading up to the Keeneland Summer Sale, most of Kentucky was silently at prayer, hoping that 1985 was an aberration and that 1986 would be better, and would save their bank loans and their shareholders.

But it was another bloodbath. Robert Sangster, Niarchos and the Maktoums would not bid against each other, and the gross for the sale crashed from $137 million to $104 million. The average cost of each yearling plunged to $411,755 per head, as opposed to $537,000 per head in 1985, and $600,000 in 1984. This was dire. The market was off nearly a third in twenty-four months.

There were some nice horses for sale, nice horses which were born a couple of years too late. The sale-topper was a Northern Dancer full-brother to Storm Bird, purchased for $3·6 million by Sheikh Mohammed. Robert Sangster did not raise his catalogue and it was announced that the colt would be trained by Vincent O'Brien. But such prices were rare. Only half a dozen went for over $1·5 million and the Arabs bought four of them. Below that there were twenty-four yearlings which fetched between $800,000 and $1·4 million. The Arabs bought seventeen of them.

Sheikh Mohammed and his brothers spent $40 million on fifty-seven yearlings and they proved their absolute devotion to the Northern

Dancer line, as taught to them by Robert, Vincent and John. They bought another Northern Dancer colt; four yearlings by Nijinsky; seven by the new Northern Dancer sire of the moment, Danzig; three apiece by Nureyev and Lyphard; and a couple apiece by Storm Bird and Shareef Dancer. They also bought single yearlings by The Minstrel, Topsider and Northern Baby. Every last one of those stallions was a son of Northern Dancer.

It was strange to see Robert Sangster's name tucked down among the also-rans among the purchasers – just three yearlings to his own account, for less than $3·5 million. But it was better to be there than scratching around on the consignors' list, which looked as if it had been French-kissed by the angel of death. The rate at the top of the table where Warner Jones and Lanes End Farm were ensconced was around $6 million a dozen. Windfields were next with $5·5 million for nine; in ninth position was Spendthrift Farm with ten sold for only $2,310,000. Three spots below them was Tom Gentry, with just a shade over $2 million for his ten. North Ridge Farm sold only four and received $1,325,000 for them. And the latter three needed the money.

Three weeks later the entire circus moved to upstate New York for the annual yearling sales at America's most famous spa town, Saratoga, where they have been racing thoroughbreds since 1863. In 1985 Saratoga's prices had held up, despite the instant recession at Keeneland. Now horse breeders from all over the United States were gathered here, once more hoping against hope that it was all a ghastly illusion, that the men from Ballydoyle would renew their rivalry with the Sheikhs; that Saratoga, in a similar vein to its French counterpart Lourdes, would answer their prayers and produce a miracle.

Once more all of the main players were in town, Robert and his men, all the Princes of Dubai and the principal buyers from Saudi Arabia, Wayne Lukas and his boys. The horses were here too, yearlings by Alydar, Northern Dancer, Storm Bird, Blushing Groom, Halo, Seattle Slew, Nureyev, Conquistador Cielo and Spectacular Bid. Saratoga had the goods, no doubt about that. The only issue was whether the buyers were prepared to lock horns in the ring. The results were shattering, confirming all of the most dark and grim fears of the cynics and obliterating the hopes of those who felt it might yet all come right. The market crashed an unbelievable 27·7 per cent, the average for a yearling plummeting from the 1985 high of $259,000 to $187,000. Only five yearlings fetched more than $1 million, none more than $1,625,000.

The *Bloodhorse*, the trade magazine of American breeders, revealed that the entire yearling industry during 1986 had experienced a '$50 million shortfall'. In one memorably poignant paragraph it asked of Saratoga, 'Where, oh where, were the boys of summers ago (1983–85) who were throwing bids of three, four, five, seven, 8·25, 10·2 and 13·1 million at each other to get the same kind of pedigrees we sent into the ring this summer?' And the answer was easy. They were right there in Saratoga. But they were not paying. Before the days of the early nineteenth century, when the big side-wheelers came cruising up the Hudson river to Albany to bring New York society to 'take the spa waters' of Saratoga, it was always said that the area should be left strictly alone, since the local Iroquois Indians were likely to hand the white man his scalp. Something comparable happened to the American breeders in the sales ring in 1986.

And who had caused the crash? Probably the man who had started the boom, Robert Sangster. Certainly Sheikh Mohammed and Stavros Niarchos had contributed, but they had *joined* Robert, having some of their expensive horses in partnership at Ballydoyle. Those facts are indisputable. The truth was, Kentucky thought the dream-world created by the bidding wars was the real world. They were unable to foresee that it might one day end. And now they were about to reap the whirlwind.

The breeders emerged battered from the sales. Men who had been paying the big prices for nominations were aghast to find the yearlings selling for less than they cost to produce. In some cases, hundreds of thousands of dollars less. As Joe Thomas once poetically put it: 'See those Nijinskys going through the ring for around $200,000? Remember it costs $250,000 to go to the sonofabitch. Somebody's gonna be unpleased.'

Even the Northern Dancer market had essentially collapsed. Two years ago at Keeneland his yearlings averaged around $3·5 million each. In 1985 they averaged $1,465,000. This year they had averaged $1,115,625. The most expensive of them at Saratoga fetched only $1,325,000. Nijinsky, with all the main 1986 Derby winners to his credit, averaged $1,005,909, at Keeneland, down sixty per cent against 1985 when they averaged $2,969,444. The million-dollar-yearling game was over. No man in his right mind was going to pay upwards of $750,000 for a service to a stallion when the market might not buy the yearling for much more than $300,000. And, more to the point, the man who did want him might not have a serious opponent in the ring. At best, the horse-breeding business has never been a game for men in short pants. Right now it was absolutely lethal.

Spendthrift's shares crashed on the Stock Exchange, hitting two dollars in the fourth quarter of 1986. The writs began to fly as the mountainous debt of over $50 million became known. The original private investors, whose $1 million stakes had been converted into Spendthrift stock, were furious. Allegations of fraud were being bandied around. The syndicate which controlled Affirmed, including the most devoted friends and clients of Cousin Leslie, Mr and Mrs Louis Wolfson, decided the stallion must be relocated. Like the 'Slew Crew' they were nervous that an injunction might hit and the stallions be held as collateral. Brownell was fired. But the man who replaced him as president, Timothy T. Green, was himself fired after only sixteen weeks in the job. He had, he admitted, reported to the US Securities and Exchange Commission that Spendthrift, as a public corporation, was concerned about certain business practices by Brownell Combs 'involving stallion syndication management agreements'.

Acres and acres of land had to be sold and watching it all from the great white-pillared mansion was Cousin Leslie. He was eighty-five years old now and time had mellowed him. The sadness of his life's work being destroyed was stronger than his desire to wreak some terrible revenge on Brownell. He sat on the little side-porch where he had pulled off so many massive coups in the past and he sometimes sipped a glass of bourbon before dinner. He longed for the old days when Spendthrift was run as a private kingdom, for the days when the great champion Nashua stalked the paddock to the left of the main drive, when Majestic Prince was king of the sales ring, when Raise a Native set the records. Cousin Leslie could still chuckle when he recalled old Clem, Nashua's devoted black groom, telling groups of awestruck visitors, 'Now, this here horse you're looking at is not no ordinary horse. This here horse is the great *Nashua*. Which means that this here horse is *a king*. Which is why he ain't gonna pay you no never mind, because Kings don't pay *no one* no never mind.'

They were all gone now. Everything was going now. Nothing could save Spendthrift. Chief executives came and went, but the heart had gone out of the place. It could not function without the massive presence of Cousin Leslie, shouting, cajoling and selling, selling, selling. It needed his energy. It needed him, but as a young man, not as this wistful old gentleman, sitting on the side-porch staring out over the dogwood trees at the lovely views which had bewitched so many great racehorse owners of the past. All he could do was to wonder what had happened and why, and to mourn for the days when he alone bought the stallions, at the *right* price. He did not need a goddamned private, goddamned jet aircraft. And people *knew* who he was and what he stood for, and that he had a *good* goddamned deal for 'em.

He always said the same thing when pressed upon the subject, 'Spendthrift Farm was very personal to me. I still live here. But nothing's the same. I don't even look at it the same from this side-porch.' After the traumas of 1986, Cousin Leslie sometimes became very within himself because the loss of Spendthrift Farm and its memories of his life with Dorothy were slowly breaking his heart. And he sometimes heard the sound of distant trumpets, 'DAH DAH DAH ... DAH DAH-DAH ... DAH DAH-DAH ... DAH DAH-DAH, DAAAH ...'

There were, however, some Kentuckians still with money to spend. One of these was J. T. Lundy, the new master of Calumet. He had paid the big price for Secreto and now he stepped forward to purchase another stallion for a major sum of money. This one was named Mogambo, a chestnut colt by Mr Prospector out of the 1977 Champion US Two-Year-Old Filly, Lakeville Miss. In her day, she had been a terrific racer, winning the Coaching Club Oaks, and finishing second in the other two legs of the US Fillies Triple Crown, the Acorn Stakes and the Mother Goose Stakes. It all formed a wonderful pedigree, although Mogambo had been just short of the best as a racehorse. As a two-year-old he had won the Champagne Stakes, but had been beaten by Storm Cat and Danzig Connection in the Young America. At three, Mogambo won the Gotham in New York, but was beaten into second place in the Wood Memorial, the Jerome Handicap, the Jersey Derby and the Jamaica Handicap. The verdict on him would be that he just lacked a touch of class.

Dr Bill Lockridge, back in the game after the catastrophe at Ashford, was one of the first men in to try to buy the son of Mr Prospector. He went to the owner, Peter M. Brant, with an offer on behalf of a client for $8 million, on the basis that Mogambo could probably stand at $40,000. Spread over five years that made a $200,000 share and, therefore, an $8 million stallion. Not a penny more. But the polo-playing paper tycoon thought that was not enough. He wanted $10 million, but wavered around on nine. 'The trouble was,' says Dr Lockridge, 'I could not see how Mogambo could possibly stand for any more than $40,000. And I would not go higher than eight. I would be reasonably sure that he was mine for $9 million though.' A few weeks later Dr Lockridge was stunned to see Mogambo had been sold to go to Calumet, with a valuation of $16 million. 'I found that absolutely amazing,' said the

Texan veterinarian. 'But then I found quite a few things pretty amazing at around that time.'

Buying stallions on the other side of the Atlantic was a little more soundly based. John Magnier's judgment of Last Tycoon had been correct. The colt came out and won the William Hill Sprint at York, and then travelled to Santa Anita to contest the Breeders' Cup Mile and he won it brilliantly. In a tough battle with the Californian Palace Music, a five-year-old son of The Minstrel, Last Tycoon got home by a head. John Magnier valued him highly and proposed to stand him at 35,000 Irish guineas. This gave the new stallion a value of more than $10 million, which was very high given the climate in the States. But John Magnier had been right before and the Brethren trusted him to be right again. Last Tycoon was, after all, the world mile champion and probably the fastest horse in Europe over lesser distances. As a racehorse he was utterly superior to Mogambo, his pedigree was deeper, much classier, and much more likely to be that of a stallion. J. T. Lundy, however, had valued Mogambo identically.

It was, to be sure, a time of changing values and, although it was less common in England than in the States for breeders to have bitten off more than they could chew, there was one Englishman on the verge of what he might very easily have described as an 'arse-gripping situation'. At the very height of the market in 1984, Robert Sangster had purchased one of the most historic racehorse training grounds in the country, the 2300 acres which surround the Wiltshire mansion of Manton. Here the folklore of racing stretches back for more than a century. Old Alec Taylor trained here, sending out Sefton to win the 1878 Derby. His son, young Alec Taylor, who was born in 1862, sent out three Derby winners from here, including Gay Crusader and the sire of Hyperion, Gainsborough. Their sire, the mighty Bayardo, who won the St Leger of 1909, was also trained at Manton. Old local horsemen, who heard the tale from their own fathers, will still tell you of the day Bayardo lost the Goodwood Cup by a neck – at 20–1 ON – giving thirty-six pounds away to the winner, Magic.

Joe Lawson took the place over in 1927 and in a long career he trained the 2000 Guineas winners Orwell and Court Martial, and he put the eighteen-year-old Lester Piggott up to win the 1954 Derby on Never Say Die. The gigantic gambler and trainer George Todd sent out Sodium to win the St Leger in 1966. Robert Sangster was not buying just history, he was buying proven ground, over which great champions had been prepared, and he hoped that one day his entire operation would be centred here, for both breeding and racing.

He chose his trainer with immense care, inviting the young steeple-chase wizard Michael Dickinson to give up training over the jumps and to enter the world of flat-racing full time. Michael had already carved himself a piece of history by training the first *five* home in the 1983 Cheltenham Gold Cup and at the conclusion of the 1984 jumping season he came to Manton. He quickly demonstrated the ability to spend money on a thoroughbred establishment, on a scale which would have received candid admiration from Franklin Groves of North Ridge Farm. Granted formal permission to plant trees, Michael popped thirty thousand of them into the ground, causing the boss to observe that he 'did not do things by halves'.

Manton had been an old, grey place when Robert bought it, but under the free-spending hands of Michael Dickinson it turned into nothing less than a showpiece, with its three covered rides, its yearling yard, its big American-style barn. Five hundred of the acres were laid out as gallops, eleven separate ones. There were two all-weather gallops, one of nine furlongs. Six of them had a semi-automatic irrigation system and they were all joined by six miles of stone-dust roads. Guards and security men patrolled the place, since the young master was extremely conscious of the clear need for total secrecy.

By June 1986 the place had cost a conservative £10 million. Robert later thought it might have been closer to £12 or even £14 million. Michael had already conducted a world tour, talking to trainers, making notes and planning his strategy. He was one of the greatest note-takers on this planet. A ball-point pen in his writing hand became atomic powered. With Ballydoyle in the doldrums, entering a season in which they would not have one two-year-old good enough to take a place on the 1986 Irish Free Handicap, Robert brought van-loads of yearlings into Manton, some of them home-bred from the great Coolmore stallions, some of them hand-picked from the sales by the little Irish genius PP Hogan, Robert's most devoted friend and advisor. Michael thought he had all the time in the world, but when a place costs this kind of money, you need results, fast. Michael might have been quick with his ball-point, but he was not swift enough to catch that one.

By season's end he had trained just four winners. Manton stood in serene splendour, one of racing's greatest-ever white elephants, the expenditure column making one of the most fearsome bits of reading since Sheikh Mohammed went berserk with his cheque book at the 1983 Keeneland Sales. The trouble was Michael Dickinson did not

really understand Robert Sangster. If he had loosened up a bit, told a
few stories and tried to cheer Robert up, it might have been different.
But he was not able to do that. He scarcely touched alcohol and as
Robert drove morbidly along the great driveways which lead to the main
house, past endless gallops and trees which had cost him a fortune, the
ghosts of great champions of the past stood before him. But there were
none at Manton. The place had become, for him, like the valley of
death. And he sacked Michael Dickinson at season's end, saying simply,
'We were not able to communicate.' The financial settlement was more
than fair to the outgoing trainer.

With no classic winner since El Gran Senor in the high summer of
1984; with the virus still playing havoc in Vincent O'Brien's yard; with
Danny Schwartz gone, and Golden Fleece dead with no insurance
money; with The Senor still losing fortunes because of infertility; with
the $13·1 million yearling, now named Seattle Dancer, showing nothing
much as a two-year-old; with three young stallions at Coolmore with
no runners yet on the track; and now Manton draining money hand
over fist ... well, Robert thought they had better head back to the
drawing board. Before it was too late. He personally did not feel like
plunging millions more into the purchase of yearlings, and he doubted
whether Vincent and John did either. But they had to do something.
Robert Sangster's luck had, for the first time, temporarily deserted him.
That much was painfully obvious. His new wife, Sue, also loved to
parade in front of the crowds on the end of a winning horse's lead-rein,
but, unhappily, her opportunities were less frequent these days.

They held another council of war and they consulted with Dermot
Desmond, the creative Dublin stockbroker and friend of John Magnier.
As a result they decided, as Spendthrift Farm had done before them,
to float a public company, in Ireland. They would each put in a bundle
of money, around the $1 million mark, and they would go to the public,
on the Dublin Stock Exchange, relying on their fantastic record to carry
such an issue forward. The scheme would be to buy yearlings at the
sales and have them all trained by the greatest trainer in the world,
under the same corporate ownership. They could point to their great
successes of the past, demonstrating how they had bought and bred
great classic winners and marketed them as stallions for fortunes. They
could point to colossal profits at various times during their years
together. And above all they would show total confidence by investing
their own money in this great Irish enterprise. It might, thought John
Magnier, be propelled by sheer patriotism, with Irish racing fans from

Cork to Donegal buying the stock in the one international commodity in which their little country was demonstrably the world master – thoroughbred racehorses.

The timing was clearly not perfect. The crash of the yearling market meant that stallion prices must fall. In the USA this was about to happen. In less volatile Europe it would take a little longer, because the debts were not so pressing. But time was running out for the Kentucky stallion masters, who were faced with breeders now saying, 'I will not pay that much money to go to that sire. His yearlings won't sell. He's not worth it, and no one else will pay it either, unless they happen to be crazy.' Farms with $200,000 stallions were being told by their clients to charge $100,000 or 'no deal'. Even Seattle Slew would not fill at $750,000. Affirmed, with no world-class runners, would shortly go under $80,000. Conquistador Cielo was under fire at Claiborne. Spectacular Bid had been so relatively unsuccessful with two crops of three-year-olds running, he was threatening to go off the charts altogether: in pretty short order his stud fee was heading downwards in a bee-line from $150,000 to $15,000. Devil's Bag, the $36 million two-year-old of 1982, was having his fee slashed downwards from $200,000 to $100,000 before he had even had a three-year-old runner. And there were those who thought he was excessively expensive at that, since he was neither good enough nor sound enough to win a major race at the age of three himself.

No one had one shred of sympathy for the stallion men. They had ridden the good times like rodeo artists and now their greed was about to backfire. There were literally hundreds of shareholders being told their 'seasons' were no longer worth what they once were, and that they could not be sold at the old price. Nonetheless, they still owed their annual instalment on the capital purchase price. Over at Spendthrift some twenty-five per cent of all of their investors were non-horsemen, in very tenuous financial positions. It was much the same at Gainesway. George Harris, now under siege in his air-conditioned haven above New York's roaring Lexington Avenue, estimated that about thirty per cent of his clients owed money on their instalments, but could not sell their nominations. 'It was', he recalls, 'a bit bloody gloomy.'

The accelerating factor in this whirlpool of diminishing returns was that a stallion without a full book of mares will soon have few runners on the track, and few runners usually means very few winners. That is the end of any stallion. The farms *had* to fill them or see them simply collapse as assets, if not now, then in forty-eight months' time. Better to have fifty-five mares to a stallion at $40,000, than seventeen at

$150,000, the latter course of action being a certain road to ruin. At the end of 1986, if you had a two-year-old by Northern Dancer who had won six graded stakes, setting track records in all of them, and you had asked any farm in Lexington for $36 million for him, they would have called Lexington County Hospital and had you declared temporarily insane. 'Goddamnit, *boy!* No horse is worth that. Y'hear me? *No horse!*'

Even Cousin Leslie was heard to remark, 'They never were worth that kind of money. It was all just too much goddamned money.'

The bank loans were also becoming a colossal problem. Some farms had borrowed against the value of stallions. As these were now crashing, the banks were phoning to say they were not covered by enough collateral. Like banks the world over, they are always quick to lend you an umbrella when the weather is fine. As soon as it starts to rain, they want it back. And, boy, was it raining in the Bluegrass! Compounding the problem, some banks had been lending against stallion shares. Now both they and their clients were in big trouble. Tom Gentry owed the Citizens Fidelity Bank and Trust of Lexington nearly $14.5 million which he did not have. Farms which two years previously would have been judged unbuyable, valued at $20,000 an acre, were suddenly appearing on the market. Buyers were not plentiful.

And into this crisis of finance and confidence Robert and his men were proposing to take a public company. It should not be underestimated how closely the worlds of Tipperary and Kentucky and Maryland were intertwined. For years they had provided each other with the oxygen of life, both in the realms of buying and selling. With the market in Kentucky down, the market in Ireland could easily follow. Prices could not possibly hold up in Tipperary when the stallions are operating for half price in Lexington. In any event, the entire flotation exercise would rest on the shoulders of Vincent. It was he, the magician and hero of so many magic moments, who would be required to do it over again, now on behalf of the Irish public. The way things were going, even if he did manage to pull it off, perhaps with an expensive yearling bought for around $2 million, what would it now be worth as a stallion? The days of the $1 million yearling market were, after all, plainly over. And that meant the days of the new $20 million stallion were also over.

Robert and his partners recruited the Chairman of the Irish Racing Board Michael Smurfit to join them in their new enterprise. They also brought in the Irish cattle magnate John Horgan and they named the company Classic Thoroughbreds, investing more than £4 million between them. Vincent would be chairman, but there was a subtle change here in that Robert and John were no longer the principal executives as they had been for so many years in their private operation. Now they were just big shareholders, not decision-makers. Their names were there to give the public confidence but essentially Vincent O'Brien, the biggest shareholder, must make the major decisions alone. The shares were 'floated' in the spring of 1987 at thirty pence each, and institutions and private shareholders invested £12 million (Irish). In Michael Smurfit they had located one of Ireland's richest men, the principal owner of a vast international paper and packaging empire. He had been brought up in Ireland and his father Jefferson Smurfit had been one of Vincent O'Brien's first owners back in the late 1940s. Michael remembers a very good horse of his, named Patricksell, which won at Cheltenham. There was a great deal of romance in the return of the family to Ballydoyle.

But now they were in an extremely high-profile operation. The eyes of the Irish nation were focused on them as never before. Every time Vincent would run a horse in 1988, there would be thousands of small investors saying things like, 'One of my horses is going today at Leopardstown. I think Vincent likes him very much.'

For a while it seemed that this mass public ownership would obscure the real hard truth of the venture, but in the end it did no such thing. They all knew, deep down, that for the kind of money they were going to spend at the 1987 sales, they *must* find a great classic winner to finance it. Otherwise all of the money would be lost, which would be a bitterly unattractive prospect. And so, with their eyes wide open to the odds so stacked against them, with the market crashing around their ears, at the lowest possible ebb of their collective fortunes, with the stakes standing at about $1·4 million each, Vincent, Robert and John rolled the dice again.

=== 15 ===

The Harder They Fall

The year 1986 in the Bluegrass had been full of omens, and most of them had been extremely dreary. But, as the nights drew in and the big racehorse breeders began to close ranks and reduce the costs of their colossally mortgaged stallions, news of an unexpected auction sent an electric current of nervousness clean around the outer freeway which circles the city of Lexington. It was an auction which in a sense affected everyone – though no one would attend it. For it would take place on the upper east side of New York beginning at 7 p.m. on the evening of 17 November. The venue was Sotheby's and the bidding would be ferocious, with millions of dollars being offered for one of the finest collections of Old Masters drawings to appear on the market in years. They had been lovingly collected from all around the world since 1972. Everyone knew they were their owner's pride and joy, his most treasured possessions. He was John Ryan Gaines, master of Gainesway Farm on the Paris Pike and the biggest controller of thoroughbred stallions in the United States.

John Gaines selling his art collection? The rumours swept across the Bluegrass. It was not as if he were selling two or three of them, just to tide himself over a minor cashflow problem. John Gaines was selling them all. Just three months after the yearling market had crashed at Saratoga, following Keeneland, it seemed as if the biggest, best-run, best-advertised racehorse farm in central Kentucky may be in trouble. If you considered the disaster area of Spendthrift, you could easily have drawn the conclusion that the two biggest stallion stations in the United States were in trouble. There was a roster of around forty at Gainesway, and it included some of the immortals and half of the history of modern thoroughbred racing: Blushing Groom stood here, alongside Vaguely Noble and Lyphard. There was Bunker Hunt's Exceller, who had beaten Seattle Slew in one of the most awesome battles ever seen at Belmont

Park; there was the wonderful French miler Riverman, sire of the peer-less racemares Triptych, Detroit and Gold River; there was the Kentucky Derby winner Cannonade; the French Derby and Washington International winner Youth; there was one of Robert's first purchases, Transworld, winner of the Irish St Leger in 1977; there was Sharpen Up, Lemhi Gold, Temperence Hill, Ruffian's brother Icecapade. Nijinsky's first son to 'hit' in America, Czaravich, stood here. So did Big Spruce, who had been taken apart by Secretariat; and the big, hard-running Bates Motel, and Green Dancer.

If John Gaines needed 'outside money', where could that possibly put the rest of the community? Of course no one knew whether he had long planned to sell the collection at the end of 1986. But these were very anxious people here, and everyone thought the worst. Some tried to shrug it off, as people will, by saying, 'It's only a few old drawings, not like they was great paintings of racehorses or nothing. Probably wouldn't fetch more'n an average yearling at Keeneland.' 'Guess he just got fed up with 'em. Wants to get some new ones, probably wants to get some good pictures of his stallions.' 'I heard one of them's of Claude Monet, that twelve-furlong horse sired by Affirmed over in England. Can't understand why Mr Gaines wanted a picture of him in the first place.'

It was not until the *Lexington Herald-Leader* ran a report on the sale – about a third of the size of the four-column report that appeared in the *New York Times* – that residents of Kentucky realized the magnitude of the John Gaines sale. Leonardo da Vinci's *Child With A Lamb*, three sketches on a five-by-eight-inch piece of paper dating from around 1500, fetched a record price of $3·6 million from a London dealer bidding on behalf of California's J. Paul Getty Museum ('Goddamnit, his daughter-in-law Jacqueline Getty *owned* Bates Motel, you'd a thought they'd'a had more sense!'). A drawing called *Dance* by Henri Matisse fetched $935,000; Rembrandt's *View of Houlewaal* fetched $957,000; Raphael's *Five Apostles* $605,000; Armand Hammer paid $440,000 for Albrecht Durer's *Satyr's Family* (1505); *Little Jump* by Edgar Degas went to Tokyo for $1,100,000; Gauguin's *Young Girl and a Fox* went for $341,000; Vincent van Gogh's *Head of a Peasant Woman* was sold for $319,000. There were three other Rembrandts, works by Canaletto, Cézanne, Sir Anthony Van Dyke, Edouard Manet, Picasso, Tiepolo, Turner, Veronese and Claude Monet.

At the end of the sale, the international art dealers who attended Sotheby's had spent $21,280,000. Aside from one or two local wits, like Cousin Leslie ('Pity Sheikh Mohammed wasn't there, they'd'a fetched

$41 million'), the Lexington horse breeders were shaken by that. Somehow art represented real money, not lunatic dreams, like racehorses. And the man whose stallion price list would take the biggest battering in the new era of cheaper 'nominations' had been driven to sell his beloved collection. That is how it was seen in the Bluegrass. And they may have been right. Fourteen months later John Gaines sold Gainesway Farm for a whole lot less than the Old Masters drawings.

With the icy winds of January now cutting across the flat eastern shore of Maryland, freezing the paddocks of Windfields Farm, Northern Dancer faced up once more to the rigours of the breeding season. He was twenty-six now and his fee was still $375,000 (no foal guaranteed). His heart was no longer in his job though, and after a very few coverings – he only put two mares in foal – it was decided that Northern Dancer would be retired. He was still bold in spirit, but he was very sway-backed and he was uninterested in the ladies who came to visit. He was also, by most people's estimation, the greatest stallion who ever lived. Breeding technocrats had already worked out that early in the twenty-first century his name would appear in the pedigrees of fifty per cent of all the racehorses in the free world. He had sired one hundred and thirty-seven stakes winners and one hundred and twenty of his sons were standing at stud in various parts of the world.

With Nijinsky also growing old now, it would be one of the younger stallions who would perhaps step forward to take on his mantle and, before the new racing season was more than a few weeks old, two of them had staked their claims for serious recognition: Nureyev and Storm Bird. A beautiful bay filly named Miesque came out and won the 1000 Guineas at Newmarket and seventeen days later won the French 1000 Guineas at Longchamp. She ran in the colours of Stavros Niarchos, the principal owner of her sire, Nureyev. At the same meeting, the French 2000 Guineas was won by Soviet Star, a son of Nureyev, owned by Sheikh Mohammed.

Then Storm Bird struck with one of the very best fillies trained in England for years. She was a tall, elegant grey named Indian Skimmer and in six weeks she won the Pretty Polly Stakes at Newmarket by four lengths, the Musidora Stakes at York by four lengths, the Prix Saint-Alary at Longchamp by two and half, and then, in one of the most devastating exhibitions of speed seen all season, she took *four lengths* off Miesque to win the French Oaks. Indian Skimmer too was owned by Sheikh Mohammed, having cost him 350,000 guineas as a yearling.

Storm Bird's second 'hit' came at Royal Ascot when Bluebird, owned by Robert Sangster and trained by Vincent O'Brien, won the King's Stand Stakes five-furlong sprint by an easy four lengths, which made him, for the moment, the fastest horse in the country. Curiously, he and Indian Skimmer shared another ancestor: they had the same great-grand-dam, Home By Dark, herself the dam of the sensational American filly Dark Mirage, who won nine in a row back in 1968 and was the first winner of the US Fillies Triple Crown.

Bluebird, with his royal blood, was a very welcome success for Vincent, because things were again not going terribly well at Ballydoyle. He had sent out his best middle-distance colt, named Entitled, to run second in the Irish 2000 Guineas, in which he was beaten half a length. Then he was well beaten in the Derby, finishing fifth behind Reference Point. Both Entitled and Reference Point were by the 1971 Derby winner Mill Reef, but the winner was four lengths faster.

There was better news of the $13·1 million yearling, the one by Nijinsky out of My Charmer (Seattle Slew's mum). He was now three, and named Seattle Dancer, and he had achieved two distinctions which were not forthcoming from the second highest priced yearling ever sold, Sheikh Mohammed's $10·2 million purchase Snaafi Dancer: Seattle Dancer had (a) run in races and (b) won two of them. He did not of course live up to expectations, but then it would have been gigantic odds against him doing that. But he won the Gallinule Stakes at the Curragh and he won the Derby Trial at Leopardstown. He went to the French Derby as favourite, but finished sixth behind Natroum, six lengths adrift. They gave him one more try, in the Grand Prix de Paris in late June over ten furlongs and he short-headed the future Arc winner, Trempolino, out of second place, behind Risk Me.

Seattle Dancer never looked as if he was in love with racing and had the disconcerting habit of continually swishing his tail during the final stages. He had, however, the most wonderful pedigree and conformation and he could run in top company, so they decided to retire him to their new Ashford Stud in Kentucky, to stand alongside Storm Bird and El Gran Senor. His fee would be $20,000. Six hundred and fifty mares and they'd be home free on the purchase price – albeit with a cross-eyed stallion.

Back in Lexington, the name Alydar was just about going up in lights. The Calumet stallion, with his fourth crop of three-year-olds on the track, had been siring a steady stream of top horses, the Champion Two-Year-Old Filly Althea, the four-times Grade I winner Miss Oceana, Saratoga Six, Red Attack and Talinum. Now in 1987 he had sired the winner of the Kentucky Derby and the Preakness – a colt whose speed and courage had already captured the hearts of the nation. His name was Alysheba and he was causing his sire to become one of the very few leading stallions who might ride out the crash, without bankrupting his shareholders. With Alysheba, Alydar had accomplished what only a select group of stallions had ever done: he had sired a dual-classic winner, who was faster than he was himself.

The question was, could any feat by any stallion possibly stop the slide in prices at the Keeneland Sales? The answer was: no. The average plunged again by 9·5 per cent to a figure of $372,000 for each yearling. In 1984 the figure was $600,000. A total of sixteen yearlings sold for seven figures, ranging from $3·7 million to $1 million. The 'millionaires' represented only six per cent of the sale, the lowest such percentage since 1982. At that time it was being referred to as the 'exotic' end of the market. Right now it was more 'quixotic', and anyone who was breeding purely for the old upper end was almost certainly tilting at windmills.

The Brethren from Ballydoyle, as Ireland had come to know and love them, were not really there, except in the guise of Classic Thoroughbreds, the Irish public company. Vincent, careful now with the public purse, bought but four: for $1·4 million a full-brother to Secreto, who had dealt them that death blow on Epsom Downs three years before; for $1·25 million another Northern Dancer from a Chilean mare; for $750,000 a Nijinsky colt from Family Fame; and for $310,000 a colt by Alleged out of a Northern Dancer mare. The Irish trainer had also made a gallant attempt to land the sale-topper, a colt by Northern Dancer out of Secret Asset, but it was no good. Sheikh Mohammed had too many guns and there was no 'truce' with the directors of the new Classic Thoroughbreds. He took the colt home for $3·7 million, with Robert the underbidder. In the good old days of all-out war, they would have blazed on, to tumultuous cheers from the crowd, but it was different now. The money was no longer their own and they could not play fast and loose with it.

As the hammer crashed down at $3·7 million, Robert seemed very forlorn. He just stood there for a few minutes, looking at the old places around the auditorium where he had once stood shoulder to shoulder with Vincent and John and Danny Schwartz, where he had rallied his men to bid on, no matter the price. What days they had been. He glanced up at the lighted numbers board. It could take eight digits now, thanks entirely to him, but it may never do so again. And now he,

Robert, had given way at $3·7 million on a colt they really wanted. He walked over to join John Magnier and they left the arena together, two veteran gladiators. They had changed this little world, between them, but there were new people here now. Centre stage belonged to the Bedouin prince from Dubai. It was very hard for John and Robert, and they were both seized by an overpowering sadness. Robert thought of the words Danny Schwartz uttered back in 1984: 'The way we operate, we actually *need* one royally bred colt to win the Derby, or a comparable race, every single year, otherwise we'll go bust.' And that was before the stallion market crashed.

Now they had not had such a racehorse for three years, since El Gran Senor – and he was infertile, and the one before that was Golden Fleece and he was dead, and the insurance company had *still* not paid out. All they could do was to hope and pray the stallions came through – Lomond, Caerleon, Storm Bird, King's Lake, Be My Guest, Sadler's Wells; perhaps Thatching, Last Tycoon, or Tate Gallery, or Salmon Leap. Every one of them had the blood for it. They had made no mistakes there. 'What we need', said Robert thoughtfully, 'is a bloody good slice of luck.'

Meanwhile the princes from Dubai charged ahead. Sheikh Mohammed bought twenty yearlings for almost $19 million, hardly ever straying from the blood of Northern Dancer. Of the top-priced eight he bought – ranging from $3·7 million down to $900,000 – two were by the Dancer himself and five were by his sons Danzig, Nureyev, Nijinsky, and El Gran Senor. Dubai Bloodstock bought another eight, for $6,325,000 (six of them were by sons of Northern Dancer, one was by a grandson, and the last was by Alydar). Sheikh Hamdan's Shadwell Estate Company bought twelve for over $6 million (nine of them by sons of Northern Dancer).

Robert Sangster, the man who had begun it all, was listed as buying just one yearling, for $300,000. It was a filly by Northern Dancer out of his own mare Detroit, who had won the Arc, a lifetime ago, it seemed. He was just buying out a partner who had owned the breeding right to the old champion.

If things were not absolutely inspiring with the dissipated army of Sangster's men, they were a sight worse for Tommy Gentry, who had gone spectacularly bust. The king of the party-givers, who had person-ally taken $35 million out of this sale in the past five years, had had his yearlings seized by the receivers of the Citizens Fidelity Bank. Seven of them had grossed $2,487,000 towards his debt of $14·4 million.

Somehow or other he had managed to sell five on his own account which grossed $895,000. But how Tommy, with that massive income, had actually managed to spend all of his profits plus another $14·4 million, will remain one of those mysteries of the thoroughbred breeding world. 'Tommy Gentry? Bankrupt? After all those fantastic sales? That's like telling me Calumet were going bust.'

Calumet were spending money, that's what Calumet were doing. J. T. Lundy had bought into the Fasig Tipton Sales Company, which runs the yearling auctions at Saratoga, and, with his co-director Peter Brant (seller to Calumet of Mogambo), he came up with a plan to get that Saratoga average way up, to tell the world that this sale was second most important, after Keeneland, and that they had stopped the unstoppable slide in values. On the face of it, the Saratoga Sales results suggested exactly that. The gross was up twenty-two per cent to nearly $47 million, and the average price per yearling was up twenty-nine per cent to $241,603 on the year. But the main reason for this was that Calumet had entered the sale as a major consignor, having traditionally raced all of their own stock. Here at Saratoga, fifty-one years ago, Warren Wright had bought the yearling Bull Lea for $14,000. In the ensuing years he sired nine champions and three Kentucky Derby winners for Calumet, including the fabled Citation. Alydar's own dam, Sweet Tooth, has a 3 X 3 Bull Lea cross in her pedigree. Now here was J. T. Lundy, married to, but separated from, Warren Wright's granddaughter, selling the farm's young stock, the descendants of Bull Lea, at auction. The half-brother to Alydar (by Seattle Slew) went for $2 million, a daughter of Alydar from My Juliet went for $1·6 million, and a daughter of Secreto out of Sugar and Spice was sold for $1 million. They received $1·5 million for a Seattle Slew colt out of the great Calumet champion of 1979, Davona Dale, in whose pedigree Bull Lea appears *three* times.

Altogether, the eight Calumet yearlings sold fetched $7,760,000, which bumped up the Saratoga 'take' no end. They were worth more than double the dollars received by the second highest consignor and they caused the average to go to $241,000. Without them, the average would have been $210,000.

The leading buyer at the sale was an unusual name to appear in such a position. It was the Axmar Stable of Robert and Betty Marcus, of West Palm Beach, Florida. They bought the half-brother to Alydar, two Alydar colts and one Alydar filly for $3,375,000. But the question being asked was not, who bought them? Or even, for how much? It was, had that Calumet consignment been sold at all? Seven of the eight yearlings ended up in Calumet racing partnerships, all involving Axmar Stables. And the last one of the eight, the Alydar colt from Reverse and Count, had been listed as 'bought' for $285,000 by Frederic and Paul Gussin, of Washington, who were shortly to become partners in some of the great Calumet mares and future yearlings. Why, people wondered, did J. T. Lundy want to 'cash out' Calumet's priceless assets? He could not have needed the money. He inherited a farm with no debt, Alydar was making a fortune, and the mares belonged to the farm, free and clear. Had his purchases of stallions been so out of line he needed money to pay for them? Or was there something going on at Calumet that no one knew about? Whatever, everyone thought there was a major credibility gap over the sale of those Calumet yearlings. People believed that the new partnership, which had bought Fasig Tipton, had just run them through the ring to build up the averages and make everything look a whole lot better than it was. The *Bloodhorse* magazine was very scathing on the subject and there was a certain amount of embarrassment when Calumet's continued ownership came to light.

It mattered, however, very little what they or anyone else tried to do about the situation. The only statistic that mattered was the one at Keeneland, the traditional barometer of the health of the industry, and there the average price for a yearling was now $372,000, when, thirty-six months ago, it had been $600,000. That one was carved in marble, no ifs, ands or buts. It was a dreadful concern for everyone in the industry, and the pressure from the banks was mounting. Anyone with a big debt was under siege, because the banks, which had been so eager to lend during the boom years, were now exposed, with everyone's stallion collateral caving in around them. Loan officers at banks all over Kentucky were demanding that their clients sell, which was impossible without losing fortunes. The breeders wanted to hang on, just for a while until the prices went back up, but the bankers were not buying that. They were beginning to believe that they might not go up again ever, which is why they claimed Tommy Gentry's yearlings. John Gaines had solved any problems he might have with loans or shareholders who would not pay their instalments by selling the drawings, but most breeders had no such extra collateral. They just had the horses and many a Kentucky night was spent cursing the private jets, and the huge expense accounts, and the limousines, and the big Mercedes – little items which had become more or less routine when times were good and the big bucks were rolling, out in the Bluegrass.

Over in Ireland the mood was not much better. Vincent was unable to get the horses into the kind of shape only he understood. The virus would not leave the yard and the big winners had, for the moment, dried up. The horses were never quite as well as he needed them and the ones that could run were always down with some minor illness. Even Bluebird, the hero of Royal Ascot, had his colours lowered as prospective sprint champion. To claim this title there are three more English races that need winning: the July Cup at Newmarket, the William Hill Sprint at York, and the Vernons Sprint (still sponsored by Robert's family firm after twenty-one years) at Haydock. The same horse won them all, a Northern Dancer colt owned by Sheikh Mohammed named Ajdal. He beat Bluebird by about a length at Newmarket, and then by more than six lengths at York. Ajdal's appearance in England was a bit of a surprise for some, because this was the colt from Native Partner, who had been left on the auctioneer's block at $7·5 million at Keeneland when Sheikh Mohammed thought he was being 'run-up' by the vendors in 1985. However, as many prospective buyers had learned, when the prince from Dubai wants something, he *really* wants it. He had gone back to the vendors, who were probably in shock at their loss in the sales ring, and negotiated a private deal, which brought Ajdal to England.

Sheikh Mohammed had a predictably excellent 1987. His filly Unite won the English and Irish Oaks, Soviet Star returned in the high summer and won the Sussex Stakes at Goodwood. Victory in the Prix de la Forêt in France gave the colt three Group I successes and a big future as a stallion at Dalham Hall. Sheikh Ahmed al-Maktoum, the youngest of the four brothers, owned a top-class colt called Mtoto which won the Eclipse Stakes.

But the real high drama on the track happened in the United States in the Breeders' Cup. Miesque spreadeagled them in the Mile and, as the sun lit up the hills to the south-west of Hollywood Park, the enormous crowd prepared to watch one of the truly great battles: between two Kentucky Derby winners, Nijinsky's son Ferdinand who won in 1986, and this year's winner, Alysheba. It took place in the $3 million Breeders' Cup Classic, over one and a quarter miles on the dirt. There were twelve in the field, including last year's winner Skywalker; the Canadian three-year-old Afleet, who had won the Jerome at Belmont Park; Judge Angelucci who had won $1 million in 1987; and Candi's Gold, winner of the Silver Screen. This was easily the biggest race to be run in the USA all season, because the Horse of the Year title was on the line, as well as the $1,350,000 first prize. Ferdinand came to it off three straight victories including the Hollywood Gold Cup. Alysheba had won the $600,000 Super Derby at Louisiana Downs eight weeks previously. Clashes between respective winners of the Kentucky Derby are rare. For this one, all of the chips were on the table. Bill Shoemaker would ride Ferdinand. Chris McCarron would handle Alysheba. It was as if every race which had been run all season in north America had been but a preliminary for this clash of the Titans.

The starter sent them away at 2.41 p.m. Pacific Daylight Time and all around the world the satellites beamed the picture into millions of homes – and they watched Judge Angelucci, Charlie Whittingham's pacemaker for Ferdinand, battling it out in the lead with Candi's Gold. They went the quarter in twenty-three flat; the half in 46·4 seconds; three-quarters in one minute 10·2 seconds; and the mile in a breathtaking one minute 35·4. And now the race was on, as Bill Shoemaker drove Ferdinand up into third place on the inside, with Alysheba coming fast now on the wide outside.

The huge California crowd was up and shouting Shoemaker home, and inside the furlong pole he struck the front, racing fiercely past the two embattled leaders. At the sixteenth pole Ferdinand was clear, but McCarron had Alysheba flying. It was like one of those old Westerns – 'Watch your back!' – and the crowd sensed what was happening and the sound was like thunder, a totally American roar of anguish: there's nothing like it anywhere in the world. Shoemaker glanced back and immediately drew his whip, and still Alysheba charged on. Now they were level, locked in deadly combat as they struggled through the dying strides of the race. The crowd went absolutely wild as Bill Shoemaker booted Ferdinand home, by a nose. Everyone who witnessed that race knew they had seen an epic, one which would live on in memory for all the years of their lives. For sheer, bone-tingling excitement, there's nothing quite like one of those classic American battles on the dirt.

Every time there was one of these races, which captivated all of the horse-racing world, Kentucky hoped anew. These two sons of Nijinsky and Alydar, grandsons of Joe Thomas's Northern Dancer and Cousin Leslie's Raise a Native, had just done the job of ten advertising agencies. They had provided millions of dollars of publicity for the Kentucky breeding industry. Surely now, somehow, the yearling prices must rise again? How could ANYONE fail to be moved by the grace, the gallantry and the speed of these great racehorses? How could anyone not want one just like Ferdinand and Alysheba?

Kentucky never quite grasped that the lunatic prices were gone.

Period. The big players were not going to do it any more. Already the word in the Bluegrass was not 'Profit'. It was another, more sinister, sadder word: 'Dispersal'. With Tom Gentry bankrupt, Spendthrift heading that way, and John Gaines considering selling Gainesway, the next big crash must clearly be Bluegrass Farm, the great sprawling thoroughbred empire of Bunker Hunt. He was under the whip from the banks for other reasons, but the value of the horses was going down fast. His friend and mentor, who stood his top stallions Vaguely Noble, Exceller and Youth, was Gaines himself. And Bunker was not short of careful advice.

Before the old year was out, it was announced that the entire bloodstock holdings of Mr Nelson Bunker Hunt, located at Bluegrass Farms, Kentucky, would come under the auctioneer's hammer on the morning of 9 January 1988. There were five hundred and eighty horses in this massive thoroughbred empire, which, before Robert and Sheikh Mohammed had arrived, had been easily the biggest in the world. Bunker had built it with care and devotion, and an almost blind love of the animals, over a period of thirty-five years. The tough, burly Dallas oil man, who had shaken out Wall Street twice in his lifetime in the silver market, was always said to be, privately, the most enormous pussy-cat when it came to those horses. His brother Herbert says it almost broke his heart to sell them and he was unable to attend the sale, because he could not bear to let anyone see him that upset. Through all the terrible trials and dramas of the dreadful losses in the market, the losses in the oil fields, the humiliations he suffered financially, no one had ever seen him cry before.

He knew that a racing stable could be rebuilt, a broodmare replaced, or even a trainer. But an empire like this? Built upon mares who had raced for their value, upon stallions who had won Derbys, fought for great championships? His philosophy had always been to breed from top racemares, with pedigrees occupying a very secondary place in the scheme of things. By so doing he had home-bred Dahlia, Youth, Empery and Exceller. Bunker's heroes had taken generations to create. They had come from France, Ireland and England as well as America, and they had taken his time, his money and his judgment down all of the years. It was an empire and to quote C. William Beebe, somewhat opportunistically, 'Surely, another heaven, and another earth must pass, before such a one can be again.' That's how it seemed to Bunker, as he sat alone in his office in Dallas that January morning, watching the clock, knowing that the auctioneer's hammer would soon crash down

for the first time, and then it would never stop. And in his mind he
heard it, like the melancholy thud of the guillotine.

It was a freezing morning and the world of thoroughbred breeding
was gathered in the Keeneland sales ring. It was a remarkable sight for
a January sale – which are not normally attended by the main players.
Everyone was there: the familiar representatives of the Maktoums,
Robert Sangster, and the two biggest American investors, Wayne Lukas
and the aircraft tycoon Allen E. Paulson. It was just like the July crowd,
with overcoats. There were two hundred and eighty-one broodmares,
one hundred and sixty-eight yearlings, one hundred and thirteen two-
year-olds, older horses, a stallion, and one solitary foal, four-days-old,
still a bit unsteady, but walking bravely around the ring beneath a red
blanket bearing in white letters the words 'The One and Only NBH-
Bred in 1988'. It was the most total dismantling of a bloodstock operation in living memory.

One by one the auctioneer 'knocked them down'.. But there was a
respectful silence as a groom led in the eighteen-year-old Dahlia, still
with her slightly skittish, elegant look, her dished face, her Arabian head
and her slim white blaze. In her time she had beaten the toughest colts
and fillies in the business, winning the Irish Oaks, the King George
VI and Queen Elizabeth Stakes (twice), the Washington International,
the Grand Prix de Saint-Cloud, the Benson and Hedges Gold Cup
(twice), the Man O'War Stakes and the Canadian International. On her
day, and there were many, she had been the best racehorse in the world.
She had heard the roar of the crowd at Longchamp, Ascot, the Curragh,
York, Belmont Park, Toronto and Hollywood Park. She had been ridden
by the best, by Bill Pyers, Lester Piggott and Bill Shoemaker. She had
produced for Bunker an excellent racehorse in Dahar, who won over
$1·2 million and stood as a stallion at Bluegrass. But now, on this cold,
cheerless morning, she was being sold, an ageing broodmare, barren to
her last cover to Lyphard. Men who had watched her greatest victories
came into the arena just to see her for the last time. Everyone was
hoping she would be bought by a top Kentucky farm, where she would
be cared for into her declining years. No one wanted her to be shipped
abroad. In the end she was sold for $1·1 million to Allen Paulson, owner
of the lovely Brookside Farm out in peaceful Versailles, and you could
almost hear the sigh of relief in the ring.

Within a very few minutes the telephone rang in the Keeneland office
and an anonymous voice asked, 'I wonder if you would be kind enough
to tell me who bought Hip Number 125?'

'Certainly, sir . . . That mare went to Mr Allen Paulson.'

'Thank you . . . Thank you very much.'

Bunker Hunt replaced the receiver and he smiled for the first time that morning. His terrible sadness was not lessened, but he needed to know that Dahlia was safe.

Next they sold her filly foal of 1987 by Northern Dancer for $1·3 million, and later they sold the top racemare Sangue, and then Nobiliary who had boldly chased home Grundy in the 1975 English Derby. By the end of the second day they were all gone and Bunker was richer by some $46 million. But his legal fees were running at $3 million a month, and there were grim discussions with the IRS, and the mountainous debt had to be serviced. Dahlia had been evicted, essentially, by bankers, which, for a mare who had run her heart out for $1·5 million in the mid 70s, was a rather depressing irony.

Three weeks later Nelson Bunker Hunt was presented with America's Eclipse Award as the leading breeder of 1987. He was also honoured in Europe as the breeder of Triptych, the racemare who had just won four Group I races to become the all-time leading money-winner on that continent. 'I would like, above all things,' said Bunker, 'to believe that one day I could come back into the thoroughbred-breeding business. It's been a big part of my life.'

Soon the land and buildings of Bluegrass Farm would go the way of the horses and upon the immediate horizon there were other sudden 'dispersals' being scheduled. Kinghaven Farms would sell everything, as would James P. Ryan's Ryehill Farm in Maryland. Everett Lowrance would sell up in Oklahoma, and Elmer Whitaker would sell the entire stock of Bwamazon Farm out in Winchester, Kentucky. In the latter part of the year there was a real shock when Robert Brennan announced he was selling the entire breeding stock of his tri-state Due Process Stable – one hundred and ninety horses, mares, two-year-olds and yearlings, in another January sale in Lexington. There would be no reserves on any of them. Bob Brennan was board chairman of International Thoroughbred Breeders Inc. and he owned Garden State Park in New Jersey, and Philadelphia Park in Pennsylvania. His departure from the world of breeding was almost as scary as John Gaines's sale of the Old Masters. 'Everything has become disoriented,' he said. 'The perceived value that was put on breeding stock was out of line . . . The beauty of the auction market is that you find out what the horses are really worth, not what you hope they're worth.'

The words were spoken by a very rich, acutely intelligent man, one of Wall Street's 'Masters of the Universe'. They were not however echoed by the 'hardboots' in Kentucky, where the word 'auction' no longer possessed even a semblance of beauty. Out there in the Bluegrass the sales were anticipated much as Hitler awaited the fall of Berlin.

It was also the worst time for the directors of Classic Thoroughbreds in Ireland. Throughout the second half of 1987, Vincent O'Brien had combed the sales of America, England, Ireland and France to find the yearlings which would launch the public company. Altogether he had bought thirty-eight of them, for either a full or partnership interest, but none of them would have run before the Keeneland Sales began. It was 1976 all over again, when they had lost some of their original investors because they *had* to go back to the sales again before any of the two-year-olds had run. The budgets were now carefully planned and the business-man-chairman of the finance committee, Michael Smurfit, had pencilled in the sum of only $4 million to spend in Kentucky. They were operating on limited finances now, because they had to stick with the cash that they had in the company.

Upon arrival Vincent was considering buying perhaps six or eight with the money, two for around the million mark, and perhaps four for $300,000 to $400,000. His views however changed dramatically when he went to visit a Nijinsky colt from the mare Crimson Saint. He was alone now, except for his son and assistant, Charles, but he needed no encouragement from anyone for this most striking individual. He had the look of Nijinsky about him, a big bold eye, and the short elegant head of his sire, right down to the white star on his forehead. He had Nijinsky's deep bay colour, with four jet-black points. There was no white about his feet or hooves, and he had the most terrific sweep of muscle across his quarters. His front legs were absolutely correct, he had a grand sloping shoulder and he stood stock still, with his ears pricked forward. Vincent, for a brief flashing moment, thought he was looking at the young Nijinsky at another sale, exactly twenty years ago.

For the first time for several seasons, here was a colt who 'spoke' to the master of Ballydoyle. The trouble was, he could not speak to the master of Classic Thoroughbreds' purse, Dr Michael Smurfit, and Vincent felt that, as chairman, he might have to take matters into his own hands. But this was not like the old days when he and Robert would have gone to the wall for this fellow. This was 1988 and he had to be careful, but he nonetheless resolved that he would go to $2·5 million for this particular son of the 1970 Triple Crown winner.

The colt was consigned by Crystal Springs Farm. The catalogue described it thus: 'Agent for Barry L. Weisbord, trustee for Tom Gentry. Debtor.' So the colt was actually owned by the Citizens Fidelity Bank and Trust Company of Lexington, who were valiantly trying to get back the remainder of the $14·4 million Tom had once owed. They had seized his bloodstock, but with a brilliant sleight of hand, the wily Thomas had hung on to Crimson Saint, from whom he had already sold yearlings for over $11 million. His big pay-day of $7 million from Sheikh Mohammed, back in 1985, was for a colt from this mare, which was later named Laa Etaab but could not run a yard. Vincent was fervently hoping that Sheikh Mohammed would remember this fact vividly when they led the yearling into the ring. Tommy Gentry was fervently hoping that Sheikh Mohammed would have forgotten this fact entirely when they led the yearling into the ring.

But there would be plenty of keen buyers for him. Crimson Saint had already bred the blisteringly fast Secretariat sprinter Pancho Villa and the outstanding West Coast stakes winner Terlingua, dam of Storm Cat. Vincent was certain that D. Wayne Lukas, who had trained Terlingua, would not be far away when the bidding commenced. And nor was he. When Lot Number 269 made his entry it was clear that the Californians were very determined. For a while they duelled with Aaron U. Jones, but Vincent came in as the price rose towards $2 million. He bid $1·9, Wayne answered. Vincent bid $2·1, and Wayne answered again. Vincent went to $2·3, but it did not work. Wayne said $2·4. And Vincent O'Brien bid his outside limit: $2·5 million.

The Californian hesitated. Vincent silently implored him to say no more. But the great West Coast trainer bid $2·6 million for the son of Crimson Saint. Vincent fought his conscience. His judgment was right on the line here, but he knew he would rather go home with this colt than any other twelve horses in this sale.

He stood quietly as the auctioneer asked him: 'Will you go one more, sir?' And he tilted his head on one side thoughtfully, a familiar gesture to all who know him. Then he bid $2·7 million.

Wayne caucused briefly before he bid $2·8. And again the auctioneer asked the Irish trainer to 'go one more'. Vincent looked down at his catalogue. Then he looked up again, with just a flicker of a nod. 'Two point nine, I'm bid,' said the auctioneer.

Wayne Lukas did not hesitate this time. And he hit back instantly. '*Yeah!*' yelled the bid-spotter Charlie Richardson.

'*Three million I have! Now will ya gimme three one, three one, three one . . . will ya gimme three one-one-one?*'

Vincent O'Brien thought hard. He did not have the money for this kind of battle. God, would he have given a lot to have Robert and Danny and John at his shoulder right now? Telling him to get on with it, telling him to get the goddamned colt. But the old operational team was gone. Robert was a only minority shareholder now. Vincent was essentially on his own and he was $600,000 beyond his limit.

Now he looked down at the colt standing with that bold, fearless eye of his on the rostrum. And he nodded his head at $3·1 million.

Wayne Lukas caucused and bid again. Vincent nodded immediately. *'Three point three million I have!'*

But now the Californians did not hesitate. They bid $3·4 million instantly. Vincent knew he had to stop. He could go no more. The auctioneer implored him to try one last bid, but he could not do so in his new position as chairman of a public company. He stared once more at the colt, who flicked his ears. The hammer was raised, the auctioneer was shouting: 'I'll sell him *now!* I'll sell him for three point four million dollars to Charlie.' But in that split-second, with some kind of divine reflex, Vincent O'Brien raised his catalogue.

'Yeah!' bawled the bid-spotter.

'Three and a half million I'm bid,' shouted the auctioneer. Wayne Lukas shook his head and the hammer crashed down, and another son of Nijinsky was on his way home to Tipperary.

It was the highest price paid at the sale. It helped to stop the decline, but the year's average nevertheless dived for the fourth year in a row to $367,838. The gross receipts fell under $98 million, their lowest point since 1981. Only a dozen yearlings fetched a million dollars. Sheikh Mohammed and his brothers spent a little over $29 million for thirty-eight, Vincent spent a total of $4·3 million for four, and Wayne Lukas went through just about $10 million for twenty-one head. The drop in overall sales had not been too bad, but the breeders had lost fortunes, because their yearlings were born of the high 1985/86 prices, set before the market realized what was happening. These were probably the most expensive yearlings ever bred, many of them from 'nominations' that went with wildly expensive shares.

The top of the Sires' League for Keeneland was occupied as ever by Northern Dancer, with his last major group, seven of them, averaging $945,714. Mr Prospector was next on $800,000. They were followed by *five* of Northern Dancer's sons, Nijinsky, Topsider, El Gran Senor (small crop, big prices), Nureyev and Danzig, their averages ranging from around $500,000 to $640,000. Seth Hancock's two $36 million stallions of the early 80s were strictly nowhere: Devil's Bag was in eighteenth place with an average of $241,000, and Conquistador Cielo was thirtieth with an average of $178,000. Welcome to the Valley of Death. Their shares cost $900,000 each. Even Storm Bird, with the magnificent Indian Skimmer batting for him in Europe, could average only $220,000 for each of eight. It was a brutally tough market for sellers.

Robert Sangster had bought seven yearlings for himself and he did the bidding on a Northern Dancer filly from Betty's Secret. This full-sister to Secreto was the top-priced filly of the sale at $1 million. She would, however, run under the flag of Classic Thoroughbreds. The remainder of Robert's purchases totalled $2,375,000, and he split them between Vincent and the new trainer installed at Manton, his old friend from Lambourn, Barry Hills. Significantly, five of them were fillies. Robert, the first of the big spenders, was preparing for a new career.

In his heart Robert knew he could no longer compete with the men from the Middle East. No one could really, unless about five people, with $100 million to lose apiece, were prepared to give it a try. No, Robert was preparing to become an owner-breeder, a seller in the market. For years now he had collected fillies, beautifully bred fillies from the great American sales. He had always been a successful breeder, ever since the days of Swettenham in Cheshire. Now he had a huge portfolio of breeding rights to a new generation of stallions, heavy with the blood of Northern Dancer. He may have seen his fortune diminish during the past few trying years, but he still had the shares and he still had the mares. He could, if he so wished, breed dozens of top-class foals, virtually for nothing, from sires like El Gran Senor, Storm Bird, Sadler's Wells, Caerleon, Lomond, The Minstrel, Last Tycoon and the rest.

He joined up with Vincent as they left the sales ring and they grinned at each other: Vincent because he was situated, rather shyly, at the top of the buyers' chart having bought the most expensive yearling at the sale. Very few people realized that the second highest priced colt in the sale was the one by Northern Dancer out of Detroit. It was sold for $2,450,000 and the consignor was Swettenham. The mare was Robert's. The two old campaigners were, somehow, right up there again, in different roles.

It was a deeply nostalgic moment for Robert as he walked across the parking lot, because he knew he may not pass this way again. The great sales pavilion loomed behind him in the warm evening. It had been the scene of so many unforgotten battles of the past fourteen years, but in his heart he knew he would not return, not as a major buyer, not as one of the gladiators of the industry. The days of the Tipperary raiders were over. He stopped for a few moments, out by the hedge towards Bluegrass Field, and he looked back at the pavilion, alone with his thoughts for a few seconds. Vincent was silent. He knew what his old friend was thinking. Then he said softly, 'Come on, Robert. It's over now. Let's go home. At least we're still top of the table.'

16

Running Out of Cash

There hammer blows to the cashflow system had driven Robert Sangster back onto the ropes for the first time in his fighting career. As a breeder he was still under control, and dangerous, still able to manoeuvre. As a big-league yearling buyer he was on the canvas and the ref was into the count. There was no way he would beat it. The original business, which he had schemed and masterminded with John Magnier all those years ago, was effectively finished. To compete against Sheikh Mohammed would have required £20 million of rock-solid cash to be spent in the sales ring annually. That meant a huge stallion deal – selling one of them, that is – every single year. The first and worst of the hammer blows was that they had had no such animal since 1984: the lean, sad years at Ballydoyle, where there had been so much sickness, had ended the dream.

The second blow was that the last two payments on Storm Bird totalling $14 million were not forthcoming. They were compensated with Ashford Farm and with shares in a high-earning horse, but that was not a big hunk of *cash*.

The third was Golden Fleece's syndication money coming in at the rate of £4 million a year (some of it in home-bred yearlings to sell) had ceased abruptly upon his death, with twenty-eight mares not covered in his second year. That alone was a £2·8 million deficit, and there was another £8 million missing over the next two years. The insurance was *still* not paid out.

For the Irishmen there was the added problem of El Gran Senor, who might have fetched $60 million for three-quarters of him, but had earned only $2·8 million for his fourteen mares, payable in October 1985. Another huge lump of cash had gone, though Robert had come out whole on this one, having sold some of his shares in $2 million packages in conjunction with those of Sadler's Wells. The insurance companies had to settle with individuals for the fertility failure of The Senor, but the absence of cash income for Vincent and John and Coolmore on this stallion was very serious.

None of it was their fault. It was bad luck on a truly majestic scale and it cost them the back-up cash their brilliance and judgment *should* have earned them, to carry them through the lean years. It would have driven many an operation down altogether. But in this case there was one powerful lifeboat in Tipperary and that was Coolmore Stud. Right now it was shouldering its way through tumultuous seas, with green water cascading over the bow. The skipper, fighting to hold her steady, was John Magnier and the entire future of the operation rested on the performance of five of his young stallions. John, as the stallion master, had the final word as to which of the expensive racehorses actually stood at Coolmore and tried to earn a living. Storm Bird and El Gran Senor did not count in this context because no one had any options. The Senor was unsaleable, and Storm Bird's financial entanglements were too complicated.

The first three of the five, upon whom John Magnier had essentially staked his reputation yet again, were Lomond, the 2000 Guineas winner out of Seattle Slew's dam My Charmer; Caerleon, Nijinsky's hard-running son out of Royal Glint's sister Foreseer; and Sadler's Wells, the tough, resolute son of Northern Dancer from Fairy Bridge. All three of them had won classics. The fourth one was Woodman, the $3 million two-year-old of 1985 who had been hit by the virus late in the season after winning three decent races in a row. This one was by the superb American sire Mr Prospector and thus a grandson of Raise a Native. His dam was Playmate, a full-sister to the great US champion filly and broodmare Numbered Account. The pedigree was irresistible to John, whether or not Woodman had fully proved himself on the racecourse. He had proved himself to John, which was all that counted, and he was sent to stand at Ashford, alongside Storm Bird and The Senor. His first-two-year-olds would run in 1990. The fifth was Last Tycoon, whom John had bought in 1986. His first two-year-olds would also appear on the track in 1990. But the foals were outstanding in conformation, as was the Breeders' Cup Champion Miler himself.

For a stallion owner, times such as these try men's souls. There are always people willing to 'crab' a stallion before his three-year-olds have run, and there are always two sides to the argument:

LOMOND

Criticism: Lacked pace. Never won a race after the 2000 Guineas.

Magnier's answer: 'Perfect pedigree. He was three-quarters of a length away from *two* one-mile classics. Blood and guts. What more do you want?'

CAERLEON

Failed to catch Shareef Dancer in the Irish Derby, may have lacked resolution.

Magnier's answer: 'Ran one of the bravest races of the season to win the Benson and Hedges Gold Cup. Classy enough to win the French Derby. Great pedigree. Great looks.'

SADLER'S WELLS

Dead lucky to win the Eclipse. Would not have done so if Time Charter had had a clear run.

Magnier's answer: 'Time Charter was one of the best racemares of the last thirty years. No disgrace even he had gone down by a neck to her. But Sadler's kept going, won the race. Wonderful pedigree, classic winner, heart like a lion. Don't be daft.'

WOODMAN

Never proved himself in England. Well beaten in the Dewhurst. Could have been just an Irish 'flash in the pan'.

Magnier's answer: 'Ever tried running flat out for nearly a mile with pneumonia?'

LAST TYCOON

Don't you think he might be too expensive?

Magnier's answer: 'Since he's the fastest horse in Europe and the Mile Champion of the World, and one of the best-looking stallions in Ireland, with one of the best pedigrees in the world, he'd hardly be cheap, would he?'

This was the kind of banter John Magnier dealt with on a daily basis. His was the essential voice of Coolmore. And by these five horses he would live or die as the recognized authority on excellence in the breed; he was the leading judge of which stallion would pass it on, which racehorse never would. Now with the cash problem driving Robert out of the yearling market, he had no option but to trust John to breed their own new champions and thus perpetuate the most exciting stallion business in Europe.

John got off to a sensational start at the end of 1987 when Lomond topped the list of all the First-Season Sires standing in the British Isles. He had four individual stakes winners and three other winners: they won twelve races between them for a total of £190,000 in prize money. Right behind him in the league table came Caerleon, with two brilliantly fast sons, Caerwent and Careafolie. Back in eighteenth place was the horse who had beaten him on that grim day at the Curragh, Shareef Dancer. The saddest news was that the leading Second-Season Sire was the late, great Golden Fleece, with only twelve mares covered in his second crop. He had fourteen winners of twenty-two races, and they won nearly £190,000. John always shook his head when the name of the 1982 Derby winner was mentioned. And the gesture had nothing to do with money.

In the middle of all of this he had actually found time to swoop and purchase another stallion, the very moderately bred Ahonoora, who had sired a stream of tough, fast horses for the Irish National Stud. This was an extremely unCoolmore-like horse. He did not have the blood for it, being by the terribly disappointing sire Lorenzaccio, who had left for Australia ten years previously without ever having sired one single winner of an English Group race. Consistency was his speciality. The dam, Helen Nichols, was a five-furlong sprinter from a very ordinary family. The one touch of real class in the entire bottom half of Ahonoora's yawn-inducing pedigree was that Helen Nichols's sire, Martial, was a son of Calumet's Kentucky Derby winner Hill Gail and thus a grandson of the immortal Calumet stallion Bull Lea. Which, even so, made the odds about 7000–1 that Ahonoora would make a decent stallion. Step forward the man who accepted those odds to a £1 and collect £7000. Ahonoora, from the day he began his new career, began to sire high-class winners, Park Appeal, Park Express, Princess Athena and Indian Ridge. John Magnier never missed one of them. And then in 1987 Ahonoora sired Don't Forget Me, the horse which won the English and the Irish 2000 Guineas. The owners wanted him to come to Coolmore and since one of them was John Horgan, John Magnier's pal from County Cork, an agreeable deal was made. But the stallion Magnier wanted was Don't Forget Me's sire, Ahonoora.

He could not be talked out of it either. Every Irishman associated with the farm had an opinion on this one and the arguments against paying the big asking price of £7 million (Irish) were strong. He was the type of sire whose early winners could dry up and then his market value would crash because he did not have the pedigree to sustain his own price. Anyway, he had never been a champion-class racehorse.

'Jesus, he was beaten about twenty times by Double Form.'

'Three times,' said Magnier. 'Twice by a length or less. And he beat Double Form twice, once by a half length when he won the Stewards' Cup.'

John had analysed all of Ahonoora's winners and there was a pattern to the stallion. From sprinting mares he sired sprinters, from milers he sired milers, from mares who ran further, he got horses that went further. To John this meant Ahonoora was regularly injecting his off-spring with speed, with a touch of winning class and with his own toughness and courage. There were a lot of good sprinters around in 1978 and '79 and Ahonoora had faced up to seventeen hard races, always in top company, and he never once gave way without a fight. John had seen stallions like this before. They sire a lot of fast horses from moderate mares – the Americans call it 'Cheap Speed'. The gamble was: could Ahonoora perform this genetic miracle with the classy mares he would be given at Coolmore?

'Not worth the trouble of finding out – not at £7 million,' was the opinion of some. But John Magnier thought it was. He had an obdurate, slightly unreasonable belief in this horse. He was *going* to buy him. And he was going to have to raise the £7 million, which he achieved in an ingenious way. He went into partnership with the Segenhoe Stud in New South Wales for half each. Ahonoora would cover the Northern Hemisphere season in Ireland at £45,000, and the Southern Hemisphere season in Australia. John had him at half-price, which confirmed entirely what most people in Ireland already knew: Mr and Mrs Magnier did not breed many stupid sons.

His first call was to Robert and he told him that in his opinion he should buy three shares in the horse. It would cost him over £500,000 (Irish) personally, but he, John, had real faith in this horse and in the special kind of well-bred mare he intended to send to him. It was complicated but it made sense to Robert, if John was correct.

'I'd trusted him for nearly twenty years,' said Robert. 'And I believed him now. He had a real "thing" about that horse and I told him to put me in for three.'

While Robert worked out his breeding plans for the 1988 season, John wrestled with his own plans for Ahonoora. He was basically looking for mares by top stallions who represented a weak branch of once-great families, because he believed Ahonoora would inject speed into them. In partnership with Vincent and John Horgan, he owned just such a mare himself. She was by Alleged and her name was Rose of Jericho. She had never been on the racecourse, but her dam, Rose Red, had won a race at two by five lengths, and *she* was by Northern Dancer. Robert and his team had bred her in 1979 from one of their Northern Dancer seasons, from a mare called Cambrienne. This was a truly brilliant family. Cambrienne was the dam of Critique, and *his* full-sister Cambretta had foaled four Group winners, plus the dam of the brilliant miler Markofdistinction. Cambrienne herself was out of the Dewhurst winner Torbella, who also foaled the Champion Miler Carlemont. The entire family was crammed with excellent runners of the not-too-distant past. It was just that Rose Red and Rose of Jericho were rather letting the side down. In John Magnier's opinion Ahonoora was the man to wake this group up and he pencilled in the mating: 'Rose of Jericho, in foal to Thatching, to Ahonoora 1988.'

John's judgment was on the line for this one, rather than his reputation, because Ahonoora was a proven classic sire. It was the other five stallions, mentioned earlier, upon which so much depended. The pressure upon Vincent was no less, because he was trying to get the Classic Thoroughbreds' thirty-eight two-year-olds on the track and he knew that he had to find a good horse in this group or there was no possibility that the public company could survive.

Robert himself, regardless of the inevitable stresses of his worldwide horse-racing conglomerate, was in rather a relaxed mood, having recently sold Vernons Pools which he owned entirely. There had been several interested parties since the death of his father in 1986, but in the end Robert cashed out for £90 million. This sizeable sum of money enabled him to pay off his bank debts – many of them as a result of the expenditure on Manton – make his settlements on the children, and settle down to become a commercial breeder. He still had stakes in Classic Thoroughbreds and an enormous amount of money tied up in Coolmore, but he knew he would not have to face the annual heart-stopping battles in the sales ring in order to survive in the game. His future was in the cool and cunning business of helping to 'make' the stallions John Magnier selected.

He owned over a hundred mares in Ireland and England and the trick
was to present them to the right stallions. He had shares, breeding
rights and ownership in almost all of them at Coolmore and its environs,
which was the shining residual from his battles at Keeneland, Ireland
and Newmarket during the past dozen years.

John Magnier had the daily worry of watching the results of the
stallions on a global basis. It was Vincent, however, who still had the
rough end of the job, sending out young horses he had selected, to take
on the Arab hordes in the big races in England and Ireland. It was an
unenviable task, but 1988 was better than 1987. He won the Irish 2000
Guineas with a Storm Bird colt which ran in Robert's colours, the
$650,000 1986 Keeneland purchase, Prince of Birds. He beat Vincent's
other runner Caerwent by a neck and in the long-term it was a pretty
good result since the Coolmore men owned the sires of both. Later in
the season, Dark Lomond won the Irish St Leger, which did his sire
no harm whatsoever. Meanwhile, the two-year-olds came out and a few
of them won. The best of them was Saratogan, a chestnut colt by El
Gran Senor from the grey mare Partia. He was beaten in his only start
in Ireland, but Vincent sent him over for the Dewhurst, in which he
was a fast-finishing third, half a length behind the dead-heaters Prince
of Dance and Scenic – both by Sadler's Wells.

Vincent was a bit fed up, but John Magnier was, metaphorically, about
to become hysterical. His stallions were performing sensationally.

STORM BIRD had the winner of the Irish 2000 Guineas and Indian
Skimmer was showing herself probably the best ten-furlong runner in
Europe, winning the Sun Chariot Stakes, the Phoenix Champion Stakes
and the Champion Stakes. The stallion finished fourth of the two hundred listed sires on the championship table.

CAERLEON was the Leading Sire in Europe, and the Leading Sire of
Two-Year-Olds. In addition to Caerwent, Careafolie won the Gladness
Stakes, Casey won the Park Hill Stakes. Caerleon had thirteen two-year-
old winners including Corwyn Bay, who won the Anglesey Stakes and
the Cartier Million. At Royal Ascot Gloriella won the Queen Mary
Stakes.

LOMOND had a classic winner in his first crop with Dark Lomond's
three-length victory over thirteen rivals in heavy going up the Curragh.
His son Kneller won the Jockey Club Cup, the Doncaster Cup and
the Tote Ebor Handicap. His daughter Inchmurrin chased home the
outstanding Magic of Life in the Coronation Stakes at Royal Ascot but

won the Child Stakes at Newmarket. In France the two-year-old filly
Oczy Czarnie won the Group I Prix de la Salamandre at Longchamp.
Lomond finished eighth of the two hundred.

SADLER'S WELLS, in addition to siring the first two in the Dewhurst,
was third leading sire of two-year-olds, and second leading first-season
sire. He was already the height of fashion, eighteen of his yearlings
having made more than 100,000 guineas at the sales in Newmarket and
Ireland.

EL GRAN SENOR, from his terribly small first crop, sired two Group
I horses: Saratogan and the winner of the William Hill Futurity, Al
Hareb. If his fertility could be improved and he could sustain that strike
rate, he would be the best stallion in the world.

So they faced up to 1989, each of them with their own set of priorities:
John to get the best possible mares to the stallions, Robert to plan his
mare's matings as well as he could and to keep Manton kicking along
under Barry Hills, and Vincent to try to coerce one of these two-year-
olds to run for his life in the spring of the year. Vincent also persuaded
Robert to join him in taking a quarter share in the $3·5 million Nijinsky
colt for which he had risked everything at Keeneland.

It was a tough time at Ballydoyle, but a mere picnic compared to the
lot of big Brownell Combs, who had sold out his 4·6 million shares in
Spendthrift to his sister for a nickel each, which wouldn't hardly pay
the Visa card bill for more than a couple of months. Also, in February
1989, poor old Brownell was standing trial before a Federal Court in
San Francisco in a case which alleged securities violations stemming
from a Spendthrift private stock offering. Fourteen people who claimed
to have lost $12 million in their investments in Spendthrift had brought
the case and were attempting to prove they had been defrauded, because
the farm's value had been exaggerated. Brownell was one of several
Spendthrift defendants and he took the stand on 20 March, pleading
that it was the downturn in the thoroughbred market which wiped the
farm out.

In mid May Brownell Combs and his financial advisor Garth Guy
were acquitted of all charges that they had defrauded anyone, but it was
too late to save Spendthrift. The farm had already filed for protection
from its creditors under Chapter 11 of the Federal bankruptcy code,
with assets – all that remained of their land, horses, stallion rights, and
so on – of only $5·8 million, and unsecured creditor claims of $38
million. Three banks were on the edge of their chairs worrying about

their secured claims, which brought the total owing to around $50 million. It did not look as though any individual Spendthrift shareholders would get a nickel, despite Brownell's heavy holdings in the five-cent US coinage.

On 17 July the sale of Spendthrift's land and assets was completed. A bankruptcy judge in Lexington approved the sale for $5·25 million. The reign of the Combs family on this historic thoroughbred-breeding ground which borders the old Ironworks Pike was over. Two grave-stones, each with a cast bronze statue set onto the granite, were left standing in front of the stallion barns. One marks the spot where Nashua was buried, the other is the grave of Raise a Native. They are silent sentinels to the best of times in the thoroughbred industry – '*Hey, boy!* You bring them mint-*juleps* over here.' But it was all gone now, even Brownell's home had been sold. Prince Khalid Abdullah purchased the old two-hundred-and-eighty-acre Myrtlewood Farm for $3 million and another piece of Combs history slipped into oblivion. The legacy of those great Spendthrift stallions will live long into the next century, for as long as men pore over the pedigrees of racehorses. But the most enduring piece of folklore will surely be the fall of the Combs family from the pinnacle of the thoroughbred industry. How could it possibly have happened? Greed? Mismanagement? Or was it always one of those operations that could not function without its progenitor? Most people think it was probably a combination of all three. Certainly as Cousin Leslie grew old, the savvy went out of the place. No one tuned into the fact that it was the foreigners that counted and that meant acquiring a top Northern Dancer stallion. Spendthrift completely missed that. The young Leslie Combs would have been the first to act on that simple truth, but in the late 1970s they had somehow missed it.

The old man was never the same after the court hearings and less than a year afterwards, on 7 April 1990, Cousin Leslie died at the age of eighty-eight. The Kentucky he left behind had little in common with the Kentucky he moved into, back in the 1930s. There was now a stampede to get *out* of the horse business. There were over eighty horse farms for sale in the Bluegrass area, in Fayette County, Bourbon County, Woodford County (Versailles and Midway) and the surrounding areas. There were forty-one listed on the Lexington Board of Realty's multiple listing service and dozens more for sale privately. The local realtors call them 'turnkey' horse farms, which means fully developed for equine breeding, and they ranged in size up to one thousand acres. The prices ranged up to $25,000 an acre.

The sun was not shining bright on the old Kentucky homes. There were now empty paddocks where once there had been royally bred mares and foals. 'For Sale' signs were up on the edges of paddocks where ex-champions had roamed as stallions. There was beginning to be a significant unemployment problem in the area. John Gaines sold the five-hundred-acre Gainesway Farm to the South African coal-mining and boat-building tycoon Graham Beck, who owned four thousand acres of thoroughbred-breeding land in the Cape region of South Africa. At the time of the sale he owned two hundred and fifty mares, twelve stallions and had one hundred horses in training. John Gaines agreed to stay on for a while as chief executive officer, running the farm for Mr Beck, who around the same time also bought four hundred and eighty acres near Midway from the land-dispersal sale of Nelson Bunker Hunt.

Wichita Farm, a four-hundred-and-fifty-two-acre horse farm which is situated between Keeneland Racecourse and Calumet, was ordered by the court to be auctioned off, just as the Union Bank of California won a court order to foreclose on its parent company, Warrenton Farms for failure to pay a $13·3 million mortgage. Shadowlawn Farm, which occupied five hundred and twenty-one acres in Woodford County, and stood the winner of the 1984 Prix de l'Arc de Triomphe, Sagace, was ordered up for a Master Commissioner's Auction. Harry and Phyllis Ranier, the owners, had been trying to avert foreclosure after a civil action and everyone felt extremely sorry for them. They had also stood at stud the winner of the inaugural Breeders' Cup Classic, Wild Again, and the sprinter Fast Gold. Normandy Farm came up for sale. Warnerton Farm sold four hundred and eighty acres of their six-hundred-and-forty-acre spread in Claremont County to help pay creditors of the extremely prominent thoroughbred breeder Marvin L. Warner. There was a complete dispersal of the family's North American Thoroughbred breeding and racing stock.

Tom Gentry, ordered by the court to sell his horses and stallion shares to satisfy the claims of Citizens Fidelity Bank and Trust, now had to sell his own three-hundred-acre farm to his children. The two-hundred-and-sixty-five-acre Crimson King Farm out on the Yarnallton Pike, near Lexington, was purchased by First Security National Bank and Trust for a little under $1 million, with the intention of selling it on. The Salmen family announced an intention to reduce its bloodstock holdings forthwith. The six-hundred-acre Golden Chance Farm near Paris, birthplace of the 1981 and 1984 US Horse of the Year, John

Henry, was put on the market by the Lehmann family, with a complete dispersal of its thoroughbred stock. And the Kentucky trainer Forrest Kaelin and his wife sold their one-hundred-and-fourteen-acre farm and training centre near Louisville.

Over on the eastern shore of Maryland, the two-thousand-acre Windfields Farm, home to Northern Dancer for most of his life, was closed down shortly after the retirement of its most exalted resident. Charles Taylor, son of E. P. Taylor, kept one barn and a huge paddock, with a round-the-clock staff, to care for the great stallion for the remaining months of his life. The other stallions were moved away as various parcels of land were sold up, all around The Dancer. The Minstrel went to Kentucky, and Assert went to Ashford, once more under the wing of Robert's men. Northern Dancer led a peaceful but lonely life in 1989 and 1990. He wanted for nothing, but he missed the activity of the farm and often seemed very depressed. But perhaps at twenty-nine he was just old and disinterested. He never knew, of course, that he had set the world of thoroughbred racing alight for two decades, driving avaricious men into paroxysms of greed and acquisitiveness.

To the end he still held his head high, slightly cocked, sniffing the wind, in his utterly unmistakable pose. But at 6.15 on the morning of 16 November 1990, before the sun rose above the great estuary of the Delaware river, Northern Dancer died. It had been over a quarter of a century since the little warrior had burst out of the pack and smashed the track record in the Kentucky Derby; twenty years since his son Nijinsky became the only winner of England's Triple Crown in fifty-five years; ten years since the offer of $40 million was made for him to leave Windfields; and seven years since Robert and his men drove Sheikh Mohammed to bid $10·2 million for one of his rare sons who could not run. And now he had gone, but only in body. His spirit will live on for at least another century where ever men race throughbred horses. History will forever be his friend.

By special arrangement with the Canadian government, his remains were transported back north across the border to the horse cemetery at Windfields Farm, Oshawa, near Toronto. There he was buried, entirely, alongside the barn where he was foaled and close by the stallion barn in which he covered his first two books of mares. The cemetery is also the last resting place of the great broodmare South Ocean, the dam of Storm Bird.

Meanwhile, back in Ireland Vincent O'Brien was still trying desperately to bring his best two-year-old Saratogan to peak form for the 2000

Guineas at Newmarket. He sent him out to win a maiden at the Curragh in April and then to win the Dermot McCalmont Tetrarch Stakes. But the colt ran terribly below form in the Guineas and finished ninth, beaten nine lengths behind Sheikh Hamdan's Nashwan. He tried to restore the horse to winning form in the much easier Irish 2000, but he was beaten into sixth place behind Sheikh Mohammed's Shaadi. In the Phoenix International Stakes, Saratogan could do no better and he was sent to race in California. The skids were under Classic Thoroughbreds, on the basis that the horse business is the most awful treadmill. To stay in it you have to buy. But if your first big batch of horses, in Vincent's case thirty-eight of them, do not provide a major stallion, then you need another huge injection of cash. But something has to be happening on the track, otherwise the shareholders lose confidence.

Shortly before the 2000 Guineas the stock, in eager anticipation of a victory for Saratogan, hit an all-time high of forty-one pence. But by the year's end, in which none of the three-year-olds had come through, the stock had plunged to eleven pence. Classic Thoroughbreds reported a first half-year loss to June 1989 of around $8·3 million. There was but one bright star on the horizon for the beleaguered Irish shareholders: the $3·5 million colt, now named Royal Academy, could run. He had hacked home in a maiden race at the Curragh by ten lengths. And, although he had been beaten four lengths in the Dewhurst Stakes behind Dashing Blade, his sixth place was very promising. He was still immature in appearance and Vincent felt he would improve through the winter. Whether he could improve sufficiently to win a classic, and save his parent company from extinction, was a matter of pure conjecture.

The year 1989 had been very moderate indeed for Vincent. His name did not appear on the list of Top Twelve Trainers in England and Robert's name had now vanished completely from that of the Top Twelve Owners. That list was headed by Sheikh Mohammed and Sheikh Hamdan, followed by Prince Khalid, and then Sheikh Maktoum al-Maktoum. Then came the Aga Khan, followed by Sheikh Mana al-Maktoum. The Arab horses had essentially dominated the season, particularly Nashwan who had won the 2000 Guineas, the Derby, the Eclipse and the King George VI and Queen Elizabeth Stakes. Curiously, for all of their massive buying in the sales ring, this one had been home-bred from a mare Sheikh Hamdan bought from the Queen.

At the Keeneland Sales that year the Sheikhs had invested yet another huge amount of money, nearly $40 million on fifty-five yearlings. Their main rival in the ring was Wayne Lukas and the names of both Vincent and Robert were missing from the buyers' list. It was the sale which would offer the very last two colts by Northern Dancer: one from the Champion English mare Mrs Penny, the other from Gleaming Smile, a mare from the family of Alydar. It was, of course, clear that the one from Mrs Penny would almost certainly top the entire sale, and it was no surprise when the Japanese stud owner Zenya Yoshida paid $2·8 million for him. Mr Yoshida had, after all, a history of romantic purchases. It was he who had bought the yearling Wajima from the very last crop of Bold Ruler back in 1973.

The other colt was not as good-looking, nor as dramatically well-bred, and it sold for $700,000 to the Irish trainer Tommy Stack. Whoever had bought it had almost certainly done so for sentimental reasons. Now, who, in all of the world, might have quietly told Tommy to buy the colt, in memory of a thousand battles, and a thousand dreams? Which two men in all of this world had hearts so soft they would part with that kind of money out of a sense of paralysing romanticism? The colt did not even look as if he might make a racehorse, but they shipped him 'home' to the Golden Vale of Tipperary, to the land of so many of his relatives, and when his name, Il Corsaro, was registered with the Irish Turf Club, the principal owner was listed as ... Robert Sangster, backed up by that of John Magnier.

You may occasionally hear that the new money which has dominated the racehorse industry these past twenty years has stripped the sport of its heart and soul, but try not to believe it. Robert and John enjoyed the reputations of being the toughest dealers in the game, but to listen to Robert on the subject of that colt you would not have thought so: 'We just thought we should have the colt brought home to Ireland. We'll never sell him, whether he can run or not. But one day, he'll be in a field, and we may be able to say: "There he is, the last son of Northern Dancer in all of the world".'

The 1989 sale at Keeneland actually saw a rise in the market. The buyers were a little more selective and reduced the number of yearlings sold, but it had the desired effect on the average, sending it up from $367,000 in 1988 to $399,000. But the atmosphere remained the same: dead gloomy. And President Reagan's tax reforms had made it even more difficult to tempt outsiders back into the business.

For the new year the stallion prices would dive yet again. Devil's Bag, the $36 million two-year-old, was on his way down from a $200,000 covering fee which would eventually hit $20,000. Conquistador Cielo was traversing a similar highway. Spectacular Bid was on his way down from $150,000 to $15,000. Saratoga Six was heading for $7500 from $75,000. Seattle Slew had dived from $1 million to $750,000 and would ultimately hit $120,000. The working figure among the industry's statisticians was a drop of around sixty per cent.

Things were however looking quite remarkably cheerful around Coolmore, where the new Prince of British stallions was being acclaimed throughout the industry. He was Sadler's Wells, who occupied the runner-up position on the Leading Sires table. The Champion was Blushing Groom thanks to Nashwan, but in only his second crop Sadler's Wells had sired the outstanding winner of the French and Irish Derbys, Old Vic. In twenty-four months he had sired ten individual stakes winners, four of them Group I winners. On the table which lists the Second-Season Sires, Sadler's Wells was so far in front it was hard to find the runner-up. His offspring had won nearly £850,000. The next one on the list had only just cleared £300,000.

Caerleon too was right up there in fifth place on the main Sires table, and the only sad issue in a wonderful breeding season was that Ahonoora had died in Australia, after an apparently minor accident in his paddock, which turned out to be a hopelessly broken rear-hind pastern. He was only fourteen years old. But stallion men live with these kind of body-blows, and John Magnier shrugged and pressed on.

The final stop of the year for him was the December sales where Rose of Jericho, and her Ahonoora foal, were coming up for sale. John did not particularly want to part with the mare, but his partners did, and she went through the ring for £42,000, sold to Robert Sangster. John immediately asked if he could come back in and Robert let him have fifty per cent. The foal then went through the ring for 52,000 guineas and was 'pinhooked' by Paul Shanahan, of County Tipperary, to sell on as a yearling in 1990.

As the new breeding season commenced and John Magnier coped with the running of the now gigantic Coolmore breeding operation – they had a total of thirty-six stallions under their control – Vincent O'Brien prepared Royal Academy for his three-year-old career. It is difficult to describe how much was riding on this one horse. For a start, the colt probably represented the only chance of survival there was for Classic Thoroughbreds. He was, thus far, the only one of the big intake of young stock which had shown any pretensions of running with the very best. He still had a few pounds to find, but Vincent believed he was improving and that he would demonstrate toughness and courage when asked. He came out early in the season and won the Dermot

McCalmont Tetrarch Stakes, before trying for the Irish 2000 Guineas, where he would meet the very superior winner of the English Guineas, Tirol. This fast son of the Coolmore sire, Thatching, had dealt with a high-class field at Newmarket, beating the unbeaten European two-year-old champion from France, Machiavellian, by two lengths.

He proved no less formidable at the Curragh, winning the Irish Classic, but by only a neck from Royal Academy, who had looked to have the race sewn up a furlong from home. But he ran on boldly to the line, in a solid performance, and Vincent was very pleased with him. The St James's Palace Stakes at Royal Ascot came next and, in the one display of mulishness he demonstrated in his whole life, Royal Academy announced, formally, that he was not doing this. He refused, flatly, to go into the stalls and the field went off without him, Shavian winning a very high-class contest from Rock City. Vincent O'Brien could not understand what had happened and, since Royal Academy refused to discuss it, they put his Royal Ascot petulance down to a little quirk in his mind. 'He probably didn't like all those bloody hats,' was the verdict of his groom. But Vincent would not want to see behaviour even remotely like that, ever again. Neither would the shareholders of Classic Thoroughbreds.

For his return to the races they decided to sharpen him up and put him back to six furlongs in the July Cup at Newmarket, where he would meet the Royal Ascot winner Great Commotion and Rock City. Here on this undulating course, Royal Academy would have his mettle well and truly tested by the very steep hill about three furlongs out before the ground flattens out for nearly a furlong coming to the line. Thus a winner on the 'July Course' needs to begin his run on the hill and then accelerate away along the flat. This is inclined to sort them out a bit and it explains why so many of the great speed-merchants of this century have won it – they include Diadem, Diomedes, Honeyway, Abernant, Vilmoray, Right Boy, Thatch, Thatching, Moorestyle and Never So Bold.

Royal Academy was bidding for an important little corner in racing history and the race, as usual, was run at a cracking good gallop. As they came to the bottom of the hill, Vincent's horse improved his pos-ition, chasing after the leaders, Great Commotion and Rock City. He had too much speed for both of them and he struck the front at the top of the rise, and kept on very strongly to win it by three parts of a length from Great Commotion with Rock City a neck away third.

Vincent kept him sprinting and aimed him next for the old Vernons Sprint Cup at Haydock, now sponsored by the English bookmaking firm

Ladbrokes, which had provided the £90 million for the Sangster coffers. Here Royal Academy ran into one of the fastest horses to race in Europe in many years, Dayjur, who beat him by a length and a half having gone clear of the field early. But Royal Academy had chased him with immense determination, closing hard all the way to the line, with Pharaoh's Delight five lengths back and Great Commotion another four lengths behind him.

There was now no further doubt in Vincent's mind. This was a very fast horse, who had improved all year, but now needed a mile to show his true excellence. There was only one such race left to establish the horse as a world-class racer and that was the Breeders' Cup Mile, 'on the weeds', as they say in New York, at Belmont Park in October. It would be a long journey and a rough race on the tight inside turf track, and Vincent was not at all sure how the sweet-tempered Royal Academy would cope with that particular brand of American fire. But he was running out of options. Victory at Belmont would give this $3·5 million yearling a big stallion value. It was his one chance of lasting glory and the Irishman knew that he must take it. The problem was, his stable jockey John Reid fell and broke his collarbone three weeks before the race and would not be fit in time to ride. It would not be that simple to find a rider who could get the tall, elegant Royal Academy round Belmont Park, in an almost certain roughhouse on the turn, and then get him clear in the straight to use his great speed. 'I'm not sure about that at all,' mused Vincent. 'The only one you'd be absolutely sure of would be Lester. But he's been retired for five years. I don't think I'd go to an American for this. We need finesse and horsemanship, and such men are hard to find.'

While Royal Academy had spent the summer preparing for the biggest day of his life in New York, several other racehorses, all sons or daughters of the Coolmore stallions, had been grabbing their opportunities with both hands. Belmez, the powerful son of El Gran Senor, beat out Old Vic, the dual-Derby-winning son of Sadler's Wells, in a sensational battle for the King George VI and Queen Elizabeth Stakes at Ascot. Salsabil, a daughter of Sadler's Wells, had won the 1000 Guineas and the Oaks, and had then beaten the colts in the Irish Derby. Storm Bird had sired a colt named Summer Squall who won the second American classic, the Preakness Stakes at Pimlico, and then Go And Go, a son of Coolmore's Northern Dancer stallion Be My Guest, won the last leg of the US Triple Crown, the Belmont Stakes.

In a sense, all of them had been created by Vincent. For he had trained all of the sires, The Senor (whose fertility rate was now up to seventy per cent), Sadler's Wells, Storm Bird and Be My Guest. And sometimes, as he sat reading in his study – the great man was seventy-three years old now – he pondered those awesome battles he had been tackling all of his life. No trainer had ever achieved what he had achieved. No trainer ever would. And he gazed at his paintings of the horses, hanging poignantly from the walls of Ballydoyle. And sometimes he heard the roar of the crowd at Newmarket as Storm Bird fought his way clear of To-Agori-Mou; and he lived again the murderous last thirty yards of the Derby when El Gran Senor had lost to Secreto. 'Could I have changed it, if I could have lived it again?' Such plaintive thoughts from such a glittering past so often loomed in his mind. But as the autumn leaves turned to gold across the Vale of Tipperary, he cast them aside and his thoughts turned to the west and the United States. For the first time in six years he was up to his eyes in the full-blooded drama of a world-class contest which would be conducted before a global television audience of millions.

Could Royal Academy, the colt upon whom he had staked his entire reputation with a $3·5 million bid, made in the sabre-flash of a split second in the Keeneland ring, finally prove him right? It was as if everything that he had ever accomplished was on the line for this one race. For years, people had been saying that Vincent may be finished, that it was time for him to retire. What more did he want anyway? Only he knew that given the chance, given the absence of illness in the yard, he could still prepare a horse for a major race better than any man alive. He had done it, dozens of times. He had made men fortunes. He had created greatness on the track. He had created dynasties among thoroughbreds. For him, as for Northern Dancer, history must surely be his ally.

He had forgotten nothing. He could still see the signs; he knew the moods of the thoroughbred. He knew precisely how much work to give them; he knew their wiles and guiles. He could spot an improving horse faster than any other trainer. He sometimes thought he could see into their souls. He had seen into the soul of Royal Academy. And he knew this horse would run for him. He knew the colt would run to within an inch of his life for him, just as his own father Nijinsky had done. He also knew that on 27 October Royal Academy would be ready. All he needed was a jockey.

Back in Kentucky the summer sales had been a nightmare. The year's average crashed by almost $50,000 to a new low of $352,000, around the level of 1982. The gross income for the sale was $82 million, the lowest since 1980. The Maktoums were holding the entire place together, buying sixty-four yearlings for almost $34 million. That was more than forty per cent of the entire sale. The highest price was $2·9 million for a colt by Seattle Slew, purchased by a Japanese property man.

And hardly had the final hammer crashed down when it was learned that America's Eclipse Award-winning breeders for 1989, Mr and Mrs Franklin Groves of North Ridge Farm, were getting out of the thorough-bred business completely. Their one-thousand-one-hundred-and-thirty-acre showpiece was being sold within four weeks, with all of the farm's assets, the sixty-five broodmares, the forty-six foals, all of the yearlings, twelve racehorses and their shares in the stallions The Bart, Seattle Song and Tsunami Slew. And the best crop of big pin-oak trees for miles around. The giant stallion barn, constructed with a view to fifty-six stallions, had never been filled. The great edifice which domi-nated the perfectly laid brick paths had never been occupied by more than four stallions. The great visions of Mr Groves, nurtured at the height of the market, lay in ruins. His corporation, S. J. Groves and Sons, had run into difficulties in a massive highway-building programme in Georgia. North Ridge was a wholly owned subsidiary and since it was not making big profits it had to go. Franklin Groves could not sustain the financial outlay such an operation requires, with the thoroughbred sales on such a downward curve. The buyer would be the international businessman Kenneth T. Jones, a native of North Carolina whose main residence was in Guam.

The situation was marginally, but not much, better in Europe. At Tattersall's Highflyer Sales in Newmarket, the aggregate total had crashed from £36·5 million in 1984 to £24 million in 1990. The follow-ing year, with a reduced catalogue, it would collapse to £12 million. In 1990 Robert attended the sale with another Irish advisor, the mercurial and inventive vet from the village of Killenaule, near Coolmore, Dr Demi O'Byrne, cousin of Paul Shanahan. For several years Demi had gone with the team to Keeneland as an advisor and there was little he did not know, or could not somehow fix, about a thoroughbred horse. He could treat any injury, cope with any problem. And if the condition was 'impossible', he'd still come up with a way of getting the horse sound. As they say of him in McCarthy's pub in the village of Fethard, 'You'd never quite know what he was tinkin' of next.'

What he was very definitely tinkin' of, in the early autumn of 1990, was the quality of the yearling which John, Vincent and John Horgan had bred from Rose of Jericho, the one by Ahonoora. The Coolmore Stud veterinarian had seen the colt often up at the Ballykelly Stud, owned by cousin Paul, near Cashel, and in his opinion Robert should definitely buy him and race him. Since Robert now owned fifty per cent of the dam, he agreed to do so and when the chestnut colt came into the ring Robert instructed the BBA to 'buy him'. The price was 56,000 guineas and he named him, rather wittily Robert thought, after the Tipperary vet, Dr Devious.

At exactly this time, another Englishman, Mr Lester Piggott, former jockey, was also in regular communication with Tipperary. John Magnier had suggested to him that he return to race-riding, since he was clearly 'bloody miserable' doing anything else. Lester had decided to consult his old friend and mentor Vincent O'Brien, for whom he had ridden so many great races. 'Actually, Vincent,' he said, 'I was thinking of making a comeback. What do you think?'

Vincent's lightning brain flickered. But he stayed calm. 'Well, now, Lester . . . how's your weight?'

''Bout the same. I'm riding work every day. I'm still fit.'

Vincent recalled the words written by Dick Francis in Lester's biography: 'How long, I asked him, would he have gone on being a jockey if it hadn't been for growing older, if he could have stopped time and stayed young? A wry smile. No hesitation. "A thousand years," he said.'

The trainer knew what it meant to Lester and how there was only one way he could ever be truly happy. He also knew that if Lester came back, he could ride Royal Academy. But he took it very carefully. 'I think you could do it very easily,' he said. 'And if you are serious why wouldn't you come over here and we'll have some lunch in Dublin?'

Lester accepted and the two great legends of the English and Irish Turf met in a private room at the Berkeley Hotel. The meeting meant a lot to both of them and over a glass of champagne the memories flooded back. Vincent spoke to him very thoughtfully and at the end of their meeting the great jockey said, 'I'll do it. I'll apply for my licence right away.'

They drove out to the airport together and on the way Vincent asked him, 'Will you come over again next Saturday and ride four for me at the Curragh?'

Lester just nodded and the profound gratitude he felt showed only in his eyes, which filled helplessly with tears, perhaps because he knew that after all the years, and all that had happened to him, including his jail sentence for tax evasion, Vincent O'Brien still believed in him.

The Jockey Club returned his licence within days and Lester rode two winners at Chepstow on his second day back in the saddle. Then he went over to the Curragh to ride for Vincent and, amidst scenes of near pandemonium at the racecourse, he won on all four of them. He then accepted an invitation to ride Royal Academy in the Breeders' Cup Mile at Belmont Park, New York, on 27 October. But he made the journey without Vincent, who was ill with 'flu and forbidden by his doctor to travel. Jacqueline and Charles O'Brien travelled to New York for the showdown 'on the weeds'. And they met Lester in the giant clubhouse stand at Belmont, as they had done before in so many different places down the years.

The race was absolutely critical for everyone concerned: for Lester at fifty-four, to show he was still tough enough for this kind of international battle; for Jacqueline and Charles, to show that her husband and his father was still the master; and for all the thousands of shareholders in Classic Thoroughbreds all over Ireland who were praying for this victory, crowded around television sets in all the tiny villages, of Limerick and Cork, of Waterford and Kerry, up in Kildare, all around the Curragh, and in West Meath, and in every bar in Dublin. And, most of all in the Golden Vale of Tipperary. Demi O'Byrne remembers his television refusing to tune into the English station and he packed everyone into the car and drove at high speed across country to a pub three miles away.

It was impossible to imagine what anyone could possibly have been doing if they were not watching the race. Inside the Cashel Palace Hotel they were jam-packed around the set. No one was serving anyone. McCarthy's for the only time in its entire history was stone silent as men who knew nothing of the outside world beyond horses watched the jockeys get mounted in the tree-shaded paddock of Belmont Park close to the statue of Secretariat. The entire Irish nation had stopped. It was holding its breath, as only Ireland can for a horse race. Could Vincent and Lester do it again, just one more time? As they had with Sir Ivor, Nijinsky, Roberto, The Minstrel and Alleged? Lester grinned at Jacqueline. They did not have to say much. Lester was well briefed, and he said, 'Don't worry about it. I'll find my way round.' And Jacqueline looked up at him and she just said quietly, 'For Vincent.'

A whole clutch of top American riders were in the race, McCarron, Lopez, Delahoussaye, Samyn and Santos, Cash Asmussen. The Champion US Grass Horse Steinlen, trained by Wayne Lukas, was there,

Paul Mellon's Who's To Play, winner of three of four starts on the grass, now ridden by Jerry Bailey, François Boutin's Priolo from Chantilly. But the big New York crowd knew Piggott and they knew the name O'Brien and they sent Royal Academy off as 5–2 favourite, despite the fact that his rider was riding Derby winners before most of the rest of them were born.

The starter sent them away at 3.49 Eastern Daylight Time, 8.49 in the evening in Tipperary. Royal Academy, drawn in the number one gate, broke slowly, swerved to the right, just as the outside horses swerved inwards, too early. Priolo nearly went down as a horse crashed into him and Lester reined in hard, picked his course and settled back in last position. They flew along the back stretch, the quarter in twenty-two and change; the half in under forty-six seconds. Still Piggott was at the rear of the field. Expensive Decision led them into the home turn with the outsider Itsallgreektome trying to improve. The field bunched, then lurched inwards, and this time Steinlen came off worse as a horse cannoned into him. Piggott eased wider as Royal Academy came to the top of the turn in eighth position.

Down along the rail it was a real rough race, with Expensive Decision under Jean-Luc Samyn leading them towards the home stretch. Itsallgreektome worked his way forward, coming to challenge the leader in the final yards of the turn. But Samyn's horse would not give in and the massive crowd roared as they joined battle. The dust and the whips were flying, and behind them the field, hurtling in a crazed half-circle at forty miles an hour, bunched again, the intensity of the drama as always obscuring the lethal nature of these big-money sagas.

No one saw the dark ex-Newmarket miler, Markofdistinction, almost go down in the scrum. But he did, with terrifying suddenness, right in front of Royal Academy. Markofdistinction stumbled, swerved right as if he had been shot. Piggott picked up the danger in about one-hundredth of a second, hardened his grip, instinctively sitting a fraction higher in the saddle, ramming his knees into his colt's shoulder blades, tugging on the right-hand rein in one lightning movement – the strength of a longshoreman, the touch of a violinist. No one could do it *quite* like Lester. Royal Academy knew what he meant and he ducked right with exquisite timing, away from the near-certain collision, and on into the great unknown, hard down the course chosen for him by the old maestro.

'Expensive Decision along the rail has it by a *half*,' yelled the New York commentator. 'Itsallgreektome in second as *down the stretch they come!*'

The race for the Breeders' Cup Mile was now erupting with excitement and the crowd was already on its feet as the announcer shouted: 'There is a *wall* of horses here – and Lester Piggott and Royal Academy have six lengths to find ... but they're launching their rally *right now* ... and Royal Academy is *thundering down the centre of the track.*'

Sure enough, there they were, far back, five horses wide, the Kelly-green colours with the sash of gold of Classic Thoroughbreds. And they were travelling like a bat out of hell. Lester Piggott had the son of Nijinsky perfectly balanced, running clean down the outside of the field on that same glorious, powerful stride which had carried him up the hill at Newmarket. Inside the three-sixteenth pole Lester went to the whip, hitting Royal Academy four times rhythmically as they hurtled over the ground.

The crowd almost went wild. Every eye at Belmont was on the Irish horse and again the announcer called the race as if no one else was taking part, 'And Lester Piggott is *flailing* away at Royal Academy ...'

Three and a half thousand miles away, a hundred Irish right feet hit the wooden floor of McCarthy's and the time-honoured roar of '*Come on, Lester!*' split the air beyond the saloon and into the silent village street outside – as the old master drew his whip again. Four times more he whacked Royal Academy, with long, right-handed swipes in quick succession. And now he had the colt firing along perfectly on that smooth, but delicate action that few opponents could resist.

He was flying over the ground, still in the middle of the track, slicing into the lead of the American outsider Itsallgreektome. Even the massed ranks of the New York bettors in the giant grandstand were screaming for the Irish favourite, but the finish line was looming ahead and fifty yards out the American was still in front. And now Piggott put down his whip and, crouching low, he drove the son of Nijinsky through the dying yards of the race to snatch victory, right at the wire, by a desperate, heart-stopping neck.

The first two were running separate races, split by almost the entire width of the Belmont track and mass confusion broke out in the stands, since no one was quite sure which horse had won. The thousands who saw the race at a slight angle from the wire thought Itsallgreektome had hung on. Those in line with the post thought Lester had got up. No such doubts existed in McCarthy's. '*Lester's wonnat!*' they yelled. No dispute. No doubts whatsoever in there. Just as there had been none when he had driven Roberto home by a short-head in the 1972 English Derby, nor when he had forced The Minstrel to victory in 1977. Mind you, in 1968, when Piggott had come from far back on Sir Ivor to win the Washington International in the States, they had still all roared '*Lester's wonnat!*' without even seeing the race, all huddled around McCarthy's ancient, crackling radio.

The fact was Lester *never* misjudged those tight finishes and they were counting their winnings in McCarthy's long before the result of the photograph was announced, and long before Jacqueline O'Brien led Royal Academy into the winners' circle to rapturous applause. The standing ovation for Piggott lasted more than five minutes and at the end of it Charles O'Brien, with his arms around his mother, was saying over and over, 'I don't think *any* other rider could have got him home today . . .'

Jacqueline, tears of joy streaming down her face, was willing herself not to blurt out the real truth – that no other trainer apart from *her* husband could possibly have produced this long-striding horse, on this day, thousands of miles from home, on a strange, tight little track, to run the greatest race of his life – the first and last time Royal Academy would have such an opportunity in a contest of such world stature. Vincent had even masterminded the comeback of the long-retired jockey, whom he believed was the one rider who could bring the horse home.

Back at Ballydoyle, still nursing the mother and father of a head-cold, Vincent dragged himself out of his chair and poured himself a medicinal tot of whisky and water. The fire crackled cheerfully as he stood beneath the portraits of his old champions and he reflected, inevitably, upon the lonely night at Keeneland when he had gone $1 million above his limit to buy Royal Academy. He resisted the urge to spring into the air and click his heels together, but he sipped his whisky luxuriously and he smiled at the television upon which Lester Piggott now looked so over-poweringly happy. The eulogies were raining down upon the veteran English jockey: 'genius, 'greatest rider in the history of the universe' 'not even Lazarus . . .' and so on. And Vincent himself, as the principal owner with Robert Sangster, as well as the purchaser and the trainer, felt obliged to join them. 'Very nice, Lester,' he said softly to the empty room. 'I thought you rode him very nicely indeed.'

17

The Magic Touch of the Irish

The famous New York victory of Royal Academy meant, almost certainly, a new stallion for John Magnier. But on that historic night at Belmont Park there was perhaps an even more significant victory for Coolmore: that of the French-trained colt, In The Wings, who won the Breeders' Cup Turf championship over one and a half miles, by a hard-fought half length from the Canadian Triple Crown winner With Approval. The sire of In The Wings was Sadler's Wells and the massive prize money of £560,000 to the winner made the white-faced son of Northern Dancer the Champion Sire of Europe for 1990. His big stars of the season were Salsabil and Belmez. In The Wings had already won the Coronation Cup at Epsom in June. Wherever you looked, there was a son or a daughter of this phenomenal stallion winning a major race.

This was the heir-apparent to Northern Dancer and Nijinsky. In his brief career Sadler's had sired the winners of one hundred and fifty races, and nearly £4·5 million in prize money. He had sired eleven stakes winners in his first crop, a feat never achieved before by any stallion, not even Northern Dancer. Home-bred by Robert Sangster from tiny Fairy Bridge, Sadler's Wells had cost little and would earn huge amounts of money for all of his principal shareholders, the biggest of whom was Robert, who could breed several mares to him free, for the rest of his life. For the 1991 season Sadler's would sell and fill at £100,000 (Irish), which was probably the biggest stud fee in the world, except for Alydar who was in excess of $250,000.

Last Tycoon finished as the Leading First-Season Sire, Caerleon sired another thirteen stakes winners and, from out of the blue, Woodman emerged as the top sire of two-year-olds in the entire world – two of them were future classic winners. Thus Robert, John and Vincent were the owners of by far the most successful stud farm there has ever been; a farm with not just one great sire, but with a selection of possibly eight, all of whom Robert could breed from free, indefinitely. Even the giant breeding emporiums of the Bluegrass rarely if ever had more than two at one time – Spendthrift had Raise a Native with Nashua and then Seattle Slew; Claiborne had Forli with Nijinsky, and later Mr Prospector; Gainsway had Vaguely Noble and Lyphard; and Windfields had Northern Dancer with The Minstrel; even Darby Dan with Ribot in residence never had one to match him until His Majesty in the 1980s.

Only Calumet, with Alydar standing peerlessly, covering gigantic books of almost one hundred mares per year at over $250,000 each (over $25 million income per annum) could possibly be earning money on the scale of Coolmore. Alydar, like Sadler's Wells, could not stop siring big winners. In addition to Alysheba, the leading earner in history with $6,679,242 worth of prize money, Alydar had also sired another great champion in Easy Goer. This chestnut son of a Buckpasser mare finished second in the Kentucky Derby, and the Preakness, but won the Belmont, the Whitney and the Travers at Saratoga, the Woodward Stakes and the Jockey Club Gold Cup. Another son Criminal Type won the Hollywood Gold Cup and the Metropolitan of 1990 and was voted Horse of the Year. Alydar could sire them in Europe too. In the same crop as Easy Goer was Alydaress who won the Irish Oaks, and Cacoethes, runner-up in the English Derby and winner of the King Edward VII Stakes at Royal Ascot. It would be hard to exaggerate the alarm at Calumet, less than three weeks after the 1990 Breeders' Cup, when Alydar kicked back in his stall and fractured the cannon-bone in his right hind leg.

The hero of one of the greatest horse races ever seen in the United States – the 1978 losing battle with Affirmed – almost went berserk with the pain. It happened on Tuesday night, 13 November, and they called in one of America's best-known bone surgeons Dr Larry Bramlage, formerly of Ohio State University. Dr Bramlage elected to operate on the Wednesday morning at 9 a.m. in the Calumet clinic and over a period of several hours, using a bone graft, steel plate, five pins and a fibreglass cast, they repaired the terrible injury. Fixation pins were driven through the bone into the cast, to enable Alydar to walk on the cast rather than on the leg. Vets came in from all over the Bluegrass to help the stricken stallion. Dr William Baker was there. Dr Linda Rhodes, the Calumet vet, refused to leave Alydar, and sat with him all through the Tuesday night and all through Wednesday. One and a half hours after the operation, Alydar was moved to the convalescent stall, and under sedation he was placed in a sling, to keep the weight off his hind legs. But it was clear that he hated it and all through the night Linda had to keep sedating him more, to prevent him becoming frantic.

By Thursday morning it was plain that they would have to either go on sedating him indefinitely or take him out of the sling, which they finally did. By now the insurance company had representatives at the farm and hundreds of people were appearing at the gates of Calumet waiting for bulletins on the champion sire of the United States. His value was astronomical. In 1987 he had covered ninety-eight mares at $310,000, the following year he covered another ninety-eight, and in 1989 he covered ninety-seven. J. T. Lundy had sold fifteen lifetime breeding rights to him for $2·5 million *each*. To Calumet, over the next four years, he represented $100 million. He was breeding more mares than any other stallion in the entire country.

Out of the sling Alydar was slightly disoriented, off balance, ill at ease with himself. After fifteen minutes, he stumbled on his foreleg and was unable to catch his balance with his hind leg. Alydar crashed to the ground, now mortally wounded. He seemed to know it was the end for him. He lay there very quietly, looking up, with that deep, bold eye of his. And Dr Baker wept as he put the great stallion down. Linda Rhodes was inconsolable.

They buried Alydar, formally, at the farm cemetery the following day. He was laid to rest alongside his great-great-grandfather Bull Lea and his great-grandfather, the Kentucky Derby winner Ponder. Seven other winners of the Run for the Roses were also buried in the little Calumet graveyard, begun by Warren Wright. But the Wright family would bury no more horses there. Within a few weeks it became clear that Calumet, unaccountably, shockingly, was in the deepest possible financial trouble. All the millions made for them by Alydar were apparently gone. Within weeks J. T. Lundy was announcing a major reduction in the stock of Calumet. One hundred horses were to be sold, a sale which took place on 15 January 1991.

Almost immediately Lyle Robey, the farm's general counsel, who served as the board's secretary-treasurer, resigned. J. T. Lundy himself resigned. It then emerged that Calumet's own land was heavily mortgaged and that it owed something close to $60 million. Two lawsuits came in demanding the return of two stallions, Wild Again and Talinum. By late June it was estimated that Calumet owed $70 million. There were writs demanding millions of dollars flying around all over the place, from the Midlantic Bank of New Jersey, from Axmar Stable, from Equus

Unlimited Insurance, from Schroder Bank and Trust. William Allen of Florida issued a writ claiming Calumet had sold a yearling of his without informing him of either the birth or the sale. White Birch Farm claimed they had not even been paid for Mogambo. The Riggs National Bank of Washington sued for nearly $10 million, First City Bank of Houston were owed almost $45 million against the land, and Mutual Benefit Life Insurance were in for $20 million. Calumet filed for Chapter 11 Bankruptcy protection on 11 July. By the autumn it seemed that the debt could be as high as $120 million. The syndicate which controlled Affirmed and had moved here from the beleaguered Spendthrift, moved him again, to Jonabell Farm.

A lot of older members of Kentucky society watched the proceedings with nothing short of horror, privately thanking God that Lucille Markey had not lived to witness the final disgrace of this citadel of Bluegrass breeding. It was the Mutual Benefit Insurance company which finally finished Calumet. They filed a lawsuit in Fayette Circuit Court to foreclose on the farm. They also sued Mrs Bertha Wright and all four of her children and three of their spouses, including J. T. Lundy. The documents which bankrupted the legendary thoroughbred nursery were delivered by the Constable, a man who had lived near Calumet all of his life. 'I just feel so badly handing this to you,' he said to Ron Sladon, the farm's new secretary-treasurer. 'It was a truly terrible moment for both of us,' said Mr Sladon. 'There were tears streaming down the Constable's face.'

The finances of the farm during the reign of J. T. Lundy had been nothing short of a catastrophe. At one point they were spending more than $1 million a month running the place. In the boom years it had been even higher and Lundy, the chief executive, was paying himself something in excess of $1 million annually in commissions. Alydar's future breeding ability was heavily mortgaged and, when the stallion died, the dam which held back the creditors burst. The whole of central Kentucky had been stunned by the demise of Spendthrift, and truly shocked by the sale of Bluegrass Farm, and Gainesway, and then North Ridge. But the collapse of Calumet was beyond anyone's belief or their innermost dreads.

Back in Europe, the sun that was not shining upon the old Kentucky homes was blazing down upon Coolmore, because Caerleon, the former Lionheart of York, had a real-live prospect to win the English Derby. He was a magnificently balanced chestnut colt named Generous, from a mare by the Preakness Stakes winner Master Derby. Generous was

a very tough customer indeed. As a 50–1 outsider he had fought his
way home in the Dewhurst Stakes to the delight of his owner, Prince
Fahd Salmon, a direct descendant of Prince Faisal ibn Turki, the grandfather of Ibn Saud. The suave, American-educated Prince Fahd played
an extremely important role on behalf of the Saudi Royal family during
the Gulf War and it was difficult for him to get to the races in the early
part of the season, but he and his cousin Prince Mohammed planned
to be at Epsom in full force on Derby Day. Generous was trained by
the droll Berkshire sportsman and wit Paul Cole at the training grounds
which surround the historic racing mansion of Whatcombe high in the
Downs. He and Prince Fahd had bought the estate together several
years previously and in the early spring they both hoped fervently that:
one, Generous would soon join Trigo, Blenheim, Blakeney and Morston
on that triumphant journey from Whatcombe to glory on Epsom Downs;
and two, Stormin' Norman Schwarzkopf had well and truly stitched up
Saddam Hussein before the start of the Flat.

Victory for Generous would of course be a tremendous boost for
Caerleon and would almost certainly make him Champion Sire. And as
a joint owner of Coolmore, Robert had a huge vested interest in victory
for the Whatcombe colt. History too would appreciate such a feat of
training and racing. For Generous, through his great-grandfather
Northern Dancer, has a direct ancestral line back to Blenheim, who
worked over these great downland gallops back in 1929 and '30. Blenheim's grand-dam was the grey speedball Mumtaz Mahal, who some
say was the fastest filly who ever lived and who was also prepared at
Whatcombe. History has tidy habits.

Some of the main rivals to Generous were also by Coolmore stallions:
Marju by Last Tycoon, and Hector Protector, Woodman's brilliant son,
who had won the French 2000 Guineas.

In the days leading up to the Derby, Robert was full of optimism and
it was in a mood of intense goodwill that he invited his closest circle of
friends to join him at one of the most formal sports dinners of the
season in England, the Earl of Derby's annual dinner, an all-male black-
tie affair at London's Savoy Hotel, traditionally attended by the Senior
Steward of the Jockey Club and many of his fellow members, five days
before the Epsom classic.

More than twenty of them gathered companionably at Robert's suite
in the Berkeley Hotel just to the north of Belgrave Square – among
them Nick Robinson, Charles Benson, Bobby McAlpine ... and,
except that he was annoyingly late, Billy McDonald. They were sipping

Roederer Cristal very elegantly, with unusual decorum, when Billy swung breezily through the doorway and walked into a sofa.

'Christ,' said Robert. 'He's smashed.'

'No, no, not me, I'm fine,' retorted the hero of so many brilliant touches in the sales ring, the man who had done so much to create Sadler's Wells.

Robert, however, knew better. And, as is customary on such occasions, he had a plan. There were two big cars waiting to transport them to the Savoy and he briefed one of the drivers carefully. 'When Mr McDonald gets into the back, wind up the glass partition which separates you from the passengers and turn the heater up to flat-out in the back,' he instructed. 'There's a fighting chance he will nod off to sleep on the journey and he can stay in the back of the car until the dinner's over. Look after him, he might not look it but he is a very valuable commodity.'

So they set off in convoy, cruising past Buckingham Palace and down the Mall, with Robert hoping against hope Bill was now unconscious in the mobile hot-house that tracked them. Right off Horse Guards, Charles Benson observed that Bill's head had disappeared.

'He's gone, Robert,' he reported. 'No further danger.'

The cars pulled up at the river entrance to the hotel. Everyone got out. Robert instructed his driver about times of departure and they left the slumbering Billy in the back of the rear car.

Seated at the table, Robert was just beginning to relax when Charles spotted a familiar figure weaving between the tables. 'Jesus Christ, Robert,' he said. 'It's him.'

Robert held his nerve, pointed to a chair and said sternly to Billy, 'Now listen, old pal. This is a very formal group. Sit down where I tell you, drink little and remember that if you embarrass me, I will not be responsible for my actions.' And, grinning, he stuck the right fist that had flattened Tiny Davies so long ago gently under Billy's chin.

'I'm all right. Do'n worry, I'm all right.'

Seated at the table, Nick Robinson between Robert and Billy, everything was fine. Billy, chastened, had a couple of glasses of wine and said practically nothing. As dinner drew to its close, the Toastmaster bid this august gathering to 'be upstanding, and pray silence for the Loyal Toast'.

Each man raised his glass. 'The Queen,' they intoned, that age-old chivalrous touch which dates back into the mists of British aristocracy. It is somehow, at any dinner involving the Stewards of the Jockey Club, a rather sacred moment. And then everyone sat down. Well, nearly everyone. Billy remained on his feet and, raising his glass, he gazed around at the gathering, pausing to draw breath.

'I just wanna say', he said firmly, 'that I wanna take this opportunity . . . while we're toasting the Queen . . . to remember and raise a glass to Bill Shoemaker.'

All conversation ceased. Every eye was upon Robert's wayward guest. The Senior Steward, the Earl of Hartington, seated at the very next table, looked as if he might die of shock. His jaw fell as he stared at the Irish-born bloodstock agent from California, a masterpiece in impropriety.

'As I 'spect you know, Bill is very ill in hospital . . . and I just wanna put his name forward, with His Majesty's . . . er . . . Her Majesty, as a true example of . . . greatest jockey . . .'

He got no further. Robert lunged left, right across Nick's lap seized Billy's jacket and dragged him down. The hissed, furious word 'asshole' was not heard beyond the Sangster group. Billy recovered and gamely tried to get up again. 'Whassamatter, do'n you like Bill?' he enquired. 'Whassamatter? . . . He's one of the greatest jockeys in the history of . . .'

'*Shut up!*' said Robert.

'Her Majesty wouldn't have minded,' mumbled Billy. 'She likes him . . . she 'preciates him . . . always has done . . .'

Another piece of folklore had taken its place in the rich annals of the life and times of Billy McDonald, hereafter referred to as 'Billy's Toast'.

Five days later Generous won the Derby by five lengths. The twelve furlongs was too far for Last Tycoon's son Marju (owned by Sheikh Hamdan), who nonetheless ran very bravely and beat the rest of them. Generous then went on to complete the modern Triple Crown, by winning the Irish Derby and the King George VI and Queen Elizabeth Stakes. Caerleon's place at the pinnacle of the 1991 Champion Sire's table was made utterly impregnable when his daughter Caerlina won the French Oaks. Marju had his day when he came out at Royal Ascot and won the Group I mile event, the St James's Palace Stakes. At the same meeting young Dr Devious, who had already won a race at Newbury, chased home Dilum in the Coventry Stakes, and Robert, warming to his new role as a commercial breeder, immediately accepted an offer for him. However, an unknowing veterinarian 'spun' the horse, declaring the Doctor to be not sufficiently sound of wind and limb.

In the American classics, John Magnier's judgment of Woodman again proved spot-on. The Ashford stallion's son Hansel won both the

Preakness Stakes and the Belmont. The master of Coolmore was so excited by this he began to write the 1992 sales brochure two months early, writing boldly against the name Woodman: World Champion Juvenile Sire in 1990 with his First Crop. Against this he elected to run a picture of the world, shot from the moon. He then spent three hours surrounded by record books and wrote again, 'The First Stallion for over a Century to Sire Two Individual Winners of Three Classics in his First Crop.' And Hector Protector, who won *five* Group I races, was not Woodman's only triumph in Europe. Another son, the two-year-old Mujtahid, won the July Stakes at Newmarket and the Gimcrack Stakes at York. It was an amazing performance by the new stallion Woodman, who had run only three times in his life. The key to this brilliance rested of course in Woodman's pedigree, emerging as he did from one of the best female lines ever bred by the Phipps family of the United States, the owners of both Bold Ruler and Buckpasser.

In the middle of the summer, however, Robert, John and Vincent had to cope with the impending collapse of Classic Thoroughbreds. Even the heroic run of Royal Academy had not been enough to save them. It would have done back in the old days when stallion prices were so enormous. If he had won the inaugural running of the Breeders' Cup Mile in 1984, his brilliant pedigree (Nijinsky–Crimson Saint) would have seen him safely on an American farm for possibly an $80,000 nomination (over five years a $400,000 share would have made him a $16 million sire). But times were very different in 1991. He went to Coolmore with a valuation of approximately the same as his cost, $3·5 million.

The main directors of Classic Thoroughbreds, who were unable to buy yearlings in either 1990 or 1991, had to haul up the white flag in August of the year. The company had accumulated losses of $10·2 million and the share price stood at a rather dismal 3·5 pence. The ordinary investor had lost eighty-eight per cent of his original stake and at an Extraordinary General Meeting in the Berkeley Court Hotel, Dublin, Michael Smurfit said, 'After three disastrous years we have come to the conclusion that enough is enough. This noble and unique experiment has not been a success. The underpinning of values, by purchasing only top-quality horses, does not occur – due to the unprece- dented decline in the value of thoroughbreds these past three years. It is a decline which unfortunately continues ... There is little point in proceeding with the purchase of any further horses.'

About one hundred shareholders turned up and when they heard that there was cash in the bank – about £1 million – many of them suggested 'we keep racing until the last penny's gone'. Being Irishmen, several of them wanted to keep the horses and send the best of them jumping. 'There'll be a couple of fine leppers in there somewhere!' shouted one man.

John, Vincent and Michael Smurfit were all on the top table facing the shareholders, but Robert, who was ten minutes late after playing in a pro-am tournament at his boyhood course of Hoylake, had to sit at the back of the room. 'The blighters,' he observed, 'did not even save me a chair.' The enterprise had cost him around £915,000. But the Sangster luck had held, of course. He still owned a quarter of Royal Academy, personally, which was worth, even in this market, about £500,000. Vincent was the biggest loser. He had paid £1·9 million for his fourteen per cent stake.

There were few recriminations. Vincent had done his best and had gone to the 1988 Keeneland Sale with, essentially, the last of his big spending money to buy several horses. In the end he spent almost all of it on just one. Even then he had the courage to back his judgment. Even with the last throw of Classic Thoroughbreds' dice, he bought them an international champion, which he trained to beat the world on one magical afternoon at Belmont Park. The words that Robert Sangster had uttered, thirty years previously in the Kardomah Coffee House in Liverpool, were still correct: 'Best trainer in the world'. You could also add, without fear of an argument, 'Best judge of a yearling'.

It was a deep irony that 1991 was probably the best year since the 1970s to buy thoroughbreds. Keeneland crashed again, the average plunging to $320,000, from $352,000 in 1990. The gross also fell drastically from $82 million to $73 million. Money was pouring out of the business. The gross take at Tattersall's Highflyer sales in Newmarket collapsed spectacularly from £24 million to £12 million. The highest-priced lot was for £380,000, which compared very moderately with the £2·4 million paid in 1982. It was now estimated that as many as four hundred thoroughbred farms may be for sale in the Bluegrass. The unemployment was becoming extremely serious. There were empty paddocks all through Bourbon and Lafayette counties. The word 'foreclosure' was heard a great deal more often than the phrase 'great stallion'. The 'For Sale' signs were becoming a blight upon the countryside. The eternal spring of Kentucky was over.

Back in Europe there was a wonderful crop of two-year-old racers making a truly dramatic season. Miraculously, Robert was right in the thick of it once again. He had a beautiful home-bred colt named Rodrigo de Triano (named after Christopher Columbus's lookout). He was by El Gran Senor and he won both the Champagne Stakes at Doncaster by three and a half lengths from River Falls, and the Middle Park Stakes at Newmarket by a length from Lion Cavern. The two victories saw him the highest-rated English colt on the Free Handicap.

Robert finally sold Dr Devious for $400,000 to Mr Luciano Gaucci, in whose colours the son of Ahonoora and Rose of Jericho proceeded to win the Dewhurst Stakes. Demi O'Byrne was very disappointed that Robert had parted with him, but it seemed like a lot of money at the time. The Doctor's half-brother Archway, by Thatching, was also running and he won the Greenland Stakes at the Curragh, getting up on the line after being left at the start. The family was looking superb, and Robert owned the first two dams, Rose of Jericho (with John) and Rose Red.

The Coolmore stallion Lomond, whom John had moved to the Ashford Stud in Kentucky, also came up with a tremendous filly, Marling, who won the Cheveley Park Stakes. But the greatest drama was taking place in France, where François Boutin's chestnut colt Arazi had just won the Prix Robert Papin, the Prix Morny, the Prix de la Salamandre, and the Grand Criterium. These victories so impressed Sheikh Mohammed that he persuaded the American owner Mr Allen Paulson to part with fifty per cent of the horse for a sum reported to be $9 million. It seemed a huge amount of money, but in the Breeders' Cup Juvenile, with $1 million on the line, Arazi produced a performance that was nothing short of breathtaking. He raced through almost the entire field and drew off in the stretch to win by five lengths against the best colts in the USA. He was lauded in America and in Europe as the best two-year-old to run in America since Secretariat.

This would be the colt who would stand between Robert and the classics, because being by Blushing Groom he would surely go for the more prestigious English 2000 Guineas rather than the French equivalent, and there he would meet Rodrigo de Triano. Still, Robert was a tremendous sportsman and he said flatly, 'If we have to race him, we'll race him ... I'll be happy to beat Dr Devious though!'

Robert was somehow right back on top of this game, and only with a desperate last-minute throw of $9 million had Sheikh Mohammed managed to rejoin him in the classic big league for the 1992 season. Even the $13·1 million yearling Seattle Dancer had managed to come through with a very fast two-year-old named Seattle Rhyme, winner of the Racing Post Trophy at Doncaster. In some books this was the winter favourite for the Derby. The extent of their success was well-nigh unbelievable: Seattle Rhyme was a product of Robert's most expensive stallion, which they practically owned in his entirety. It was also quite incredible that Robert had owned and bred Rodrigo, who was by another of their top stallions; and that they had bred Dr Devious, owned his dam and his grand-dam, and had owned his sire. And that they also owned Caerleon, the Champion sire of the Derby winner Generous, as well as Sadler's Wells and Lomond, and Last Tycoon, and Storm Bird and Be My Guest – *and* the 'world champion two-year-old sire, Woodman'.

Never, in all of the history of the Turf, had one group of horsemen, in one stud-farm operation, owned and been responsible for the breeding of such overpowering brilliance. No one had ever seen anything like it. All of those battles in the sales ring, all of those months of planning, the near-mystical eye of Vincent, and the uncanny instincts of John Magnier, had created the finest bloodstock empire in history. And Robert Sangster was one of the three lynchpins of the organization. It had been launched into the major league with his money. He had backed them without flinching. He had weathered the lean years at Ballydoyle when the virus had struck down the yard. And he was still, somehow, at the top.

In fact, during 1991, one of the few disappointments he suffered was with a filly named North Wind, trained by Barry Hills. He owned her in partnership with Her Royal Highness Princess Michael of Kent. This had come about when the Royal filly, Spirit of the Wind, had failed to win a race for either of her trainers, Henry Candy and John Dunlop, and the Princess had asked Robert whether he would be interested in sharing a foal – that is, she would retire Spirit of the Wind, breed her to Lomond, and she and Robert would own the offspring together. The problem was that Spirit of the Wind could not get out of her own way, she was so slow. And she was by the American stallion Little Current, who had proved to be a truly ineffective sire. A very slow filly, by a failed stallion? It did not sound all that hopeful, but in England it is slightly awkward turning down members of the Royal family. And Robert, against his better judgment – John Magnier would have laughed at the silliness of the idea – agreed to go ahead, and he put up one of his precious nominations to Lomond and they became partners.

They named the filly foal North Wind, put her in training and to Robert's amazement she could run. She won a maiden at Newbury and finished third in both the Cheshire Oaks and the Nassau Stakes. Her last race was very poor, however, and she looked to have concluded her career. At this point Princess Michael wanted to buy Robert out, as cheaply as possible, so that she could have the filly as a future brood-mare. And as usual it was difficult to turn the Royals down. Robert was firm about the price, but he ended up feeling he had been on the wrong end of the deal from start to finish.

Princess Michael, however, had been very much on the right end of the deal, for she had acquired Spirit of the Wind for nothing during a trip to America. Visiting in the mid-west, she had telephoned John Galbreath, the immensely wealthy Ohio construction magnate, who owned not only the Derby winner Roberto and the great Kentucky stud farm Darby Dan (where Tommy Gentry's father, Olin, was the man-ager), but also the Pittsburgh Pirates baseball team. He was well into his eighties and he fielded the phone call from this unknown 'relation of the Queen's'.

Mr Galbreath, who had been a good friend of Her Majesty's for many years, thought, like Robert, that he should do what he could for 'this Princess'. He invited her to his home in Ohio, which sits in the middle of hundreds of acres outside the city of Columbus, which he practically built. He flew her and a lady he thought was her secretary down to Darby Dan direct to Bluegrass Field in his private Gulfstream jet and showed her all of the stallions. Still not quite knowing who she was, the grand old gentleman offered her a yearling filly as a gift, which Princess Michael accepted with some alacrity, and he arranged to fly this daughter of Little Current back to England for her. It took him months to find out who she actually was and one night, at a dinner at the house, an English guest mentioned this filly, of Darby Dan breeding, which was now in training in Berkshire with Henry Candy.

Now, Mr Galbreath had never understood why the Queen had a relation with an Austrian accent. 'But she told me she was a princess, all right,' he said. 'I remembered that much.' Now he was informed, formally, that the lady in question was actually married to a cousin of the Queen; to the brother of the Duke of Kent.

Mr Galbreath was deeply unimpressed by this. 'I'll be damned,' he said. 'You mean she doesn't even live in Buckingham Palace? I only gave her the filly because I kinda thought she must have been Princess Margaret!'

The fact that North Wind had shown some speed was entirely due to the influence of Lomond and as the year ended Robert reflected upon the sheer excellence of his stallion operation. For the past few years, as a major consignor at the sales, he had been selling, worldwide, including Australia, some $20 million of foals and yearlings annually. He had also stabilized his racing empire and appointed a new trainer to Manton. This was the twenty-eight-year-old Peter Chapple-Hyam, who had worked for several years as assistant to Barry Hills and was now given the opportunity to take over the running of a major racing yard. He was married to the pretty, dark-haired Australian daughter of the second Mrs Sangster, Jane Peacock, who had also worked for Robert for several years. They made a good team because Peter knew precisely what he was doing and Jane was an excellent horsewoman, who could ride those racehorses at work and made a major contribution to the operation. She was also, like most Australian sports, a shrewd punter and on the rare occasions that she put her own money down, she was apt to collect. Big.

Peter had trained both Rodrigo and Dr Devious to their two-year-old victories and the entire racing community in England was watching to see whether the cheerful, thick-set young master of Manton could prepare a young horse to win an English classic. Thanks to the years of work by both Michael Dickinson and Barry, Manton was now as good a training ground as anywhere in England, with superb gallops of deep downland turf. Michael Dickinson had even put in an American bend, for when they were preparing horses to race in the United States. Altogether Peter Chapple-Hyam would train sixty horses for Robert and a dozen for the Italian Luciano Gaucci who had bought Dr Devious.

In the not-to-distant future Robert planned to centralize his entire operation here, bringing in all of the mares and foals and yearlings. He already had his computerized records, of breeding and ownership, going back nearly twenty years at Manton, under the care and control of his trusted assistant, Wendy Cousins, the daughter of his first trainer. It was very characteristic of Robert Sangster to nurture these old links with days past. Wendy had been a child when he and Eric had first conducted their raids on the handicap prizes at Ayr and Haydock. But she had worked for him both at the Isle of Man and Manton and through her he always stayed in touch with her father. Also his loyalties to the Irishmen in Tipperary remain unbreakable. He had the same secretary for thirty years. On the occasions when Billy McDonald embarrassed him, he always forgave, because he never forgot his debt to him. On the occasions when Charles Benson had needed cash to fight off the bookmakers, Robert had usually helped. Charles would do anything for Robert.

Even his wife Sue had on one unforgettable occasion been prepared to make the supreme sacrifice to save the sometimes-errant life of Billy McDonald. Well, in a manner of speaking she had. It happened during a winter holiday in Barbados, quite late at night on the beach outside Robert's house. They were gazing out at the distant lights of Michael Smurfit's yacht when, quite suddenly, Billy announced that he was fed up to the teeth with all this vodka. 'Dat bloddy boat of Smurfit's is packed with Château Petrus,' he shouted. 'And I'm going out there to get a decent bottle.'

With which, he flopped into the water and began a rather inexpert stroke towards the yacht which was about half a mile away. Slowly the sounds of his flailing arms grew fainter. Until, harsh on the soft, warm Caribbean night air, came a waterlogged Irish roar: *'Oi'm bloddy drownin'. Fock it!'*

'Oh, that's rather a pity,' said Charles, languidly. 'He hasn't even got the Petrus.'

'Jesus,' said Sue, whipped off her skirt and knifed into the water, swimming a strong crawl to the aid of the exhausted Billy. Somehow she got him on his back, grabbed his hair and dragged him the two hundred yards back to the shore, telling him all the way that if he wriggled, belched or spoke she would leave him. She dragged him through the shallows and deposited him, poleaxed with tiredness, upon the sand. 'I'd say he owes you,' said Robert. 'None of us could have done that. Shame about the Petrus, though!'

By any standards, you would have to say that Robert Sangster's creed of absolute loyalty to his friends, colleagues and staff had always served him well. He gave it, and he received it. As Arthur Hancock's secretary might have put it, 'Most everyone has a real soft spot for Robert.'

No such creed, however, existed at Calumet Farm, under the reign of J. T. Lundy. As the big wooden notice board was nailed up close by the farm gates announcing the total auction of the estate in March 1992, there were many who blamed the unravelling of this thoroughbred empire on JT's total disregard for the Calumet traditions, and on his propensity to lose loyal long-serving staff. Key people who had been there for more than a generation had left soon after he became president. Margaret Glass retired, the farm manager Melvin Cinnamon went to Overbrook Farm, Ewell Rice who had worked with the Calumet yearlings since 1939 went to Claiborne. Young people, far less experienced at the highest level of horse breeding, were brought in. Farm managers came and went. Visitors were no longer welcome. Relations of Lundy's prospered from their dealings with the farm. Especially his son Robert, who was earning large commissions, and his sister Kathy's insurance agency. Breeding rights to the Calumet stallions were not maintained with the same tight control as before. J. T. Lundy approved the expenditure of $500,000 a year on the lease of a private jet. It was not unknown for the travel and entertainment bills, mostly his own, to match that figure.

There was a certain amount of grim laughter around Lexington when the first $40 million of the debt became known in the spring of 1991. At that time there was just about $400 in the Calumet bank account. In the final months other stallions had to be moved. Secreto went to Airdrie to stand at a fee of $7500 when the foal stands. Talinum went to Claiborne, Criminal Type went to Lane's End, and Mogambo was sold for $1·1 million. The rest of the mares, foals and yearlings were sold at a Keeneland dispersal, one hundred and twenty-three of them for just over $10 million – a mere drop in the ocean against the massive debt.

Now the farm was being sold and on 26 March thousands turned out to see the final curtain brought down on the Wright family's ownership. The auction was conducted by Swinebroad-Denton of Lexington and the J. P. King Auction Company, and by that morning they had received formal notice of the interest of five different parties. The auction took place in a gigantic red-and-white-striped tent and the place was packed with two thousand people long before the proceedings started. At 10.40 a.m. a private plane touched down at Bluegrass Field and from it stepped the rather dashing figure of sixty-four-year-old Henryk de Kwiatkowski, the man who had owned the $36 million Conquistador Cielo. Limping slightly from an old polo injury and walking with a cane, Ricky had flown from his home in the Bahamas. He had, he said, always wanted to buy Calumet and that was his mission today.

When bidding started it took just twelve minutes. The auctioneer started off at $10 million and Ricky came in at $11 million. A group representing some wealthy Calumet neighbours took him on and bid up to $16·7. But Ricky was an old hand at auctions. He immediately raised the bid to $17 million and his opponents folded their hand. Calumet Farm had passed from the descendants of Warren Wright into the hands of another horseman, cut far more in the mould of the founder himself than any of the Wright children and grandchildren would ever be. The main tract of seven hundred and sixty-three acres bought, he stayed around to purchase another thirty acres for $175,000, as well as the 'Calumet' name for $210,000. 'This is', he said, 'the crowning achievement of my life.' And the crowd, sensing an historic purchase by a man who would perhaps rebuild Calumet to its former glory, leapt to its feet and clapped and cheered the Polish-born aviator.

He did not bid for the devil's red-and-blue Calumet colours, which were snapped up by a Brazilian for $12,000, because of course the de Kwiatkowski silks of white with red cross-belts, and scarlet polka dots on the sleeves, have become extremely well known in their own right. Ricky raced a second Belmont Stakes winner Danzig Connection, as well as the American filly Sabin, who reeled off eight stakes victories in nine starts in 1984. He also raced the Nijinsky filly De La Rose who was voted US Champion Grass Filly in 1981, and Danzig who ran only four times but made a wonderful Claiborne stallion.

Altogether the Calumet sale raised $19 million. They even sold the beautiful old horse van which had driven most of the Calumet Derby winners in its time. The Kentucky Derby Museum bought it for $72,000. The Eclipse Award won by Alydar's son Criminal Type (Horse of the Year 1990) went for $4500. It was a bitter-sweet day, and the question remained unanswered: where had the Calumet fortune gone? Frittered away on a huge overhead, jet planes and too-expensive horses? Perhaps. But that's a real hard way to get rid of upwards of $200 million – that is, Alydar's entire earnings and the $100 million-plus debt.

After the sale Henryk de Kwiatkowski toured the farm and assured everyone that their jobs were safe. 'I do not want to change things,' he said. 'I'd just like to put Calumet back at the top.' Within hours of the sale the phones were ringing. Former employees wanted to come back. Everyone was trying to help pick Calumet off the floor and back into the winner's circle.

Meanwhile, back at Manton, Dr Devious had been sold again, a procedure he was getting rather used to, since he had now been sold four times, once in every year of his life. A less tough and resilient character might have been excused suffering from some kind of a complex. But Luciano Gaucci had received an offer of $2·5 million for him from Mrs Jenny Craig, the California-based head of a major international weight-loss chain which she had founded in Australia in 1983. Jenny's husband, Sidney, the bearded chairman and chief executive of the corporation, was due for a birthday and she wanted to give him a racehorse which had a serious chance in the Kentucky Derby. She paid out the big money and the Doctor was shipped in late April to Churchill Downs to be trained by another Californian, Ron McAnally, who already trained twenty horses for Mr Craig.

Peter Chapple-Hyam thought that was the last he would see of him and he settled down to prepare Rodrigo de Triano to win the 1992 2000 Guineas. This would prove a rather daunting task since Rodrigo had been well beaten into fourth place, after weakening in the last hundred yards of his prep race, the Greenham Stakes at Newbury. But the ground was soft that day and for the Newmarket classic the young trainer hired the veteran Lester Piggott to wear once more the green-and-blue silks of Robert Sangster, colours he had not worn regularly since the 1980 season.

The 2000 Guineas had not been a lucky race for Robert and Lester, operating as a team. Three times the ex-champion jockey had been beaten in this race in the Sangster silks: once on The Minstrel, once on Try My Best, who finished last as the hottest favourite for forty years in 1978, and again on Night Alert, who finished fourth to the disqualified Nureyev. Robert himself had won the race in 1983 and '84 with Lomond and El Gran Senor, but on those occasions Pat Eddery rode. This year, however, the race looked infinitely winnable. Dr Devious and Arazi had both gone to the Kentucky Derby, which was being run on the same day. Seattle Rhyme was injured and Lion Cavern, the French-trained winner of the Greenham, was staying in Chantilly in preparation for the French 2000 Guineas.

Robert and Lester, old friends who had fought a lot of wars together, grinned at each other cheerfully in the paddock. 'A waiting race,' said the youngest trainer in the classic to the jockey who had ridden three Derby winners before he was born. Lester grinned again, as Peter legged him up. The old maestro landed upon Rodrigo's back, as ever, like a snowflake. Then he nodded curtly and did what he always did – rode off to do precisely whatever he liked.

The early pace in this straight one-mile championship was set by Thourios and he had half the field exhausted by the time they hit the two-furlong pole. Pursuit of Love, under the South African rider Michael Roberts, hit the front running down the hill, by which time Lester Piggott was flying from the very back of the field. Inside the final furlong Rodrigo shot past the leader and, with an exquisite piece of timing and riding, went away to win Lester's thirtieth classic by two lengths.

Peter Chapple-Hyam and Robert were beside themselves with joy, the trainer because of his fairy-tale start to his first season with Robert's three-year-olds. And Robert, 'because I feel a bit like Lazarus, after the barren years ... and because of Lester winning this race for me at last . . . and because it's so great for The Senor . . . and for Peter . . . and for Manton . . . because of everything, really . . . I just feel very, very happy.'

Everyone at Newmarket was delighted for him. Dozens of people rushed to congratulate him, people he hadn't spoken to for years showed up to shake his hand. Most everyone has a soft spot for Robert. As Cousin Leslie would almost certainly have phrased it, 'That ole dog can still hunt.'

That night there was more brilliant news for Peter Chapple-Hyam. Both Arazi and Dr Devious got well beat in the Kentucky Derby, finishing seventh and eighth, the Doctor in front. And Ron McAnally, the trainer who had kept John Henry winning millions of dollars until he was Horse of the Year at *nine*, made a decision. 'This Doctor', he said, 'ought to go right back to England. He doesn't like the dirt track and he ain't gonna start liking it. Get him back on the weeds where he's comfortable.' At that moment Peter knew that Dr Devious was on his way home to Manton to be trained, hopefully, for a shot at the English Derby. Sidney Craig called and the arrangements were made very quickly. The sooner the horse was back on the soft green turf of Wiltshire, the better for everybody.

Rodrigo went to Ireland a couple of weeks later and won the Irish 2000 Guineas with another fast finishing sprint through the final two hundred yards. He was immediately made favourite for the Derby and Chapple-Hyam found himself nursing a set of deeply divided loyalties. Firstly he wanted to win the Derby for Robert and for Manton more than he wanted fresh air to breathe. But in his horseman's heart he believed that Dr Devious might stay the mile and a half better. Rodrigo plainly had fantastic pace and if any jockey could coax him home at Epsom it was surely Lester Piggott, nine times winner of the race. He had done it before with horses which really were bred to go only a mile and a quarter, but it was not easy, because Rodrigo may not even go that far. His sire, El Gran Senor had *just* got home in 1984, albeit it a short-head behind Secreto. But the blood on his dam's side was almost all that of the sprinter. No one could possibly look at Rodrigo's pedigree and say truthfully, 'I think he'll go twelve furlongs.' Worse yet, Robert did not especially want to be beaten by Dr Devious, a horse he had sold as a two-year-old for about one-sixth of his value now.

But there is only one Derby in any horse's life and owners who have not run have been known to spend, subsequently, a lifetime wishing they had. What if Rodrigo did stay? What if he came out and won the

Arc in October? What then? R. E. Sangster, the man who funked the Derby! Fat chance. Robert, however coyly he made his decision known to the public, was *always* going to Epsom, win, lose or draw. Lester Piggott was more circumspect than most of the connections about whether the colt would stay. But Rodrigo was favourite, his owner was a fearless gambler and Lester knew where he would be on Derby Day – all dressed up in those green-and-blue silks, going for his tenth Derby and his third successive classic victory on Rodrigo de Triano.

As things turned out, Lester's celebrity was a bit of a liability to the son of El Gran Senor. The crowd kept cheering him all the way from the paddock. The photographers were driving the horse mad and there was a loud and ignorant mob at the start, jeering at the horses who were reluctant to enter the stall, jeering at Lester who was trying to control the very excited Rodrigo, who was now awash with sweat. This was one of those Derbys that was lost before it was raced. Lester rode Rodrigo very tenderly, knowing his cause was hopeless and quickly finding out that the colt did not really relish running downhill. In the end they finished ninth.

Out in front of the race at Tattenham Corner was Sheikh Maktoum's Twist and Turn, but once into the straight, Dr Devious came rolling down the outside, hit the front and went away to win the two hundred and thirteenth English Derby by two easy lengths. It was clear from three furlongs out that he was the only one in the field who would genuinely run a mile and a half. For a split second Robert, the man who had sold a Derby winner halfway through the horse's career, felt as if he had been slammed in the solar plexus. But he rolled with the punch and, as the Doctor charged over the winning line, Robert was grinning again. Freddie would have been proud.

No one knew quite what to say to him, but they did not require any tact. Robert walked over to Peter, put his arm round his shoulders and he said, 'Well done, Pete, a great job with the horse. You can do it for me next year, if you've got time!'

Everyone laughed, and Robert said what he usually said at times such as this, 'Come on, let's go and have a drink.' And he led them all away, towards a champagne bar, walking with his head held forward, chatting away, a study in irredeemable resilience. Never once throughout that late afternoon did he betray one flicker of remorse at having sold the Doctor. And on the way back to Manton for dinner that evening he was full of optimism.

Later, standing outside as the sun set quite high along a ridge of the

Downs, he gazed out over this majestic English country property. Its views were as pleasant as they had been at far-away Swettenham. One of the estate workers walked by. 'Evening, Mr Robert. Bad luck today ... but Rodrigo will be back.'

Much had changed in all of those years since first he had entered the Sport of Kings, but attitudes had stayed the same. And he did still own the dam of Dr Devious, whom he could breed to Sadler's Wells, or Woodman, or The Senor, or any of the other great stars of Coolmore. He would not have wanted to exchange places with Sheikh Mohammed, who had effectively driven him out of the sales ring, but who still had not owned a horse which had finished in the first three in the English Derby. Nor had the Sheikh won the Arc. And he had spent $9 million for half of Arazi, which was looking very suspect. And that very morning it had been confirmed that 'The Curse of Snaafi Dancer' lived on ... Don Johnson's Crescent Farm, which had consigned the $10·2 million colt, had just filed for Chapter 7 Bankruptcy. In fact the two top colts the Sheikh had ever owned, Belmez and Old Vic, were both by stallions he, Robert, had owned, bred and raced, The Senor and Sadler's Wells. So, for that matter was his older brother's great filly Salsabil.

The truth was, whichever way anyone looked at it, the Irishman had outmanoeuvred the Sheikhs in their choice of bloodstock. The sharp, sure instincts of Vincent, and John, and Phonsie, and Bob and Demi, and PP Hogan, had been too much for the raiders from the Middle East. The giant breeding empire of Coolmore was on top of the world and Robert was sitting up there with it. The key to their success rested in the green hillsides of Tipperary and Limerick. It rested in the know-ledge of these horsemen, whose judgments of pedigree and confor-mation had been handed down for generations. Vincent had created those sensational seasons of the late 70s and early 80s from a yard with only around sixty horses, not the hundreds and hundreds the Sheikhs had trained each year. In late October 1982, all at the same time, there had resided on the estate of Ballydoyle the following future stallions: Golden Fleece, Assert, Danzatore, Salmon Leap, Lomond, Caerleon, Solford, and the new yearlings El Gran Senor, Sadler's Wells and Secreto.

Robert thought of PP whose sight was now failing, out in the village of Bruff. And of Phonsie who was probably casting a late fly upon the water somewhere north of Coolmore. And of Vincent who had helped to breed the Doctor. And of Demi who was probably regaling them right now in McCarthy's with the story of how he had begged Robert not to sell. And of John who had bought Ahonoora. And he looked again at the neatly typed list of the mares which Wendy had left for him, with their prospective foals and some prospective matings. He thought again of the new foal by Sadler's Wells they were due to get from Rose of Jericho next spring. And he skipped through the pages and saw again the names of all the other stallions he was breeding to – Alleged, Caerleon, Be My Guest, Seattle Dancer, Woodman and Bluebird, Royal Academy and Lomond. Born of American blood, they had all learned their trade in Tipperary. Each one of them was blessed with a little touch of Irish magic.

That was the one ingredient Sheikh Mohammed had missed: the Irish magic. The estimated $750 million which the Princes of Dubai had spent on yearlings had not been able to buy that for them. The mystical brilliance of the Irish with thoroughbreds is as elusive as the Bedouins' ancient mastery of the desert.

'By God,' thought Robert, 'the Sadler's Wells foal from Rose of Jericho is going to be born in Tipperary. I've a bloody good mind to keep him, if he's a colt, and race him. It would be a huge gamble – but John would go for it, and we could end up with one helluva stallion. Just imagine if he could run like the Doctor, with a Northern Dancer cross in his pedigree . . . Wouldn't that be something?'

'Sorry, Robert,' said Benson. 'I didn't quite catch that?'

'Oh, nothing really. I was just thinking I might roll the dice on the track, one last time, with a very expensive horse, before I become a real commercial breeder.'

That ole dog, he could still hunt.

Epilogue

The traditional final Group I race of the season in the British Isles was run at Newmarket on the clear, chill Saturday afternoon of 17 October 1992. And, as it has done so often in the past one hundred and fifteen years, the Champion Stakes brought down the curtain on British racing at the highest level in spectacularly dramatic fashion. Still out there, still running for his life after seven months in hard training, Rodrigo de Triano, under the green-and-blue silks of Robert Sangster, swooped to victory by a neck over Sheikh Hamdan's game, but outclassed Riverman colt, Lahib.

The dual 2000 Guineas classic winner thus added over £200,000 more to his prize money of £400,000 for the season and this gave Robert's Swettenham Stud in 1992 its first-ever title of Leading British Breeder. The horsetrader from the Wirral thus stepped forward, formally, to join the most celebrated order of men who had not only won this honour before him, but who had also *shaped* the breed down all of the seasons of the twentieth century – men like the distant Earls of Derby and Rosebery; the old Aga Khan and his grandson, Karim, the present Aga Khan; Monsieur Marcel Boussac; Major Lionel Holliday; E. P. Taylor and Paul Mellon. It is doubtful, however, whether, in the fullness of time, any one of them will have exerted quite the same influence on the pedigrees of future thoroughbred generations as Robert Sangster, who financed the Irish buying spree which created the irresistible march of Northern Dancer. The trademarks of the little Canadian stallion have already been embossed upon the pages of the Stud Book, which now contains so many champions of identical characteristics – sons and grandsons of the Dancer, none of them overbearing in size, but all possessed of a wicked turn of foot and a will of steel.

Rodrigo gave Robert his Championship with a victory at Newmarket that was a near-duplicate of his triumphs in both the English and Irish

2000 Guineas, and in Europe's other top ten-furlong race, the Juddmonte International Stakes at York in August. Under the hard driving of Lester Piggott, he came with a finishing kick that could not be withstood by any other horse and he ran the race out with iron determination. The son of El Gran Senor, with five Group I races now to his credit, thus became the first horse for twenty-one years – since Brigadier Gerard in 1971 – to win both the 2000 Guineas and then, half a year later, the Champion Stakes. Not even Nijinsky had the constitution for that. Rodrigo's triumph came eighteen years after Robert, Vincent and John had first joined forces in their bold attempt to corner the market on the Northern Dancer breed. In the ensuing years they had seen many would-be imitators, not least the Arabian Princes from the Sheikhdom of Dubai and the Kingdom of Saudi Arabia, who tried to emulate their every move.

When the market finally crashed in the late 1980s it hit everyone, because stallion and mare values plummeted across the board. But it hit the Arabs hardest, because they had spent ten times more money than even the millions Robert and his partners had poured into the business of racing and breeding. The difference between the two camps was, of course, the Merlin of Tipperary, Vincent O'Brien, who achieved more than all of the Arabians put together with about one-twentieth of the horses. Robert elected to follow the star of Vincent right at the beginning and he never strayed from that course. He kept the faith through all weathers, from The Minstrel to Royal Academy.

Robert started with an investment of approximately £2 million, and at the height of the market in 1984 and 1985 this was probably worth something close to $350 million worldwide. There were bank loans to be serviced, of course, but these were settled upon the sale of Vernons Pools. Even as the market crashed further, into the 1990s, his accountants assiduously calculated the value of Robert's international bloodstock empire, and on the day Rodrigo wrapped up the British season the figure stood at a conservative $157 million – a quite remarkable total given the world bloodstock recession and the wildly fluctuating values of breeding stallions.

By the conclusion of 1992, Robert had banked close to £1·5 million in prize money for the season, which took care of the bulk of the training fees and expenses. In addition he had sold his annual $20 million worth of yearlings, which gave him a return of roughly 13·5 per cent on his investment. Plus, of course, he had the chance once more to fight for the big prizes of the future, with at least fifty of his blue-blooded homebred yearlings on their way into training at Manton, with Peter Chapple-Hyam, the tough, blunt young trainer who prepared with such brilliance both Rodrigo and Dr Devious for their 1992 triumphs.

And, as October wore on and the yearling markets of Europe continued their catastophic decline, Robert played his last big-money ace for the season – he sold Rodrigo de Triano for $6·2 million cash to the Japanese, in the absence of a comparable offer from the British Isles. 'As I have always stressed,' he said cheerfully, 'the strength of a big investment in thoroughbred horses is its global appeal. There's always someone, somewhere, who will have the money for a classic stallion prospect. I am a horsetrader and right now I'm very happy with my situation.'

Over at Coolmore, the great broodmare band of Robert Sangster was preparing to deposit almost one hundred foals on the ground – they would have dams like Fairy Bridge, Rose of Jericho, Hot Princess, Sex Appeal and Detroit – and they would be by stallions such as Sadler's Wells, Caerleon, Lomond, Royal Academy, Woodman, Storm Bird, Bluebird and Seattle Dancer. All bred, essentially, with no stallion fees involved. Still overseeing the great Irish breeding empire was John Magnier, who had masterminded the growth of the modest Fethard Stud in 1974 into the sprawling three-thousand-acre domain it is today. Along the way, John Magnier's astute intelligence was recognized by a political buccaneer of similar flair in Mr Charles Haughey, the Prime Minister of Ireland. He created John a Senator of Ireland, and the Tipperary horseman sat upon many a Parliamentary Council during his tenure of office.

Vincent O'Brien too was recognized as perhaps the finest brain in the entire history of horse training, and he was awarded a Doctorate from the National University of Ireland. At the height of his powers he was known universally in Ireland, and especially in McCarthy's Bar, simply as 'Himself'. By early 1992, now in his mid-seventies and still training, he was known throughout Ireland, with respect and affection, as 'Dr O'Brien'.

Tom Cooper died in July 1990, and PP Hogan is not seen much these days – the sharp eyes which made him so valuable to Robert have dimmed sadly with age. Robert still calls him, though. Phonsie is quietly retired, fishing the local rivers, and Dr O'Brien is spending more time on the golf course, often with John.

Occasionally Robert comes over for a few days and even more occasionally the three men can be seen standing at the top of the

Ballydoyle gallops watching the horses work. Their talk always seems a bit conspiratorial, their laughter private to themselves, a certain remoteness suggesting they have much to say, but only to each other. It is perhaps the type of close camaraderie which settles only upon men who have fought many battles together. Somehow these three diverse personalities had made the lunatic world of the thoroughbred racehorse actually work, profitably and with dazzling success. At times they had gambled everything. They had accepted their losses and they had maximized their victories.

Their reunions upon the quiet hillside at Ballydoyle have become, by necessity, rare. For the world of the thoroughbred marches ever forward, sometimes pointing towards America, sometimes towards France, and sometimes towards home, towards Ireland. But the memories will never fade. And the beauty of the land touches all three of them still. The rain never daunts them. And sometimes they stand watching the horses as they have done so many times before; times when the stakes were higher and the risks appalling. And still, in the late spring mornings, when thunder showers sweep the fields of the Golden Vale and the sun fights its way out from behind the swiftly moving clouds above Mount Slievenamon, the rainbow arches again over the Vale, settling, from their viewpoint, brightly upon the broad acres of Coolmore. And Jacqueline still rushes for her camera to catch again the glorious pastel lights over the pastures.

But Robert no longer utters his droll and teasing remarks to Vincent and John about 'the end of the rainbow'. No need. These three, above all other horsemen, have been there.

Patrick Robinson
October 1992

Index

Laurence Olivier

A Biography

Donald Spoto

'Rivetingly interesting, admirably researched and exquisitely written – an altogether wonderful book'   Sir John Gielgud

'A work of subtle critical insight, warm, human, and always highly readable'   *New Statesman*

In the first biography of Laurence Olivier to appear since his death, Donald Spoto reveals the man behind the mask of the flamboyant, heroic actor. Based on meticulous research and many previously unpublished documents, this is the first full portrait of our greatest man of the theatre.

This is Orson Welles

Orson Welles and Peter Bogdanovich

This is the book that Welles ultimately considered his auto-biography, but it's a memoir like no other. At once accessible, entertaining and revealing, Welles and Bogdanovich's collaboration is an unforgettable collection of penetrating, fascinating and often hilarious conversations undertaken over many years, on both sides of the Atlantic. With *This is Orson Welles* the master illusionist and self-confessed 'faker', in his own words, 'puts the record straight'.

'The Art of Bogdanovich's interrogation conceals itself in the ease of good friends talking, yet it elicits from Welles answers which show us his position and his character under the arc-light thrown upon them by his brilliant tongue . . . Such humorous charm is captivating'   Philip Glazebrook, *Spectator*

'This is a book you must beg, borrow or steal . . . Welles pulls no punches: reading it is like being a privileged guest at his table, savouring that inimitable voice, as the pearls drop in abundance'
                                        Bryan Forbes, *Mail on Sunday*

'Fascinating. A treasure-trove of insights'   John Lahr

'Welles at his roaring best'   *New York Times Book Review*

ISBN 0 00 638232 0

☐	THE SCARS OF WAR Hugh Manners	0-586-21129-2	£7.99
☐	GUERRILLAS Jon Lee Anderson	0-00-637567-7	£6.99
☐	DEATH PLUS TEN YEARS Roger Cooper	0-00-638103-0	£6.99
☐	CAVALIERS AND ROUNDHEADS		
	Christopher Hibbert	0-586-09008-8	£7.99
☐	HAUGHEY Bruce Arnold	0-00-638104-9	£6.99
☐	CORPORATE CLOAK AND DAGGER James Croft	0-00-638067-9	£7.99

All these books are available from your local bookseller or can be ordered direct from the publishers.

To order direct just tick the titles you want and fill in the form below:

Name: _____

Address: _____

_____

Postcode: _____

Send to: HarperCollins Mail Order, Dept 8, HarperCollins *Publishers*, Westerhill Road, Bishopbriggs, Glasgow G64 2QT.

Please enclose a cheque or postal order or your authority to debit your Visa/Access account –

Credit card no: _____

Expiry date: _____

Signature: _____

– to the value of the cover price plus:

UK & BFPO: Add £1.00 for the first and 25p for each additional book ordered.

Overseas orders including Eire, please add £2.95 service charge.

Books will be sent by surface mail but quotes for airmail despatches will be given on request.

24 HOUR TELEPHONE ORDERING SERVICE FOR ACCESS/VISA CARDHOLDERS –

TEL: GLASGOW 041-772 2281 or LONDON 081-307 4052